Archaeology, Cultural Heritage, and the Antiquities Trade

CULTURAL HERITAGE STUDIES

UNIVERSITY PRESS OF FLORIDA

Florida A&M University, Tallahassee
Florida Atlantic University, Boca Raton
Florida Gulf Coast University, Ft. Myers
Florida International University, Miami
Florida State University, Tallahassee
New College of Florida, Sarasota
University of Central Florida, Orlando
University of Florida, Gainesville
University of North Florida, Jacksonville
University of South Florida, Tampa
University of West Florida, Pensacola

Cultural Heritage Studies
Edited by Paul Shackel, University of Maryland

The University Press of Florida is proud to announce the creation of a new series devoted to the study of cultural heritage. This thematic series brings together research devoted to understanding the material and behavioral characteristics of heritage. The series explores the uses of heritage and the meaning of its cultural forms as a way to interpret the present and the past. The series highlights important scholarship related to America's diverse heritage.

Books include important theoretical contributions and descriptions of significant cultural resources. Scholarship addresses questions related to culture and describes how local and national communities develop and value the past. The series includes works in public archaeology, heritage tourism, museum studies, vernacular architecture, history, American studies, and material cultural studies.

Heritage of Value, Archaeology of Renown: Reshaping Archaeological Assessment and Significance
    Edited by Clay Mathers, Timothy Darvill, and Barbara J. Little (2005)
Archaeology, Cultural Heritage, and the Antiquities Trade
    Edited by Neil Brodie, Morag M. Kersel, Christina Luke, and Kathryn Walker Tubb (2006)

Authors interested in contributing to the Cultural Heritage Studies series
should send inquiries to:
Paul A. Shackel
Department of Anthropology
1119 Woods Hall
University of Maryland
College Park, MD 20742
Phone 301-405-1422
Fax 301-314-8305
Email: pshackel@anth.umd.edu

Archaeology, Cultural Heritage, and the Antiquities Trade

EDITED BY

NEIL BRODIE, MORAG M. KERSEL, CHRISTINA LUKE,

AND KATHRYN WALKER TUBB

FOREWORD BY PAUL A. SHACKEL

University Press of Florida

Gainesville/Tallahassee/Tampa/Boca Raton

Pensacola/Orlando/Miami/Jacksonville/Ft. Myers/Sarasota

First cloth printing, 2006
First paperback printing, 2008

23 22 21 20 19 18   8 7 6 5 4 3

A record of cataloging-in-publication data is available from the Library of Congress.
ISBN 978-0-8130-2972-6 (cloth)
ISBN 978-0-8130-3339-6 (pbk.)

The University Press of Florida is the scholarly publishing agency for the State University System
of Florida, comprising Florida A&M University, Florida Atlantic University, Florida Gulf Coast
University, Florida International University, Florida State University, New College of Florida,
University of Central Florida, University of Florida, University of North Florida, University of
South Florida, and University of West Florida.

University Press of Florida
15 Northwest 15th Street
Gainesville, FL 32611-2079
http://upress.ufl.edu

Contents

Illustrations

TABLES

MAPS

Foreword

There is an international heritage crisis: archaeological sites are being looted at an increasing rate and the illicit antiquities trade is escalating throughout the world. Looting and the antiquities trade severely affect those who wish to know the social history of a place and culture. As plunder escalates, so do the number of participants in the trade, and the battle for heritage protection becomes increasingly personal for all those involved. *Archaeology, Cultural Heritage, and the Antiquities Trade* provides many in-depth case studies in which the authors show the complex realities of a tough and sometimes losing battle.

With the growing interest in heritage throughout the world, many people and governments are becoming more aware that archaeological sites and objects of antiquity are components that may be used in the creation of group and national identities. The Harris Poll sponsored by the Society for American Archaeology in 2004 provides some indication about what Americans think about archaeology. Overwhelmingly, people are supportive of archaeology and endorse laws that protect archaeological sites and artifacts. They believe that archaeology is important to our society: almost all of those interviewed believe that archaeological resources on public lands should be protected by laws. Americans also believe that public funds should be used to protect and preserve archaeological resources, and almost two-thirds of those interviewed believe that objects of antiquity should not be removed from a foreign country without permission from the government of the relevant country.

The poll showed also that about one-third of the American public has been to an archaeological site, and the majority of those polled have visited museums with archaeological materials. While the public sees archaeological objects as important and worthy of saving, the illicit trade and the destruction of archaeological sites continue at a significant rate. Most people understand the value of archaeological objects, but they are often unaware of the fact that without context, the objects lack the critical correlates that would aid in understanding the social past. This lack of understanding of context is often reinforced by art museums when they display artifacts as "art" objects. The goal of these "art" exhibitions is to foster an appreciation of the objects for their aesthetic value rather than to interpret the larger story they can help unfold when their context is clear. Some museums also exhibit looted objects and monuments, and several authors in this volume address the ethical issue of acquisition and display of these materials. An ethical dilemma is how museum policies differ from the more general trade in antiquities as practiced in the private sphere.

In this same vein, several of the chapters in this volume pose difficult questions with regard to the perceived value of antiquities before and after museum exhibitions of such materials. Museum displays that emphasize the aesthetic value of artifacts help to create a demand for these objects. The wealthy museums, thus, become agents that can set the agenda for the illicit trade of antiquities. It is clear that professionals and professional organizations dealing with antiquities need to make a better effort to share with interested communities the value of context and the importance of scientific techniques to record the context of artifacts. Only a common understanding about the value of archaeological remains can translate into beneficial public policy with regard to museum exhibition.

Many other complex issues related to the antiquities trade are addressed in this book. For instance, those who remove antiquities from an archaeological site without regard to scientific methods are often seen as looters and are condemned by professionals archaeologists. Does the profession have a right to dictate how descendant communities use archaeological resources, especially in the case of "subsistence digging?" Do indigenous peoples have a right to use these resources as they see fit? Does economic relief justify the extraction of archaeological materials? Should the outside developed communities impose their views on how to use the material remains of descendant communities? These are all questions without clear answers, and they present a challenge for the professional community.

The war on cultural heritage is alive, and destruction of significant cultural resources may be a devastating loss to a nation as well as to the world. For instance, the demolition of the two Bamiyan Buddhas by the Taliban was an effort to erase the history of Buddhism in Afghanistan. In much the same way, the looting that occurred immediately after the fall of Saddam Hussein's regime helped to destroy a significant portion of the Iraq's cultural heritage. Artifacts related to early civilization have been taken from areas that are within the modern boundaries of Iraq, and these items are now part of the illicit antiquities trade.

The past is important for supporting a group's identity, and the preservation of cultural heritage is important for sustaining communities. Lessons of intolerance can be learned from the destruction of the Bamiyan Buddhas. However, the looting of the Iraqi museums and libraries in 2003 and the continued destruction and looting of sites may have long-lasting and unpredictable consequences. We hope we can look at these incidents and use them as lessons learned to help change society in a constructive and positive way.

The issues raised in this volume show that there are no easy answers to stopping the destruction of archaeological sites or to slowing the illicit antiquities trade. The authors provide a wide array of case studies showing the complexity of dealing with these issues in different cultures. It is only by making these issues more public and sharing these concerns with a larger audience that we can make significant headway to change values and attitudes. *Archaeology, Cultural Heritage, and the Antiquities Trade* takes a major step in this direction.

Paul A. Shackel
Series Editor

Preface and Acknowledgments

The looting of archaeological sites and the resultant loss of knowledge is fact. This volume provides a review of the current issues surrounding the destruction of archaeological sites and the illicit trade in antiquities. The concerns surrounding access to and preservation of archaeological heritage are underscored by graphic examples of pillage over the last decade in Afghanistan and Iraq. Authors address those concerns by relating archaeological looting to the antiquities market and by advocating a proactive role for the archaeological and anthropological communities. Preservation and interpretation of archaeological heritage are increasingly becoming a political enterprise.

Such contributions are crucial if the debate is to continue in a constructive vein. Without the input of new information and the development of fresh analytical perspectives, the debate will lose impetus and relevance. These studies offer important insights for those who engage in the practice of archaeology and related subjects. As such, the book's interest transcends disciplinary boundaries, and it is invaluable to students and educators alike.

The editors would like to thank all the participants in the two sessions at the Fifth World Archaeological Congress in Washington, D.C., in June of 2003 from which many of these chapters originated. We would like to thank Joan Gero and Claire Smith for encouraging and facilitating our participation in the congress. We are extremely grateful to all the contributors to the volume for adding their voices to the debate.

Neil Brodie acknowledges the generous support of the McDonald Institute for Archaeological Research at the University of Cambridge and particularly the cheerful help of Jenny Doole.

Morag M. Kersel thanks the Department of Archaeology and Lucy Cavendish College at the University of Cambridge for financial assistance in attending the World Archaeological Congress. She would also like to thank Jenny Doole for her sage advice and helpful recommendations.

Christina Luke thanks the Department of Archaeology and the Writing Program at Boston University for encouragement and support.

Kathryn Walker Tubb would like to thank University College London for making attendance at the World Archaeological Congress possible and also to thank Peter Ucko and Jonathan Tubb for their support.

Introduction

NEIL BRODIE

There is a booming international trade in antiquities of all kinds, and from all countries of the world. Many of these antiquities are removed destructively from archaeological sites, monuments, or cultural institutions, illegally exported from their countries of origin, and converted into legal commodities through a series of commercial transactions and exchanges across jurisdictions. The conversion is facilitated by different stolen property laws and limitation periods and ensured through forged documentation and corrupt officials. Most antiquities are bought and sold without a documented find spot (provenience) or ownership history (provenance); trading histories thus become so complicated and so obscure that it is almost impossible to identify definitively any antiquities that have been stolen or illegally exported. By the time these "unprovenanced" antiquities enter the salesrooms and museums of Europe and North America, where they command veneration and high prices, the destructive and illegal circumstances of their initial acquisition have been long forgotten.

But although the trade in antiquities flouts national and international laws, it does not end there. Unscientific digging aimed at recovering salable antiquities extirpates the stratigraphies and contexts of archaeological sites, destroying archaeological information and, ultimately, historical knowledge. When these antiquities are redeployed in public or private collections as "art," shorn of their contextual relations, they are then forced to conform to Western conceptions of artistic production and consumption, with all the ideological and political baggage that such conceptions entail. For many archaeologists, working in an intellectual tradition that acknowledges at least some degree of objectivity about the past, this uncritical insertion of ancient products into modern cultural frames is anathema. But archaeologists are not alone. Many anthropologists and art historians take a similarly jaundiced view of the type of cultural appropriation and revaluation that marks the antiquities trade, which some claim is implicated globally in maintaining "Western" structures of political dominance.

Some of the issues raised by the antiquities trade were discussed in June 2003 at two sessions convened at the Fifth World Archaeological Congress (WAC) in Washington, D.C. One session was organized by Christina Luke and Morag Kersel, the other by Neil Brodie and Kathryn Walker Tubb. Most of the contributions to this book are expanded versions of papers first presented there, although chapters 4 and 10 were specially commissioned, and chapter 1 was first presented in February 2004 at the Australian War Memorial, Canberra, to mark the fiftieth anniversary of the Hague Convention.

ARCHAEOLOGICAL HERITAGE: A THREATENED RESOURCE?

The damage caused "on the ground" to archaeological sites and monuments by unrecorded and unsystematic excavation is well documented by a large number of studies that have utilized archival and literature research, field survey, photographic testimony, and informant interviews (see, for example, Atwood 2004; Brodie et al. 2000; Coggins 1969; Gill and Chippindale 1993; Graepler 1993; Gutchen 1983; Lafont 2004; Meyer 1973; O'Keefe 1997; Paredes 1998; Renfrew 2000; Schick 1998; Stead 1998; Toner 2002; and papers in Brodie et al. 2001; Brodie and Tubb 2002; Heilmeyer and Eule 2004; Leyten 1995; Messenger 1999; Schmidt and McIntosh 1996; Tubb 1995; Vitelli 1996). More evidence is provided here in chapter 8, in which Christopher Roosevelt and Christina Luke describe a survey of burial tumuli in the Güre-Uşak region of western Turkey where the Lydian Hoard was discovered, famous—or infamous—because of its acquisition by the Metropolitan Museum of Art in the 1960s and subsequent return to Turkey in 1993 (Brodie et al. 2000: 8–10; Kaye and Main 1995). Roosevelt and Luke make the important point that although the destruction caused by looting is clear on the ground—in the form of ransacked tombs—it is hard to assess just what has been lost, in terms of both material and historical information. Nevertheless, despite the losses, there is still something to be learned from what is left: the spatial patterning of the tumuli themselves throws light on the political geography of Lydia during the Lydian and Persian periods of the seventh through fourth centuries B.C. In similar vein, Luke and John Henderson provide an account in chapter 7 of the damage caused to the archaeological heritage of the Lower Ulúa Valley of northwest Honduras by looting to feed a thriving market for Maya material.

The point made by Roosevelt and Luke that no estimate is possible of material lost from a looted site, or of what the accumulated material losses mean in terms of wasted information, is an important one. All that remains is an unknowable number of lacunae in the historical evidence, each one of indeterminate size and significance. Occasionally, however, there are glimpses of what might have been. For example, it has long been hypothesized that the inception and subsequent spread of the Eurasian Bronze Age was dependent upon trade and, ultimately, efficient means of long-distance bulk transport (Childe 1958: 78–80). Overland, this meant the introduction of domestic pack animals from outside the region: horses from the north and donkeys from the south. However, the archaeological evidence required to test this hypothesis is scarce (Brodie, in press). Thus it is galling to find a continuing series of terra-cotta models of pack animals appearing for sale on websites for a few hundred dollars each. These models are devoid of context and are of uncertain authenticity. Even if they are genuine, it is sometimes questionable what species they represent and what the exact or even approximate date of their manufacture was. They are useless for the task at hand. Had they been found in controlled excavations, they would be provenienced, dated, securely identified, and perhaps able to contribute to our understanding of the development of overland trade and the articulation of a continent-wide metal-using economy. As it is, the best they can do is decorate a mantelpiece.

In chapter 14, Lena Mortensen emphasizes that archaeologists are not the only stakeholders in archaeological heritage and that lost historical knowledge is not the only issue—illegal digging also has a political aspect. In many areas, archaeological sites or objects are constitutive elements of foundational narratives that help group identities to cohere and perhaps legitimize territorial claims (see papers in Kane 2003); thus rights of access to or ownership of archaeological heritage have become highly charged political issues.

The complexities of the situation are best illustrated by the site of Sipán, in Peru (Alva 2001: 92–93; Atwood 2004; Kirkpatrick 1992; Watson 1999). Here, in 1987, local diggers out looking for antiquities to sell discovered a rich Moche tomb in a decayed mud-brick pyramid. The looting frenzy that followed attracted a host of characters—archaeologists, collectors, dealers, local inhabitants, looters, and law enforcement officers—with a variety of motivations and sometimes incompatible agendas, but all making claims on the site. Arrests were made in the United States and some of the contents of the looted tomb were recovered, though most material slipped through the judicial net. The looted tomb also excited the interest of Peruvian and foreign archaeologists, and a scientific excavation ensued. Money was raised to build a "local" museum for the finds, which opened in 2003, though at the town of Lambayeque, about forty kilometers away from the village of Sipán itself. The archaeological discoveries and the new museum have proved a boon for the regional tourist economy, but most of the money seems to be bypassing Sipán to be spent in the towns of Lambayeque and Chiclayo. Understandably, the inhabitants of Sipán are resentful. They face tough times as traditional sources of employment in the sugar industry are being lost, and they regard archaeologists as thieves who are stealing their rightful inheritance of the tombs. They say the tombs contain valuables that were left to them by their ancestors for use in hard times (Atwood 2002).

The appearance of good quality Moche artifacts on the market stimulated demand, and during the late 1980s and 1990s illegal digging intensified throughout the Moche heartland of northern Peru. But public opinion in Peru is divided. The Sipán material also appeals to the imagination and historical sensibility of many Peruvians, for whom the finds are a rediscovery of lost heritage and a source of ethnic pride. Patrols were organized in many areas of northern Peru and have had some success in bringing looting under control (Alva 2001: 94–95; Atwood 2003), but there is still no public consensus. Attitudes toward archaeological heritage are differently structured or at least affected by ethnic affiliation and economic circumstance as well as by outreach by museums and other cultural institutions (Alva 2001: 95).

The plight of the Sipán villagers reveals a powerful argument in favor of the antiquities trade, which is that it can support what has been called "subsistence digging" (Hollowell-Zimmer 2003; Matsuda 1998; Paredes 1998). Poor rural farmers or agricultural laborers, who are often dependent upon the cultivation and uncertain sale of cash crops, can sometimes supplement their income through digging up and selling artifacts from archaeological sites. In these situations, attempts to stifle the trade appear to value the integrity of archaeological heritage more than human well-being, and perhaps life, even though in the long term subsistence digging is unsustainable (as once the archaeological resource is looted out, it cannot be replaced).

One solution to subsistence digging has been to develop archaeological heritage as an educational resource or tourist attraction, as with the site and finds of Sipán, so that jobs are created and local people benefit financially. This is a sustainable use of archaeological heritage, though not one without problems (Nalda 2002: 219–26; Stark and Griffin 2004). However, in some areas that are being badly looted, state-sponsored antiquities or museum services are staffed by members of a dominant social or ethnic group, sometimes outsiders, and so local people continue be alienated and there is no incentive for them to stop digging. Indeed, it can even be the case that state authorities will turn a blind eye to digging, either because it is—conveniently—destroying the heritage and thus the identity and political presence of a minority group (often that of the looters themselves), or because it provides an income supplement at no cost to the state and quiets the local population. In other words, while in the short term subsistence digging may bring some economic relief to an underprivileged or oppressed community, in the longer term it may simply perpetuate or worsen social inequality. Mortensen explores some of these issues in chapter 14, where she provides an account of the negotiations that took place in 2000 and 2001 during the preparation of a management plan for the Maya site of Copán, in Honduras, and describes the interest groups that were involved.

The opinions of the subsistence diggers themselves are not often heard, and there is an uneasy sense here that the entire debate over the commercialization of archaeological heritage is embedded within a larger postcolonial or postimperial discourse, so it is important that in chapter 5 Julie Hollowell reports on the Sivuqaq and Savoonga Native corporations. These corporations own St Lawrence Island and thus all archaeological objects buried there. Hollowell describes how artifacts are legally excavated and sold and considers the consequences both for the archaeological heritage and for archaeological research. She also discusses a recent initiative of the islanders to take control of the distribution and marketing of artifacts out of the hands of outside dealers and intermediaries.

It is pointless, even reprehensible, to punish subsistence diggers for a crime that mainly benefits individuals higher up the trading chain, who are often corrupt officers of the local or national government, of customs or archaeological services, or even of the law enforcement agencies charged with protecting archaeological heritage. Indeed, members of these organizations may even sanction, organize, or provide resources to support the digging. Subsistence digging will stop only when rural populations are in safe possession of their own land and are able to receive a fair price for their agricultural produce, which in turn requires the abolition of tariffs and other trade barriers that are currently maintained by the world's main trading blocks. In the meantime, archaeologists working in such areas can do their best to employ local labor and to encourage public involvement (Brodie 2002: 12–13; Hollowell-Zimmer 2003: 50–53).

It is important to remember that not everyone who illegally or destructively digs up an archaeological site is a subsistence digger. The British nighthawks, who visit sites after dark with their metal detectors, U.S. relic hunters looking for Native American artifacts to sell, and the infamous Italian *tombaroli* all operate in G8 countries—the richest countries in the world. In chapter 6 Robert Hicks advocates a two-pronged strategy of law enforcement and public engagement that is particularly suited to discouraging or even eliminating archaeological looting in those countries; the strategy is of potential use in modified or adapted form in poorer countries too.

First, Hicks looks at improving methods of law enforcement. Although national and international laws outlaw archaeological looting and unauthorized trade, they offer few guidelines on how archaeological theft should be investigated and documented on the ground or about how damage should be assessed. Hicks presents a model investigative protocol for use by law enforcement officers and archaeologists when confronted by an illegally excavated site—what he accurately terms a crime scene. The second prong of Hicks's strategy is to enroll public support for the statutory protection of archaeological heritage. Education is important here, but he moves beyond public education to public engagement and describes how students might be involved in a role-playing investigation based on the aforementioned investigative protocol.

Some of the worst examples of archaeological looting in the past thirty years have occurred in countries suffering from the public disorder and economic disruption that follow the breakdown of central authority during wartime. In these circumstances, law enforcement is weak and buried artifacts are a ready source of cash for people who have seen their homes and their livelihoods destroyed. Two high profile cases are Iraq, discussed by Brodie in chapter 10 and Tubb in chapter 16, and Afghanistan, addressed by van Krieken-Pieters in chapter 11; Cambodia, Congo, and Somalia have also suffered. If looting could be discouraged or stopped in such circumstances it would seriously diminish the amount of illicit material reaching the market. In chapter 1, Lyndel Prott discusses the 1954 Hague Convention for the Protection of Cultural Property in the Event of Armed Conflict, which was drafted with this aim in mind, particularly its First Protocol, which places an obligation on States Parties not to remove cultural objects from territories occupied during wartime, and the 1999 Second Protocol, which extends this obligation to Parties engaged in civil war, and establishes that violations of the Convention are criminal offenses and provides rules for the prosecution of offenders (Boylan 2002; O'Keefe 2004). Unfortunately, although 114 states had ratified the Hague Convention as of 2005, there were only ninety-two States party to the First Protocol and thirty-six to the Second Protocol, and neither the United States nor the United Kingdom was party to the Convention or to either of its Protocols (although in May 2004 the United Kingdom did announce its intention to ratify the Hague Convention).

THE ANTIQUITIES MARKET

It is often said that the antiquities market is a fact of life—that people have always bought and sold antiquities and will continue to do so. It is true that precious or exotic materials are often in demand, but this is for a luxury market, an institution that is normally considered distinct from the art market, which subsumes the antiquities market. The art market is, in fact, an unusual phenomenon that appears only as part of what Alsop has termed a rare art tradition (Alsop 1982).

Alsop has chronicled how visual "art" as we know it, which he describes as "art-as-an-end-in-itself" (as distinct from "art-for-use-plus-beauty"), has appeared as a cultural form only five times at most in human history, on each occasion as part of a rare art tradition, an integrated system that includes the practices of critical or scholarly review, collecting, and trade besides the actual production of art. "Art-as-an-end-in-itself" cannot, apparently, exist by itself or for itself. Within a rare art tradition, the collecting and study of art enjoy a logical priority over the market. Art history is necessary to establish a hierarchy of quality (and thus value) and to establish criteria for investigating authenticity.

Art collecting provides the competitive demand that drives the market (Alsop 1982: 139).

Alsop's study is concerned with visual art, but that is not always a dominant art form. In many societies the musical, verbal, and performance arts are considered to be more accomplished than the visual, and the same was probably true in the past. It was not until the nineteenth century that visual art achieved its present cultural preeminence in Europe and the United States, possibly due to changing social attitudes about property and ownership (Coutts-Smith 1991: 17). A painting or art object can be owned, or at least appropriated, in a way that a dance performance or poem cannot. Preziosi (2002: 43) suggests that for the past century and a half, the commodification and aestheticization of artworks have been mutually implicated, so that the present Western system has grown from its Renaissance roots to a monstrous florescence that combines "swollen luxuriance with swollen influence" (Alsop 1982: 24). Thus the present-day art market is a historical formation that owes more to the consumerist urge of late capitalism than to the natural predispositions of consumers themselves. As such, it is socially constructed and open to amelioration through intervention. It is not an abstract entity operating mechanically in conditions of antiquities' scarcity according to the immutable laws of microeconomics.

In chapter 9, Morag Kersel analyzes the structure of the global antiquities market and identifies what in functional terms may be characterized as three separate markets through which artifacts may pass on their journey from the ground to the collector. They are, respectively, archaeologically-rich (source), transit, and destination markets. These markets are circumscribed but not necessarily physically discrete exchange networks. Sometimes geography does have a role to play, and in some locations actual marketplaces do emerge—Hollywood Road in Hong Kong being a notorious example, where anything from Chinese dinosaur eggs to colonial furniture can be bought (though much of it is probably fake). But different types of markets can also coexist in space, most obviously in the United States, which is a large destination market for material originating overseas but also a large source market for Native American material. In chapter 12, Pachauri describes some of the tribulations faced by a source country, in this case India, when infiltrated by the antiquities trade.

In destination markets, antiquities can be bought by private transactions, at galleries or fairs, by mail order, and even on the Internet (Brodie 2004; Tubb and Brodie 2001). Many antiquities are sold at public auction, in the United States and United Kingdom mainly at Sotheby's, Christie's, and, in London only, at Bonhams. In 1997 Sotheby's stopped their London sales of Mediterranean and West Asian antiquities after senior staff members were accused of being knowingly implicated in the sale of smuggled antiquities (Watson 1997).

Auction sales of antiquities are generally thought to represent the high end of the market and to provide a good estimate of market size. In chapter 4, however, Peter Watson refutes this conventional wisdom when he shows that there is a high-volume "hidden" trade bypassing the auction houses—and that it involves many objects that are higher-priced than those appearing at auction. Hollowell makes a similar point in chapter 5 with regard to ivory artifacts, and it is a phenomenon that has been noticed before. In her study of ancient Greek vases, for example, Nørskov notes that during the 1970s and 1980s museums had already purchased several Classical pieces direct from dealers for sums in excess of a million dollars before the first piece to pass the million-dollar mark at public auction was sold in New York in 1988 (Nørskov 2002: 291).

Watson and Hollowell suggest that the true function of an auction sale is to set a price standard for the larger market. The price of an object on the open market normally reflects the prevailing conditions of supply and demand, but so many antiquities are derived from illegal sources that supply is often shrouded in secrecy, and thus not quantifiable, and hence normal price-setting mechanisms cannot prevail. The problem is compounded when previously unknown classes of material appear on the market for which there is no precedent to guide prices. An auction can also be used to establish the pedigree of an object (Smith 1989: 39–40), a useful function in the antiquities trade. If there are doubts over the authenticity or provenance of an antiquity, these may be reflected by hesitant bidding. Conversely, doubts are dispelled by a healthy hammer price. Watson shows how auctions may actually be used to "launder" antiquities when dealers consign and buy back their own stock in order to provide a sales history—an important constituent of provenance. Auctions also allow vendors to remain anonymous, and so can buyers, who may appoint an agent to represent them in the auction room. The context of anonymity allows sellers of dubious reputation to participate, facilitates the dispersal or accumulation of major collections without unduly affecting prices, and can even cover tax avoidance (Smith 1989: 37).

Several international conventions have been drafted and adopted in recent decades with a view to regulating the antiquities trade, notably the 1970 UNESCO Convention on the Means of Prohibiting and Preventing the Illicit Import, Export and Transfer of Ownership of Cultural Property, the 1995 UNIDROIT Convention on Stolen or Illegally Exported Cultural Objects, and the 2001 UNESCO Convention on the Protection of the Underwater Cultural Heritage. It is a further indication of the competing interests that are vested in archaeological heritage that the United States did not ratify the 1970 UNESCO Convention until 1983, thirteen years after its adoption by UNESCO, and other major market countries dragged their feet for more than thirty years; that Convention was finally ratified by the United Kingdom in 2002 and implemented by Switzerland in 2004 (see Gerstenblith, chapter 3, for further discussion).

In view of this time lag between the drafting of a regulatory instrument and its widespread adoption, Marina Papa Sokal makes an important contribution in chapter 2 with her historical account of the negotiations that preceded the 1983 implementation of the 1970 UNESCO Convention in the United States as the Convention on Cultural Property Implementation Act (CPIA). Laws are not "natural" and they are not set in stone, and it is clear from Papa Sokal's account that they are very much contingent upon the political realities of the antiquities trade. There are powerful constituencies of interest whose views must be taken into account, ranging from domestic lobbying groups to international opinion, and although the final law is a compromise, it is also provisional and open to renegotiation.

In chapter 3, Patty Gerstenblith describes what other legal measures are available to discourage or combat the trade and thus protect heritage at its source. The recent convictions of Frederick Schultz in the United States and Jonathan Tokeley-Parry in the United Kingdom have reaffirmed that it is an offense under the respective stolen-property laws of those countries to trade in objects that foreign governments consider to be state property, even though U.S. and U.K. policy permit some degree of private ownership. The recent ratifications of the 1970 UNESCO Convention by the United Kingdom and Switzerland have renewed interest in the efficacy of international conventions and the manner of their implementation, which can vary considerably. In the United Kingdom, for example, it was felt that no new laws were necessary for implementation, while in Switzerland the 1970 UNESCO Convention was implemented through the 2003 Cultural Goods Transfer Act, which follows the lead set by the 1983 U.S. CPIA in allowing import controls to be imposed on selected categories of material through bilateral agreements.

ART, THE ART COLLECTOR, AND THE ART MUSEUM

The material object that is traded—the antiquity—is central to the debate. The term "antiquity" is no longer a common one in archaeological usage (where the more mundane "artifact" is preferred), but it does convey a sense of the archaeological artifact as collectible art object, and it is probably for this reason that "antiquity" is commonly used in market and collecting circles. In the concluding chapter 17, Neil Brodie and Christina Luke describe how, starting in the fifteenth century but particularly since the late nineteenth century, artists have imagined the aesthetic qualities of different categories of archaeological material. Art collectors have followed in their wake and have now claimed antiquities as their own. The financial ramifications of this appropriation and the negative implications for research are only just beginning to be investigated and understood, but it is clear that the imputation of aesthetic excellence and its consequence of high monetary value together bias the judgment of an antiquity's original purpose, significance, and value (Gill and Chippindale 1993; Vickers and Gill 1994). In analyzing the motivations and justifications of antiquities collectors, Brodie and Luke also point to the almost fetishistic power of the antiquity to transform personal and social values, while in chapter 16 Tubb considers some of the psychological aspects of collecting.

Nevertheless, although the private collector cannot be dismissed, it has long been recognized that museums, particularly art museums in the United States, play *the* central role in creating a demand for unprovenanced antiquities. They do this both by the indiscriminate acquisition that fuels the market—either directly by purchase or indirectly through gift or bequest—and by modes of display that emphasize the singularity of objects and discount the importance of archaeological context.

The art museum can be distinguished from other museums in that unlike a natural history or anthropology museum its purpose is not considered to be primarily educational; instead it is intended to allow contemplation of art in a space that is not cluttered with intrusive didactic aids (Bennett 1995: 10–11; Duncan 1995: 16–17). Although U.S. art museums have a long tradition of educational programming (Einreinhofer 1997: 102–13; Zolberg 1994), most education takes place outside the gallery through public outreach or inside the gallery through guided tours, and once alone, the art museum visitor is expected to possess the aesthetic disposition and knowledge necessary to appreciate what is on display without further visual prompting. The mission of the art museum was clearly stated in 1968 when the American Association of Museums published *America's Museums: The Belmont Report*, which claimed that art museums "aim to provide the esthetic and emotional pleasure which great works of art offer. This is a primary purpose of an art museum. It is assumed that a majority of the people who come regularly to art museums come to be delighted, not to be taught, or preached at, or 'improved' except by the works of art themselves" (quoted in Weil 1999: 235).

This distinction between the educational and the aesthetic purposes of museums may have blurred somewhat by the end of the twentieth century, but it is still deeply embedded in the definition of a museum offered in Section 272 of the 1996 U.S. Museum and Library Services Act (amended in 2003): "The term 'museum' means a public or private nonprofit agency or institution organized on a permanent basis for essentially educational or aesthetic purposes."

Thus there is a rift within the U.S. museum community. On one side stand

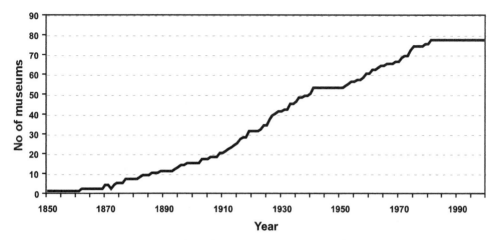

Figure Intro.1. Increasing number of U.S. art museums with collections of archaeological material originating in countries outside the United States (data from Art Museum Network website; Loebl 2002).

the art museums, with their commitment to the unfettered object; on the other side stand the natural history and anthropology museums, with their belief in the importance of context. The division is not absolute—for example, in chapter 2 Marina Papa Sokal records that some art museums lined up with anthropology museums during negotiations over the CPIA—but it does nevertheless have a general relevance.

Throughout the twentieth century, the number of art museums in the United States collecting archaeological material increased steadily (fig. Intro.1), and by the end of the century attendance figures were rising and collections were still growing (Harris 1999: 33). Most art museums contain large quantities of archaeological material, and the burgeoning growth of the art museum sector has undoubtedly been the underlying cause of the expanding antiquities trade over the same period. Unfortunately, this growth coincided with a sharp reduction in the legitimate supply of antiquities as countries, particularly newly independent countries, took steps to secure their archaeological heritage and to prevent its flow abroad. A small amount of material from old private collections reached the market, but as the twentieth century wore on, art museums were increasingly forced to acquire unprovenanced antiquities.

Inevitably, over the past few decades, several art museums have been caught in possession of stolen or illegally exported antiquities and have returned them, usually voluntarily but occasionally after a court case (table Intro.1). There are more claims outstanding. The propensities of art museums to acquire unprovenanced material have also attracted media attention. In 1995 Harvard's Arthur

M. Sackler Museum bought 182 Greek vase fragments of uncertain provenance, even though it had adopted a strong acquisitions policy in 1971 (Robinson and Yemma 1998). Acquisitions of the Boston Museum of Fine Arts (Boston MFA) have come under particularly close scrutiny, though not, it should be said, because the Boston MFA has been particularly unusual or remiss in this regard but because of the persistent inquiries of its local newspaper, the *Boston Globe*. In 1997 the *Globe* complained about many objects in a new permanent exhibition of Maya material, and two Malian terra-cottas, suggesting that they might have been exported from Guatemala and Mali illegally (Yemma and Robinson 1997). The MFA replied that the pieces were in the United States before 1983, when the CPIA took effect, and that therefore no U.S. laws had been broken. Then in 1998 the *Boston Globe* revealed that although the MFA had adopted an acquisitions policy in 1983, which was intended to guard against the acquisition of dubious objects, it had nevertheless between 1984 and 1987 purchased 73 classical Greek and Roman antiquities, of which only ten had any clear provenance (Robinson 1998).

The museum community is well aware of the potential for destructive synergy between the museum and the market and has taken steps to prevent it by formulating codes of ethics and practice to guide the acquisitions policies of museums and the commercial involvement of their employees. It is important that museums take a strong position on the antiquities trade, not only because of their active involvement but because they set a moral tone that others will follow. In the words of the United Kingdom's Museums Association, there is a "kind of ethical body language expressed by the museum around issues of openness, stewardship, honesty, humility and inclusivity." Its behavior must be exemplary.

Colin Renfrew discusses museum acquisitions policies in chapter 13. One of the first explicit statements of an ethical acquisitions policy was by the University of Pennsylvania Museum of Archaeology and Anthropology, which announced in April 1970 that it would no longer acquire an antiquity without convincing documentation of the item's legitimate pedigree. The Field Museum in Chicago followed suit in 1972. It is significant that both of these institutions can be broadly characterized as anthropology or natural history museums, with their commitment to an educational agenda.

Today there are three ethical codes or statements that are relevant for U.S. museums, drafted by the International Council of Museums (ICOM), the American Association of Museums (AAM), and the Association of Art Museum Directors (AAMD), but the nature and strength of their requirements vary.

Table Intro.1. Returns of Stolen or Illegally Exported Archaeological Artifacts by U.S. Art Museums

Date of return	Museum	Date of acquisition	Piece	Country of origin	Reference
1974	Newark Museum	1971	Roman mosaic	Syria	Miller 1998
1986	Kimbell Art Museum	1979	Bronze Nataraja	India	Shankar 2001, 34
1993	Metropolitan Museum of Art	1960s	Lydian Hoard	Turkey	Kaye and Main 1995
1997	Metropolitan Museum of Art		Stone head	Cambodia	ICOM 1997, 11
1998	Denver Art Museum	1973	Mayan wooden lintel	Guatemala	Schuster 1999
1999	Metropolitan Museum of Art		Stone sculpture	India	Shankar 2001, 35
1999	Asia Society	1978	Stone relief	India	Shankar 2001, 35
1999	J. Paul Getty Museum		Greek pot; two pieces of Roman sculpture	Italy	Lee 1999
2002	Honolulu Academy of Arts		Two stone heads	Cambodia	ICOM 1997, 11
2002	Princeton University Art Museum	1985	Stone relief	Italy	Lufkin 2002

Note: Date of acquisition included only when known.

ICOM has taken an active oppositional stance toward the trade in unprovenanced antiquities, and this is reflected in its code of ethics (ICOM 2004), which is carefully worded to guard museums against acquiring objects that might first have been obtained in destructive or illegal circumstances. Articles 2.3 and 2.4 state:

2.3. Provenance and Due Diligence

Every effort must be made before acquisition to ensure that any object or specimen offered for purchase, gift, loan, bequest, or exchange has not been illegally obtained in, or exported from, its country of origin or any intermediate country in which it might have been owned legally (including the museum's own country). Due diligence in this regard should establish the full history of the item from discovery or production.

2.4. Objects and Specimens from Unauthorised or Unscientific Fieldwork

Museums should not acquire objects where there is reasonable cause to believe their recovery involved the unauthorised, unscientific, or intentional destruction or damage of monuments, archaeological or geological sites, or species and natural habitats. In the same way, acquisition should not occur if there has been a failure to disclose the finds to the owner or occupier of the land, or to the proper legal or governmental authorities.

In practice, however, the ICOM code is largely ignored by U.S. art museums, which look to the AAM and the AAMD for ethical guidance. The AAM's statement on the ethics of acquisition is briefer than ICOM's and far less specific: "Acquisition, disposal and loan activities are conducted in a manner that respects the protection and preservation of natural and cultural resources and discourages illicit trade in such materials" (AAM 1993). There are no direct recommendations in the AAM's statement, although in the introduction to its code the AAM does ask that museums comply with applicable international conventions, which would include the 1983 CPIA, and in the afterword it emphasizes that individual museums should frame their own codes of ethics, which should conform with the AAM code and expand on it through the elaboration of specific guidelines.

One museum that did just that was the J. Paul Getty Museum (True 1997: 139). In 1987 its board of trustees ratified a policy with two main guidelines. First, the museum would not rely on documents of provenance provided by dealers, as such documents had in the past, and to the museum's cost, sometimes proved to be fake. Instead, the museum would communicate its intention to purchase a piece to the relevant authorities of the country in question so that they would have an opportunity to register an objection. Second, the museum would excuse itself from time limits placed on its liability by the statute of limitations. In other words, if it could be demonstrated that a piece in the Getty's collection had been stolen, then the museum would return the item to its rightful owner irrespective of whether the limitation period had expired (in which case the museum would be under no legal obligation to do so; True 1997: 139). In November 1995 the Getty's policy was strengthened with a requirement that the museum would no longer acquire any object that had not been published or otherwise documented prior to 1995 (True 1997: 139). Unfortunately, the welcome that originally greeted this amendment turned sour when, six months later in June 1996, the museum acquired the Barbara and Lawrence Fleischman collection of Classical antiquities, which had been published in 1994, just one year before the Getty's 1995 cut-off date—by the Getty itself (Kaufman 1996)!

Art museum directors, including Philippe de Montebello of New York's Metropolitan Museum of Art (Kaufman 1999) and James Cuno of the Art Institute of Chicago (Cuno 2001), offer two arguments or justifications for the acquisition of unprovenanced antiquities that have possibly been looted. The first is that museums should not be bound by foreign laws that are counter to their interest and that may also be contrary to established U.S. law. The second is the so-called rescue argument—antiquities on the market are already out of the ground, the context has already been destroyed, and so by acquiring them the museum is rescuing material that would otherwise be destroyed or lost from public view.

The art museums' opposition to foreign patrimony laws was already evident in the 1970s, as Marina Papa Sokal makes clear in chapter 2, and it has continued since. In 1998, the central thesis of an *amicus curiae* brief prepared by the AAM in support of the collector Michael Steinhardt was that U.S. museums should not be subject to foreign patrimony laws, which the AAM defined as laws vesting ownership of archaeological heritage in the state and/or barring the export of archaeological heritage (AAM 2000: 77, 99; see also Lyons 2002; Shapreau 2000). The AAM's stated objection to patrimony laws was that they are antithetical to fundamental principles of U.S. law (AAM 2000: 77), but it can be no coincidence that these laws also place a strong constraint on the freedom of museums to acquire antiquities. This is because although all U.S. museums undertake not to acquire stolen property, it is usually impossible to prove that an unprovenanced antiquity is stolen, as usually understood in U.S. law, in that it is the private property of an individual person or an organization. Thus an unprovenanced antiquity is an acceptable (in the sense of low-risk) acquisition. However, if an antiquity is removed from a country with a patrimony law that vests ownership in the state, it becomes stolen public property, which is easier to identify and reclaim than stolen private property. As most unprovenanced antiquities that appear on the market are from states with patrimony laws, these laws pose a clear threat of restitution to museums that might be caught in un-lawful possession after an unguarded acquisition. The possible financial loss that such restitutions might inflict, about U.S. $1.5 million in the case of the Lydian Hoard, is a powerful deterrent to the acquisition of unprovenanced material.

Patty Gerstenblith discusses patrimony laws in chapter 3, where she reports that the conviction of Frederick Schultz in 2002 confirmed that one type of foreign patrimony law—state ownership of antiquities—is recognized by U.S. criminal courts (see also Gerstenblith 2002), and so the force of the art muse-ums' argument has been lessened.

In 2004 the Association of Art Museum Directors published its *Report of the AAMD Task Force on the Acquisition of Archaeological Materials and An-cient Art,* which contains seven guidelines to assist museums in the preparation or revision of acquisition policies (AAMD 2004). There is no specific refer-ence to the applicability of foreign patrimony statutes, as might be expected in light of the Schultz decision. Guideline C1 does recognize that the "status of a work of art under foreign law may bear on its legal status under U.S. law" but also notes that "the law relevant to the acquisition of archaeological materials and ancient art has become increasingly complex and continues to evolve." The AAMD guidelines contain nothing to discourage the acquisition of material when there is reasonable cause to believe that its original recovery involved the destruction or damage of an archaeological site or monument (as required by the ICOM code). Indeed, on the face of it, the requirement in guideline D that member museums should not acquire any archaeological material or work of ancient art "known to have been 'stolen from a museum, or a religious, or secu-lar public monument or similar institution'" or "known to have been part of an official archaeological excavation and removed in contravention of the laws of the country of origin" seems carefully worded to allow the acquisition of mate-rial from unofficial excavations—in other words, looted antiquities.

The AAM's Steinhardt brief acknowledged that the looting of archaeologi-cal sites is a serious problem but argued that the solution lies in "international cooperation and extensive internal efforts by source countries" (AAM 2000: 99, note 6). There was no admission or even hint of the role played by museums in stimulating the trade and, by extension, the looting. The AAMD guidelines do concede some connection: in guideline E they recommend that museums should not acquire unprovenanced antiquities that cannot be documented out of their country of origin for at least ten years, for fear of providing a mate-rial incentive to looting. Nevertheless, there is reluctance on the part of the art museum community to acknowledge or even investigate the causal relationship that exists between museum acquisitions (demand) and the looting of archaeological sites (supply). Unfortunately, art museums are the only institutions in a position to initiate such an investigation, either internally or externally by allowing outside researchers access to their accession records, and this has not often happened (Coggins 1998: 436).

When the *Boston Globe* questioned the legitimacy of the Boston MFA's Greek and Roman antiquities, the MFA refused to reveal the identities of dealers who supplied material and thus blocked the *Globe*'s investigation (Robinson 1998). The MFA's answer to the *Globe*'s article, when it came, was in the pages of *Minerva*, a glossy magazine published by New York–based antiquities dealer Jerome Eisenberg. Emily and Cornelius Vermeule (he being retired curator of Classical antiquities at the MFA) showed how most of the MFA's Bronze Age material had been acquired in the late nineteenth and early twentieth centuries through what were then legitimate channels (Vermeule and Vermeule 2004). But the *Globe* questions had been about late twentieth-century acquisitions of Classical Greek and Roman material, not early twentieth-century acquisitions of Bronze Age material, and the evasion of the *Minerva* article was disingenuous. In any case, demonstrations of past probity do little more than show how standards have lapsed over the intervening period. This is effective public relations but hardly fair scholarship.

Although art museum directors continue to justify dubious acquisitions on the grounds of legality and rescue, Alan Shestack, a former director of the Minneapolis Institute of Arts and the Boston MFA, has offered what is perhaps a more pragmatic reason, which is that art museum directors are responsible to their boards of trustees and can be fired if strict adherence to an ethical acquisitions policy causes desirable pieces to be passed over (Shestack 1999: 98). In answer to this, it has been argued that in law trustees have a fiduciary obligation to ensure that the museum they serve does not incur a financial loss through having to deaccession material for purposes of restitution, as has happened several times in recent years. This obligation can only be met by the implementation of acquisitions policies that embody strong diligence procedures to guard against the acquisition of illegal material (Gerstenblith 2003).

Art museum acquisitions make a positive and direct impact upon the antiquities market, but as Paula Kay Lazrus emphasizes in chapter 15, their exhibitions have a more indirect, though still important, effect. Modes of display aimed at creating an aesthetic presence promote the desirability and monetary value of antiquities, and so help commodify them. The empty context of an art museum vitrine is intended to focus attention on the object, to let the object speak for itself. But the object can only take voice from its context, which in the absence of anything else is provided for antiquities by the architectural grandiloquence of the museum, designed to evoke in the visitor a proper sense of respect, or even awe, for the artworks contained therein, or by extension from the elitist connotations or symbolism of other objects on display.

Art museums tend to fill up with objects that are emblematic of high social status (Belk 1995: 152–55; Duncan 1995: 59, 63). This is for two reasons. First, museum collecting is a filtering process, whereby exemplary or high quality objects are selected for collection, and poorer quality objects are rejected. The term "museum quality" is used in trade advertisements to denote pieces of exceptional interest or quality. The second reason is the propensity of museums to accept the private collections of wealthy patrons, which usually comprise artifacts that are valued because of their preciosity and that have been assembled to enhance their owner's reputation as a person of "taste." For Belk, "'Museum quality' more often than not also means museum inequality. In museums and collections we consecrate not just taste, but the taste of the elite and powerful" (Belk 1995: 155; see also Bennett 1995: 11). Perversely, by consecrating their taste, what might otherwise be considered as wasteful expenditure by the social elite, particularly on objects of decorative art, can be justified as being for the public benefit (Harris 1990: 136). Thus if the museum display of antiquities alongside other artistic trappings of wealth and power is predicated largely or entirely upon the criterion of aesthetic merit, the message received by the visitor/consumer might be that the possession and transaction of equivalent pieces can form a legitimate route to social advancement or a socially approved sign of cultural attainment.

The commodifying effects of display are highlighted by Luke and Henderson in chapter 7, where they note that sales of Ulúa-style marble vases from Honduras increased after an exhibition of vases in 1992 at the Houston Museum of Fine Arts. Increased market activity following from exhibitions has been noticed before. In chapter 13, Colin Renfrew discusses the unfortunate consequences of a 1976 exhibition of Cycladic figurines at the Badisches Landesmuseum in Karlsruhe, Germany. It was reported that the looting of archaeological sites in Niger worsened after the Vallées du Niger exhibition of archaeological material from West Africa toured Mali, Burkina Faso, Nigeria, Mauritania, Conakry Guinea, Niger, and France between 1993 and 1998 (Gado 2001), and in August 2003, the month the Metropolitan Museum's exhibition "Art of the First Cities—The Third Millennium B.C. from the Mediterranean to the Indus" closed, its positive impact on the market for West Asian antiquities was already being noted in the trade press (*Antiques Trade Gazette* 2003: 31).

Even if exhibitions are structured around the historical or social significance of artifacts, or their use or function, rather than their perceived aesthetic importance, the trade will almost certainly seize upon bumper exhibitions of high-quality archaeological material to promote and create demand for similar objects. The museum is in a quandary, as even a well thought-out and informative exhibition may act to promote antiquities as desirable commodities and may ultimately provoke an upturn in archaeological looting. One answer to this quandary is provided by Lundén (2004: 238), who suggests the creation of display contexts that in themselves draw attention to the dubious origins of exhibited objects: "To present an object on its own in a showcase creates certain notions. To present it in a reconstruction of its ancient context creates others. To put it on display poking out of the crate in which it arrived at the museum from, for example, a Swiss dealer is to create yet other notions."

Occasionally, exhibitions of archaeological looting have been displayed at museums (see, for example, Graepler 1993), but such exhibitions have been few and far between and usually for only a limited period of time. For a full public understanding of the threats posed to archaeology by looting, an explanation of the issues should be an integral and permanent part of all exhibitions, particularly those that are promoting antiquities as works of art.

The debate over the role of art museums in facilitating or stimulating the trade in unprovenanced antiquities is polarized, and art museums are often held to be good or bad, to have responsible or irresponsible acquisitions policies, and so on. But like the "market," the "museum" should not be treated as an abstract entity imbued with a will and a purpose of its own. In a generic sense the "art museum" is a social institution, but the policies and practices of individual museums are determined by the actions of their governing and curatorial staffs, who are themselves embedded in larger social networks, including those that constitute the trade.

Conclusion

The antiquities trade transforms monetary, aesthetic, legal, personal, and social values. The causes and consequences of these transformations form the subject matter of this book. The chapters that follow investigate different aspects and components of the antiquities trade and its regulation and consider the roles played by collectors and museums in perpetuating it. No firm recommendations or positive conclusions are offered, largely because the trade and the transformations it entails are still poorly understood phenomena. In view of this, the concluding chapter makes some outline proposals for future research. The damage caused on the ground to archaeological sites and monuments is already well documented, and the sale and collection of unprovenanced antiquities is equally so. The need now is for concerted research into the social relationships that constitute the trade and its institutions. But this will not be easy. Access to relevant sources of information will routinely be blocked, and inquiries will face obfuscation. Yet until the trade is rendered transparent, it is hard to see how it will be abated.

BIBLIOGRAPHY

AAM. "AAM Code of Ethics for Museums." Available at <http://www.aam-us.org/museumresources/ethics/coe.cfm>, accessed October 23, 2004 (1993).

———. "Brief of *Amici Curiae* American Association of Museums, *et al.* in support of the appeal of claimant Michael H. Steinhardt." *International Journal of Cultural Property* 9 (2000): 76–105.

AAMD. "Report of the AAMD Task Force on the Acquisition of Archaeological Materials and Ancient Art." Available at <http://www.aamd.org/papers/documents/June-10FinalTaskForceReport_001.pdf>, accessed October 23 2004 (2004).

Alsop, Joseph. *The Rare Art Traditions.* London: Thames and Hudson, 1982.

Alva, Walter. "The Destruction, Looting and Traffic of the Archaeological Heritage of Peru." In *Trade in Illicit Antiquities: The Destruction of the World's Archaeological Heritage,* ed. Neil J. Brodie, Jennifer Doole, and Colin Renfrew, 89–96. McDonald Institute Monograph. Cambridge, U.K.: McDonald Institute for Archaeological Research, 2001.

Antiques Trade Gazette. "Egypt and Bactria Are Ancient Favourites." *Antiques Trade Gazette,* August 16, 2003, 31–32.

Atwood, Roger. "Stealing History." MotherJones.com, May–June 2002. Available at <http://www.motherjones.com>, accessed September 23, 2003.

———. "Guardians of the Dead." *Archaeology,* January–February 2003, 43–49.

———. *Stealing History: Tomb Raiders, Smugglers, and the Looting of the Ancient World.* New York: St. Martin's Press, 2004.

Belk, Russell W. *Collecting in a Consumer Society.* London: Routledge, 1995.

Bennett, Tony. *The Birth of the Museum.* London: Routledge, 1995.

Boylan, Patrick J. "The Concept of Cultural Protection in Times of Armed Conflict: From the Crusades to the New Millennium." In *Illicit Antiquities: The Theft of Culture and the Extinction of Archaeology,* ed. Neil Brodie and Kathryn W. Tubb, 43–108. London: Routledge, 2002.

Brodie, Neil J. "Introduction." In *Illicit Antiquities: The Theft of Culture and the Extinction of Archaeology,* ed. Neil Brodie and Kathryn W. Tubb, 1–22. London: Routledge. 2002.

———. "Export Deregulation and the Illicit Trade in Archaeological Material." In *Legal Perspectives on Cultural Resources,* ed. Jennifer R. Richman and Marion P. Forsyth, 85–99. Walnut Creek, Calif.: AltaMira, 2004.

———. "The Donkey: An Appropriate Technology for Early Bronze Age 1 and Transport and Traction." In *A Colloquium on the Prehistory of the Cyclades,* ed. Neil J. Brodie, Jennifer Doole, Giorgos Gavalas, Colin Renfrew, and Katie Boyle. McDonald Institute

Monograph. Cambridge, U.K.: McDonald Institute for Archaeological Research, in press.

Brodie, Neil J., Jennifer Doole, and Colin Renfrew (eds.). *Trade in Illicit Antiquities: The Destruction of the World's Archaeological Heritage*. McDonald Institute Monograph. Cambridge, U.K.: McDonald Institute for Archaeological Research, 2001.

Brodie, Neil J., Jennifer Doole, and Peter Watson. *Stealing History*. Cambridge, U.K.: McDonald Institute for Archaeological Research, 2000.

Brodie, Neil J., and Kathryn W. Tubb (eds.). *Illicit Antiquities: The Theft of Culture and the Extinction of Archaeology*. London: Routledge, 2002.

Childe, Gordon. *The Prehistory of European Society*. London: Penguin Books, 1958.

Coggins, Clemency. "Illicit Traffic in Pre-Columbian Antiquities." *Art Journal* 29, no. 1 (1969): 94–98.

———. "A Proposal for Museum Acquisition Policies in the Future." *International Journal of Cultural Property* 7 (1998): 434–37.

Coutts-Smith, Kenneth. "Some General Observations on the Problem of Cultural Colonialism." In *The Myth of Primitivism*, ed. Susan Hiller, 14–31. London: Routledge, 1991.

Cuno, James. "The Whole World's Treasures." *Boston Globe*, March 11, 2001.

Duncan, Carol. *Civilising Rituals: Inside Public Art Museums*. London: Routledge, 1995.

Einreinhofer, Nancy. *The American Art Museum: Elitism and Democracy*. Leicester: Leicester University Press, 1997.

Gado, Boubé. "The Republic of Niger." In *Trade in Illicit Antiquities: The Destruction of the World's Archaeological Heritage*, ed. Neil J. Brodie, Jennifer Doole, and Colin Renfrew, 57–72. McDonald Institute Monograph. Cambridge, U.K.: McDonald Institute for Archaeological Research, 2001.

Gerstenblith, Patty. "United States v. Schultz." *Culture without Context*, issue 10 (Spring 2002): 27–31.

———. "Acquisition and Deacquisition of Museum Collections and the Fiduciary Obligations of Museums to the Public." *Cardozo Journal of International and Comparative Law* 11 (2003): 409–65.

Gill, David W. J., and Christopher Chippindale. "Material and Intellectual Consequences of Esteem for Cycladic Figures." *American Journal of Archaeology* 97 (1993): 601–59.

Graepler, Daniel. *Fundort: Unbekannt. Raubgrabungen Zerstören das Archäologische Erbe*. Munich: Walter Bierung, 1993.

Gutchen, Mark. "The Destruction of Archaeological Resources in Belize, Central America." *Journal of Field Archaeology* 10 (1983): 217–28.

Harris, Neil. *Cultural Excursions: Marketing Appetites and Cultural Tastes in Modern America*. Chicago: University of Chicago Press, 1990.

———. "The Divided House of the American Art Museum." *Dædalus* 128, no. 3 (1999): 33–56.

Heilmeyer, Wolf-Dieter, and J. Cordelia Eule. *Illegale Archäologie?* Berlin: Weißensee, 2004.

Hollowell-Zimmer, Julie. "Digging in the Dirt: Ethics and 'Low-End Looting.'" In *Ethical Issues in Archaeology*, ed. Larry J. Zimmerman, Karen D. Vitelli, and Julie Hollowell-Zimmer, 45–56. Walnut Creek, Calif.: AltaMira, 2003.

ICOM. *One Hundred Missing Objects: Looting in Angkor.* Paris: ICOM, 1997.

———. *ICOM Code of Ethics for Museums*, 1986. Amended, Paris: ICOM, 2004.

Kane, Susan (ed.). *The Politics of Archaeology and Identity in a Global Context.* Boston: Archaeological Institute of America, 2003.

Kaufman, Jason. "Getty Decides Publishing Equals Provenance." *Art Newspaper*, no. 61 (1996): 17.

———. "To the Greater Glory of Antiquity?" *Art Newspaper*, no. 92 (1999): 18–19.

Kaye, Lawrence M., and Carla T. Main. "The Saga of the Lydian Hoard Antiquities: From Uşak to New York and Back and Some Related Observations on the Law of Cultural Repatriation." In *Antiquities Trade or Betrayed: Legal, Ethical and Conservation Issues*, ed. Kathryn W. Tubb, 150–62. London: Archetype-UKIC, 1995.

Kirkpatrick, Sidney D. *Lords of Sipan.* New York: Morrow, 1992.

Lafont, Masha. *Pillaging Cambodia: The Illicit Traffic in Khmer Art.* Jefferson, N.C.: McFarland, 2004.

Lee, Donald. "Getty Returns Three Stolen Works." *Art Newspaper* no. 90 (1999): 1, 3.

Leyten, Harrie (ed.). *Illicit Traffic in Cultural Property: Museums against Pillage.* Amsterdam: Royal Tropical Institute, 1995.

Loebl, Suzanne. *America's Art Museums.* New York: W. W. Norton, 2002.

Lufkin, Martha. "While Princeton Doesn't Need to Be Asked." *Art Newspaper* no. 128 (2002): 16.

Lundén, Staffan. "The Scholar and the Market: Swedish Scholarly Contributions to the Destruction of the World's Archaeological Heritage." In *Swedish Archaeologists on Ethics*, ed. H. Karlsson, 197–247. Lindome: Bricoleur Press, 2004.

Lyons, Claire L. "Objects and Identities: Claiming and Reclaiming the Past." In *Claiming the Stones: Naming the Bones*, ed. Elazar Barkan and Ronald Bush, 116–40. Los Angeles: Getty Research Institute, 2002.

Matsuda, David J. "The Ethics of Archaeology, Subsistence Digging, and Artifact Looting in Latin America: Point, Muted Counterpoint." *International Journal of Cultural Property* 7 (1998): 82–97.

Messenger, Phyllis M. *The Ethics of Collecting Cultural Property.* Albuquerque, N.M.: University of New Mexico Press, 1999.

Meyer, Karl E. *The Plundered Past.* London: Readers Union, 1973.

Miller, Samuel C. "A Syrian Odyssey: The Return of Syrian Mosaics by the Newark Museum." *International Journal of Cultural Property* 7 (1998): 166–69.

Nalda, Enrique. "Mexico's Archaeological Heritage: A Convergence and Confrontation of Interests." In *Illicit Antiquities: The Theft of Culture and the Extinction of Archaeology*, ed. Neil Brodie and Kathryn W. Tubb, 205–27. London: Routledge, 2002.

Nørskov, Vinnie. *Greek Vases in New Contexts: The Collecting and Trading of Greek Vases—An Aspect of the Modern Reception of Antiquity.* Aarhus, Denmark: Aarhus University Press, 2002.

O'Keefe, Patrick J. *Trade in Antiquities: Reducing Destruction and Theft*. London: Archetype/UNESCO, 1997.

———. "The First Protocol to the Hague Convention Fifty Years on." *Art, Antiquity and Law* 9 (2004): 99–116.

Paredes Maury, Sofia. "Surviving in the Rainforest: The Realities of Looting in the Rural Villages of El Peten, Guatemala." Foundation for the Advancement of Meso-American Studies, (August), 1998. <www.famsi.org/spanish/reports/95096/section05.htm>, accessed October 18, 2004.

Preziosi, Donald. "Hearing the Unsaid: Art History, Museology, and the Composition of the Self." In *Art History and Its Institutions: Foundations of a Discipline*, ed. Elizabeth Mansfield. London: Routledge, 2002.

Renfrew, Colin. *Loot, Legitimacy and Ownership: The Ethical Crisis in Archaeology*. London: Duckworth, 1999.

Robinson, Walter V. "New MFA Link Seen to Looted Artifacts." *Boston Globe*, December 27, 1998.

Robinson, Walter V., and J. Yemma. "Harvard Museum Acquisitions Shock Scholars." *Boston Globe*, January 16, 1998.

Schick, Jürgen. *The Gods Are Leaving the Country*. Bangkok: White Orchid, 1998.

Schmidt, Peter R., and Roderick J. McIntosh (eds.). *Plundering Africa's Past*. London: James Currey, 1996.

Schuster, Angela M. H. "Maya Art Return." *Archaeology*, January–February 1999, 16–17.

Shankar, Ajai. "The Threat to Cultural Sites in India from Illegal Excavation." In *Trade in Illicit Antiquities: The Destruction of the World's Archaeological Heritage*, ed. Neil J. Brodie, Jennifer Doole, and Colin Renfrew, 33–36. McDonald Institute Monograph. Cambridge, U.K.: McDonald Institute for Archaeological Research, 2001.

Shapreau, Carla J. "Second Circuit Holds That False Statements Contained in Customs Forms Warrant Forfeiture of Ancient Gold Phiale—Hotly Contested Foreign Patrimony Issue Not Reached by the Court: United States v. An Antique Platter of Gold." *International Journal of Cultural Property* 9 (2000): 49–76.

Shestack, Alan. "The Museum and Cultural Property: The Transformation of Institutional Ethics." In *The Ethics of Collecting Cultural Property*, ed. Phyllis M. Messenger, 93–102. Albuquerque, N.M.: University of New Mexico Press, 1999.

Smith, Charles W. *Auctions: The Social Construction of Value*. London: Harvester Wheatsheaf, 1989.

Stark, Miriam T., and P. Bion Griffin. "Archaeological Research and Cultural Heritage Management in Cambodia's Mekong Delta: The Search for the 'Cradle of Khmer Civilisation.'" In *Marketing Heritage: Archaeology and the Consumption of the Past*, ed. Yorke Rowan and Uzi Baram, 117–42. Walnut Creek, Calif.: AltaMira, 2004.

Stead, Ian M. *The Salisbury Hoard*. Stroud, U.K.: Tempus, 1998.

Toner, Mike. *The Past in Peril*. Tallahassee, Fla: Southeast Archaeological Center, 2002.

True, Marion. "Refining Policy to Promote Partnership." In *Antichità Senza Provenienza II*, ed. Paola Pelagatti and Pier Giovanni Guzzo, 137–46. *Bolletino D'Arte* Supplemento 101–2 (1997).

Tubb, Kathryn W. (ed.). *Antiquities Trade or Betrayed: Legal, Ethical and Conservation Issues*. London: Archetype-UKIC, 1995.

Tubb, Kathryn W., and Neil J. Brodie. "From Museum to Mantelpiece: The Antiquities Trade in the United Kingdom." In *Destruction and Conservation of Cultural Property*, ed. Robert Layton, Peter G. Stone, and Julian Thomas, 102–16. London: Routledge, 2001.

Vermeule, Emily T., and Cornelius C. Vermeule. "The Bronze Age in Boston: A Catalogue of Documented Antiquities." *Minerva*, January–February 2004, 43–44.

Vickers, Michael, and David Gill. *Artful Crafts*. Oxford: Clarendon Press, 1994.

Vitelli, Karen D. (ed.). *Archaeological Ethics*. Walnut Creek, Calif.: AltaMira, 1996.

Yemma, John, and Walter V. Robinson. "Mayan Art of Questionable Origin in Boston Museum." *Boston Globe*, December 3, 1997.

Watson, Peter. *Sotheby's: Inside Story*. London: Bloomsbury, 1997.

———. "The Lessons of Sipán: Archaeologists and Huaqueros." *Culture without Context*, issue 4 (Spring 1999): 15–20.

Weil, Stephen E. "From Being *about* Something to Being *for* Somebody: The Ongoing Transformation of the American Museum." *Dædalus* 128 no. 3 (1999): 229–58.

Zolberg, Vera L. "An Elite Experience for Everyone: Art Museums, the Public, and Cultural Literacy." In *Museum Culture: Histories, Discourses, Spectacles*, ed. Daniel J. Sherman and Irit Rogoff, 49–65. London: Routledge, 1994.

1

Protecting Cultural Heritage in Conflict

LYNDEL V. PROTT

The 1954 Hague Convention for the Protection of Cultural Property in the Event of Armed Conflict and its associated Protocols are among the great humanitarian legal instruments, together with the Geneva Conventions and those on Genocide and Torture, that were developed in the twentieth century in order to try to minimize the inhumanity of warfare. The Preamble of the Hague Convention states a simple and important philosophy: "damage to cultural property belonging to any people whatsoever means damage to the cultural heritage of all mankind." This is more than ever the case: the whole world was concerned by the destruction of the Buddhas of Bamiyan and the looting of the National Museum of Iraq in Baghdad.

THE INSTRUMENTS

The Hague Convention sets out major obligations for warring states (Boylan 2002; O'Keefe 2004). In relation to the potential destruction of cultural property the Convention provides that a State Party to the Convention must respect cultural property in its own territory as well as that of other states; must refrain from any use of the property and its immediate surroundings for military purposes, and must refrain from directing any act of hostility against it. The only situation in which this rule may be waived is where military necessity imperatively requires it.

Other obligations are also set forth, specifically those in relation to removal of cultural property. States party to the Convention must prohibit, prevent, and if necessary put a stop to any form of theft, pillage, or misappropriation of and any acts of vandalism directed against cultural property. They must refrain from requisitioning movable cultural property. Most important, in the current context of Iraq, occupying forces must as far as possible support the competent national authorities of the occupied country to protect cultural property, and if it proves necessary to preserve cultural property situated in occupied territory and damaged by military operations, the occupier must as far as possible, if the competent national authorities are unable to do so, take the most necessary measures, in close cooperation with such authorities.

There are also important provisions that are in force under the Hague Convention before the conflict arises: the State Parties are to undertake training to foster a spirit of respect for the culture and cultural property of all peoples in the members of their armed forces. They are also to introduce in peacetime provisions to ensure observance of the Hague Convention into their military regulations or instructions.

As of January 2006, there are 114 states that are party to this Convention. Neither the United Kingdom nor the United States has ratified the Convention, although both signed it when it was first drawn up. Although it is not, therefore, directly in force for them, they have paid regard to its principles by including these in their officer training and military manuals. Australia has been a party since 1984, Canada since 1998.

The First Protocol

The First Protocol to the Convention, also drawn up in 1954, concerns the return of cultural property. There are ninety-two parties to this Protocol. Unfortunately, the United Kingdom and the United States are not among them, nor is Australia.

During the 1960s and 1970s, with the Cold War and the development of intercontinental ballistic missiles, enthusiasm for the Hague Convention dimmed, on the basis that precise targeting over the horizon was not possible and so some of the Convention's obligations—to target only military objectives, for example—were not realistic. That objection has disappeared with the development of more precise targeting methods. Furthermore, it became clear in the last quarter of the twentieth century that most conflicts were not state-of-the-art warfare between major powers but short-term local, though equally brutal, disputes. The conflict in the former Yugoslavia in the early 1990s caused such revulsion that sufficient impetus was given for the development of the Second Protocol to the Hague Convention.

The Second Protocol

A Second Protocol was drawn up in 1999, designed to improve the working of the Convention. This Protocol makes three major developments: a refinement of the concept of "military necessity," which creates an exception to the protection of heritage and which was drafted with the clarity necessary for military staff that some saw as lacking in the Convention itself; the much more extensive treatment of punishment of violations; and the establishment of the intergovernmental committee of twelve States Parties to supervise the workings of the protective system. A fourth important component was a major reworking of the system for increased protection of outstanding items of heritage to replace that of the Convention, which had fallen into disuse. This Protocol also specifically prohibits archaeological excavations in occupied territory, "save where this is strictly required to safeguard, record or preserve cultural property" and "in close co-operation with the competent national authorities of the occupied territory" (Article 9).

Twenty States Parties were needed to bring the Second Protocol into force, and in January 2004 Costa Rica became the twentieth State. The Protocol then came into force in April 2004. There are currently thirty-seven States Parties. Both the United Kingdom and the United States, though they had never ratified the Convention, participated actively in the negotiations, arguing that they were signatories and were actively considering ratification. Not being party to the Convention, neither can be party to the Second Protocol (Articles 41 and 42).

The Minister for Arts, Media and Sport in the United Kingdom announced in July 2003 that that country would ratify the Convention and is studying the legal issues to that end. President Clinton gave his approval to ratification and sent the Convention to the Senate Foreign Relations Committee for the next step, but there it has stalled. Neither Australia nor Canada signed the Second Protocol, although both took part in the negotiations. Canada has since acceded.

It is significant, since most major art markets are in Europe, that almost all European states are party to both the Convention and the First Protocol, and many of them are working toward ratification of the Second Protocol also; Austria and Switzerland have already ratified it. European countries, which have experienced dramatic losses of cultural property from their own territory, naturally have had understanding of the importance of an international code of law designed to mitigate the loss of cultural heritage, whether by destruction, theft, or other illegal removal.

THE DAMAGE DONE

The recent history of cultural losses shows just how important it is that citizens of all civilized countries support the international rules designed to prevent such losses. UNESCO has had to respond in the last three decades to a number of sad and notorious cases. These include Cambodia, the glorious architectural heritage of which was dismantled piece by piece as civil war and foreign invasion swept over the country; Afghanistan, where not only the famous giant Buddhas were destroyed but every piece of Buddhist art in Taliban hands; and Iraq, where terrible looting took place in 1991 and further looting has taken place since the coalition invasion in 2003.

In August 1991 Iraqi forces invaded Kuwait. The collections of the National Museum in Kuwait were quickly and systematically removed and installed in the National Museum of Iraq in Baghdad. The inventories of the collections were destroyed. To make room for these exhibitions of conquest, thousands of items from the earliest Mesopotamian civilizations were moved out of the National Museum in Baghdad to five of the provincial museums. Following the armed intervention "Desert Storm," these museums were in turn looted, by whom it is not clear, and between three and four thousand very important objects from the earliest Mesopotamian sites disappeared into the illicit trade in cultural property. Of the approximately thirty-five hundred items lost, only about seventy have been located and returned.

Iraq had been party to the Hague Convention since 1967. Of the eighteen states involved in the 2003 intervention, only two (the United Kingdom and the United States) were not party to the Hague Convention, although each made a statement prior to the intervention that historical and religious build-ings would not be targeted. While the intervention was threatening but before it began, Iraq asked UNESCO for assistance to put hundreds of sites on the World Heritage List. (Iraq had been party to the 1972 UNESCO Convention Concerning the Protection of the World Cultural and Natural Heritage since 1978, although only one site was on the list). There are 10,000 known archaeo-logical sites in Iraq, and there are estimated to be at least another 100,000 not yet registered. The requested action could not be processed in the time avail-able—sites are put on the list only after meeting strict criteria, and the process takes at least eighteen months. What is more, the use of cultural sites for military purposes is strictly forbidden by the Hague Convention, and there were press reports of the parking of tanks at Ur in the 1990–91 conflict, just as there were other reports of archaeological sites, Shi'ite holy sites, hospitals, and schools being used by the Iraqi military during the conflict in 2003. Such usage destroys the protected status of the sites under the Hague Convention.

But can we therefore simply wash our hands of the situation because of re-ports that Iraq itself, despite its adoption of the Convention, does not appear to have observed its obligations fully? Because this outstanding heritage is of importance to all humanity, the provisions of the Convention should be ob-served as far as possible whatever the stance of the enemy in this respect. Indeed, the Convention itself provides that States Parties to it are bound to follow its provisions even if one of the parties to a conflict is not a Party, if it declares that it accepts the provisions of the Convention and for as long as it applies them.[1]

We have to look here not just at "Iraqi" heritage: the importance of the heri-tage in that country can hardly be sufficiently stressed. It is unique and a source of history for many ages we do not know well. The early Mesopotamian civili-zations—Sumerian, Akkadian, Assyrian, Babylonian—and Iraq's ancient cities of Babylon, Ur, Nineveh, Nimrud, and Ashur are of primary importance in understanding the development of urban society. A high proportion of the objects looted from the provincial museums in 1991 were finds from the very earliest excavations at Mesopotamian sites—priceless as comparanda for the dating and understanding of materials from the thousands of other sites in Iraq. Floating in the market, free of their documented context, they represent an irreparable loss to science and history.

The removal of cultural property from Kuwait was also contrary to the provisions of the Convention. After the 1991 conflict, the procedure for the return of all property, including cultural, to Kuwait, was organized by the United Nations. Much was returned to Kuwait from the Baghdad museum, although there has been a claim by Kuwait that some material remains missing. During the period of sanctions imposed by the United Nations Security Council against Iraq from August 1990 to the present, widespread looting has taken place in Iraq. Pieces of relief sculpture from Sennacherib's palace at Nineveh have been offered on the international market, and coins that seem to be from the Iraqi collections have also been reported. The situation of thousands of sites not yet scientifically explored represents losses of huge importance to human history, despite the efforts of archaeologists and museum experts all over the world to try to arrest the outflow by publicizing the losses and thus trying to cut off sales and diminish the rewards of the traffickers.

THE PROTECTORS

UNESCO's assistance to Iraq was limited by the United Nations' Sanctions Committee, which did not allow the dispatch of chemicals, photographic paper, and other supplies to enable reconstitution of the inventories. However, UNESCO did release press statements warning the market of the expected transmission of illegally acquired objects for sale. In April 2002 it was also able to assist in the return of a sculpted stone head from the World Heritage site of Hatra, the piece having been seen in a dealer's window in London and identified by an expert.

Sadly, until 1990, Iraq had had an excellent record of care for this cultural heritage: it had good legislation dating from 1936 and competent professionals in its museums, and it had controlled the looting of sites. A few years of conflict, really the blink of an eye in the long history of the country, has lost to humanity critical information about our early development.

The impunity with which looted objects of Iraqi origin have been traded in art markets since 1991 has outraged archaeologists. When it became clear that conflict was again pending in this area, the archaeological community in the United States and United Kingdom made strong representations to their governments that this must not happen again and, in particular, that the fabulously important collections of the National Museum in Baghdad should be protected, as should the key archaeological sites. Archaeologists supplied information about the nature and location of this heritage of great significance to all humanity, together with lists and maps, and believed that the message had been heard.

Some preparations to this end were undoubtedly made. The invasion by the coalition partners began on March 20, 2003. On April 5, 2003, Major Christopher Varhola, a civil affairs reservist and cultural anthropologist, described to the press in Kuwait the U.S. military planning to protect Iraq's cultural heritage.[2] He said that the U.S. military had integrated into its operational planning, from top-level planners to soldiers, measures to identify and protect sites of religious, cultural, and historical importance in Iraq. Noting that Iraq's cultural heritage was priceless, he said he was in constant contact with the archaeological and anthropological communities for information so as to refine target lists and adjust military plans to incorporate cultural and archaeological considerations. Not only potential bomb damage but also that of military construction and the threat of looting were concerns addressed in the military planning. Pentagon planners, he said, had worked closely with members of the academic community to identify both the locations of concern and the kinds of military activity that might adversely affect these areas. "Army civil affairs assets" [*sic*], said the spokesman, "work closely with ground commanders to advise them of archaeological and cultural sites in their areas of operation. The institutional mechanism for this is . . . the cultural affairs officer. This is an actual position in the civil affairs units whose responsibility is to do the research, on his or her own with higher headquarters, so that he or she is aware of the targets that need to be protected" (U.S. Department of State 2003).

The concern about looting was specifically mentioned, "especially in the absence of law and order and the economic uncertainty that is inherent to any military operation of this magnitude. All around Iraq, there are a number of museums, in particular the National Museum of Baghdad, that hold priceless materials. The U.S. Military is eager to coordinate with any organization dedicated to the task of preservation, which transcends military and operational necessity" (U.S. Department of State 2003). While we can rejoice that these careful preparations for selective targeting were carried out, fully consistent with the Hague Convention, we all know that preparations to prevent the looting of the Baghdad museum did not measure up to these hopeful predictions. Four days after this news conference, U.S. forces reached and occupied the center of Baghdad. Reports are confused as to exactly what happened: some stated that one tank had been provided for protection of the National Museum but then withdrawn; at a later stage there was a report that four tanks were in the vicinity but were also withdrawn. The museum was most seriously looted. U.S. authorities said action would be taken to ensure the return of cultural property to the museum. Unfortunately, UNESCO's experience in many conflict situations shows that only the tiniest fraction of material will be returned. Interpol's rate of recovery of major, easily identifiable artworks is less than 10 percent. They state that stolen cultural property is generally out of the country concerned within twelve hours. As of September 2004, an archaeologist working with the U.S. authorities estimated that about fourteen thousand objects were still missing from the Baghdad museum, despite the establishment of a special unit (now disbanded) given the task of retrieving as much as possible. Objects of probable Iraqi origin are said to be on sale in London and other major art market locations.[3]

Could adherence to the rules of the Hague Convention at least have diminished this tragedy, even if it could not wholly have prevented losses? As indicated, although neither the United Kingdom nor the United States has ratified the Convention, both signed it when it was first drawn up. Signature of an international convention implies that a state will at least not act contrary to its provisions before ratification. Australia, the third coalition partner, has been a Party since 1984, and Poland, which also sent military support, since 1956. Observance of the minimal provisions as to respect for cultural property and assistance to local authorities to care for cultural property would have required prevention of the looting, at the very least, under Articles 4(3), 5(1), and 5(2).

The situation in Iraq is all the more tragic in that it follows the hemorrhage of cultural materials set in motion by the armed intervention of 1991.

THE RESULTS OF FIFTY YEARS' WORK

In assessing the value of the Hague Convention over the last fifty years, we can take satisfaction that it has managed to limit damage, particularly in terms of specific targeting of sites. Nonetheless, it is grim to note that whereas the 1972 World Heritage Convention, adopted some eighteen years later, now has 182 States Parties out of the 192 states constituting the international community, only 114 of them are parties to the Hague Convention. What are those other sixty-four States doing? The fact that they have signed with enthusiasm the UNESCO Convention Concerning the Protection of the World Cultural and Natural Heritage shows that they share the international interest in cultural heritage everywhere and happily promote their own sites for the World Heritage List. But it seems they are not prepared to undertake the more demanding obligations of the Hague Convention. It seems more than time for citizens of all civilized countries to stress once again the international rules designed to prevent such losses and to insist that their countries ratify these rules and apply them.

It is not sufficient to be complacent and to think that one's own country would not offend against these principles. The Hague Convention represents a moral commitment. When the director-general of UNESCO, or in due course the committee now to be established under the Second Protocol, speaks up for the principles of the Convention, they do so with far more authority when they speak for 182 of the now 192 states in the international community than when speaking for 114, 92, or 37. Joining the great conventions of humanitarian law should be a matter of pride for any state that regards itself as civilized.

We can take some satisfaction in the fact that the military in many countries is sensitized to the long-term importance of cultural heritage. We know that in the heat of battle, or because of misuse of a cultural site by the opponent that may endanger lives where it cannot be bypassed, there will continue to be some losses: the most we can hope for is to minimize them. However, it seems difficult to accept that no adequate implementation is made in a case of occupation, despite the clear terms of the Hague Convention, leading in the case of Iraq to the devastation of irreplaceable evidence of the early development of civilization in Eurasia. Preparation is not enough where there is a complete collapse at the operational stage.

On the question of looting, we need to be realistic. Looting by local populations may happen in any country where the forces of order collapse without immediate replacement. We cannot dismiss this as unfortunate but understandable in an unstable and desperate situation and assume that "after all, it's their own heritage they are destroying." More and more, there is evidence of organized criminal mafias working to plan, systematically seeking particular objects of value, using tools preassessed for smashing locks and opening secure areas, and often showing evidence of detailed information of the holdings and their location. In Iraq those mafias have now moved on to less public sites and are continuing to wreak havoc on humanity's heritage across the country. We know that such activities are likely in times of war. A clear plan to prevent them must not only be formulated in any theater of conflict but must actually be put into effect with adequate military or civil administration to implement it.

These sobering thoughts arise from the example of Iraq, but it is, of course, not the only area of conflict that gives rise to these considerations. The conflict in the former Yugoslavia has also been deadly for the region's cultural heritage: the targeting of mosques and churches by enemy forces is a horrific violation of the Hague Convention, to which Yugoslavia was a Party, and to which the new states emerging from it signified their succession. The demolition of the Mostar

Bridge, a highly visible symbol of cultural interchange, was particularly sinister, linking as it did the Christian and Muslim parts of that town.

Religious bigotry was also behind the destruction of the Bamiyan Buddhas, a grief not only in archaeological, historical, and, for the local population, economic terms but an affront to Buddhists everywhere. The conditions fostering such bigotry are beyond the reach of the Hague Convention. UNESCO supports cultural diversity, and this is where work really needs to be done. It is much too late when children raised in bitterness, without appreciation of the accumulated wealth of the world heritage for the benefit of all humanity, are armed and sent to war as young men and women with the admonition to "look after the monuments." It is not going to happen. Children have to be taught from their earliest years to appreciate the cultures of their neighbors and even of their former enemies. If they, too, can see that these things are important for them and for all of humanity, they will not have the urge to destroy, and they will preserve what can be preserved in the tragedy of conflict.

Conclusion

Do these experiences suggest that the Hague Convention is too weak and that its development was a futile exercise? Not at all. What is weak is its implementation and the will of states to adopt it and abide by it. Its weakness is that of international law generally. Added to this is the fact that it is most visible during armed conflict, a time when rationality gives way to emotion, when national governments have many major life-threatening concerns to look after for their peoples, and it is then that concentration on the Convention has been seen to weaken. When war crimes such as mistreatment and murder of POWs, and crimes against humanity such as torture, are being committed, we know that it is unlikely that the protection of cultural heritage will be respected. All these illegal acts are deplorable, but they happen and may happen again: this does not mean we should not fight, with every resource at hand, to ensure in peacetime a proper legal framework of respect for these rights and punishment of offenders and to educate in the principles of protection.

It is in peacetime that major advances have been made in developing these standards of minimizing the inhumanity of war. The Geneva Conventions were developed in 1948, when the horrors of World War II were alive in the minds of all those who had lived through six years of destruction and cruelty. The Genocide Convention was developed the same year. In 1954 the Hague Convention for the Protection of Cultural Property in the Event of Armed Conflict followed. Public outrage galvanized governments to negotiate and accept more stringent rules than existed before that conflict. The conflict in Yugoslavia led to the successful negotiation of the Second Protocol. The experience in Iraq should lead us now, when the implications of nonaction are very clear to see, to push for greater participation and implementation.

What has happened and, alas, what is still happening today on important archaeological sites in Iraq is a repetition of the same destruction suffered in any country subject to civil war, invasion, or indeed political instability or natural disaster. If we are to stop this destructive process, we must persuade all states to become party to the UNESCO conventions and protocols and to abide by their provisions. Destruction and theft may not be easy to prevent, but we know that it is impossible to reconstitute a heritage that has been largely destroyed, and extraordinarily difficult to ensure the return of objects illegally taken in times of trouble. Future generations will thank us for this effort to save their history.

NOTES

This chapter was presented on the fiftieth anniversary of the Hague Convention at the Australian War Memorial, Canberra, on February 2, 2004. The occasion was organized by the Sustainable Heritage Development Programme Research School for Pacific and Asian Studies, Australian National University, Canberra, and sponsored by Toyota.

1. Article 18(3).

2. This information is taken from the U.S. government website <http://usinfo.state.gov/topical/pol/terror/texts/03040503.htm>, accessed January 28, 2004.

3. Some had been seized in New York and Rome by September 2003; see <https://listhost.uchicago.edu/pipermail/iraqcrisis/2003-September/000356.html>; *Art Newspaper*, September 2003. Archaeologists who have worked closely with the Iraqi museum authorities for many months say it is still impossible to know exactly how many items are missing, and this is but an estimate.

BIBLIOGRAPHY

Bogdanos, Matthew. "The Casualties of War: The Truth About the Iraq Museum." *American Journal of Archaeology* 109(3) (2005): 477–526.

Boylan, Patrick J. "The Concept of Cultural Protection in Times of Armed Conflict: From the Crusades to the New Millennium." In *Illicit Antiquities: The Theft of Culture and the Extinction of Archaeology*, ed. Neil Brodie and Kathryn W. Tubb, 43–108. London: Routledge, 2002.

O'Keefe, Patrick J. "The First Protocol to the Hague Convention Fifty Years On." *Art, Antiquity and Law* 9 (2004): 99–116.

United Nations Educational, Scientific and Cultural Organization. *Convention Concerning the Protection of the World Cultural and Natural Heritage*. Paris: UNESCO, 1972.

———. *Hague Convention on the Protection of Cultural Property in the Event of Armed Conflict*. The Hague: UNESCO, 1954.

————. *Second Protocol to the Hague Convention of 1954 for the Protection of Cultural Property in the Event of Armed Conflict*. Paris: UNESCO, 1999.

U.S. Department of State. "Military Planning Includes Protecting Iraq's Cultural, Religious Heritage (Army Civil Affairs Officer Describes Measures)." *Washington File*, April 5, 2003.

2

The U.S. Legal Response to the Protection of the World Cultural Heritage

MARINA PAPA SOKAL

The worldwide looting of archaeological sites and ancient monuments has grown in the past two decades to alarming proportions (Atwood 2004). Every time an object is ruthlessly extracted from the ground and separated from its context—rather than being scientifically excavated—invaluable historical knowledge is irreparably lost. This loss is not only to the people whose cultural heritage is being devastated but also to the common history of humanity.

In this chapter I intend to discuss some of the legal remedies that have been adopted for the protection of the world cultural patrimony, both at the international level and, in greater detail, with regard to the legislation of the United States. My aim is threefold: to provide an overview of some aspects of current U.S. law regulating the international trade in antiquities in the United States; to recount the history of the political struggles and compromises that shaped the U.S. Cultural Property Implementation Act in its present form; and to offer some suggestions for possible improvements in the Act.

The need for an international effort to address the problem of the illicit trade in art and antiquities was specifically expressed at the General Conference of UNESCO in 1960, which passed a resolution calling on the director-general to prepare a report on "appropriate means of preventing the illicit export, import and sale of cultural property" (UNESCO Resolution 4.412, 11th Session).[1] Almost ten years ensued during which a number of attempts at drafting a convention were made.[2] Finally, in August 1969, a small committee appointed by the director-general completed a preliminary draft of a proposed convention, which was then circulated among the member states for comment.[3] This was followed a year later by a slightly revised text—the so-called Secretariat draft—which took into account some of the comments received (UNESCO 1970d). This new draft, like the previous one, contained a number of very stringent obligations, including a commitment by art-importing countries to enforce other countries' export control laws; furthermore, no reservations to the convention would be permitted (UNESCO 1970d: Articles 7 and 15). Not surprisingly, the United States and other major art-importing countries found it unacceptable

(Feldman 1970: 3).[4] The U.S. delegation proposed instead a far less binding alternative draft (DuBoff et al. 1976: 101; Feldman et al. 1970). After much negotiation, a compromise text was adopted, in which several of the sweeping obligations on art-importing states were replaced by more limited procedures proposed by the United States (notably Articles 7(b) and 9, to be discussed later in this chapter); at the same time, much of the spirit of the Secretariat draft was retained.[5] On November 14, 1970, the 16th General Conference of UNESCO adopted, by a 77–1–8 vote, the Convention on the Means of Prohibiting and Preventing the Illicit Import, Export and Transfer of Ownership of Cultural Property (hereinafter the UNESCO Convention).[6]

In February 1972 President Richard Nixon submitted the UNESCO Convention to the U.S. Senate for ratification, and in August of the same year the Senate gave its advice and consent by a vote of 79–0, albeit with one reservation and six understandings that I discuss later (U.S. Senate 1972a and 1972b, and 118 Cong. Rec. 27925). However, the United States did not formally accede to the Convention until April 19, 1983, after the implementing legislation had been passed. The instrument of accession was formally deposited at UNESCO on September 2, 1983, and came into force on December 2, 1983.

As is clearly stated in the first of the understandings, the UNESCO Convention is not self-executing.[7] It therefore became apparent at an early stage that new legislation needed to be enacted to implement at least two Articles of the UNESCO Convention: Article 7(b), which obliges State Parties to the Convention to prohibit the import of cultural property that has been stolen from a museum or monument in another State Party and to take steps to recover and return those artifacts; and Article 9, which says that a State Party whose cultural patrimony is in jeopardy from pillage of archaeological and ethnological materials may call on other State Parties to participate in a concerted international effort to protect the affected category of materials, through measures that may include restrictions on exports and imports.[8]

Legislation to implement Articles 7(b) and 9 of the UNESCO Convention was first introduced in the U.S. Congress in 1973, based on a draft proposed by the State Department.[9] Over the next decade, this legislation was debated in House and Senate committee hearings and went through a half-dozen successive revisions (table 2.1) before the Convention on Cultural Property Implementation Act (CPIA) was finally enacted by Congress in December 1982 (128 Cong. Rec. S 15987 and H 10755, December 21, 1982) and signed into law by President Ronald Reagan on January 12, 1983.[10] These revisions were mostly the result of compromises aimed at reconciling the goals of at least three interest groups: archaeologists and anthropologists, who were overwhelmingly in favor of the new legislation; dealers and collectors, who were almost universally

Table 2.1. Bills Leading up to the Convention on Cultural Property Implementation Act (CPIA)

Congress and bill number	Date introduced	Introduced	Date of hearings (if any)	Final outcome
93 S. 2677/ 93 H.R. 11754	Nov. 9, 1973/ Dec. 3, 1973	Sen. Fulbright/ Reps. Ullman and Schneebeli		Died
94 H. R. 14171	June 3, 1976	Rep. Green	Written comments Aug. 3. 1976 (U.S. House 1976)	Died
95 H.R. 5643a	Mar. 28, 1977	Rep. Mikva	Apr. 26, 1977 (U.S. House 1977a)	Amended in committee 95 H.R. 5643b
95 H.R. 5643b	Oct. 19, 1977	Committee report Sept. 21, 1977 (U.S. House 1977b)		Passed House unanimously Oct. 17, 1977
95 H.R. 5643b/ 95 S. 2261			Feb. 8, 1978 (U.S. Senate 1978)	Died in the Senate
96 H.R. 3403 (= 95 H.R. 5643b)	Apr. 3, 1979	Rep. Mikva	Sept. 27, 1979 (U.S. House 1980)	Died
97 S. 426 (= 95 H.R. 5643b)	Feb. 5, 1981	Sens. Matsunaga and Baucus		Died
97 S. 1723	Oct. 7, 1981	Sens. Matsunaga and Baucus	July 21–22, 1982 (U.S. Senate 1982a)	Amended in committee, added to H.R. 4566
97 H.R. 4566	Oct. 16, 1981	Committee report Sept. 21, 1982 (U.S. Senate 1982b)		Passed both houses on Dec. 12, 1982; signed into law (PL 97–446) on Jan. 12, 1983

Table 2.2. Overview of the Convention on Cultural Property Implementation Act (CPIA) in its Final Form

Overview of provisions of CPIA (19 U.S.C. §2601–2613)
(= PL 97–446, Title III, §302–314, January 12, 1983)

Definitions
19 U.S.C. §2601

Country-specific import restrictions
19 U.S.C. §2602: agreements with other state parties to impose import restrictions
19 U.S.C. §2603: emergency import restrictions
19 U.S.C. §2604: formal designations of materials covered by import restrictions
19 U.S.C. §2605: Cultural Property Advisory Committee, role in import restrictions
19 U.S.C. §2606: how import restrictions work; what Customs and importer have to do
19 U.S.C. §2608: temporary disposition of seized items
19 U.S.C. §2609(b): to whom forfeited items are to be returned
19 U.S.C. §2609(1): burden of proof

Stolen cultural property
19 U.S.C. §2607: forbids import of stolen cultural property
19 U.S.C. §2608: temporary disposition of seized items
19 U.S.C. §2609(c): to whom forfeited items are to returned; compensation
19 U.S.C. §2610(2): burden of proof

Exemptions
19 U.S.C. §2611

---

against it; and museums, which took a variety of intermediate positions.[11] Table 2.2 provides an overview of the provisions of CPIA in its final form.

STOLEN CULTURAL PROPERTY

Article 7(b)(i) of the UNESCO Convention obliges State Parties "to prohibit the import of cultural property stolen from a museum or a religious or secular public monument or similar institution in another State Party . . . provided that such property is documented as appertaining to the inventory of that institution."[12] Furthermore, Article 7(b)(ii) requires State Parties "to take appropriate steps to recover and return any such cultural property" in response to a "request of the State Party of origin."[13]

The requirement of Article 7(b)(i) was in part already satisfied by the National Stolen Property Act (NSPA), which prohibits the transportation "in interstate or foreign commerce [of] any goods . . . of the value of [U.S.] $5,000 or more" with the knowledge that such goods were "stolen, converted or taken by fraud" (18 U.S.C. §2314). However, this criminal statute explicitly excludes the case in which stolen cultural property is imported into the United States by an innocent purchaser. Likewise, long-standing state and federal law provide civil remedies for obtaining restitution of stolen property to its rightful owner; but these remedies potentially place a high burden of expense and time on the owner and fail to meet the requirement of Article 7(b)(ii) for active assistance, by the government of the importing country, in obtaining the recovery and return of the stolen cultural property.[14] For these reasons, all of the bills to implement the UNESCO Convention, starting from the first one, included specific provisions to implement Article 7(b). In fact, all the congressional documents stress that these provisions *supplement* existing civil and penal remedies and are in no way intended to *substitute* for them.[15] The basic idea was straightforward, and the language closely mirrored that of Article 7(b) itself. Importation of cultural property stolen from a foreign museum or monument would be prohibited; and legal procedures would be put in place allowing for its seizure, forfeiture, and return to the country of origin. Who could possibly object?

Surprisingly, these apparently simple provisions became the object of intense debate, as a result of a decision in January 1977 by the Fifth Circuit Court of Appeals that, in the words of the judge in the case, must have left "museum directors, art dealers, and innumerable private collectors . . . in a state of shock" (*United States v. McClain*, 545 F.2d 988 [5th Cir. 1977]), p. 991). Patty McClain and four co-defendants had been convicted under the National Stolen Property Act of transporting (and conspiring to transport) across state lines certain Pre-Columbian Mexican artifacts, knowing these artifacts to have been stolen.[16] The objects were considered "stolen" because, under Mexican law, all Pre-Columbian archaeological artifacts found within the national territory are "the inalienable and imprescriptible property of the Nation."[17] Though the appeals court overturned the defendants' conviction on certain technical grounds, their decision made clear that the court "recognizes the sovereign right of Mexico to declare, by legislative fiat, that it is the owner of its art, archaeological or historic national treasures," and that if such property were exported illicitly to the United States, it would be considered "stolen."[18]

The first congressional hearings on the CPIA bill were held in April 1977, a mere three months after the *McClain* decision (U.S. House of Representatives 1977a). The *McClain* case weighed heavily in the comments of the dealers and at least one museum. The dealers, not surprisingly, were upset that U.S. courts would enforce a foreign patrimony law (though the *McClain* decision was in fact based on the well-established legal principle of *lex rei sitae*).[19] But one museum director went even further than the dealers. Douglas Dillon, president of the Metropolitan Museum of Art (the Met) in New York, reiterated the Met's "full support" for the objectives of the CPIA bill but recommended "a few modifications" (U.S. House of Representatives 1977a: 8, 2). He raised the specter that the *McClain* decision could subject museum trustees to criminal prosecution for "mere possession of objects, allegedly covered by a foreign statute's definition of natural [*sic*] patrimony" (U.S. House of Representatives 1977a: 3, 4)—and this despite the fact that the *McClain* decision made perfectly clear that the National Stolen Property Act applies only when the individual has *knowledge* that the goods in question are stolen, which means, in this case, that the individual must be aware of the foreign patrimony law and also aware that it covers those particular artifacts.[20] On this dubious basis, the Met proposed two amendments to the CPIA bill. The first would overturn the *McClain* decision by declaring that the National Stolen Property Act would not apply to any material "where the alleged act of stealing . . . is based solely on" a foreign patrimony law (U.S. House of Representatives 1977a: 9). The second amendment was even more radical: it provided that "no claim by a foreign nation . . . shall be recognized in any civil proceeding in any Federal or State court for the recovery or return of any cultural property . . . when such claim of ownership or title is based solely on" a foreign patrimony law (U.S. House of Representatives 1977a: 9). In other words, this second provision aimed to foreclose foreign governments' existing rights, under well-established state or federal law, to seek restitution of objects through civil suits.

However, neither of these amendments was accepted by the congressional committees (U.S. House of Representatives 1977b). The dealers tried again the following year (U.S. Senate 1978: 40, 48), in 1979 (U.S. House of Representatives 1980: 42, 44 ff.), and in 1982 (U.S. Senate 1982a: 440, 448 ff., 473 ff.; see also the response of the American Anthropological Association, 558) to have included in CPIA a provision overturning the *McClain* decision, but they were unsuccessful.[21]

COUNTRY-SPECIFIC IMPORT RESTRICTIONS

Article 9 of the UNESCO Convention states that "any State Party whose cultural patrimony is in jeopardy from pillage of archaeological or ethnological materials may call on other State Parties who are affected . . . to participate in a concerted international effort" to protect the "specific materials concerned," through "concrete measures" that may include "the control of exports and imports and international commerce."[22] The U.S. chose to implement Article 9 by setting up a mechanism for the negotiation of bilateral or multilateral agreements involving import controls.[23]

Early bills (93 H.R. 11754/S. 2677 through 97 S. 426; see table 2.1) gave the president great freedom to negotiate agreements and to impose import controls, with only a limited number of "findings" needed, no time limitations, and a nonbinding consultation with an advisory committee. Predictably, the implementation of Article 9, perhaps more than any other provision of CPIA, generated heated debate and resulted in some hard-won compromises. The dealers in particular, along with some museum officials, while professing support for the principles and aims of the UNESCO Convention, raised numerous complaints; here at least, many of their concerns were addressed and to a large extent satisfied.

First and foremost, the dealers and their supporters worried about the excessive discretion conferred upon the Executive Branch in deciding whether to enter into bilateral or multilateral agreements involving import restrictions. They feared that such agreements could be used as negotiating tools for foreign-policy objectives that have nothing to do with cultural property, such as "cotton quotas, military bases, help in drug legislation, and the like."[24] They also worried that if the U.S. alone among art-importing nations were to implement the Convention, then the flow of antiquities would simply be diverted to other countries such as England, France, and Japan, thereby causing "a loss to our citizens in terms of the enjoyment of art" (statement of Douglas Ewing, U.S. House of Representatives 1977a: 31) and "a severe cultural deprivation of the American public" (statement of the American Association of Dealers in Ancient, Oriental and Primitive Art, U.S. House of Representatives 1976: 18). Indeed, despite the fact that a "concerted international effort" is specifically contemplated in the language of Article 9 of the UNESCO Convention, the early bills did not require any actions by other countries; some of those involved in the legislative process felt that, at least on this issue, the proposed implementing legislation went beyond the scope of the Convention.[25] As a result of these lengthy negotiations, a number of clauses aimed at restricting the president's freedom to enter into agreements were included in the final draft of CPIA. Among these was the requirement that the president make a series of specific findings before entering into any bilateral or multilateral agreement, including that:

- The archaeological or ethnological patrimony of the requesting country is indeed in jeopardy from pillage.
- The State Party making the request has taken appropriate measures to protect its cultural patrimony.
- Import restrictions, if applied in concert with other art-importing countries, would be of substantial benefit in deterring the pillage.
- Remedies less drastic than import restrictions are not available.
- The application of the import restriction is consistent with the general in-

terest of the international community in the interchange of cultural property among nations for scientific, cultural and educational purposes.[26]

In addition, the president "should endeavor" to obtain a commitment from the requesting country to permit the exchange of its archaeological and ethnological materials in ways that do not jeopardize its cultural patrimony.[27] Finally, the president may enter into an agreement only if the import restrictions are applied "in concert with" similar controls implemented by other nations (whether or not State Parties) that also have a "significant import trade" in similar materials. Moreover, if it is determined that these countries have not implemented such import restrictions within a reasonable period of time or are doing so ineffectively, the president is obliged to suspend the agreements until the other nations "take appropriate corrective action."[28] However, in the final draft of CPIA, a clause was added to give the president authority, in exceptional circumstances, to enter into agreements regardless of whether other countries adopt similar import restrictions (19 U.S.C. §2602(c)(2); U.S. Senate 1982b: 28).

In all cases, the agreement must be initiated by a request from the affected State Party, which must be accompanied by written documentation supporting all the required presidential findings.[29] All requests must be published in the *Federal Register* and need to be evaluated by an advisory committee (see later discussion).

If all these criteria are fulfilled, the president is authorized to impose import restrictions on specified categories of archaeological or ethnological materials covered by a bilateral or multilateral agreement.[30] The listing of materials must be "sufficiently specific and precise to insure that . . . fair notice is given to importers and other persons as to what material is subject to such restrictions."[31] After this, listed materials can be imported into the United States only if accompanied by a valid export certificate issued by the relevant State Party (19 U.S.C. §2606(a), but see exceptions later). Such agreements remain in force for up to five years, after which time the situation is reassessed. If it is found that the factors that initially prompted the agreement are still in place, the president may extend the import restrictions for additional periods of not more than five years each.[32]

The dealers' association and the Metropolitan Museum of Art also suggested that all agreements on import restrictions should be in the form of treaties to be submitted to the Senate for ratification or, alternatively, that they should be subject to congressional approval on an ad hoc basis.[33] Professor Paul Bator proposed instead a "lay it on the table" arrangement allowing ninety days for a congressional veto (DuBoff et al. 1976: 123). However, none of these suggestions was accepted by the congressional committees (U.S. House of Representatives 1977b: 12; M. Feldman's response in Du Boff et al. 1976: 115).

The United States has so far signed such bilateral agreements with the governments of Bolivia, Cambodia, Canada, Cyprus, El Salvador, Guatemala, Honduras, Italy, Mali, Nicaragua, and Peru.[34]

It should be noted that negotiating such bilateral agreements may impose heavy burdens on the resources of the requesting countries, especially in the developing world. It would be highly desirable that the application process could be streamlined. In the meantime, archaeologists could provide a useful public service by assisting the authorities in the countries in which they work in preparing the necessary documentation for their requests.

CPIA also provides for the unilateral imposition by the president of import restrictions in so-called "emergency situations" (19 U.S.C. §2603). This provision covers archaeological and ethnological material that is:

1. "a newly discovered type of material which is of importance for the understanding of the history of mankind" and which is "in jeopardy from pillage, dismantling, dispersal or fragmentation";
2. "identifiable as coming from any site recognized to be of high cultural significance," if the site is in jeopardy; or
3. "part of the remains of a particular culture or civilization," the record of which is in jeopardy "which is, or threatens to be, of crisis proportions."

However, as is the case for the bilateral agreements, the affected State Party must make a request and supply information that "supports a determination that an emergency condition exists."[35] Any such import restrictions may remain in place for not more than five years and may be extended for a further three-year period if the justifying circumstances persist.[36] It is not entirely clear why a provision for emergency action was included in CPIA—neither the House Report of 1977 nor the Senate Report of 1982 provide any explanation—but as Patty Gerstenblith (2002: 8) has suggested, it may have been in response to the final sentence of Article 9 of the UNESCO Convention, which requires State Parties, "pending [an] agreement," to "take provisional measures ... to prevent irremediable injury to the cultural heritage of the requesting State."

Cultural Property Advisory Committee

All of the bills to implement the UNESCO Convention provided for a committee of experts representing the art dealer, museum, and scientific communities to advise the president concerning requests for import restrictions. However, the precise membership and duties of this committee underwent a number of significant modifications over the course of the history of CPIA.

In the first bill (H.R. 11754/S. 2677), the size and composition of the committee were left entirely to the president's discretion. Starting in 1977 (H.R. 5643a), however, the bills provided detailed representation for the various constituencies concerned with cultural property, specifically listing a number of institutions and organizations that would nominate (or in some cases directly appoint) their candidates of choice. Among these were the American Association of Museums, the Association of Art Museum Directors, Harvard University Museums, the Smithsonian Institution, and the Metropolitan Museum of Art; the Archaeological Institute of America and the Association for Field Archaeology; and the Art Dealers Association of America and the American Association of Dealers in Ancient, Oriental and Primitive Art. The precise membership was altered from bill to bill, and the various compositions generated considerable opposition and debate from the different sides.[37] Only in the final draft, in fact, was the makeup of the Cultural Property Advisory Committee (CPAC) changed to its present form, which is composed of eleven members as follows: two representing the interests of museums; three experts in the fields of archaeology, anthropology, and ethnology; three representing dealers in archaeological and ethnological material; and three representing "the interest of the general public." No specific institution or organization is mentioned. All the members of the committee are directly appointed by the president for terms of two years (changed in December of 1987 to three years) and may be reappointed for one or more terms.[38]

CPAC's job is to investigate and assess the validity of each request for import restrictions, whether for bilateral or multilateral agreements or for emergency situations, and to advise the president on appropriate actions. Although the committee's recommendations are not binding, the president would ordinarily be expected to follow them. At the end of its evaluation, the committee must prepare a report stating its recommendation as to whether an agreement should be entered into, along with its reasons. CPAC must also review any request for extension of an agreement. The committee has 150 days to issue its report in the case of bilateral and multilateral agreements, and ninety days in the case of emergency actions. The president, whenever entering into or extending an agreement, must submit a report to the Congress containing a description of the actions taken and the reasons for any differences between presidential decisions and the recommendation of the committee (U.S. House of Representatives 1977a: 29).

EXCEPTIONS

CPIA provides two classes of exceptions to its general rules: the first concerns objects that left their country of origin sufficiently long ago; the second concerns objects that have been continuously in the United States for a sufficiently long period.

The first exception applies only to archaeological and ethnological material covered by country-specific import restrictions (whether by agreement or by emergency action), not to stolen cultural property (19 U.S.C. §2606 [b,c,d]). Though these provisions are located in a procedural section of the law (dealing with Customs action regarding material imported without a proper export license from the country of origin), they create a de facto exception to the import restrictions, as follows: The import restrictions do not apply if the importer can provide satisfactory evidence, consisting of one or more declarations under oath, that the object left the country of origin either (a) before the effective date of the import restrictions, or (b) more than ten years before the object's date of entry into the United States, provided that neither the importer nor any related person acquired an interest in the object more than one year before the date of entry.[39]

The second exception applies to all the provisions of CPIA—including those concerning stolen cultural property—and provides a "statute of limitations" for objects that have been held in the United States for a sufficiently long period (19 U.S.C. §2611). The provisions are complicated, but roughly speaking they exempt material in the following cases:

(a) if it has been imported into the United States for temporary exhibition;[40]
(b) if it has been held by a recognized U.S. museum or similar institution for at least three years, was purchased innocently, and was on exhibit for at least one year or contained in a published catalogue for at least two years or was sufficiently publicized at the time of acquisition;
(c) if it has been within the United States for at least ten years and exhibited in a recognized museum or similar institution for at least five years;
(d) if it has been within the United States for at least ten years and the country of origin has received or should have received fair notice about its location;
(e) if it has been within the United States for at least twenty years and was purchased innocently.

It is worth noting that (c) and (d) protect non-innocent parties if they are lucky enough not to be caught within ten years.[41]

OTHER ARTICLES OF THE UNESCO CONVENTION

As mentioned earlier, several other Articles of the UNESCO Convention, implementation of which might have required legislative action, were handled by one reservation and six understandings attached to the U.S. ratification of the Convention.[42] The most important of these, to my mind, concerns Article 10(a), which I shall deal with last.

Article 3

Article 3 of the UNESCO Convention states: "The import, export or transfer of ownership of cultural property effected contrary to the provisions adopted under this Convention by the States Parties thereto, shall be illicit." Commentators are extremely divided as to the meaning of this Article (see O'Keefe 2000: 42–45 for details of the debate, with citations to the original literature). The controversy centers around two major points: To what extent are the State Parties to the Convention required to give effect, in their domestic law, to the laws regulating cultural property that have been adopted by other State Parties? And what is the precise meaning of "illicit"?

One natural interpretation of Article 3 is that "it requires States, in their national law, to regard as illicit, transactions which breach the national law of another State Party whose law is in accordance with the Convention" (O'Keefe 2000: 44). In particular, art-importing countries would have to enforce, in some way, the export restrictions adopted by art-rich countries. But the precise manner in which they should do so is not clear. As O'Keefe (2000: 44–45) points out, the term *illicit* is not generally used in English-language law (*unlawful* and *illegal* are more common); it probably arose during the drafting of the Convention as a literal translation from the French *illicite*. This leaves some uncertainty as to how transactions breaching the national law of another State Party are to be dealt with: "An obligation to regard an act as contrary to law may be interpreted in several different ways. Its consequences may be criminal, leading to the extradition, fining or imprisonment of the offender; or they may be civil, leaving it open to a private citizen to seek compensation . . . or restitution of an object, or there may be effects of nullity or voidability attached to the transaction."[43]

In order to preclude all interpretations of these kinds, the United States included in its ratification of the Convention a specific "understanding" that "the United States understands Article 3 not to modify property interests in cultural property under the laws of the states parties" (U.S. Senate 1972a: VII; U.S. Senate 1972b: 2). O'Keefe is highly critical of this "understanding," considering it to be a willful *mis*understanding: "Clearly there are varying interpretations of Article 3. [But] it is a basic principle of legal interpretation that an interpretation which gives a provision some meaning should be preferred to one which renders it meaningless" (O'Keefe 2000: 42–45 and 109, quotation at 45).

Article 6

Article 6(a, b) requires State Parties to prohibit the export of their cultural property unless accompanied by an appropriate export certificate. In its ratification of the Convention, however, the United States made a formal reservation, effectively retaining "the right to determine whether or not to impose export controls over cultural property" (U.S. Senate 1972a: VIII; U.S. Senate 1972b: 3).

Article 7(a)

Article 7(a) of the UNESCO Convention obliges State Parties "to take the necessary measures, consistent with national legislation, to prevent museums and similar institutions within their territories from acquiring cultural property originating in another State Party which has been illegally exported after entry into force of this Convention." The phrase "consistent with national legislation" was suggested by the U.S. delegation.[44] In its ratification of the Convention, the United States added the following understanding: "The United States understands Article 7(a) to apply to institutions whose acquisition policy is subject to national control under existing domestic legislation and not to require the enactment of new legislation to establish national control over other institutions." In the United States, however, the only museums and similar institutions fully under the control of the federal government appear to be the Library of Congress, the National Archives, and the museums run by the National Park Service, leaving all the others free to establish their own acquisition policies.[45]

Article 13

According to Article 13 of the UNESCO Convention, the States Parties to this Convention also undertake, consistent with the laws of each state:

(a)　To prevent by all appropriate means transfers of ownership of cultural property likely to promote the illicit import or export of such property;

(b)　to ensure that their competent services cooperate in facilitating the earliest possible restitution of illicitly exported cultural property to its rightful owner;

(c) to admit actions for recovery of lost or stolen items of cultural property brought by or on behalf of the rightful owners;

(d)　to recognize the indefeasible right of each State Party to this Convention to classify and declare certain cultural property as inalienable which should therefore ipso facto not be exported, and to facilitate recovery of such property by the State concerned in cases where it has been exported.[46]

Some aspects of this article are confusing. For instance, how does paragraph (b) apply to cultural property that is illicitly exported *by* its rightful owner (e.g., an Italian collector selling a Renaissance painting at auction in London without the proper export license from the Italian government)?[47] The most important part of this article, however, as concerns archaeological objects, is paragraph (d), which requires State Parties to recognize the national patrimony laws adopted by other State Parties that declare certain archaeological material to be the property of the State. It is noteworthy in this regard that the U.S. State Department in its letter submitting the Convention to the president, as well as the Senate committee in its report recommending ratification of the Convention, both state: "Presumably, the relevant law in the United States would recognize the validity of foreign legislation declaring certain cultural property within the jurisdiction of a foreign state to be inalienable. Illegal removal of such property without consent of the owner should be recognized as theft" (U.S. Senate 1972a: XI; U.S. Senate 1972b: 6). In other words, they have made clear, *five years before the McClain case*, the basic principle underlying the *McClain* decision.

However, these documents go on to say that Article 13(d) "is not self-executing . . . and in the absence of Federal legislation, the decision in each case would be governed by state law."[48] Therefore, in order "to avoid any appearance of a commitment broader than intended" (U.S. Senate 1972a: XI; U.S. Senate 1972b: 6–7), the United States attached to its ratification the following understanding: "[that] the means of recovery of cultural property under subparagraph (d) are the judicial actions referred to in subparagraph (c) of Article 13, and that such actions are controlled by the law of the requested state, the requesting state having to submit necessary proofs."

It is perhaps worth noting that if the proposals of Douglas Dillon and the dealers to prohibit certain civil actions by foreign countries had been adopted, the United States would very likely have found itself in violation of Articles 13(c, d) even as qualified by this formal "understanding."

Article 10(a)

As previously noted, the most significant of the understandings, in my view, concerns Article 10(a) of the UNESCO Convention, according to which each State Party undertakes, "as appropriate for each country, [to] oblige antique dealers, subject to penal or administrative sanctions, to maintain a register recording the origin of each item of cultural property, names and addresses of the supplier, [and] description and price of each item sold."[49] The U.S. ratification added the understanding that the words "as appropriate for each country" permit each State Party "to determine the extent of regulation, if any, of antique dealers" and declared that "in the United States that determination would be made by the appropriate authorities of *state and municipal* governments" (emphasis added; U.S. Senate 1972a: X, 1972b: 5–6).[50]

Because of this understanding, none of the drafts of CPIA even purported to implement Article 10(a); and this, in my opinion, is one of the most glaring flaws of CPIA in its present form. Certainly the obligation to maintain a register showing date and country of purchase would be a significant deterrent to the illicit trade, especially if it were open to inspection by potential purchasers.[51] And this record-keeping would not be in any way burdensome to legitimate dealers, because these are records that they would presumably keep anyway for their own business purposes. It is worth mentioning that other countries have such laws, for example Italy and France.[52]

But insisting that this regulation be done at the state and local level is tantamount to guaranteeing that it will not be done at all (and that is presumably the unspoken purpose of the understanding). In the unlikely event that New York City or New York State were to enact such a registration law, the Madison Avenue dealers could simply move to New Jersey. Moreover, the threat to do so would almost certainly deter the city or state government from enacting such a law in the first place. The illicit trade in antiquities is a national—indeed, international—problem and needs to be addressed as such.

RECOMMENDATIONS AND CONCLUSIONS

CPIA is a significant effort by a major art-importing country to stem the illicit trade in antiquities, but it is inadequate in several important ways.

One crucial limitation is that import restrictions can be applied, even in emergency situations, only to nations that are State Parties to the UNESCO Convention. This may leave some countries in a vulnerable position, as in the case of Afghanistan, which was not a Party to the Convention until September of 2005 and which has seen its cultural patrimony systematically depleted by more than twenty years of almost continuous war. Moreover, the requirement for a formal request from the government of the affected country, which applies even to emergency actions, fails to address situations such as civil war, coup d'état, the temporary absence of a recognized government (as in the case of Iraq recently), or an unwilling government (as in the case of Afghanistan under the Taliban), where it would be difficult or impossible to put together the necessary documentation for a request.[53]

The five-year limit on import restrictions, for both emergency action and bilateral/multilateral agreements, may not allow enough time for the import restrictions to make a durable positive impact or for the CPAC adequately to assess their efficacy, and it gives dealers an incentive simply to hold the material temporarily outside the United States, awaiting the expiration of import restrictions. Furthermore, the frequent renewals impose a heavy burden on the requesting country in providing documentation to justify extensions.

The requirement that "objects of archaeological interest" be at least 250 years old (see note 30) has no basis in the UNESCO Convention itself and unfortunately excludes important archaeological material in many parts of the world.[54] For instance, O'Keefe (2000: 36) notes that "for countries such as Australia and New Zealand, the 250-year rule would exclude the entire archaeological evidence of early permanent European settlement."[55] O'Keefe (2000: 36) also observes that, curiously, the domestic American law governing the protection of archaeological resources requires only that the object be at least one hundred years old.[56]

Most important, however, the nonimplementation of Article 10(a) relinquishes what could be a powerful deterrent to the illicit trade in antiquities. The argument that the antiquities trade should be regulated at the state and municipal level is specious, as virtually all the objects in question fall under the congressional authority to regulate foreign and interstate commerce. It is worth noting that Switzerland, like the United States, has a federal system, in which significant powers are reserved to the individual cantons; despite this, the Swiss implementing legislation fully carries out Article 10(a).[57]

However, even if some of these flaws in CPIA were corrected, the legislation would still fall far short of what would, in my opinion, be a truly adequate regulation: namely, demanding that each object have a documented provenance back to a specified cutoff date and making the rebuttable presumption that objects without such documentation are illicit. Unfortunately, we are at present very far from getting this kind of legislation, so we need to face the facts: as long as there exists a less than strictly regulated market in archaeological objects, there will be powerful incentives for looting and pillage.[58] It is therefore urgent to consider, simultaneously, measures that would reduce the total global demand for purchase of antiquities: first, by greatly reducing the appeal of private collecting, through campaigns aimed at raising public awareness about the problem of pillage; and second, by giving museums and educational institutions wider access to antiquities through means other than purchase on the private market. Among these are long-term loans, widely traveling exhibitions, strictly controlled museum-to-museum sales or exchanges of duplicate objects, and joint excavation projects with art-rich countries (in which the finds could be fairly shared between the country of origin and the foreign contributing institutions).

Museums in particular, in their role as public educators, should adopt strict codes of ethics and careful acquisition policies, and where these are already in place, should commit themselves to strengthening the often too-vague guidelines and to observing them adequately. Indeed, museums have the responsibility to lead the way in setting the ethical standards in the art world.

Moreover, the resources currently invested in the purchase of antiquities could be effectively channeled instead into sponsoring new research and excavations, conservation projects, educational and training programs for local populations in art-rich regions, construction of on-site museums, and the development of responsible cultural tourism—all in order to help create, at least in part, a sustainable economy for local peoples out of their cultural resources while preserving their historical heritage. Indeed, if some of the social cachet attached to antiquities collecting could be eliminated from public opinion, this might not be such a utopian vision.[59]

Fundamentally, I believe that the goal of any international legislative effort should not be primarily to keep *every* archaeological artifact in its country of origin—in fact, carefully monitored movement of art among museums and other public institutions in different countries is highly desirable—but rather to make sure that the object is scientifically excavated, that its full context and history are recorded, and that the public and scholars have access to it.[60] Ultimately, I do not think it is really relevant whether a find from Pompeii (especially if it is a duplicate) ends up in a museum in Naples, Italy, or in Naples, Florida, as long as the integrity of its context is maintained and it is kept in the public domain.

It seems to me that the long-term task for archaeologists must be to sensitize both citizens and politicians to the immense loss to our historical patrimony that is being caused by the illicit trade in antiquities. With such an awareness it should be possible to devise effective measures to protect the world's cultural heritage, and to make that heritage widely available to people around the world in a safe and democratic way.

Acknowledgments

I wish to thank the editors Neil Brodie, Morag Kersel, Christina Luke, and Kathryn Walker Tubb for all their hard work in organizing the World Archaeological Congress sessions and putting this book together. I also wish to thank Patty Gerstenblith, Ellen Herscher, Cindy Ho, Claire Lyons, Patrick O'Keefe, Lyndel

Prott, and Lucille Roussin for their friendship and for all their encouragement and support. In particular, I wish to thank Patty Gerstenblith, Christina Luke, Patrick O'Keefe, Lyndel Prott, and Rick St. Hilaire for their thoughtful and thorough comments on earlier drafts of this chapter. A special thanks to Professor James Nafziger for providing me with some important and much-needed documents and to Morag Kersel for help in tracking down some references. I am also grateful to the staff of the archives and of the library at UNESCO, Paris, for their kind help with my many requests.

But my greatest debt of gratitude goes to my husband Alan Sokal for his genuine interest, unfailing support, and generous advice, not to mention his efficient secretarial assistance.

Needless to say, these people are not responsible for my views or for my mistakes.

Notes

1. As early as the 1920s and 1930s, attempts were made in the League of Nations to negotiate international instruments to protect cultural heritage. Indeed, in 1936–38 a draft Convention for the Protection of National Historic Artistic Treasures was circulated among the member states for comments; but several art-importing nations (notably the Netherlands, Sweden, the United Kingdom, and the United States) raised objections, and further negotiations were ultimately derailed by the outbreak of World War II. After the war, an important step was the adoption in 1954 of the Hague Convention for the Protection of Cultural Property in the Event of Armed Conflict. For further details of the pre-1960 history, see Prott chapter 1; Prott and O'Keefe 1984: 44–45 and 72–74; Prott and O'Keefe 1989: 708 ff.; Prott 1983: 337–38.

2. In particular, in April 1964, UNESCO for the first time appointed an ad hoc Committee of Experts with the task of drafting some preliminary recommendations for a convention (O'Keefe 2000: 13; UNESCO 1969b).

3. UNESCO 1969b, often referred to as the "preliminary" or "original" draft. According to the accompanying report (UNESCO 1969a: 2), "a principal expert and four consultants from various parts of the world have worked together on the preliminary draft of the convention here submitted to Member States for comment."

4. Rogers and Cohen (1975: 317) report that the U.S. "resisted [this draft] vehemently." For other countries' replies, see UNESCO 1970b and 1970c.

5. In those cases where the stringent obligations were maintained in the final text of the Convention (albeit sometimes in difficult-to-interpret form), the United States managed to limit their impact by inserting "understandings" in its ratification of the Convention. See the discussion of Articles 3, 10(a), and 13 later in this chapter.

6. The full text of the Convention can be found in numerous places, including O'Keefe 2000 and the UNESCO website <www.unesco.org>. For a history of the UNESCO Convention, see Bator 1982; Fraoua 1986; Gordon 1971; Prott 1983; Rogers and Cohen 1975. For a more recent and thorough analysis of the Convention, see O'Keefe 2000.

7. "The United States understands the provisions of the Convention to be neither self-executing nor retroactive" (U.S. Senate 1972a: VI).

8. U.S. Senate 1972b, statement of Mark B. Feldman: 11–12. A brief discussion of other Articles of the Convention appears later in this chapter.

9. S. 2677, 93rd Congress, 1st session (1973). The State Department consistently supported the implementing legislation. Mark B. Feldman, deputy legal advisor for the U.S. Department of State, was particularly active and tirelessly championed all the bills that were introduced to implement the Convention. See, for instance, DuBoff et al. 1976: 111 ff; U.S. House of Representatives 1977a: 80; U.S. Senate 1972b: 11–12; U.S. Senate 1978: 27–28.

10. 19 Weekly Comp. Pres. Doc. 58 (January 17, 1983). See also U.S. Senate 1982b. In addition to the bills listed in table 2.1, on September 16, 1982, Rep. Edgar introduced 97 H.R. 7127, which was almost identical to the earlier bill 95 H.R. 5643b. But by that time the Senate committee had nearly completed work on the revised bill 97 H.R. 4566, so that 97 H.R. 7127 was ignored. Interesting contemporaneous comment on the House and Senate hearings, as well as on the subsequent implementation of the CPIA, can be found in the column "The Antiquities Market" that appeared regularly in the *Journal of Field Archaeology*, edited first by Karen D. Vitelli (1974–83) and later by Ellen Herscher (1983–87), Timothy Kaiser (1990–93), and now by Christina Luke and Morag Kersel (2005).

11. Some notable exceptions to the general standpoint of archaeologists were Douglas Fraser, professor of art history and archaeology, Columbia University (U.S. House of Representatives 1977a: 102); Leopold Pospisil and Michael D. Coe, both professors of anthropology and, respectively, director of the Division of Anthropology and curator at the Peabody Museum of Natural History, Yale University (U.S. House of Representatives 1977a: 128, 69); and George Preston, professor of art history, City College, City University of New York (U.S. House of Representatives 1977a: 129).

Trade organizations, together with individual dealers and collectors, campaigned strenuously against all of the bills. Among the organizations involved were the American Association of Dealers in Ancient, Oriental and Primitive Art, the Art Dealers Association of America, and the National Antique and Art Dealers Association of America.

Museums and associated organizations in favor of the legislation included the Association of Art Museum Directors, the Field Museum of Natural History in Chicago, the International Council of Museums, the Minneapolis Institute of Art, the Peabody Museum of Archaeology and Ethnology at Harvard University, the Smithsonian Institution, the University of Pennsylvania Museum of Archaeology and Anthropology, and the National Small Museums. The Cleveland Museum and the Indiana University Art Museum supported the bills with some reservations. Voicing opposition were the Art Museum at Princeton University, Brooklyn Museum, Boston Museum of Fine Arts, Seattle

Art Museum, Museum of Art and Archaeology of the University of Missouri, Kimbell Art Museum in Fort Worth, Craft and Folk Art Museum of Los Angeles, the Everson Museum of Art in Syracuse, and the Bowers Museum in Santa Ana, California. The position taken by the New York Metropolitan Museum of Art is discussed later in this chapter.

12. Unfortunately, this provision does not cover artifacts stolen from as-yet-undiscovered archaeological sites or from sites that have not yet been fully excavated and documented.

13. Article 7(b)(ii) also provides that "the requesting State shall pay just compensation to an innocent purchaser or to a person who has valid title to that property." This provision is adjusted to the needs of civil law systems, in which an innocent purchaser of stolen property is protected after a certain lapse of time, but is ill-adapted to legal systems based on Anglo-Saxon common law, in which an innocent purchaser cannot ordinarily obtain valid title to stolen property. For this reason, the U.S. ratification of the UNESCO Convention included an understanding stating that "the United States understands that Article 7(b) is without prejudice to other remedies, civil or penal, available under the laws of the states parties for the recovery of stolen cultural property to the rightful owner without payment of compensation. The United States is further prepared to take the additional steps contemplated by Article 7(b)(ii) for the return of covered stolen cultural property without payment of compensation, except to the extent required by the Constitution of the United States, for those state parties that agree to do the same for the United States institutions." See O'Keefe 2000: 62–69, for a detailed discussion of this issue in a comparative international context.

In the preliminary and secretariat drafts, Article 7 contained much more stringent and sweeping obligations. It required State Parties to prohibit the import of cultural property not accompanied by an export certificate (c), to impose penalties for violation of this prohibition (e), and to sequestrate, when possible, cultural property illicitly introduced into their territory (f). These provisions generated much controversy and opposition, notably from the U.S. delegation (UNESCO 1970b: 22; see also Bator 1982: 379). The Committee of Experts set up a working party to draw up a new draft covering the whole of Article 7, which was split into five separate Articles, namely Articles 6 to 10 of the final draft (UNESCO 1970e: 4–5). Article 7 of the Convention is indeed the product of much negotiation and compromise.

14. O'Keefe 2000: 64 notes that "Article 7(b)(ii) clearly places the onus on the State of import to act at the request of the State of origin; refusal to act on the ground that other options are available to the dispossessed owner would be, in my view, a breach of the Convention."

15. Thus, the 1972 Senate report recommending ratification of the Convention states that "Article 7(b) does not affect existing remedies available in state or federal courts. The purpose is to provide a framework for special Government [co]operation" (U.S. Senate 1972a: VIII; U.S. Senate 1972b: 4). Similarly, the Senate report accompanying the final version of the CPIA bill states: "Implementation of Article 7(b) of the Convention affects neither existing remedies available in State or Federal courts nor laws prohibiting the theft and the knowing receipt and transportation of stolen property in interstate and foreign

commerce . . . including the possible recovery of stolen property for the rightful owner in the courts without payment of compensation" (U.S. Senate 1982b: 33; see also U.S. House of Representatives 1977b: 16).

16. *United States v. McClain*, 545 F.2d 988 (5th Cir. 1977), hereafter called McClain I; and *United States v. McClain*, 593 F.2d 658 (5th Cir. 1979), hereinafter called McClain II. For detailed discussions of the McClain case, see Gerstenblith 2001; Rosecrance 1986. For a different view of the McClain case, with which I personally do not agree, see Ewing 1999; Fitzpatrick 1983; and McAlee 1983. It is worth noting that the legal principles behind the *McClain* decisions were recently reaffirmed in *U.S. v. Schultz*, 17 F. Supp. 2d 445 (S.D.N.Y. 2002): 8–11, and 333 F.3d 393 (2nd Cir. 2003): 398–407.

17. Mexican Federal Law on Archaeological, Artistic and Historic Monuments and Zones, 6 May 1972, Article 27, as cited in McClain I: 1000.

18. McClain I: 992. The defendants' first conviction was reversed by the Court of Appeals because the district court judge had instructed the jury that "since 1897 Mexican law has declared pre-Columbian artifacts . . . to be the property of the Republic of Mexico," while the appeals court's analysis of Mexican law suggested that "not until 1972 did Mexico enact a law declaring *all* archaeological objects within its jurisdiction, movables and immovables, to be the property of the Nation" (McClain I: 992). Upon retrial, the defendants were once again convicted, and they again appealed, alleging that the judge's instructions to the jury concerning Mexican law were erroneous. The Court of Appeals reversed their conviction on the substantive count of transporting stolen property, on the grounds that because of the uncertainties in the meaning of the various Mexican laws, "the defendants may have suffered the prejudice of being convicted pursuant to laws that were too vague to be a predicate for criminal liability under our jurisprudential standards" (McClain II: 670). But the appeals court upheld their conviction on the conspiracy charge, because "it is abundantly clear that they conspired to bring in [from Mexico] at least one other load [of Pre-Columbian antiquities], and most likely a continuing stream of articles. . . . Their plans regarding those loads and the conduit itself were clearly illegal under any view of Mexican law, including that presented by their own witnesses" (McClain II: 671).

19. See, for instance, the testimony of Douglas Ewing, then president of the American Association of Dealers in Ancient, Oriental and Primitive Art, and testimonies by Alan Brandt, Andre Emmerich, and Peter Mark (U.S. House of Representatives 1977a: 35 ff., 45 ff., 38 ff., 42 ff.).

20. "[O]ur decision to refer to foreign declarations of ownership . . . poses the possibility, of course, that similar exportations from different countries might lead to different results in the United States. But the National Stolen Property Act has a specific scienter requirement—knowledge that the goods are stolen—that protects a defendant who might otherwise be trapped by such differences. . . . [T]he specific scienter requirement eliminates the possibility that a defendant is convicted for an offense he could not have understood to exist" (McClain I: 1002). See also Bator in U.S. Senate 1978: 219.

21. Around the time of the enactment of CPIA and for some years later, a number of attempts were made to overrule *McClain* by amending the NSPA. In September 1982,

Senators Dole, Moynihan and Matsunaga introduced a bill (S. 2963, 97th Congress, 2nd session) to amend NSPA (18 U.S.C. §2314 and §2315) as it applies to stolen archaeological material, along the lines proposed by Douglas Dillon and the dealers. Similar legislation was introduced also in the 98th Congress (S. 1559); and in March 1985, Senators Dole and Moynihan introduced yet another bill (S. 605, 99th Congress, 1st session) with the same purpose. Also in 1982, as a companion bill to S. 2963, Senator Bentsen introduced the Cultural Property Repose Act (S. 3102, 97th Congress, 2nd session). It would have created a regime of repose against claims by a foreign government to recover archaeological and ethnological material that had been in the United States for five or more years (128 Cong. Rec. 30819). In 1985, Senator Mathias introduced again a similar bill (S. 1523). None of these bills ever passed Congress. See also Fitzpatrick 1983: 864; Gerstenblith 2001: 221 n. 111; Rosecrance 1986: 312 n. 9.

22. This Article effectively replaces the stringent provisions contained in Article 7(c) of the Secretariat draft (see note 13 above) with an ad hoc system of export and import controls covering only archaeological and ethnological materials. Article 9 is almost entirely based on the alternative draft proposed by the U.S. delegation, including the restriction of import/export controls exclusively to archaeological and ethnological materials and not to other types of cultural property (see DuBoff et al. 1976: 114; Feldman et al. 1970: 4; statement of M. Feldman in U.S. Senate 1978: 17 ff.). According to Bator (1982: 339), the U.S. position was supported by a number of Western European and Latin American countries, including Mexico.

23. Some commentators are highly critical of the U.S. approach: "There is nothing in Article 9 of the 1970 Convention to suggest that a further agreement is necessary. The United States interpretation reduces the 1970 UNESCO Convention to an 'agreement to agree,' an interpretation which might be surprising to the delegates to the Special Committee of Governmental Experts, who might have considered that their task at Paris in 1970 was in fact to make the agreement, not to agree to make others" (O'Keefe 2000: 110; Prott and O'Keefe 1989: 797). These commentators also point out that negotiating a series of bilateral or multilateral agreements with all the major art-importing states can be very burdensome on art-rich countries.

24. Andre Emmerich in DuBoff et al. 1976: 110; see also James McAlee (120) and James Nafziger (105). And see statements of Douglas Ewing, president of the American Association of Dealers in Ancient, Oriental and Primitive Art (U.S. House of Representatives 1976: 17–23, 1977a: 32–33, 1980: 40), and memorandum of Paul Bator (U.S. Senate 1978: 191 and U.S. House of Representatives 1980: 19).

25. See Paul Bator memorandum (U.S. Senate 1978: 193 and U.S. House of Representatives 1980: 21) and Douglas Ewing statements (U.S. House of Representatives 1977a: 33–34, 1980: 40, 43; U.S. Senate 1978: 47).

26. 19 U.S.C. §2602(a)(1)(A–D). The last finding directly reflects the language contained in the preamble of the UNESCO Convention.

27. 19 U.S.C. § 2602(a)(4). This provision was first introduced in 1977 in the revised H.R. 5643. It was specifically suggested by Douglas Dillon (U.S. House of Representatives

1977a: 38). For further comments on this clause, see the memorandum of Paul Bator in U.S. Senate 1978: 193–94 and U.S. House of Representatives 1980: 21.

28. These provisions, in 19 USCS §2602(c)(1) and (d), were first introduced in 1981 (S. 1723).

29. 19 U.S.C. § 2602(a)(3). The dealers insisted that the documentation be provided in writing. See the testimony of Douglas Ewing, U.S. Senate 1982a: 453.

30. 19 U.S.C. § 2601 defines objects of archaeological interest as those which are "(I) of cultural significance; (II) at least 250 years old, and (III) . . . discovered as a result of scientific excavation, clandestine or accidental digging, or exploration on land or under water." It defines objects of ethnological interest as those which are "(I) the product of a tribal or nonindustrial society, and (II) important to the cultural heritage of a people because of its distinctive characteristics, comparative rarity, or its contribution to the knowledge of the origins, development, or history of that people." See discussion later in the chapter for a comment on the 250-year limitation.

31. 19 U.S.C. §2604. The materials are designated by the secretary of the treasury in consultation with the director of the United States Information Agency (now the Bureau of Educational and Cultural Affairs, Policy, Cultural Heritage Office at U.S. Department of State).

32. The first three bills introduced in Congress (H.R. 11754 and S. 2677 in 1973; H.R. 14171 in 1976; and H.R. 5643a in March 1977) gave the president authority to enter into bilateral and multilateral agreements with requesting States with no time limitations. At the hearings on April 26, 1977, Douglas Ewing, representing the American Association of Dealers in Ancient, Oriental and Primitive Art, complained that Congress was granting authority in perpetuity to the Executive Branch to enter into agreements for import controls and that these agreements could themselves extend in perpetuity. He recommended that Congress's grant of authority to the Executive Branch to enter into agreements should be limited to a five-year trial period, after which, as he put it, "Congress will be in a position to assess just how wisely the State Department has used its powers under the bill and can then determine whether it is necessary or desirable to continue those extraordinary powers for an additional period of time" (U.S. House of Representatives 1977a: 32, see also 38). He also urged that the agreements themselves be limited in time. Members of Congress seem to have accepted Ewing's arguments on the second point but not on the first: they agreed to place time limits on agreements but did not put any "sunset" provision into CPIA's basic grant of authority to the Executive Branch. The revised bill H.R. 5643b incorporated these changes and others and passed the House unanimously on October 17, 1977, but died for lack of action in the Senate. H.R. 5643b limits any agreement to an initial effective period of not more than five years; after that initial period, however, the president may extend an agreement for any additional periods considered reasonable. The five-year time limit for extensions was added only in the final draft of CPIA, although such a clause had previously been considered by the Committee on Ways and Means in 1977 in the markup of H.R. 5643 and had apparently been opposed by the State Department (see memorandum of Paul Bator in U.S. Senate 1978: 194). Also, at this stage, the committee specifically rejected the dealers' view that any agreement should terminate automatically

within a specific period unless there is evidence that other art-importing countries are also willing to apply import restrictions.

33. See the statements of Douglas Ewing (U.S. House of Representatives 1977a: 32, 36, and U.S. Senate 1978: 47) and Douglas Dillon (U.S. House of Representatives 1976: 51, 1977a: 6–7).

34. For a discussion of the U.S.–El Salvador agreement, see Guthrie Hingston 1999. For a discussion of the U.S.-Italy agreement, see Magness-Gardiner 2003 and Papa Sokal 2004a, 2004b. Some of these agreements have expired. For up-to-date information on renewals and new agreements, see the website of the Cultural Property Advisory Committee of the U.S. State Department, <http://exchanges.state.gov/culprop/>.

35. When the emergency provision was first introduced in 1977 (H.R. 5643b), it allowed for import restrictions to be implemented "whether or not the State party indicated in [its] request that an emergency condition exists"; Sec. 3(c)(1). This clause was eventually removed from the final draft of CPIA at the urging of the dealers. See testimony of Douglas Ewing (U.S. Senate 1982a: 456).

36. In H.R. 5643b there was no time limit on emergency import restrictions. These limitations were introduced in 1981 (S. 1723). See also U.S. Senate 1982a: 432.

37. See for instance U.S. House of Representatives 1976: 75; U.S. House of Representatives 1977a: 19, 24, 29, 37 and 70; U.S. Senate 1978: 55, 63; U.S. House of Representatives 1980: 75 ff. and 91.

38. Details of the committee are specified in 19 U.S.C. §2605(b)(1); the 1987 amendment can be found in PL 100-204, Title III, §307(c).

39. For a discussion of the "detoxification" provision, see the statement of Joseph D. Duffey, Assistant Secretary, Bureau of Educational and Cultural Affairs, Department of State, in U.S. House of Representatives 1977a: 19–20; memorandum of Paul Bator in U.S. Senate 1978: 195–96 and U.S. House of Representatives 1980: 23. The details of this provision underwent numerous modifications in the successive bills after it was first introduced in 1977 (H.R. 5643a).

40. This is pursuant to 22 U.S.C. §2459, "An Act to render immune from seizure under judicial process certain objects of cultural significance imported into the United States for temporary display and exhibition . . . ."

41. For a discussion of these statutes of limitations, see memorandum of Paul Bator in U.S. Senate 1978: 196 and U.S. House of Representatives 1980: 23 ff.; statement of Douglas Dillon, ibid.: 89; see also U.S. House of Representatives 1977a: 13.

42. A *reservation* is "a unilateral statement . . . made by a State, when signing, ratifying, accepting, approving or acceding to a treaty, whereby it purports to exclude or to modify the legal effect of certain provisions of the treaty in their application to that State" (Vienna Convention on the Law of Treaties, 23 May 1969, Article 2(1)(d); see United Nations 1980). Reservations are permitted unless the treaty in question prohibits them or "the reservation is incompatible with the object and purpose of the treaty" (Vienna Convention, Article 19). An *understanding*, by contrast, is a device by which a State declares its interpretation of certain of the treaty's provisions, without purporting to modify or limit them.

43. O'Keefe 2000: 45. O'Keefe also discusses how Article 3 is handled in the Canadian and Australian laws implementing the UNESCO Convention.

44. U.S. Senate 1972a: VIII; U.S. Senate 1972b: 3; Bator 1982: 379–80. Feldman et al. (1970: 7) explains that "the reference to 'national legislation' was inserted in this paragraph to accommodate the problems of governments, such as the United States government, which do not have legislation regulating the acquisition policy of private institutions. Thus, in the United States this provision would apply primarily to institutions controlled by the Federal Government. It is expected that private institutions would develop their own code of ethics consistent with the spirit of this provision."

45. I thank Rick St. Hilaire for drawing my attention to the extensive network of museums run by the National Park Service (NPS), which previous commentators on Article 7(a) had overlooked (see, e.g., Abramson and Huttler 1973: 965, n. 213; O'Keefe 2000: 58). According to the NPS website, "the National Park Service manages the world's largest system of museums; more than 350 national parks preserve more than 105 million objects, specimens, documents, and images" (http://www.cr.nps.gov/museums.htm). "National Park Service museum collections preserve more than 105 million items, including 34.5 million archaeological, 3.4 million historical, 1.9 million biological, 290,000 paleontological, 69,000 geological, and 28,000 ethnographic objects and specimens and more than 65 million archival and manuscript items" (http://www.cr.nps.gov/museum/centennial/treasures.html).

The Smithsonian Institution and the National Gallery of Art in Washington, D.C., are semiprivate organizations governed by independent boards of regents or trustees. See Abramson and Huttler 1973: 965, n. 213. Abramson and Huttler (1973: 966, n. 214) believe, nevertheless, that "this provision will exert powerful moral pressure on private institutions." Indeed, some museums, such as the Smithsonian Institution and the University of Pennsylvania Museum of Archaeology and Anthropology, have adopted stringent acquisition policies. For detailed analysis of Article 7(a), see Nafziger 1975 and O'Keefe 2000: 57 ff.

46. The phrase "consistent with the laws of each State" was added in the introduction of Article 13 at the urging of the U.S. delegation and applies to all the subparagraphs (Feldman et al. 1970: 17). Its goal, according to Bator (1982: 378), is "to insure that no action inconsistent with or going beyond existing domestic laws of the parties would be required." The effectiveness of Article 13, however, is seriously undermined by this clause. See also O'Keefe 2000: 85–90 for a detailed discussion of this Article.

47. The Executive Branch and Senate documents accompanying the U.S. ratification of the UNESCO Convention ignore the reference to *illicitly exported* cultural property and instead read Article 13(b) as referring to *stolen* cultural property: "Paragraph (b) contemplates the normal cooperation of law enforcement agencies and cultural services within the framework of existing law. Under U.S. procedures, the rightful owner of stolen property may be able to recover it through normal police action" (U.S. Senate 1972a: XI; U.S. Senate 1972b: 6).

48. U.S. Senate 1972a: XI; U.S. Senate 1972b: 6–7. Here they are referring to civil actions for recovery of the cultural property in question.

49. As O'Keefe (2000: 78) points out, the reference to "antique dealers" is most likely a clumsy translation from the French. Indeed, the French text of the Convention—which, along with the English, Spanish, and Russian, is equally authoritative (Article 18)—uses the term *antiquaires*, which can indeed mean "antique dealers" but in the present context is better translated as "antiquities dealers."

Bator (1982: 378) calls this "a nuisance provision." Article 10(a) also requires State Parties to "restrict by education, information and vigilance, movement of cultural property illegally removed from any State Party." For a more detailed discussion of this provision, which Bator (1982: 378) calls an "unenforceable undertaking," see O'Keefe 2000: 77–78.

50. Once again, the phrase as "appropriate for each country" had been inserted in the UNESCO Convention at the suggestion of the U.S. delegation. See Feldman et al. 1970: 17. For further discussion of Article 10(a), see also Papa Sokal 2002.

51. Here is a simple analogy: Businesses are required by federal law to maintain certain financial records, and these records are subject to audit by the tax authorities. Though this record-keeping does not make it impossible to cheat on one's taxes, it does make it more difficult.

52. Since 1931 the Italian law has required dealers in used or ancient objects to declare themselves to the local authorities and to keep a daily register of the transactions carried out, including the identities of buyers and sellers, who must show their state-issued photographic identity card (Regio decreto 18 giugno 1931, n. 773, Articles 126 and 128). The cultural property law currently in force furthermore provides that:

1. Whoever engages in commerce in the items listed in annex A of this law [which includes archaeological objects more than 100 years old] shall send to the *Soprintendente* and to the Region a copy of the declaration prescribed by Article 126 [of the 1931 law].

2. The persons indicated in paragraph 1 shall record daily in the register prescribed by Article 128 [of the 1931 law] the transactions carried out, describing the characteristics of the items bought or sold in accordance with the procedures established by regulation. The register shall be exhibited, upon request, to the employees of the Ministry [of Culture] and of the Region.

3. The *Soprintendente* shall verify, through periodic inspections at least once every six months, the proper maintenance of the register and the accuracy of the annotations contained in it (Italy 1999: Article 62).

Finally, art and antiquities dealers are required "to make available to the buyer the certificates of authenticity and provenance of the works and objects located on the premises or on exhibit" and "to provide the buyer with a photograph of the work or object together with a signed declaration of authenticity and indication of provenance" (Italy 1999: Article 63). See also D'Antone 2000 for the full text of the Italian cultural property law as compiled in 1999, along with commentary.

The French record-keeping law applies to dealers in all types of used movable objects, not just antiquities, and belongs to a section of the Penal Code aimed at discouraging the possession, transmission, or concealment of unlawfully obtained property (*recel*). It provides that "any person whose professional activity involves the sale of movable objects that are used or are acquired from persons other than the maker or dealer, who omits (including by negligence) to keep a daily register . . . containing a description of the objects acquired or held for the purpose of sale or exchange and permitting the identification of these objects and of the persons who sold or exchanged them, shall be punished by six months of imprisonment and by the fine of 30,000 euros" (France 2004, Code Pénal, Article 321-7). The same penalties apply to any person who makes inaccurate entries on the register, or who refuses to present the register to a competent authority (France 2004, Code Pénal, Article 321-8). The accompanying regulations further stipulate that the register must contain "the name and address of each person who sold, exchanged or consigned one or more objects" of the aforementioned types, "as well as the type, number, date of issue and issuing authority of the identity document produced by this person"; when the vendor or consignor is a firm, the register must contain the name and business address of the firm as well as the identity details of the person representing it (France 2004, Code Pénal, Article R321-3).

53. The situation in Iraq is covered by the 1954 Hague Convention for the Protection of Cultural Property in the Event of Armed Conflict and its protocols. Unfortunately, as of 2005 the United States is not yet a party to the Hague Convention.

54. For this reason, "the United States interpretation was seen by Canada as an unwarranted limitation of its obligations under the 1970 Convention" (O'Keefe 2000: 35–36).

55. See also the written testimony of the American Anthropological Association in U.S. Senate 1982a: 564, which points out that "Hawaii was discovered by Europeans 204 years ago; Benin was sacked in the late 19th century; interior Papua-New Guinea was not penetrated by Europeans until the 1940s."

56. The relevant law is the Archaeological Resources Protection Act of 1979; 16 U.S.C. §470bb(1). On November 17, 2003, Representatives English and Leach introduced a bill (H.R. 3497) to address some of these shortcomings of CPIA. The principal goal of H.R. 3497 is to "provide for the recovery, restitution, and protection of the cultural heritage of Iraq." (This is actually a slightly weaker version of an earlier bill, H.R. 2009, they had sponsored in May 2003.) However, H.R. 3497 would also amend CPIA to strengthen it in certain aspects, particularly in the case of emergency import restrictions. It would extend the application of emergency action to countries that are not State Parties to the UNESCO Convention; it would eliminate, in emergency cases, the need for a request from the government of the affected country and the requirement for a review by CPAC, thereby streamlining the emergency process. Moreover, the maximum length of emergency import restrictions would be increased from five to ten years, and extensions would no longer be subject to a time limit or a review by CPAC. H.R. 3497 would also extend the maximum length of bilateral and multilateral agreements and their renewals from five to ten years; the definition of an archeological object would be changed from at least 250 years old to at least 100 years old, with the notable exception of coins; and the composition of CPAC would be changed from eleven members to thirteen with the addition of

one more member representing the interests of museums and one expert in the field of conservation. These would all be welcome improvements on the current legislation. Alas, this bill died in December 2004 when the 108th Congress adjourned.

57. Switzerland 2003, Article 16(2). For more information on the history of the Swiss legislation, see Renold and Raschér 2002, and Patty Gerstenblith, chapter 3.

58. For quantitative studies of the relationship between the antiquities market and the looting of archaeological sites, see Chippindale and Gill 2000; Elia 2001; Gilgan 2001; Gill and Chippindale 1993.

59. It is important, however, to be aware of the dangers associated with the large-scale private funding of archaeology; this is obviously a difficult and multifaceted issue that requires careful analysis and debate.

60. I stress that I am advocating the controlled circulation of antiquities *only* among museums and other publicly accessible institutions. It goes without saying that I am not in any way advocating the private collecting of antiquities.

BIBLIOGRAPHY

Abramson, Ronald D., and Stephen B. Huttler. "The Legal Response to the Illicit Movement of Cultural Property." *Law and Policy in International Business* 5 (1973): 932–70.

Atwood, Roger. *Stealing History: Tomb Raiders, Smugglers, and the Looting of the Ancient World*. New York: St. Martin's Press, 2004.

Bator, Paul M. "An Essay on the International Trade in Art." *Stanford Law Review* 34 (1982): 275–384.

Chippindale, Christopher, and David W. J. Gill. 2000. "Material Consequences of Contemporary Classical Collecting." *American Journal of Archaeology* 104, no. 3 (2000): 463–512.

D'Antone, Carmelo (ed.). *La tutela dei beni culturali ed ambientali nel T.U. 29 ottobre, 1999, n. 490*. Pisa: Felici, 2000.

DuBoff, Leonard D., James A. Nafziger, Andre Emmerich, Mark B. Feldman, James McAlee, and Paul M. Bator. Proceedings of the Panel on the U.S. Enabling Legislation of the UNESCO Convention on the Means of Prohibiting and Preventing the Illicit Import, Export and Transfer of Ownership of Cultural Property. *Syracuse Journal of International Law and Commerce* 4, no. 1 (1976): 97–134.

Elia, Ricardo. "Analysis of Looting, Selling and Collecting of Apulian Red-Figure Vases: A Quantitative Approach." In *Trade in Illicit Antiquities: The Destruction of the World's Archaeological Heritage*, ed. by Neil Brodie, Jennifer Doole, and Colin Renfrew, 145–53. McDonald Institute Monograph. Cambridge, U.K.: McDonald Institute for Archaeological Research, 2001.

Ewing, Douglas C. "What Is 'Stolen'? The McClain Case Revisited." In *The Ethics of Collecting Cultural Property: Whose Culture? Whose Property?* 2nd ed., ed. Phyllis Mauch Messinger, 177–83. Albuquerque, N.M.: University of New Mexico Press, 1999.

Feldman, Mark B., et al. Report of the United States Delegation to the Special Committee of Governmental Experts to Examine the Draft Convention on the Means of Prohibiting and Preventing the Illicit Import, Export and Transfer of Ownership of Cultural Property. UNESCO House, Paris, France. April 13–24, 1970.

Fitzpatrick, James F. "A Wayward Course: The Lawless Customs Policy toward Cultural Properties." *New York University Journal of International Law and Politics* 15 (1983): 857–94.

France. *Code Pénal.* 2004. <http://www.legifrance.gouv.fr/html/codes_traduits/code_penal_textan.htm>, accessed January 15, 2005.

Fraoua, Ridha. "Convention concernant les mesures à prendre pour interdire et empêcher l'importation, l'exportation et le transfert de propriété illicites des biens culturels: Commentaire et aperçu de quelques mesures nationales d'exécution." UNESCO Doc. CC-86/WS/40. 1986.

Gerstenblith, Patty. "The Public Interest in the Restitution of Cultural Objects." *Connecticut Journal of International Law* 16, no. 2 (2001): 197–246.

———. The United States' Implementation of the 1970 UNESCO Convention. Paper presented at a seminar at the Department for Culture, Media and Sport in London, U.K., 2002.

Gilgan, Elizabeth. "Looting and the Market for Maya Objects: A Belizean Perspective." In *Trade in Illicit Antiquities: The Destruction of the World's Archaeological Heritage*, ed. Neil Brodie, Jennifer Doole, and Colin Renfrew, 73–87. McDonald Institute Monograph. Cambridge, U.K.: McDonald Institute for Archaeological Research, 2001.

Gill, David W. J., and Christopher Chippindale. "Material and Intellectual Consequences of Esteem for Cycladic Figures." *American Journal of Archaeology* 97 (1993): 601–59.

Gordon, John B. "The UNESCO Convention on the Illicit Movement of Art Treasures." *Harvard International Law Journal* 12 (1971): 537–56.

Guthrie Hingston, Ann. "U.S. Implementation of the UNESCO Cultural Property Convention." In *The Ethics of Collecting Cultural Property: Whose Culture? Whose Property?*, 2nd ed., ed. Phyllis Mauch Messinger, 129–47. Albuquerque, N.M.: University of New Mexico Press, 1999.

Italy. *Regio decreto 18 giugno 1931, n. 773, Approvazione del testo unico delle leggi di pubblica sicurezza.* 1931. <http://www.italguire.giusta.it/nir/1931/lex_15915.html>, accessed May 12, 2006.

———. *Decreto Legislativo 29 ottobre 1999, n. 490, Testo unico delle disposizioni legislative in materia di beni culturali e ambientali.* 1999. <http://www.parlamento.it/parlam/leggi/deleghe/99490dl.htm>, accessed January 15, 2005.

Luke, Christina, and Morag M. Kersel. 2005. "The Antiquities Market: A Retrospective and a Look Forward." *Journal of Field Archaeology* 30(2): 191–200.

Magness-Gardiner, Bonnie. "Long-term Archaeological Loans from Italy: Summary of Roundtable Discussions." *American Journal of Archaeology* 107, no. 3 (2003): 477–81.

McAlee, James R. "The *McClain* Case, Customs, and Congress." *New York University Journal of International Law and Politics* 15 (1983): 813–38.

Nafziger, James A. R. "Article 7(a) of the UNESCO Convention." In *Art Law, Domestic and International*, ed. Leonard D. DuBoff, 387–94. South Hackensack, N.J.: Fred B. Rothman and Company, 1975.

O'Keefe, Patrick J. *Commentary on the UNESCO 1970 Convention on Illicit Traffic*. Leicester, U.K.: Institute of Art and Law, 2000.

Papa Sokal, Marina L. "Stemming the Illicit Trade in Antiquities." *Culture without Context,* Issue 11 (December 2002): 26–27.

———. "USA and Italy Sign Agreement to Protect Italian Archaeological Materials." *Accordia Research Papers* (Accordia Research Institute, University of London) 9 (2004a): 183–88.

———. The Plundering of Archaeological Sites in Italy. Paper presented at the 6th International Conference on Italian Archaeology, Groningen, Netherlands, April 2003. (2004b). Publication forthcoming in proceedings.

Prott, Lyndel V. "International Control of Illicit Movement of Cultural Heritage: The 1970 UNESCO Convention and Some Possible Alternatives." *Syracuse Journal of International Law and Commerce* 10, no. 2 (1983): 333–51.

Prott, Lyndel V., and Patrick J. O'Keefe. *Law and the Cultural Heritage*, vol. 1: *Discovery and Excavation*. Abingdon, Oxfordshire, U.K.: Professional Books, 1984.

———. *Law and the Cultural Heritage*, vol. 3: *Movement*. London: Butterworths, 1989.

Renold, Marc-André, and Andrea F. G. Raschér. The Swiss Draft Legislation on the International Transfer of Cultural Objects. Paper presented at a seminar at the Department for Culture, Media and Sport in London, U.K., 2002.

Rogers, William D., and Rosalind C. Cohen. "Art Pillage—International Solutions." In *Art Law, Domestic and International*, ed. Leonard D. DuBoff, 315–24. South Hackensack, N.J.: Fred B. Rothman and Company, 1975.

Rosecrance, Barbara B. "Harmonious Meeting: The *McClain* Decision and the Cultural Property Implementation Act." *Cornell International Law Journal* 19 (1986): 311–46.

Switzerland. Loi fédérale sur le transfert international des biens culturels. June 20, 2003. This statute can be found at <www.admin.ch/ch/f/rs/444_1>, accessed May 12, 2006.

United Nations. *Vienna Convention on the Law of Treaties*. Treaty Series, vol. 1155 (1980): 331.

United Nations Educational, Scientific and Cultural Organization. *Means of Prohibiting and Preventing the Illicit Import, Export and Transfer of Ownership of Cultural Property*. Preliminary report prepared in compliance with Article 10.1 of the Rules of Procedure concerning Recommendations to Member States and International Conventions covered by the terms of Article IV, paragraph 4, of the Constitution. Document number SHC/MD/3., 1969a.

———. Preliminary Draft Convention Concerning the Means of Prohibiting and Preventing the Illicit Import, Export and Transfer of Ownership of Cultural Property. Document number SHC/MD/3 Annex., 1969b.

———. *Means of Prohibiting and Preventing the Illicit Import, Export and Transfer of Own-*

ership of Cultural Property. Final report prepared in compliance with Article 10.1 of the Rules of Procedure concerning Recommendations to Member States and International Conventions covered by the terms of Article IV, paragraph 4, of the Constitution. Document number SHC/MD/5., 1970a.

―――. *Replies to circular letter CL/2041 and to document SHC/MD/3 received from States on 27 January 1970*. Document number SHC/MD/5 Annex I., 1970b.

―――. *Analysis of General Observations and Comments Made by Member States Which Involve Proposals to Amend the Preliminary Draft Convention, document SHC/MD/3*. Document number SHC/MD/5 Annex II., 1970c.

―――. *Revised Draft Convention Concerning the Means of Prohibiting and Preventing the Illicit Import, Export and Transfer of Ownership of Cultural Property*. Document number SHC/MD/5 Annex III., 1970d.

―――. *Report of the Special Committee of Governmental Experts to Examine the Draft Convention on the means of Prohibiting and Preventing the Illicit Import, Export and Transfer of Ownership of Cultural Property*. UNESCO House, 13–24 April 1970. Document number 16 C/17 Annex II., 1970e.

U.S. House of Representatives. *Written Comments on H.R. 14171. Subcommittee on Trade, Committee on Ways and Means*. 94th Congress, 2nd sess., Microfiche number H782-38., 1976.

―――. *UNESCO Convention on Cultural Property: Hearings before the Subcommittee on Trade, Committee on Ways and Means*. 95th Congress, 1st sess., April 26, 1977. Microfiche number H781-46 (1977a).

―――. *Implementation of the Convention on Cultural Property. Report of the Committee on Ways and Means to accompany H.R. 5643*. Report 95-615. 95th Congress, 1st sess., September 21, 1977 (1977b).

―――. *Cultural Property Treaty Legislation. Hearings before the Subcommittee on Trade, Committee on Ways and Means*. 96th Congress, 2nd sess., September 27, 1979. Microfiche number H781-20 (printed 1980).

U.S. Senate. *Convention on Ownership of Cultural Property. Message from the President of the United States Transmitting the Convention on the Means of Prohibiting and Preventing the Illicit Import, Export, and Transfer of Ownership of Cultural Property*. Executive B, 92nd Congress, 2nd sess., February 2, 1972. Microfiche number S385-2 (1972a).

―――. *Convention on Ownership of Cultural Property*. Report of the Committee on Foreign Relations. Executive Report 92–29, 92nd Congress, 2nd sess., Microfiche number S384-11 (1972b).

―――. *Hearings on H.R. 5643 and S. 2261 before the Subcommittee on International Trade of the Senate Committee on Finance*. 95th Congress, 2nd sess., February 8, 1978. Microfiche number S361-31 (1978).

―――. *Hearings before the Subcommittee on International Trade of the Committee on Finance*. 97th Congress, 2nd sess., July 21 and 22, 1982. Microfiche number S361-13 (1982a).

―――. *Miscellaneous Tariff, Trade, and Customs Matters: Report of the Committee on Finance to accompany H.R. 4566*. Title III. Implementing Legislation for the Convention on the Means of Prohibiting and Preventing the Illicit Import, Export and Transfer of Ownership of Cultural Property, 21–34. Senate report 97-564. 97th Congress, 2nd sess., September 21, 1982. Microfiche number S363-8 (1982b).

————. *Hearing before the Subcommittee on Criminal Law of the Committee on the Judiciary on S. 605*. Senate hearing 99-589. 99th Congress, 1st sess., May 22, 1985. Microfiche number S521-56 (printed 1986).

United States v. McClain, 545 F.2d 988 (5th Cir. 1977), 593 F.2d 658 (5th Cir. 1979).

3

Recent Developments in the Legal Protection of Cultural Heritage

PATTY GERSTENBLITH

The opening years of the twenty-first century have seen considerable progress in the use of the legal system to combat the looting and destruction of archaeological sites, while at the same time illuminating significant deficiencies in the ability of both the international and national legal regimes to respond effectively to cultural heritage crises. The intentional destruction of the Bamiyan Buddhas and of other forms of representational ancient art by the Taliban in Afghanistan in 2001, which compounded the years of damage inflicted on the Afghan cultural heritage through war and lack of central governmental authority, constituted one threat. The war in Iraq in 2003 and its aftermath have demonstrated again the vulnerability of cultural heritage and particularly archaeological sites to the same elements of war and civil unrest. This chapter first sets out the methodical, incremental progress that has been made, primarily in the United States, British, and Swiss legal systems, and then contrasts this progress with the inability of these legal systems to respond effectively to sudden crises.

The scientific recovery of archaeological artifacts through controlled excavation is crucial to our understanding of and ability to reconstruct the past. Ancient sites are composed of different layers or strata that represent distinct chronological periods. The horizontal and vertical excavation and documentation of architectural features, objects, and faunal and floral evidence within the context of each stratum permits the full reconstruction of associated remains. It is only through an understanding of a site's stratigraphy and the ability to associate contemporary remains that the full historical, cultural, and archaeological record of the past can be retrieved and utilized to increase our understanding of the past. It is incumbent upon us to preserve these remains so that future generations can continue to enjoy and learn from the past.

Thefts of art works from both public and private collections and the looting of antiquities from archaeological sites are major international crimes. Archaeological sites throughout the world are looted to supply archaeological objects for sale on the international art market.[1] The ultimate purchasers of these objects—museums and private collectors—provide the financial incentive for the looting of sites. The availability of both civil and criminal legal consequences for those who trade in and collect undocumented antiquities decreases the demand for such objects. This, in turn, reduces the supply by depressing the financial incentives of middlemen, who encourage the looting, and ultimately depresses incentives for the actual looters. While it is not the only solution to the problems of theft and looting of cultural materials, the legal system in Western market nations is one essential element in the attempt to reduce the losses that result from these illegal activities.

RECENT PROGRESS IN THE LEGAL REGIME TO PROTECT CULTURAL HERITAGE

The McClain/Schultz Doctrine

In 1977, the United States government prosecuted several dealers under the National Stolen Property Act (NSPA) for conspiring to import and trade in archaeological artifacts that were stolen from Mexico.[2] Mexico had enacted legislation in 1972 vesting ownership of all undiscovered archaeological objects in the Mexican nation. Removal of such objects without permission was therefore theft, and if such objects were brought to the United States, they retained their character as stolen property. The U.S. Court of Appeals for the Fifth Circuit analyzed the Mexican vesting law to determine whether it was truly an ownership law or whether it was merely regulatory in nature. The court concluded that the 1972 law was a vesting statute that utilized terms that were sufficiently clear for a U.S. citizen to understand (*United States v. McClain*, 545 F.2d, at 997–1004). While the defendants were acquitted on the substantive counts, their conviction for conspiring to violate the NSPA was affirmed (*United States v. McClain*, 593 F.2d, at 670–72).

The art collecting community reacted strongly to the *McClain* decision and, through its chief supporter in Congress, Senator Daniel Patrick Moynihan, tried without success to amend the NSPA so as to exclude from its definition of stolen property archaeological objects where "the claim of ownership is based only upon a declaration by the foreign country of national ownership . . . ."[3] The *McClain* doctrine was utilized over the ensuing twenty-five years in several civil claims for the recovery of stolen archaeological objects. The courts that confronted the validity of the *McClain* doctrine consistently held that its doctrinal underpinning was correct, and in those cases in which the doctrine's prerequisites were satisfied, the stolen archaeological artifacts at issue were returned to their country of origin.[4] However, most of these cases ended in out-of-court settlements or were not appealed, and so there was no definitive decision from a federal appellate court on the *McClain* doctrine after the *McClain* decision itself.[5]

In 1997, the United States Customs Service sought the forfeiture from New York collector Michael Steinhardt of a fourth-century B.C. gold phiale that had been taken illegally from Italy. The trial court ordered the forfeiture on the bases both that the phiale was stolen property, because it was taken in violation of Italy's national ownership law, and that the phiale had been imported illegally into the United States, because of material misrepresentations concerning its country of origin and value on the Customs import documents.[6] When the decision was appealed, the U.S. Court of Appeals for the Second Circuit affirmed the lower court's decision, relying exclusively on the material misrepresentations on the Customs documentation, while sidestepping the more complex question of whether the phiale was stolen property (*United States v. An Antique Platter of Gold*, 184 F.3d 131, 134 [2d Cir. 1999]).

However, within a short time—in 2001—the U.S. attorney for the Southern District of New York indicted the prominent dealer Frederick Schultz. Until shortly before the indictment, Schultz had been the president of the National Association of Dealers in Ancient, Oriental and Primitive Art (NADAOPA). As far back as the original *McClain* decisions, this organization had taken a leading role in submitting *amicus* briefs in support of the positions of dealers and collectors in acquiring and dealing in undocumented antiquities. NADAOPA has opposed most (if not all) of the bilateral agreements and emergency actions that the United States has taken to prohibit import into the United States of illegally exported designated archaeological and ethnological materials pursuant to its ratification of the 1970 UNESCO Convention on the Means of Prohibiting and Preventing the Illicit Import, Export and Transfer of Ownership of Cultural Property (UNESCO Convention).[7]

The Schultz indictment alleged that he had conspired to import, deal in, and possess antiquities stolen from Egypt in violation of Egypt's Law 117, which vested ownership of antiquities in the Egyptian nation (*United States v. Schultz*, 333 F.3d 393). As this was the single count of the indictment, the court was forced to address the *McClain* doctrine. As the case was brought in New York, the court's decision would clarify the law in the jurisdiction that is the heart of the art market in the United States and that is one of the largest centers for the art trade in the world. The case thus had considerable significance for the question of whether the law of the United States would be an effective tool in the attempt to diminish the destruction of archaeological sites throughout the world through the adoption of disincentives to trading in looted artifacts.

The indictment charged that Schultz and his co-conspirator, the English restorer Jonathan Tokeley-Parry, had conspired to remove stolen antiquities from Egypt and sell them in London and New York. While Tokeley-Parry was responsible for the theft of numerous artifacts, the most prominent of those that featured in Schultz's trial was the head of the Eighteenth Dynasty pharaoh Amenhotep III (Watson 2002: 21–26). Tokeley-Parry covered the head to disguise it to look like a souvenir replica so that it could be smuggled out of Egypt. Schultz offered it for sale for U.S. $1.2 million. Tokeley-Parry kept extensive autobiographical notes of his transactions with Schultz and included descriptions of how they "assigned" these antiquities to the "Thomas Alcock collection," an "old" collection that Schultz and Tokeley-Parry had fabricated. They manufactured old labels to endow an aura of authenticity to their claim that the collection had been established in the 1920s, long before the enactment of Law 117 (Bohlen 2002; *United States v. Schultz*, 333 F.3d, at 396). These facts, portrayed in considerable detail at Schultz's trial, also presented an interesting glimpse into the workings of the New York antiquities market and should provide clues for future investigations of such operations.

Before the trial, Schultz moved to dismiss the indictment on the grounds that antiquities subject to a national ownership law no longer constituted stolen property once they were removed from their country of origin and, in the alternative, that the Egyptian law was not truly an ownership law but was rather an export regulation. Two friend of the court (*amicus curiae*) briefs were submitted concerning Schultz's motion to dismiss: one in support of Schultz by NADAOPA, Christie's, and other dealers' associations; and the second in support of the U.S. government's position by the Archaeological Institute of America and other archaeological and preservationist organizations.

The disagreements between the parties and the respective *amici* focused on the proper characterization of antiquities illegally excavated and removed from a country despite a national ownership law; the characterization of Law 117; and the effect of the enactment of the Convention on Cultural Property Implementation Act (CPIA) on the *McClain* decision's interpretation of the NSPA.[8] After two lengthy hearings on these questions, the court issued its opinion in January 2002, holding that property taken in violation of a national ownership law is still stolen property, even after entering the United States; that enactment of the CPIA had no effect on the earlier *McClain* doctrine; and that Law 117 is truly a national ownership law (178 F. Supp. 2d 445 [S.D.N.Y. 2002]).

The trial then proceeded; Schultz was convicted and later sentenced to serve thirty-three months in jail, pay a fine of fifty thousand dollars, and return those antiquities still in his possession to Egypt. Schultz's appeal to the U.S. Court of Appeals for the Second Circuit squarely presented the crucial issues of whether antiquities subject to a national ownership law and removed without permission constituted stolen property even after entering the United States and what the criteria are for determining whether a foreign law is truly a vesting law, rather than a regulation, which would not be enforced by U.S. courts. The appellate court upheld Schultz's conviction; its opinion is worth analyzing to point out the essential elements of this type of stolen property claim (333 F.3d 393 [2d Cir. 2003]).

The criteria that the court established to determine the proper characterization of a foreign ownership law focused on two elements. First, was the law on its face an ownership law? Second, was the law internally enforced within Egypt as an ownership law (333 F.3d, at 399–402)? The first element was easily satisfied by the court's inspection of the wording of the statute, which clearly vested ownership of newly discovered antiquities in the nation and permitted private possession to continue only for those antiquities discovered before the effective date of the statute. The second element required two Egyptian government officials to testify concerning internal enforcement of Law 117. Dr. Gaballa Ali Gaballa, then secretary general of Egypt's Supreme Council of Antiquities, and General El Sobky, director of criminal investigations for the Egyptian Antiquities Police, described the operation of the law, the regular investigation and prosecution of individuals who traffic in antiquities within Egypt, the various fines and prison sentences available for violations of the law, and the government's seizure and retention of all newly discovered antiquities (333 F.3d, at 400–402, 407–8). Having determined that the law is a true ownership law, the court then confronted Schultz's substantive arguments.

After reviewing earlier case law, including the *McClain* and *Hollinshead* decisions, the appellate court examined whether the property taken in violation of a national ownership law was "stolen property" for purposes of the NSPA. The court held that the NSPA should be interpreted broadly and that it makes no difference whether the owner is foreign or whether the property was stolen in the United States or in a foreign country (333 F.3d, at 402–3). Furthermore, the court is not limited to common law definitions of stolen property (333 F.3d, at 409–10). Relying on earlier case law, the court concluded that if the property is considered stolen in a foreign country, it is still stolen property after it is brought to the United States (333 F.3d, at 402–3). The court analogized theft from a foreign sovereign to any other type of theft of property and stated:

> Although we recognize the concerns raised by Schultz and the *amici* about the risks that this holding poses to dealers in foreign antiquities, we cannot imagine that it "creates an insurmountable barrier to the lawful importation of cultural property into the United States." Our holding does assuredly create a barrier to the importation of cultural property owned by a foreign government. We see no reason that property stolen from a

foreign sovereign should be treated any differently from property stolen from a foreign museum or private home. The *mens rea* requirement of the NSPA will protect innocent art dealers who unwittingly receive stolen goods, while our appropriately broad reading of the NSPA will protect the property of sovereign nations. (333 F.3d, at 410)

Finally, the court turned to the argument that enactment of the CPIA was inconsistent with the government's interpretation of the NSPA. The court rejected this argument, noting that the legislative history of the CPIA clearly states that the CPIA was not intended to preempt or change in any way any preexisting remedies available under either federal or state law (333 F.3d, at 408).[9] Furthermore, there is no inconsistency between the CPIA and the NSPA that results. The CPIA is a civil, Customs statute; it carries no criminal punishment and results only in forfeiture of the illegally imported property. The NSPA is a broader statute, criminal in nature, and requires proof of *mens rea* (criminal intent) before it can be enforced. While there are some circumstances in which both statutes might apply, overlapping jurisdiction of statutes is not uncommon and does not mean that one statute negates the other (333 F.3d, 408–9).

Schultz attempted to argue, in particular, that the concept of "stolen property" should be limited to that property described in the CPIA section prohibiting import of stolen cultural objects that had been documented in the inventory of a museum or similar public or religious institution (19 U.S.C. § 2607). This argument, however, was patently flawed in that it would mean that one who deals in cultural objects stolen from a private collection could not be prosecuted under the NSPA—a result that Congress surely would not have intended when it enacted the CPIA (333 F.3d, at 408–9). One of the *amicus* briefs that supported Schultz suggested that application of the NSPA in this context would eviscerate the CPIA provisions allowing the U.S. government to impose import restrictions on illegally exported objects that belong to designated categories of archaeological and ethnological objects (333 F.3d, at 408; 19 U.S.C. §§2602–3). This argument was again flawed because it failed to acknowledge the distinction between theft and illegal export—a distinction that the court clearly accepted (333 F.3d, at 407–8).

The significance of the *Schultz* decision lies not merely in the conviction of a prominent dealer, whom many had considered to be reputable, and the public attention that it has attracted to this subject (see Vardi 2003). Rather, its significance lies in the fact that it is unlikely that the legal doctrine underlying the *Schultz* decision will be challenged in any serious fashion in the future. Those who deal in antiquities now have clear warning of the government's intent to utilize the *McClain/Schultz* doctrine as a method of enforcement and that it may be used in civil replevin actions for the purpose of recovery and restitution of looted archaeological objects as well as in criminal prosecutions. While litigation in this area is likely to continue and even increase, future court cases will probably focus on clarifying the nature of the ownership laws of various foreign nations and on the factual elements that are necessary for a successful prosecution, in particular the intent and knowledge of any potential defendant. The clear message that this decision sends to the art market community should decrease the desire to trade in undocumented antiquities and thereby reduce the incentives for the initial looting of sites.

U.S. Cultural Heritage Resource Crimes Sentencing Guideline

The United States took another significant, although less heralded, step by moving to ensure significant penalties for those who traffic in stolen and looted cultural objects when a new Sentencing Guideline for cultural heritage resource crimes went into effect in November 2002. The United States Sentencing Guidelines establish a range for both jail time and fines depending on the type of crime and various factors. Crimes related to cultural heritage were typically considered to be property crimes, and the sentences for property crimes are based primarily on the market value of the property involved in the crime. Because Native American cultural objects do not tend to have a high market value, a defendant who had looted a site within the United States might not receive a meaningful sentence. A judge who thought that the resulting sentence under the Sentencing Guidelines was not adequate had the discretion to add the cost of restoration and repair and "archaeological value."[10] A judge could thereby enhance the defendant's offense level and increase the sentence.[11] However, this was discretionary, and some courts viewed the determination of archaeological value as too speculative for this value to be included in the sentencing procedure.[12] It was thus difficult for the sentence to take into account the full extent of the cultural, scientific, and historical losses, which are essentially abstract values, in the determination of a sentence.

In May 2002, the United States Sentencing Commission proposed a new sentencing guideline specifically for cultural heritage resource crimes, and it became law in November 2002 (18 U.S.C. Appx. § 2B1.5).[13] The Sentencing Commission, in recommending the new guideline to Congress wrote:

> The Commission has determined that a separate guideline, which specifically recognizes both the federal government's long-standing obligation and role in preserving such resources, and the harm caused to both the nation and its inhabitants when its history is degraded through the destruction of cultural heritage resources, is needed.
> . . . Because individuals, communities, and nations identify themselves through intellectual, emotional, and spiritual connections to places and ob-

jects, the effects of cultural heritage resource crimes transcend mere monetary considerations. Accordingly, this new guideline takes into account the transcendent and irreplaceable value of cultural heritage resources and punishes in a proportionate way the aggravating conduct associated with cultural heritage resource crimes. (18 U.S.C. Appx. § 2B1.5: "Reason for Amendment")

The new guideline continues the use of commercial and archaeological values and the cost of repair and restoration in calculating a defendant's offense level, although the inclusion of archaeological value is now mandatory for any crime involving archaeological resources (18 U.S.C. Appx. § 2B1.5: Application Note 2). The guideline also creates a series of special offense characteristics, which is a list of other factors that may increase the defendant's sentence and that attempt to capture the intangible values that have been harmed through the defendant's conduct (18 U.S.C. Appx. § 2B1.5(b)(1)–(6)).

The mechanics of the guideline are fairly complex, incorporating definitions and concepts from an array of other U.S. federal statutes. The initial determination is whether a particular object fits the definition of a cultural heritage resource (18 U.S.C. Appx. § 2B1.5: Application Note 1). This definition includes: archaeological resource under the Archaeological Resources Protection Act (ARPA); cultural item under the Native American Graves Protection and Repatriation Act (NAGPRA); designated ethnological material under the CPIA; historic property or historic resource under the National Historic Preservation Act; commemorative work; and object of cultural heritage (18 U.S.C. Appx. § 2B1.5: Application Note 1).[14] If the object involved in the defendant's crime is a cultural heritage resource, then there is an enhancement in the defendant's base offense level (18 U.S.C. Appx. § 2B1.5(a)).

If the crime itself involved one or more additional enumerated factors, then the offense level is again increased. These additional factors include whether the offense involved a particular type of object, including human remains; funerary objects; cultural patrimony or sacred object, as defined by NAGPRA; archaeological or ethnological materials designated under the CPIA; cultural property as defined by the CPIA; and Pre-Columbian monumental or architectural sculpture or mural (18 U.S.C. Appx. § 2B1.5(b)(3)).[15] Another enhancement is triggered if the crime took place at a particular designated location, such as a site listed on the World Heritage List; a national monument, park, cemetery, memorial, or marine sanctuary; a National Historic Landmark; or a museum, including museums both in the United States and abroad(18 U.S.C. Appx. § 2B1.5(b)(2)).[16] Finally, there are additional enhancements if the defendant has "engaged in a pattern of misconduct involving cultural heritage resources," if the defendant used or threatened to use a dangerous weapon in committing the crime, or if the crime was "committed for pecuniary gain or otherwise involved a commercial purpose" (18 U.S.C. Appx. § 2B1.5 (b)(4)–(6)).

Because the new Sentencing Guideline applies only to crimes committed after November 1, 2002, there have been few opportunities to use it so far in a sentencing procedure.[17] However, it applies to anyone convicted of trafficking in cultural objects stolen from the National Museum of Iraq in April 2003 or looted from Iraqi archaeological sites in violation of Iraq's national ownership law. While applicable only to crimes prosecuted in the United States, this Sentencing Guideline could perhaps serve as a model to other nations that may be grappling with the difficulty of incorporating the intangible values of cultural heritage into a meaningful criminal sentence for those who damage or destroy cultural heritage.

Recent Ratifications of the UNESCO Convention

In 2002 and 2003, significant progress was made in the number of market nations that have ratified or otherwise joined the 1970 UNESCO Convention.[18] These states include Denmark, Japan, Sweden, Switzerland, and the United Kingdom. Switzerland enacted new legislation that took effect on June 1, 2005, while the British Parliament enacted a new Dealing in Cultural Objects (Offences) Act 2003.

The British legislation creates a new offense for dealing in "tainted cultural objects."[19] One commits this offense by "dishonestly deal[ing] in a cultural object that is tainted, knowing or believing that the object is tainted" (ch. 27: sec. 1, subsec. 1). The statute defines a "tainted object" under the following circumstances: "(2) A cultural object is tainted if, after the commencement of this Act—(a) a person removes the object in a case falling within subsection (4) or he excavates the object, and (b) the removal or excavation constitutes an offence" (ch. 27: sec. 2, subsec. 2). Subsection 4 refers to objects removed from "a building or structure of historical, architectural or archaeological interest" or from an excavation (ch. 27: sec. 2, subsec. 4). For purposes of the statute, it does not matter whether the excavation or removal takes place in the United Kingdom or in another country or whether the law violated is a domestic or foreign law (ch. 27: sec. 2, subsec. 3).

While the enactment of this legislation is certainly a welcome step in efforts to prevent illegal dealing in stolen and illegally excavated cultural objects, it largely represents a codification of the law under which Schultz's co-conspirator, Jonathan Tokeley-Parry, had previously been convicted (*R. v. Tokeley-Parry*). However, the British statute uses an expansive definition of "tainted" objects as those resulting from illegal excavation as well as those that are stolen. Therefore the British statute applies even where the foreign nation does not have an ownership law but protects its archaeological sites only through a prohibition of unlicensed excavation. A British court would not then need to engage in an extensive analysis of foreign law to determine whether it is truly in the nature of an ownership law. This result would be broader than the *McClain/Schultz* doctrine, as the action in removing the archaeological object only has to constitute an offense under local law and not necessarily theft.

The new Swiss legislation is called the Federal Act on the International Transfer of Cultural Property.[20] It implements the UNESCO Convention in a manner that is closer to the U.S. model of implementation, through use of import restrictions, rather than following the British model of expanding the criminal law.[21] The new Swiss legislation permits the Swiss Federal Council to enter into agreements with other nations that are party to the UNESCO Convention to protect "cultural and foreign affairs interests and to secure cultural heritage" (Federal Act, Article 7). The Federal Council can also take additional measures when a "state's cultural heritage [is] jeopardized by exceptional events" (Federal Act, Article 8).

The other significant change in the Swiss legislation is its definition of "due diligence." Article 16 sets forth the following definition:

> In the art trade and auctioning business, cultural property may only be transferred when the person transferring the property may assume, under the circumstances, that the cultural property:
>
> a. was not stolen, not lost against the will of the owner, and not illegally excavated;
>
> b. not illicitly imported. (Federal Act on the International Transfer of Cultural Property: Article 16, § 1)

A clear definition of due diligence under Swiss law is significant because of the Swiss good faith purchaser doctrine, which permits the transfer of good title even of stolen goods to a good faith purchaser. The phrase "under the circumstances" requires that one who wishes to claim to have acted in good faith must have considered all the circumstances of the transaction, including the extent to which stolen art objects and particularly looted archaeological objects are present in the art market. Article 16 also imposes additional obligations on those who are active in the art trade to maintain written records concerning their acquisition of cultural property, to acquire a written declaration from sellers concerning their right to dispose of the object, and to inform customers of existing import and export regulations of other nations that are UNESCO Convention parties (Federal Act, Article 16, § 2).

Since the time that the United States ratified and then implemented the UNESCO Convention through enactment of the CPIA, there has been some debate about the necessary steps that a nation must take to be considered an effective State Party to the Convention.[22] As has been demonstrated, the United Kingdom and Switzerland have chosen different paths, with Switzerland following more closely, although not identically, the U.S. model of entering into a series of bilateral and potentially multilateral agreements. The United Kingdom chose instead to rely on an expansion of its criminal law (in a manner that brings British law into line with, although exceeding, the U.S. *McClain/Schultz* doctrine), its current system of export licensing, and European Union trade regulations. It will be necessary and interesting to conduct studies in future years of the effectiveness of these different models in terms of amount of illegal cultural materials recovered and returned to their country of origin from the United States, United Kingdom, and Switzerland and the number of criminal prosecutions brought and their effect on the operation of the market in the United Kingdom.

RECENT CRISES IN THE PROTECTION OF CULTURAL HERITAGE

Two events, almost precisely two years apart, have demonstrated that no matter how much progress is made, there are some threats to the cultural heritage that both the international and national legal regimes are almost entirely unable to thwart. The first of these occurred in March 2001 when the Taliban destroyed not only the two Bamiyan Buddhas but also many of the cultural objects with human figural representations housed in various Afghan museums. The blatant and well-publicized destruction of the Buddhas aroused a worldwide chorus of condemnation. Despite this attention and frantic efforts by UNESCO and other governments to intercede, the Taliban proceeded with their destructive plans.

There is no international force that could have prevented these actions, and there is even some question as to the applicability of international legal instruments, such as the 1954 Hague Convention for the Protection of Cultural Property in the Event of Armed Conflict (Hague Convention), to this circumstance.[23] While the Second Protocol to the Hague Convention, completed in 1999, was intended (among other objectives) to clarify that the Convention applies to internal conflicts, such as occurred in the former Yugoslavia in the 1990s (Second Protocol, Article 22), it is not clear that the Convention would apply in a situation that does not involve armed conflict at all. Even if the Convention did apply, the only punishment would be a war crimes trial held after the fact. Although some of the Yugoslav leaders have now been charged with and convicted of intentional destruction of cultural property in violation of the Hague Convention, the ouster of the Taliban leadership in Afghanistan has not resulted in war crimes prosecutions of any of the individuals involved for destruction of cultural property.[24] This episode once again demonstrates the inability of the international community to respond in times of crisis to major threats to cultural heritage and the lack of enforcement in a legal regime that still largely depends on national implementation.

The events in Iraq during the second Gulf War of 2003 and in the aftermath present a more complex situation. While lacking the intentional and premeditated character of the Taliban's destruction in Afghanistan, the aftermath of the war in Iraq has pointed out significant shortcomings in the international legal regime for the protection of cultural heritage. The United States and its coalition allies seem to have avoided targeting cultural sites, in compliance with the Hague Convention. While the exact extent of any damage done to cultural sites as a result of military activities cannot be determined without an impartial fact-finding investigation, it seems from the information currently available that little or no intentional damage was caused during active hostilities.

However, the situation looks quite different when one analyzes both the immediate and longer-term aftermath of the war. As is now well known, considerable looting and destruction occurred throughout Iraq in the days that immediately followed the fall of the Saddam Hussein regime. Despite repeated warnings to the United States government that such looting would ensue upon the collapse of the Iraqi government, virtually nothing was done to prevent this chaos. All of the major cultural institutions in Baghdad were vandalized (Lawler 2003; Russell 2003). The current estimate of archaeological artifacts stolen from the National Museum of Iraq is approximately fifteen thousand, although the exact number will likely never be known (George 2005).[25] Significant portions, currently estimated to be 60 percent, of the collections of the National Library, Archives, and other cultural repositories in Baghdad were stolen or suffered destruction through vandalism and burning.

The 1954 Hague Convention is not clear as to whether it imposes an obligation on a military force to prevent looting and vandalism by the opposing military or civilian population, at least before a transition from a state of military activity to one of occupation has occurred.[26] Nonetheless, it is now clear that the U.S. occupation of Iraq would have proceeded much more smoothly if thought had been given to the prevention of looting and chaos, with an almost complete breakdown of civilian police authority, at least in Baghdad. The cultural loss to the Iraqi people, and indeed to the entire world, is incalculable.

Outside Baghdad, looting occurred at numerous government buildings, including museums and particularly site museums, such as at Nineveh and Nim-

rud. By May and June of 2003, a UNESCO team and another team of archaeologists sponsored by *National Geographic* magazine were able to make some
nonsystematic assessments of the cultural situation both in Baghdad and at
archaeological sites throughout Iraq (Russell 2003). The looting and vandalism
had by then been halted within Baghdad and, to a large extent, at the significant sites in the north. The situation in the south was and is still quite different.
While a few sites, such as Ur and Babylon, were eventually placed under guard
and given adequate protection, many other significant sites in the south, such
as Fara, Isin, Larsa, Umm al-Aqarib, Umma, Mashkan Shapur, and Nippur, suffered considerable damage (Banerjee and Garen 2004; Ho 2005; Shakir 2005).
According to Professor McGuire Gibson of the University of Chicago, looting
started at these sites as soon as the war began in March and the Iraqi forces
were withdrawn from the region. Two years later, guards have been placed at
a handful of sites, although their level of training, a lack of equipment, and
the difficulty of communication with government officials in Baghdad leave the
situation very uncertain. Numerous other sites clearly remain unprotected. It
will likely never be known how many objects were looted in this fashion and,
even more important, what losses to our understanding of the past we have suffered.

Other types of damage to archaeological and historic structures have also
occurred. Probably the most severe is the damage done to the well-known site
of Babylon caused by the construction of a military base directly on the site.
When the military camp was constructed, sections of the site were leveled to
create space for helicopter landing pads. In addition, vibrations from the helicopters reportedly destabilized the ancient structure. Sandbags filled with dirt
from other archaeological sites were used at Babylon. As the bags deteriorate,
the archaeological artifacts in the transported dirt mix with the in situ artifacts.
The ensuing confusion of the archaeological strata renders impossible any future study of both the "imported" artifacts and the artifacts that are found at
Babylon itself (Curtis 2004; Russell 2005). This construction seems to be a clear
violation of the Hague Convention, which permits interference with cultural
property in occupied territories only when "necessary . . . to preserve cultural
property . . . damaged by military operations" (Article 5, paragraph 2).[27]

Other examples of military activity near cultural sites have been reported.
One of these is the controlled explosion of ordnance near the World Heritage
site of Hatra of the Parthian era (Crawford 2005: 6–7). These explosions are
reported to be endangering the stability of the ancient structures at this site. In
late 2004 and early 2005, the U.S. military used the minaret of the ninth-cen-
tury al-Mutawakkil mosque in Samarra as a sniper position.[28] The U.S. military
apparently chose to use the minaret as a sniper position because it provides an

excellent view of the surrounding area (Harris 2005b). When the U.S. military eventually withdrew from the minaret, the minaret was damaged in an explosion set off by Iraqi insurgents, although the damage seems minimal (Northedge 2005).

How are the international and national regimes prepared to respond to this situation? A patchwork of laws may be pieced together to inhibit the import of and dealing in cultural objects that were removed illegally from Iraq. On May 22, 2003, the United Nations Security Council passed Resolution 1483 calling on UN member states to prevent the trade in illegally removed cultural material from Iraq and to ensure the return of any such material to Iraq.[29] Many nations quickly followed with administrative measures to comply.[30] The United States, which had had sanctions on the import of all goods from Iraq since 1990, merely left these sanctions in place for illegally removed Iraqi cultural materials, while lifting the sanctions on most other more typical commercial goods (31 C.F.R. 575.533(b)(4)). However, if it were not for the fortuity of the sanctions in place since 1990, there would not have been a rapid response in the United States to the cultural crisis in Iraq.

The existing laws of most nations prohibit dealing in stolen goods. Therefore, trade in those objects stolen from a museum and for which adequate documentation exists is likely prohibited and criminalized. The circumstances of the thefts at the Baghdad cultural institutions complicate this situation because the massive vandalism also destroyed or compromised much of the documentation of the collections. Without this documentation and evidence of the ownership of these objects, it may be difficult to apply typical stolen property statutes to such objects.[31] Many nations that are party to the 1970 UNESCO Convention also prohibit the import of stolen objects that had been inventoried in the collection of a museum or other public institution (1970 UNESCO Convention, Article 7(b)(ii)). Again, however, the efficacy of such provisions depends on the availability of documentation that may have been lost or is at least unavailable for some period of time.

Nearly one hundred nations had joined the 1970 UNESCO Convention before the second Gulf War. Most of these nations prohibit the import of illegally exported cultural materials from other nations that are party to the Convention.[32] Because Iraq is a party to the Convention, these provisions should be effective in prohibiting import of objects that are either stolen from museums or looted directly from sites and are otherwise undocumented. However, the United States does not prohibit the import of cultural objects that are not stolen but are merely illegally exported from their country of origin, unless import restrictions are in place pursuant to either a bilateral agreement or emergency action under the CPIA (19 U.S.C. §§ 2602–3). For the United States to take action in emergency or crisis situations, it is first necessary for the other nation to present a request for a bilateral agreement accompanied by information that supports the statutory criteria for entering into a bilateral agreement and the criteria for demonstrating that a crisis situation exists.[33]

Despite the fact that sites have been looted from at least the mid-1990s, Iraq was unable to present a request because of the lack of diplomatic relations with the United States, another prerequisite to the bringing of a request under the CPIA. The cultural heritage crisis in Iraq has brought considerable attention to the inability of the United States to respond quickly or effectively to a crisis situation in another State Party to the 1970 UNESCO Convention. The events in Afghanistan have also demonstrated the inability of much of the world to react effectively because Afghanistan, which has been subject to political chaos for thirty years, had not, until recently, ratified the Convention and therefore could not claim even the most minimal protection for its cultural heritage.

Aside from the general sanctions, the only saving legal mechanism for the current situation in Iraq, at least as far as the United States is concerned, is the recent affirmation of the *McClain/Schultz* doctrine. Because Iraq has had a national ownership law for its antiquities since 1936, the import of any illegally excavated archaeological artifacts discovered after this date is prohibited, and the knowing dealing in such objects is criminalized under the NSPA.[34] Nonetheless, it will require a judicial analysis of the Iraqi law and of the extent of its internal enforcement, as occurred in the *Schultz* case, before it can be stated for certain that the NSPA will apply to undocumented Iraqi archaeological objects.

In May 2003, shortly after the events in Iraq, legislation was introduced in the U.S. House of Representatives that would have imposed an import ban on illegally removed Iraqi cultural materials and would have amended the CPIA to enable the president to impose import restrictions in emergency or crisis situations without need for a request from the other nation and without need for review by the Cultural Property Advisory Committee.[35] This bill drew the ire of the museum organizations, particularly the Association of Art Museum Directors, and the dealer organizations, led by the National Association of Dealers in Ancient, Oriental and Primitive Art, the organization of which Schultz had been president until shortly before his indictment. While the market community (with the exception of the coin dealers and collectors) did not openly oppose the import restriction on Iraqi cultural materials, it did oppose the open-ended duration of the restriction. The market community, which has considerably greater access to funds for lobbying efforts than do the archaeological and heritage communities, also opposed the amendments to the CPIA, which were designed to allow the U.S. government to respond more quickly and effectively in case of future cultural crises. This bill died with the end of the 108th Congress at the close of 2004.

A competing bill was introduced in the Senate, with the support of the art market community, that would have allowed the president to exercise his authority under the CPIA to restrict the import of illegally removed Iraqi cultural materials without need for Iraq to submit a request or for review by the Cultural Property Advisory Committee. This bill also adopted the language of the United Nations Security Council Resolution 1483 to define "archaeological and ethnological" material of Iraq, thus giving the terms a broader definition than that in the CPIA.[36] A similar bill passed in Congress in the fall of 2004 and was signed into law by President George Bush in December of that year.[37] The president has not yet exercised his authority under this legislation, but on May 20, 2005, he extended the declaration of emergency with respect to Iraq, thereby also extending the prohibition against import of any cultural materials illegally removed from Iraq after August 1990 (70 Fed. Reg. 29435, 2005 WL 1243182).

The irony is that both Britain and Switzerland, nations that had lagged considerably behind the United States in their efforts to stem the import and trade in looted and undocumented archaeological objects, have recently taken significant steps forward. The actions of both nations to ratify and implement the UNESCO Convention had been under consideration for several years. However, the crisis in Iraq provided the final impetus to ensure the enactment in each country of the necessary implementing legislation. The result is that it is likely that both nations, in particular Switzerland, have leapfrogged past the United States in this regard. The amendments proposed in the House legislation would merely have served to bring the United States more closely into line with the new Swiss legislation. Several of the administrative aspects of the Swiss legislation give Switzerland greater flexibility in responding to any future cultural heritage crisis in another State Party.

Conclusion

Hope for the creation of effective legal mechanisms for combating the trade in illegal antiquities and thereby encouraging the preservation of the world's archaeological heritage was raised at the same time that the global cultural heritage faced its greatest challenges in more than half a century. The lessons to be drawn are perhaps twofold. The first is that the international legal regime is not yet adequately equipped to provide a sufficient disincentive to those who engage in and profit from the looting of sites and cultural institutions. The second is that gradual, incremental change is under way, perhaps more clearly so than at any time in the last several decades. The legal systems in the major market nations are changing, while at the same time public awareness of these issues has grown significantly, in large part due to the widespread attention given to the events in Iraq. Time is clearly on the side of those who seek to preserve the cultural heritage for future generations, although the time in which to secure that heritage is limited. Whether the necessary changes in the legal system and public attitudes will occur quickly enough to preserve our cultural heritage cannot at this time be predicted.

NOTES

1. See, for example, the collection of Articles documenting the destruction of the world's archaeological heritage published in Brodie, Doole, and Renfrew 2001.

2. *United States v. McClain*. The National Stolen Property Act prohibits the knowing receipt, possession, concealment, sale, or transport of goods worth U.S. $5,000 or more "which have crossed a State or United States boundary after being stolen, unlawfully converted, or taken."

3. S. 2963, 128 Con. Rec. 12, 418, 97th Congress, 2nd session (1982); S. 605, 131 Cong. Rec. S 2611–12, 99th Congress (1st session (1985).

4. *United States v. Pre-Columbian Artifacts*; *Turkey v. OKS Partners*. In a decision that predated *McClain*, the Ninth Circuit Court of Appeals affirmed the conviction of a dealer for conspiring to deal in a Maya stela stolen from Guatemala (*United States v. Hollinshead*). In two cases, the claimant nations failed to recover the archaeological objects at issue because they were unable to prove that the objects had been excavated within their modern national boundaries (*Peru v. Johnson*, *Peru v. Wendt*; *Croatia v. Trustee of the Marquess of Northampton 1987 Settlement*).

5. The *OKS Partners* case was ultimately settled out of court after initial rulings favorable to the Republic of Turkey (Kornblut 1999). The case of the Lydian Hoard held by the Metropolitan Museum of Art in New York was also settled out of court. Both cases resulted in the return of all the looted antiquities to Turkey (Kaye and Main 1995; Özgen and Öztürk 1996).

6. The country of origin of the phiale was declared to be Switzerland, although the phiale had merely passed through Switzerland briefly on its way from Italy to New York. Its value was stated at U.S. $250,000, despite the price of U.S. $1.2 million that Steinhardt paid (*United States v. An Antique Platter of Gold*). The materially false statements violated 18 U.S.C. §§ 542 and 545. The phiale is described in Slayman 1998: 36–41. The court's holding that the country of origin was Italy, where it was discovered in modern times, should force importers to declare the country of discovery on Customs import forms. This should assist in the protection of sites in those countries as the legal system often looks, for a variety of purposes, to the law of the nation where an archaeological object was excavated.

7. November 17, 1970, 823 U.N.T.S. 231, 10 I.L.M. 289 (1971). Mr. Schultz, as president of NADAOPA, was critical of the new U.S.-Italy bilateral agreement to restrict the import of undocumented Italian antiquities into the United States (Bohlen 2001).

8. Enacted in 1983, the CPIA is the means by which the United States implements the 1970 UNESCO Convention. The CPIA implements only Articles 7(b)(ii) and 9 of the Convention and is discussed in greater detail later in the chapter.

9. The Senate Report on the CPIA states that the CPIA "affects neither existing remedies available in state or federal courts nor laws prohibiting the theft and the knowing receipt and transportation of stolen property in interstate and foreign commerce (e.g., National Stolen Property Act . . .)." (S. Rep. No. 97-564, at 33 [1982]).

10. "Archaeological value" is defined by the regulations that accompany the Archaeological Resources Protection Act, 16 U.S.C. §§ 470aa *et seq.* (ARPA) as "the value of the information associated with the archaeological resource," 43 C.F.R. § 7.14(a). This value is determined by calculating what it would have cost the government to conduct a scientific excavation at the site, if the looting had not occurred. Among other provisions, ARPA prohibits the disturbance and removal of archaeological artifacts from federally owned or controlled land.

11. For example, in *United States v. Shumway*, the court found that the fair market value of the artifacts did not adequately reflect the harm inflicted on the victim by the defendant's conduct. The defendant had not merely looted an archaeological site but had disturbed an infant burial, taking the burial blanket and leaving the skeletal remains on top of a dirt pile. The court therefore used both cost of repair and archaeological value as a way of increasing the defendant's sentence.

12. In contrast to the decision in *Shumway*, in *United States v. Hunter*, the court rejected the use of archaeological value in determining the defendant's offense level because the court did not view the defendant's conduct as particularly egregious, and it considered the government's estimates of archaeological value too speculative.

13. See also Desio 2004. The exact status of the sentencing guidelines has recently been brought into question by the U.S. Supreme Court's decision in *United States v. Booker*. The guidelines are now considered to be advisory, rather than mandatory, for judges, but they do establish the standard of reasonableness for sentences.

14. Historic property and historic resource are defined by the National Historic Preservation Act as "any prehistoric or historic district, site, building, structure, or object included in, or eligible for inclusion on the National Register, including artifacts, records, and material remains related to such a property or resource," 16 U.S.C. § 470w(5); archaeological resource is defined by ARPA, 16 U.S.C. § 470bb(1), as "any material remains of past human life or activities which are of archaeological interest" and are at least 100 years of age; cultural items include human remains, associated funerary objects, unassociated funerary objects, sacred objects, and objects of cultural patrimony, as defined by NAGPRA, 25 U.S.C. § 3001(3); commemorative work means "any statue, monument, sculpture, memorial, plaque, inscription, or other structure or landscape feature . . . designed to perpetuate in a permanent manner the memory of an individual, group, event or

other significant element of American history," 40 U.S.C. § 8902(a)(1), and includes any national monument or national memorial; object of cultural heritage means any object that is more than 100 years old and worth at least U.S. $5000 or one that is worth more than U.S. $100,000 (regardless of age), 18 U.S.C. § 668(a)(2); designated ethnological material is the product of a nonindustrial or tribal society, which is "important to the cultural heritage of a people because of its distinctive characteristics, comparative rarity, or its contribution to the knowledge of the origins, development, or history of that people" and the import of which is prohibited under either a bilateral agreement or emergency action pursuant to the CPIA, 19 U.S.C. §§ 2601(2)(ii), 2601(7), and 2604.

15. The process by which archaeological or ethnological materials are designated for import restriction is discussed in note 21. The CPIA, 19 U.S.C. § 2601(6), utilizes the UNESCO Convention Article 1 (a)–(k) definition of "cultural property." Pre-Columbian monumental or architectural sculpture or mural includes "any stone carving or wall art which (i) is the product of a Pre-Columbian Indian culture of Mexico, Central America, South America, or the Caribbean Islands; (ii) was an immobile monument or architectural structure or was a part of, or affixed to, any such monument or structure; and (iii) is subject to export control by the country of origin" and any part or fragment thereof, 19 U.S.C. § 2095(3).

16. While the Theft of Major Art Works Act defines "museum" as an institution located within the United States, 18 U.S.C. § 668(a)(1), the Sentencing Guideline expands this to include museums located in other parts of the world.

17. But see note 31.

18. The current list of parties to the Convention may be found at: <www.unesco.org/culture/laws/1970/html_eng/page1.shtml>.

19. *Dealing in Cultural Objects (Offences) Act 2003*, ch. 27. The text of the bill may be found at the website for Parliament: <http://www.uk-legislation.hmso.gov.uk/acts/acts2003/20030027.htm>.

20. The Swiss statute may be found at <www.kultur-schweiz.admin.ch/arkgt/files/kgtg2_e.pdf>.

21. The United States implemented Article 9 of the UNESCO Convention by creating mechanisms by which other States Parties could request that the United States impose import restrictions on designated categories of archaeological and ethnological materials. The request is reviewed by the Cultural Property Advisory Committee, which recommends to the president (or a designated decision maker) whether the statutory criteria for import restrictions are satisfied. If the decision maker determines that the criteria are met, the United States negotiates a bilateral agreement with the requesting nation. The agreement lasts for five years and may be renewed. If the decision maker determines that an emergency or crisis situation exists, then import restrictions may be imposed without the negotiation of a bilateral agreement (although only after the nation has brought a request for a bilateral agreement and review by the Cultural Property Advisory Committee; CPIA 19 U.S.C. §§ 2601–3). This contrasts with the broad-based implementation of the Convention by other nations such as Canada and Australia. See O'Keefe 2000: 102–6.

22. The U.S. implementation of the UNESCO Convention is considered by O'Keefe 2000: 106–9. At the time of its acceptance of the Convention, the United States stated one reservation and six understandings. The United States implemented only Articles 7(b)(ii) and 9 of the Convention and has not, for example, taken any step to establish broad export controls on U.S. cultural property.

23. In October 2003, in response to the Taliban actions, UNESCO adopted a Declaration concerning the Intentional Destruction of Cultural Heritage. The declaration calls on all states to refrain from intentional destruction and sets out actions that states can take in both war and peacetime to reduce the risk of such destruction.

24. Four former Yugoslav leaders were charged by the International Criminal Tribunal for the former Yugoslavia with willful destruction of or damage to cultural monuments during the 1991 bombing of the historic city of Dubrovnik and the destruction of the Sarajevo library (Press Release 2003a, Press Release 2003b). Pavle Strugar, former general of the Yugoslav Peoples' Army, was sentenced to eight years in prison in connection with the shelling of the historic town of Dubrovnik, a UNESCO World Heritage site. Admiral Miodrag Jokic of the Yugoslav Navy pleaded guilty to the same charges and was given a seven-year sentence. This is only the second time that a military commander has been convicted by an international criminal court for destruction of cultural property. Additional indictments are expected to be brought in connection with the siege of Mostar, including the destruction of the Mostar Bridge (Harris 2005a).

25. Initial reports of the looting of the entire collection of the museum, estimated to comprise 170,000 or more objects, turned out to be incorrect.

26. Article 4, paragraph 3, of the Convention states: "The High Contracting Parties further undertake to prohibit, prevent and, if necessary, put a stop to any form of theft, pillage or misappropriation of, and any acts of vandalism directed against, cultural property." This provision does not specify whose acts of vandalism should be prevented, but the rest of this Article focuses on the conduct of the military of the High Contracting Party. While one might interpret this provision to apply more broadly to any acts of vandalism and pillage, the lack of clarity in this circumstance is only one example of how the Hague Convention, drafted in the wake of World War II and its large-scale destruction and pillage of cultural property, is not well suited to many modern examples of warfare, despite the attempt to modernize it through the Second Protocol.

27. Neither the United States nor the United Kingdom, the two leading members of the coalition, is a party to the Hague Convention. However, they both claim to follow its provisions as a matter of customary international law. Poland, which occupied Babylon after the United States, is a party to the Convention, as is Iraq. The construction of the military camp at Babylon, utilizing U.S. federal funds, does seem to be a violation of the National Historic Preservation Act, 16 U.S.C. § 470a-2, which states: "Prior to the approval of any Federal undertaking outside the United States which may directly and adversely affect a property which is on the World Heritage List or on the applicable country's equivalent of the National Register, the head of a Federal agency having direct or indirect jurisdiction over such undertaking shall take into account the effect of the undertaking on such property for purposes of avoiding or mitigating any adverse effects."

28. The mosque, which was built between 849 and 852 by the Abbasid caliph al-Mu-tawakkil, is known as the Malwiya because of its spiral minaret.

29. Paragraph 7 of UNSCR 1483 states that the Security Council "[d]ecides that all Member States shall take appropriate steps to facilitate the safe return to Iraqi institutions of Iraqi cultural property and other items of archaeological, historical, cultural, rare scientific, and religious importance illegally removed from the Iraq National Museum, the National Library, and other locations in Iraq since the adoption of resolution 661 (1990) of 6 August 1990, including by establishing a prohibition on trade in or transfer of such items and items with respect to which reasonable suspicion exists that they have been illegally removed . . . ."

30. For example, on May 28, 2003, the Swiss Federal Council imposed a ban that "covers importation, exportation and transit, as well as selling, marketing, dealing in, acquiring or otherwise transferring Iraqi cultural assets stolen in Iraq since August 2, 1990, removed against the will of the owner, or taken out of Iraq illegally. It includes cultural assets acquired through illegal excavations. Such assets are presumed to have been exported illegally if they can be proved to have been in the Republic of Iraq after 2 August 1990" (Ordinance on Economic Measures against the Republic of Iraq). The British enacted Statutory Instrument 2003 No. 1519, which, in section 8, prohibited the import or export of illegally removed Iraqi cultural property and created a criminal offense for "[a]ny person who holds or controls any item of illegally removed Iraqi cultural property . . . unless he proves that he did not know and had no reason to suppose that the item in question was illegally removed Iraqi cultural property."

31. The American author Joseph Braude was charged with three counts for smuggling and making false statements in violation of 18 U.S.C. § 545. When he entered the United States on June 11, 2003, Braude was found to be carrying three cylinder seals of the Akkadian period (ca. 2340–2180 B.C.), which were taken from the collection of the National Museum of Iraq in Baghdad. The seals still carried the partially preserved registration numbers used by the Iraq museum's cataloguing system. Although the seals were undoubtedly stolen property, Braude was not charged under the National Stolen Property Act. Nor was he charged for violating the sanctions against importing illegally removed Iraqi cultural materials. When questioned, Braude initially denied having traveled to Iraq but he later admitted that he had been to Iraq, where he had purchased the seals. He was therefore charged under the Customs statute for making false declarations. Braude ultimately pleaded guilty and was sentenced to six months of house arrest and two years of probation. The three seals were returned to His Excellency Samir Sumaidaie, the ambassador of Iraq to the United Nations, on January 18, 2005 (U.S. Immigration and Customs Enforcement news release, January 18, 2005). Although Braude's conduct undoubtedly fell under the new Cultural Heritage Resource Crimes Sentencing Guideline for the purpose of increasing the base offense level, it seems apparent that the judge did not take the guideline into account in determining Braude's sentence.

32. See, for example, Canada's *Cultural Property Export and Import Act*, R.S.C. 1985, c. C-51, § 37.

33. The CPIA provides that the term *emergency condition*, with respect to any archaeological or ethnological material of any State Party, means that such material is:

(1) a newly discovered type of material which is of importance for the understanding of the history of mankind and is in jeopardy from pillage, dismantling, dispersal, or fragmentation;

(2) identifiable as coming from any site recognized to be of high cultural significance if such site is in jeopardy from pillage, dismantling, dispersal, or fragmentation which is, or threatens to be, of crisis proportions; or

(3) a part of the remains of a particular culture or civilization, the record of which is in jeopardy from pillage, dismantling, dispersal, or fragmentation which is, or threatens to be, of crisis proportions; and application of the import restrictions . . . on a temporary basis would, in whole or in part, reduce the incentive for such pillage, dismantling, dispersal or fragmentation. (19 U.S.C. § 2603(a))

34. Article 3 of the Iraq law states: "All antiquities in Iraq whether movable or immovable that are now on or under the surface of the soil shall be considered to be the common property of the State. No individuals or groups are allowed to dispose of such property or claim the ownership thereof except under the provisions of this Law." Article 1(e) defines antiquities as man-made "possessions" that are more than 200 years old and those that are less than 200 years old if they are of historical, national, religious or artistic value (*Antiquities Law No. 59 of 1936* and the *Two Amendments, No. 120 of 1974 and No. 164 of 1975* [Iraq]).

35. H.R. 2009, 108th Congress, 1st session (2003).

36. S. 1291, 108th Congress, 1st session (2003). This bill stated: "The term 'archaeological or ethnological material of Iraq' means cultural property of Iraq and other items of archaeological, historical, cultural, rare scientific, or religious importance illegally removed from the Iraq National Museum, the National Library of Iraq, and other locations in Iraq, since the adoption of United Nations Security Council Resolution 661 of 1990."

37. H.R. 1047, 108th Congress, 2nd session (2004). This bill is substantially the same as S. 1291 and includes the same definition of "archaeological and ethnological material of Iraq."

BIBLIOGRAPHY

Antiquities Law No. 59 of 1936 and the *Two Amendments, No. 120 of 1974 and No. 164 of 1975* (Iraq).

Archaeological Resources Protection Act (ARPA), 16 U.S.C. §§ 470aa *et seq.* (United States).

Banerjee, Neela, and Micah Garen. "Saving Iraq's Archaeological Past from Thieves Remains an Uphill Battle." *New York Times*, April 4, 2004, A16.

Bohlen, Celestine. "Old Rarities, New Respect: U.S. Works with Italy." *New York Times*, February 28, 2001, E1.

———. "Witness in Antiquities Case Tells of a Smuggling Plot." *New York Times*, January 31, 2002, B3.

Brodie, Neil, Jennifer Doole, and Colin Renfrew (eds.). *Trade in Illicit Antiquities: The Destruction of the World's Archaeological Heritage*. Cambridge, U.K.: McDonald Institute for Archaeological Research, 2001.

Convention on the Cultural Property Implementation Act (CPIA), 19 U.S.C. §§ 2601 *et seq.* (United States).

Crawford, Harriet. "Turning a Blind Eye." *Museums Journal* 105, no. 2 (2005): 6–7.

Croatia v. Trustee of the Marquess of Northampton 1987 Settlement, 203 A.D.2d 167 (N.Y. App. Div. 1994).

Cultural Property Export and Import Act, R.S.C. 1985, c. C-51, s. 37 (Canada).

Curtis, John E. "Report on Meeting at Babylon, 11th–13th December 2004." Available at <http://www.thebritishmuseum.ac.uk/newsroom/current2005/Babylon_Report04.doc>, accessed December 15, 2004.

Dealing in Cultural Objects (Offences) Act 2003. United Kingdom: Stationery Office Limited, 2003 (United Kingdom).

Desio, Paula J. "Crimes and Punishment: Developing Sentencing Guidelines for Cultural Heritage Resource Crimes." In *Legal Perspectives on Cultural Resources*, ed. Jennifer R. Richman and Marion P. Forsyth, 61–84. Walnut Creek, Calif.: AltaMira, 2004.

Emergency Protection for Iraqi Cultural Antiquities Act of 2004. Miscellaneous Trade and Technical Corrections Act of 2004, §§ 3001 et seq., H.R.1047, 150 Cong. Rec. H 9627, vol. 150, no. 127 (Enrolled as Agreed to or Passed by Both House and Senate), 108th Congress 12-07-04, Washington, D.C., 2004.

Federal Act on the International Transfer of Cultural Property. Federal Assembly of the Swiss Confederation. Geneva: Switzerland, 2003 (Switzerland).

George, Donny. Presentation of Dr. George, Director of the Iraq Museum, Iraq State Board of Antiquities and History. Paper presented at the Annual Meeting of the Archaeological Institute of America, Boston, Mass., January 8, 2005.

Harris, Lucian. "Former Yugoslav General Sent to Jail for Shelling Dubrovnik." *Art Newspaper*, February 25, 2005 (2005a).

———. "US Snipers on Samarra's Spiral Minaret." *Art Newspaper*, February 25, 2005 (2005b).

Ho, Cindy. "Heritage Lost: Looting of Archaeological Sites Continues in Iraq." <http://www.savingantiquities.org/h-feature.htm#Mashkan>, accessed March 5, 2005.

Kaye, Lawrence M., and Carla T. Main. "The Saga of the Lydian Hoard Antiquities: From Uşak to New York and Back Again and Some Related Observations on the Law of Cultural Repatriation." In *Antiquities Trade or Betrayed: Legal, Ethical and Conservation Issues*, ed. Kathryn Walker Tubb, 150–62. London: Archetype–UKIC, 1995.

Kornblut, Anne E. "In Settlement, Koch to Return Coins to Turkey." *Boston Globe*, March 5, 1999, A1.

Lawler, Andrew. "Beyond the Looting." *National Geographic Magazine*, October 2003: 58–75.

National Historic Preservation Act, 16 U.S.C. §§ 470a *et seq.* (United States).

National Stolen Property Act, 18 U.S.C. §§ 2314–15 (United States).

Native American Graves Protection Repatriation Act, 25 U.S.C. § 3001 *et seq*. (United States).

Northedge, Alastair. Commentary on the Damage to the Malwiya, Samarra, IraqCrisis List. <https://listhost.uchicago.edu/pipermail/iraqcrisis/2005-April/001176.html>, accessed April 7, 2005.

O'Keefe, Patrick. *Commentary on the UNESCO Convention 1970*. Leicester: Institute of Art and Law, 2000.

Ordinance on Economic Measures against the Republic of Iraq of May 28, 2003, SR 946.206. <www.kultur-schweiz.admin.ch/arkgt/kgt/e/e_kgt.htm>, accessed March 5, 2005 (Switzerland).

Özgen, Ilknur, and Jean Öztürk. *Heritage Recovered: The Lydian Treasure*. Istanbul: General Directorate of Monuments and Museum, Ministry of Culture, Republic of Turkey, 1996.

Peru v. Johnson, 720 F. Supp. 810 (C.D. Cal. 1989), *aff'd sub nom*.

Peru v. Wendt, 933 F.2d 1013 (9th Cir. 1991).

Press Release. "Dubrovnik Bomber in Hague Trial." *Reuters*, October 23, 2003 (2003a).

Press Release. *ICTY the United Nations* The Hague, October 23, 2003, CT/P.I.S./793e (2003b).

R. v. Tokeley-Parry, [1999] Crim LR 578 (1998).

Russell, John. "A Personal Account of the First UNESCO Cultural Heritage Mission to Baghdad." May 16–20, 2003. <www.archaeologoical.org/pdfs/papers/J-Russell/_IraqA5S.pdf>, accessed March 5, 2005.

———. Report from the Former Deputy Senior Advisor to the Iraqi Ministry of Culture. Paper presented at the Annual Meeting of the Archaeological Institute of America, Boston, Mass., January 8, 2005.

Shakir, Burhan. Public presentation of the Director of Excavations, Iraq State Board of Antiquities and History. Paper presented at the Annual Meeting of the Archaeological Institute of America, Boston, Mass., January 8, 2005.

Slayman, Andrew L. "Case of the Golden Phiale." *Archaeology* 51, no. 3 (May–June 1998): 36–41.

Statutory Instrument 2003 No. 1519. <www.hmso.gov.uk/si/si2003/20031519.htm>, accessed March 5, 2005 (United Kingdom).

Turkey v. OKS Partners, No. 89-3061-WJS, 1994 U.S. Dist. LEXIS 17032 (D. Mass. June 8, 1994).

United Nations Educational, Scientific and Cultural Organization. *Convention on the Means of Prohibiting and Preventing the Illicit Import, Export and Transfer of Ownership of Cultural Property*. Paris: UNESCO, 1970.

———. *Declaration Concerning the Intentional Destruction of the Cultural Heritage*. Paris: UNESCO, 2003.

———. *Hague Convention on the Protection of Cultural Property in the Event of Armed Conflict*. The Hague: UNESCO, 1954.

United Nations Security Council Resolution 1483. Paris: United Nations: Paris, 4761st meeting, 2003.

United States Immigration and Customs Enforcement (ICE). <http://www.ice.gov/

graphics/news/newsreleases/articles/iraqiartifact_011805.htm>, accessed January 18, 2005.

United States v. An Antique Platter of Gold, 991 F. Supp. 222, 226 (S.D.N.Y. 1997), *aff'd*, 184 F.3d 131 (2d Cir. 1999).

United States v. Booker, 125 S. Ct. 738 (2005).

United States v. Hollinshead, 495 F.2d 1154 (9th Cir. 1974).

United States v. Hunter, 48 F. Supp. 2d 1283 (D. Ct. Utah 1998).

United States v. McClain, 545 F.2d 988 (5th Cir. 1977), 593 F.2d 658 (5th Cir. 1979).

United States v. Pre-Columbian Artifacts, 845 F. Supp. 544 (N.D. Ill. 1993).

United States v. Schultz, 178 F. Supp. 2d 445 (S.D.N.Y. 2002), *aff'd*, 333 F.3d 393 (2d Cir. 2003).

United States v. Shumway, 112 F.3d 1413 (10th Cir. 1997).

Vardi, Nathan. "The Return of the Mummy." *Forbes*, December 22, 2003, 156–68.

Watson, Peter. "The Investigation of Frederick Schultz." *Culture without Context*, issue 10 (Spring 2002): 21–26.

4

Convicted Dealers

What We Can Learn

PETER WATSON

Over the past few years no fewer than four dealers in antiquities have appeared in court, in three countries, charged with offenses relating to the illegal excavation and/or illegal export and/or import of antiquities. All of them have been convicted of criminal offences, three have been jailed, and one is appealing the guilty verdict and sentence of ten years in prison.

The dealers are Jonathan Tokeley-Parry (British), Robin Symes (British), Frederick Schultz (American), and Giacomo Medici (Italian). In addition, two other dealers—Jean Louis Domercq, of the Sycamore Gallery in Geneva, and Frieda Tchacos, of the Phoenix Gallery in Zurich, were fellow defendants with Symes but did not attend court.

This is an unprecedented flurry of court activity, and it has helped throw an unusual light on the often secretive trade in illicit antiquities. In particular, this light has been shone into three areas. The first thing to say is that in each of these cases—irrespective of the country in which the antiquities originated and irrespective of where they finally came to market—Switzerland was a staging post, an *entrepôt* along the way. Jonathan Tokeley-Parry brought several of his objects from Egypt to the United Kingdom and the United States via Zurich. The same applies with Frederick Schultz. Robin Symes had several warehouses in Geneva where he stored objects. Similarly Giacomo Medici had three warehouses in Geneva Freeport where he kept his antiquities.

This is not surprising, perhaps, but it confirms—and confirms abundantly—anecdotal evidence of the past, which has always suggested that Switzerland, because of its lax laws in regard to the import and export of artistic and archaeological material, has been a major "laundering" center for illicit antiquities. We can be thankful that the Swiss have themselves recognized this and, not a moment too soon, last year introduced a new law designed to stop such trafficking (see Gerstenblith, chapter 3, for further discussion).

More interesting is the information released during the trials of both Medici and Symes regarding the extent and price levels of their inventory. According to details released by the Italian police, Medici had some ten thousand objects in his warehouses in Geneva Freeport, mainly Italian antiquities. So far, no value has been put on these objects. In the case of Symes and his late partner Christo Michaelidis, their twenty-nine warehouses contained seventeen thousand objects valued—by Symes himself—at U.S. $250 million.

Just two dealers between them had twenty-seven thousand objects. It is interesting, in the first instance, to compare these figures with the number of objects appearing on the open market, at auction. Antiquities sales at Bonhams, Christie's, and Sotheby's usually contain between three hundred and six hundred lots—five hundred lots might be considered an average figure. Bonhams holds two sales a year in London, Sotheby's holds two sales a year in New York, and Christie's holds two sales a year in each of those cities. That makes eight auctions a year or, on average, four thousand lots. However, analysis of the lots on sale shows that on average, there are 2.4 objects per lot: if we call it 2.5 to be on the safe side, this means that at the main auction houses, around ten thousand objects pass through the market every year.

Putting these figures together, we may say that just two dealers keep in stock the equivalent of nearly three years' worth of objects that appear at auction. There are roughly twenty-five firms comprising the International Association of Dealers in Ancient Art, and if only half of those—say, twelve—have stock of the order of Medici and Symes, then something like 150,000 antiquities are on the market at any one time. This seems an enormous figure, especially as the recent trials have shown that the great bulk of both Medici's and Symes's stock had no provenance. But the figures also reveal that what appears at auction is just a fraction—perhaps as low as 6.25 percent (10,000 out of 160,000)—of what is actually on the market at any one time. This, I would suggest, is a much lower percentage than has traditionally been thought, and it casts a new light on the auction market in antiquities.

We know that Medici left Sotheby's labels on many of the objects he bought at Sotheby's. We also know that he himself had sold those very same objects through the auction house. In other words, he bought back his own objects. This suggests (a) that his aim in doing this was to "launder" illicit objects through the auction house, making it appear to the gullible that he had bought these objects on the "open" market, and (b) that the function of the auction market is to set prices. Some form of open market is needed by the trade, otherwise there would be no generally accepted value for illicit objects.

A second factor concerns the price levels of these objects. At present, the overall value of the antiquities market to a company like Christie's is roughly U.S. $6 million per year. This means that if it sells 2,000 lots, or 5,000 objects in the course of its four sales, the average price per object is U.S. $1,200. Now compare that figure with the average price of Robin Symes's stock. His 17,000 objects have a combined value of U.S. $250 million, or an average value of U.S. $15,000. Even if we take the view that Symes has himself overvalued his stock by a factor of two, and that the real average value of his objects is nearer U.S. $7,000, the resulting value still means that his antiquities are typically six times the value of those sold at auction.

What can we conclude from this analysis? One real possibility is that the best antiquities rarely appear at auction but remain firmly hidden in the warehouses of the world's dealers (the Symes trial revealed that he had at least twenty-nine warehouses in London, Geneva, and New York). This supports the idea that one purpose of the auction house sales is to set prices for objects, against which all other price levels can be calculated. Rings are known to operate in other areas of the salesrooms. If they operate in this field (and that has yet to be proved), they might have the effect of setting general price levels for a business that is largely underground.

And that is a second point. It is often said that a tighter control of the antiquities market would only succeed in driving that market "underground." The figures already given show that such an argument is wrongheaded. In the first place, it is the *less* valuable objects that come onto the open market; in the second place, it follows that the market is *already* underground: perhaps as much as 93.75 percent of objects—call it 90 percent—never come onto the open market anyway.

Access to the Robin Symes inventory, which I was given by the family of Symes's late partner, throws light on several other matters. For example, the inventory is grouped into several documents, one of which was 104 pages long, with an average of thirty-four objects per page—roughly thirty-five hundred objects in all. None of these had any real provenance: some had been acquired from other dealers, but this was as far as "provenance" went. A document attached to the inventory discloses that Symes had been forced to credit the Getty Museum in Los Angeles with the sum of U.S. $8 million because objects he had sold to them between 1985 and 1995 had subsequently been shown to have been illicitly excavated and/or smuggled from their countries of origin and had to be returned.

Finally there is the case of a statue on which Symes had borrowed money. This concerns a life-size ivory head, thought to be of Apollo, the Greek god of the Sun, and dating perhaps from the fifth century B.C. Ivory sculptures, even in antiquity, were extremely rare. In ancient Greece it was the practice for exceptionally important statues to consist of ivory heads, hands, and feet, with bodies of stone or wood, which were covered in gold sheets. Such objects were known as Chryselephantine sculptures, after the Greek for gold and ivory. Ivory was so expensive in antiquity that only emperors and other major figures could afford objects made from it. Dozens of ivory fragments are known today, and some small statuettes. But only one other life-size figure is known to have survived in Italy, found at Montecalvo (again, near Rome) and now in the Apostolic Library in the Vatican. And only one set of life-size Chryselephantine sculptures survives in Greece. This includes statues of Apollo and Artemis at the Delphi Museum.

The ivory head that Symes had was initially dug up by a well-known *tombarolo*, Pietro Casasanta, of Anguillara, north of Rome on the shore of Lake Bracciano. Casasanta was once jailed for his illegal digging and provided intriguing insights into the way the illicit market operates at his level. For example, he usually had to pay an "entrance fee" for permission to dig on someone's land. This usually amounted to 25 million lire (about U.S. $18,000) plus a share of any profits on objects found. His greatest find, he said, came in 1970, when he unearthed L'Inviolata, the site of a temple cult where he found sixty-three statues, twenty-five of them life size. He even returned to this site in 1992 and discovered the famous Capitoline Triad, a six-ton marble statue of three seated gods—Jupiter, Juno, and Minerva—the only marble sculpture in which the three gods of the Triad are intact.

Casasanta found the ivory head in a field not far from a well-known archaeological landmark, the Baths of Claudius, and it was probably found in the remains of Claudius's villa. At the same time that he found the ivory head, Casasanta also found three Egyptian statues of goddesses, two in green and one in black granite, together with some piece of mosaic. "This was obviously the residence of a very rich, very important family," he said (for a fuller account of this case, see Todeschini and Watson 2003).

The interesting thing about this statue, in the context of this chapter, is that Casasanta sold it to a Munich-based Italian dealer, Nino Savoca. A fee of U.S. $10 million was agreed upon, though Savoca stopped paying after U.S. $700,000 and the two men fell out. Casasanta says Savoca claimed to have shown the object to two American museums, one of which attributed the head to Phidias, the famous fifth-century B.C. Greek sculptor, but neither establishment was willing to risk buying such an obviously looted object (besides the head, there are hundreds of tiny ivory shards, the tip of a finger, an ear, and a toe). Savoca died in 1998, and during a subsequent raid on his premises police discovered documentation that led them, among other places, to Robin Symes.

Symes, it turned out, had pledged the ivory head as part security for a loan he had for U.S. $8 million with a well-known bank. The bank was persuaded to give up the head to the Italian Carabinieri because, alongside the ivory sculpture, Symes also had two partial frescoes that had been stolen from an archaeological site near Herculaneum. The carabinieri had photographs of these frescoes in situ.

According to Symes's inventory, the ivory head was on the market for between U.S. $20 million and 30 million, showing the sort of markup that dealers can make in this area (for a general discussion of price markups, see Brodie 1998). Symes had apparently pledged it as part of a loan because still other antiquities had come onto the market, and he needed funds to make a purchase in a hurry. Not even the most successful of dealers always have ready cash.

These cases throw light on the financial levels that are obtained in the antiquities underworld, but this last instance also shows the levels of ignorance in the banks. Prior to being contacted by the Carabinieri, the (well-known) bank in question had no idea that the ivory head had been looted. This must mean that the independent expert they called in to provide a confirmation of the value of the object, who must have been an art market professional, was willing to turn a blind eye to the actual status of the head. Given the shards that accompanied the head, and its very uniqueness, there can have been no question in any expert's mind that the object was looted. But the episode does raise a new possibility: when governments, or police forces such as the Carabinieri, discover that a major object has been looted from their territory, it would not be a bad idea to circulate information among some of the banks that are known to specialize in funding art and antiquities dealers, besides circulating it to police forces, auction houses, and art loss registers around the world. This is a new form of deterrence that might just work.

BIBLIOGRAPHY

Brodie, Neil. "Pity the Poor Middlemen." *Culture without Context*, issue 3 (Autumn 1998): 7–9.

Todeschini, Cecilia, and Peter Watson. "Familiar Route out of Italy for Looted Ivory Head." *Culture without Context*, issue 12 (Spring 2003): 5–7.

Watson Peter. *Inside Sotheby's*. London: Bloomsbury, 1997.

5

St. Lawrence Island's Legal Market in Archaeological Goods

JULIE HOLLOWELL

We tend to characterize all undocumented digging as illicit looting, but sometimes it can be a legitimate activity and part of a legal trade in antiquities. In either case, ethnographic studies of these activities have much to offer archaeologists and others who have concerns about conserving the archaeological record in situ. In 1995 I began exploring an extensive legal market for archaeological materials that originates in the Bering Strait region of Alaska, the materials coming predominantly from St. Lawrence Island. The two Alaska Native corporations that own St. Lawrence Island manage their archaeological resources as a form of economic capital, allowing their indigenous shareholders to excavate sites for old marine mammal bone, walrus ivory, and artifacts to sell. People on St. Lawrence Island do not think of themselves as "looters" in any sense of the word, but as subsistence diggers of "old things."[1]

This situation provides an opportunity to take a closer look at the complex nature of an artifact and antiquities market—a legal one, at that—and some of the processes that create demand. It also clearly shows that archaeologists are one among a number of different stakeholders who make claims on the material past. First I describe the composition of this market in archaeological goods, the products it encompasses, and the range of its activities, followed by a look at some of the sociohistorical contexts that have given rise to the commodification of these excavated materials. Then I consider the effects, at least in this case, of the existence of a *legal* market on the supply and demand of these archaeological commodities and on site destruction. Finally, I return to the dilemma of subsistence digging and how archaeology might proceed under these circumstances.

LOCATION AND CULTURAL BACKGROUND

St. Lawrence Island (map 5.1) lies in the northern reaches of the Bering Sea, right in the path of major migrations of marine mammals as they funnel through the Bering Strait between Asia and North America. Paleontologists estimate that a drop of only 46 meters in sea level here would expose a land bridge several hundred miles wide linking Asia and the Americas, as it did approximately ten

Map 5.1. The Bering Strait region (adapted by the author from Fitzhugh and Kaplan 1982: 28).

thousand years ago (Hopkins 1967: 464). The bridge would not appear, as one might think, at the narrowest portion of the strait between the tiny Diomede Islands and Cape Prince of Wales (only forty miles across); here strong currents have naturally cut a much deeper channel. It would appear to the south, in the shallow waters surrounding St. Lawrence Island (Hopkins 1967: 460).

Marine mammal migrations, though sometimes fatally unpredictable, offered an abundance of food and raw materials that attracted and sustained a relatively large human population on St. Lawrence and the other Bering Strait islands over a long period, compared to many northern locales. St. Lawrence Island's most populous settlements of long ago lie adjacent to places where, for thousand of years, herds of walrus hauled out along the shore (Ackerman 1988: 61–63; Northern Resource Management and Yeti Map Studio 1984: 27). Episodic mass mortalities at these haul-out sites left literally tons of ivory and bone (Fay 1980). Over the past two millennia or more, human occupants on both sides of the strait undoubtedly gathered ivory and bone from these ancient deposits for use in trade and in local production of tools, house structures, and all kinds of utilitarian and decorative objects, supplementing the materials they procured from their own marine mammal harvests.

Today St. Lawrence Island is home to around fourteen hundred Yupik people living in two permanent villages—Gambell (Sivuqaq) and Savoonga. Gambell lies at the northwest tip of the island, only forty miles from the Chukotkan peninsula of Russia and two hundred miles from the Alaskan mainland. Savoonga sits on the northern coast, between two large former village sites—Ivetok to the west and Kukulik to the east. Family hunting and fishing camps and subsistence areas dot the entire perimeter of the island, often right next to thousand-year-old middens. Several flights a day shuttle people, mail, and other goods between St. Lawrence Island and the Alaskan city of Nome, which serves as a hub for the Bering Strait region.

St. Lawrence Island Yupik, as they prefer to call themselves, are one of many Inuit groups living in the circumpolar Arctic today. Their language, history, and cultural practices differentiate them from other Alaskan Inuit peoples—the Inupiat, who inhabit Seward Peninsula and the northern coasts of Alaska, and the Yup'ik peoples of the Yukon-Kuskokwim basin to the south—and connect them closely to the twelve hundred or so Siberian Yupik people living along the coast of the Chukotkan peninsula of Russia. Visits to and from the Russian mainland occurred regularly in times past (not always in a friendly manner, according to oral histories), until the Bering Strait closed to international travel in 1948 due to the Cold War. In 1989 the border reopened, at least for those who can muster the proper visas, and intermittent crossings by boat and plane now take place.

In the late 1920s and 1930s, Otto Geist, an adventurer-turned-archaeologist sponsored by the Alaska College, and archaeologist Henry Collins of the Smithsonian Institution conducted separate multiyear excavations at several locations on St. Lawrence Island. In Gambell, Collins documented two thousand years of continuous occupation in a series of adjacent sites known for their distinctive material culture (Collins 1937; Geist and Rainey 1936). Findings from these "type sites" allowed him to formulate an initial cultural chronology for Bering Strait prehistory (Collins 1937, 1959), one that archaeologists have continued to use and revise, incorporating new data and interpretations (Bandi 1969; Bronshtein and Plumet 1995; Dumond and Bland 2002; Gerlach and Mason 1992; Mason 2000).

The earliest documented cultural materials from St. Lawrence Island date from around 2000–2300 B.P. and include intricately engraved ivories in styles named "Okvik" and "Old Bering Sea." Except for a few pieces that have turned up on the Alaskan mainland, these artifact styles are found exclusively on St. Lawrence Island and along the Chukotkan coast of Russia. While Okvik materials are generally thought to be older, some archaeologists make a case for the overlap and contemporaneity of Okvik and Old Bering Sea styles, rather than interpreting them as consecutive cultures in a discrete linear sequence. The possibility also exists that the designs might mark distinctions among different ethnic affiliations that coexisted on St. Lawrence Island more than a millennium ago (Bronshtein 2002; Bronshtein and Plumet 1995; Mason 2000).

Around A.D. 500, "Punuk-style" artifacts appear on the Alaskan mainland and on the Bering Sea islands, less intricate in design and associated with larger habitations and an emphasis on whaling. The gradual transition to even simpler "Thule-style" artifacts, which apparently spread westward across the Canadian Arctic, occurred around A.D. 1200 and lasted until c. A.D. 1700, when the historic period ushered in many changes in technology, goods, and materials.

Archaeological information about St. Lawrence Island has come almost exclusively from sites along the coast, which typically consist of winter (semi-subterranean) and summer (above-ground) dwellings in settlements of various sizes, with associated burials, meat caches, and other features. Centuries of occupation in the same location have created middens with cultural layers several meters deep. The preservation of organic materials is excellent due to the ubiquitous permafrost, but coastal erosion has washed away large portions of many sites. What is left has been mined persistently by ivory diggers for several generations. In some places, people have even tried diving for old ivory and artifacts. No archaeological work has taken place in the island's interior, though the possibility of finding cultural evidence from yet earlier millennia at higher elevations has intrigued more than one researcher.

Figure 5.1. Okvik-style ivory figurines on display in the Alaska State Museum, Juneau (left to right: IIA-5105, IIA-4903, IIA-5106, IIA-5028; photograph by the author).

The tiny Punuk Islands, just off the southeastern tip of St. Lawrence Island, have yielded many tons of valuable old ivory since the early 1930s, when Otto Geist called the attention of local hunters to extensive underground caches. Decades of ivory mining have taken their toll. Besides depleting the stock of old ivory, I am told that digging has ruined the water table, and hunters who head to the Punuks must now carry their own drinking water. The Punuk Islands have also been the main find spot of Okvik-style figurines (fig. 5.1) so highly valued in the art world today. Only a few of these have ever been documented in situ, and it looks unlikely that any more ever will be.

The source of most old ivory appears to be caches of tusks, ivory chunks, and artifacts, but some also comes from natural deposits created by walrus fatalities in haul-out areas. Whole tusks have become harder for local ivory hunters to find, making them even more valuable on the market. One thing is certain; a great deal of archaeological information about early life and cultural interactions on the island and in the Bering Strait region will never be recovered due to the extensive undocumented digging for old ivory and, more recently, for artifacts and bone.

Subsistence as a Way of Life

Like many Arctic communities, St. Lawrence Islanders practice a mixed cash-and-subsistence economy, one that combines in flexible and innovative ways hunting and gathering, the utilization of local resources to acquire desired goods, home-based industry, and wage labor (Condon 1983: 161; see especially Nuttall 1998). The ideology and practice of subsistence permeate daily life and the annual cycle in this place where jobs are scarce and costs of living are exorbitant. Most households depend on locally procured foods for more than half their diet, derived primarily from marine mammal sources (walrus, seal, and whale) and supplemented with fish, waterfowl, eggs, green plants, and berries. Seasonal unemployment rates of up to 75 percent, along with the high costs of outfitting a subsistence hunter and of living in general, mean that people look for whatever ways they can to make ends meet. Along with carvings made from newly harvested ivory and a few other arts and crafts produced for the tourist market, the sale of old ivory, bone, and artifacts is one of the few ways people have to obtain cash that does not depend on government subsidies.

Subsistence activities are integral to cultural identity. They provide a deep connection to the land and sea, their resources, and all kinds of indigenous knowledge (e.g., about weather, hunting practices, survival skills, and animal behavior). St. Lawrence Islanders still use skin boats covered with split walrus hide when they head out after a bowhead whale. A person's worth is often judged by his or her skill in providing Native foods to the family or village. The right to continue to practice a subsistence lifestyle occupies a focal place in the ongoing struggles for Native sovereignty that St. Lawrence Islanders share with other Alaska Natives and with Inuit across the circumpolar region as well as with Indigenous peoples worldwide.

Digging for ivory and artifacts fits well with the economic landscape of St. Lawrence Island and the ideology of subsistence. During late summer, as soon as the permafrost starts to recede, people of all ages spend time at their digging spots after work, on weekends, or between other subsistence activities like fishing, hunting, drying meat, preparing skin boats, and picking greens and berries.[2] Digging for ivory and artifacts has much in common with other subsistence hunting and gathering practices found in arctic communities (for more information on characteristics of arctic economies, see Krupnik 1993 and Nuttall 1998), including a seasonal harvest; uncertainty of supply; unpredictable day-to-day returns; a strong connection to ancestral lands; and the ability to combine well with other activities (both on a daily basis, while out on a hunt, and in the overall scheme of things). St. Lawrence Islanders also justify digging as subsistence-related because it transforms local resources into cash that people can use to fund the escalating costs of subsistence hunting. Sometimes they refer to artifacts in the ground as gifts the ancestors left so that people today could survive in a cash economy.

A LEGAL MARKET FOR ARCHAEOLOGICAL GOODS?

St. Lawrence Island is the source of arguably one of the most extensive *legal* markets in archaeological goods in the world today. What makes this commercial use of archaeological resources legal?

Unlike in most countries, United States property laws consider archaeological materials that come from private lands (with the exception of human remains) as the property of the landowner, who then has the right to sell them on the open market. In contrast, on public (state and federal) lands in the United States, excavating without a permit has been illegal since the Antiquities Act of 1906, and any archaeological resources that come from the ground belong to the state. Relic collectors and amateur archaeologists have long taken advantage of this inconsistency between private and public property, conducting legal digs in sites on private land and selling or swapping materials at "relic shows." Today more than a dozen U.S. states, including my home of Indiana, require anyone who knowingly digs into an archaeological site, even one located on private land, first to obtain a permit from the state.

Vast areas of Alaska remain public lands, but in 1971, as a result of the Alaska Native Claims Settlement Act, Native lands in Alaska became privately owned property, unlike tribal lands in other U.S. states. The 1971 land claims settlement gave Alaska's indigenous peoples the "right" to enroll as shareholders in Native corporations, which received land—about 11 percent of the state—and money—over U.S. $960 million—in exchange for relinquishing all future claims to aboriginal lands and title (Arnold 1978). The two Native corporations of St. Lawrence Island refused the money and chose instead to settle for more land. As a result, they received full title to the entire island and its subsurface rights. This choice left the St. Lawrence Island corporations with no capital to invest or dividends to distribute, but it gave them close to three and a half times more land than if they had taken the monetary settlement (Bureau of Indian Affairs 1977: 126–27; Jorgensen 1990: 29–30). No one on the island seems to regret this decision. In the words of one elder, "We didn't take the land claims money, and I'm glad for that. We have our land here; that money would go away, but the land won't."

Today the island is private property, owned jointly by the Sivuqaq and Savoonga Native Corporations. The Native corporations firmly restrict digging for ivory, bone, or artifacts to their shareholders but otherwise currently do little to regulate either the digging or the sale of finds. The unwritten rule is one of "finders keepers," though other informal use rules guide how people stake and maintain a claim to a digging spot.

The thirteen regional and 203 village-level Native corporations in Alaska demonstrate a wide range of responses to subsistence digging on their lands. Several have policies that prohibit or discourage digging. Others tolerate it, especially in the Bering Strait, where old ivory has long played an important economic role. At least one Bering Strait village corporation allows its shareholders to dig in most places but prohibits excavations at one highly visible significant site.[3]

The importance of commercial digging on St. Lawrence Island relates to the fact that no other location in Alaska has a comparable quantity or quality of marketable archaeological goods. Each year, dealers spend an estimated $1.5 million on the island in purchases of old ivory, aged bone, and artifacts. This figure seems large, but divided among the local population it comes to less than one thousand dollars per person. Once these materials leave the island, they move through various networks of producers and distributors to consumers (see my attempt to diagram this in figure 5.2), their values typically doubling each time they change hands.

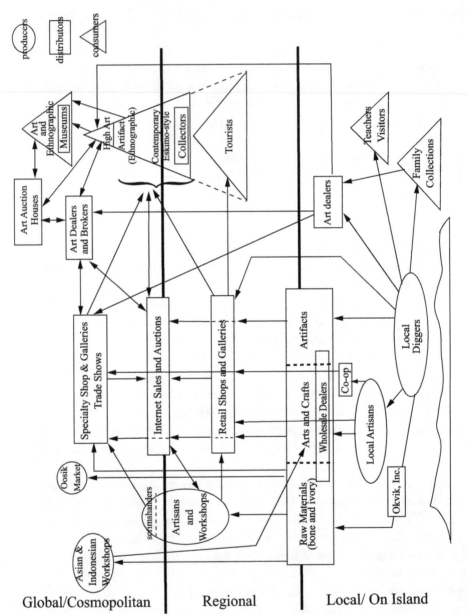

producers

distributors

consumers

Global/Cosmopolitan

Regional

Local/ On Island

Art and Ethnographic Museums

Art Auction Houses

Art Dealers and Brokers

High Art Artifact (Ethnographic)

Contemporary Eskimo-style Collectors

Tourists

Teachers Visitors

Family Collections

Art dealers

Specialty Shop & Galleries Trade Shows

Internet Sales and Auctions

Retail Shops and Galleries

Artifacts

Arts and Crafts

Co-op

Wholesale Dealers

Local Artisans

Local Diggers

Oosik Market

scrimshanders

Artisans and Workshops

Asian & Indonesian Workshops

Raw Materials (bone and ivory)

Okvik, Inc.

Figure 5.2. Diagram of the market for St. Lawrence Island archaeological materials.

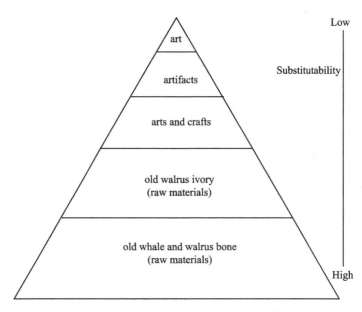

Figure 5.3. The market pyramid of low-end to high-end products (based on Moulin 1987: 143).

THE MARKET

The market for St. Lawrence Island's archaeological goods consists of an astonishing range of products, most of which end up on the Alaskan tourist market. Figure 5.3 depicts the market as a pyramid with several tiers.[4] Bulk quantities of archaeological bone and ivory sold as raw materials make up the broad, "low" end, and the few singular objects found each year that head to the art market are represented at the peak or "high" end. First I discuss the raw materials and briefly describe their transformations as they move through the market. Then I turn to worked objects sold as artifacts and collectible remnants of the past and how they surface in the market. Discussions about antiquities markets often deal only with those things that surface on the high end of the market and tend to neglect other dimensions, but in this case, and probably in others, high-end antiquities represent only one aspect of a much larger phenomenon associated with undocumented digging.

Archaeological Ivory and Bone as Raw Materials

The bulk of the market consists of old walrus ivory and marine mammal bone, gathered from old settlement sites, digging spots (fig. 5.4), and eroding middens along the coast. Local residents sell these materials by the pound to ivory and

Figure 5.4. Digging spot with the village of Gambell in the background. Note the bones drying, including a stack of whale vertebral disks (*oosevas*), used locally in arts and crafts and sold by the piece to dealers (photograph by the author).

bone buyers who typically fly out to the island to make their purchases. A handful of wholesale dealers make several trips a year to the island, and they account for the main volume of these sales.

Diggers gather close to five tons of old walrus ivory on St. Lawrence Island each year. Whole tusks have grown harder and harder to find, but by some accounts, they still comprise around half a ton of the total (somewhere between two hundred and three hundred tusks a year). The remainder consists of chunks of tusk, small pieces of scrap ivory, and thousands of walrus teeth. Buyers who come to the island pay anywhere from U.S. $30 to $120 a pound for old ivory, depending on its size, coloring, and condition. Sometimes St. Lawrence Islanders pack old ivory or artifacts with them when they travel to cities like Nome or Anchorage, where they can exchange these materials for a substance less easy to come by on the island—cash.

Walrus ivory differs significantly from mammoth and mastodon ivory (also found in the Bering Strait, though less frequently, and sold for carving) and from elephant ivory in its solid composition, which refuses to fracture in layers, and in its mottled inner core that runs the length of the tusk. All over Alaska, in tourist centers and rural villages alike, people refer to old, excavated ivory as "fossil" ivory. Old ivory, however, is not fossilized at all but mineralized from contact with iron, salt, and other substances in soil and water, a process that creates hues ranging from light tan or yellow to dark brown, mottled peach, or a deep blue-black.

By contrast, new or "white" ivory refers to recently procured ivory that has never been buried in the ground. This distinction becomes important because today, unlike old ivory, new "white" ivory cannot legally be marketed as a raw material except among Alaska Natives (a status defined, regrettably, according to 25 percent blood quantum). This policy took effect in 1972, when the United States passed the Marine Mammal Protection Act (MMPA). The act contained an exemption that allows Alaska Natives to continue hunting marine mammals for noncommercial subsistence purposes and also permits Alaska Natives to utilize byproducts from subsistence hunting to create arts and crafts for the commercial market. Since the MMPA does not apply to marine mammal materials harvested *before* the passage of the act in 1972, unworked "pre-act" ivory and bone, including any from archaeological sites, can still be sold on the open market (e.g., to non-Natives).

With the passage of the MMPA, non-Native carvers and artisans no longer had legal access to unworked new, white ivory. Many switched to using ivory from extinct sources (e.g., mammoth and mastodon) and long-buried walrus ivory. In essence, the MMPA may protect living species, but it also has had the effect of shifting market demand toward archaeological sources of ivory and bone.

The market for "fossil" ivory has a long and stable history, but the sale of large quantities of old whale and walrus bone developed relatively recently, over the past twenty-five years, in response to requests from wholesale dealers seeking a larger, cheaper carving medium. People on the island were more than happy to find a market for bones that had piled up around digging sites. Today several St. Lawrence Island entrepreneurs gather marketable bone and sort it into piles to bleach and dry. An estimated ten tons of old whale and walrus bone leave the island annually. Dealers pay from U.S. $1.25 a pound for porous whalebone to $3 a pound for walrus jawbone and other dense varieties. Though most old bone sells as a raw material, many of these pieces, particularly large whale bones, have had former lives centuries ago as components of a house or another structure. In other words, they are artifacts too—just not such finely worked ones. A few specialty bones, such as skulls, eardrums, vertebral disks, or oosiks (penis bones) sell by the piece and fetch much higher prices. The market for these "curiosities" is on the rise, and several shops now display unmodified old bones for sale, alongside an array of products created from old ivory.

Bone and Ivory in Arts and Crafts

The production of old ivory and bone from raw materials into marketable goods takes place in local, regional, and global locations and encompasses a wide range of arts and crafts.

Local production. Artisans on St. Lawrence Island, known for their skill in ivory carving and other arts and crafts, often use old bone and ivory since it is a readily available local resource (fig. 5.5). Most Native carvers prefer new or white ivory when they can get it (since it cannot be sold to non-Natives until it is worked), but they rely on old ivory for color contrast or when stocks of white ivory are low. Carvers who work with marine mammal bone always favor aged bone, as newer bone reeks of the oil that fills its pores and is more difficult to work. The majority of locally made arts and crafts are sold to wholesale dealers who in turn market them to retailers in Alaska and specialty shops across the United States.

Regional production. The wholesale dealers stockpile old ivory and bone purchased on the island in warehouses and garages in Anchorage or Juneau to sell to individual carvers or carving workshops. Regional production of archaeological bone and ivory ranges from workshops that use immigrant labor for mass production of goods for the tourist market, using blatant appropriations of Native designs and motifs, to fine artists and craftspeople who transform these raw materials into distinctive (and expensive) art forms.

"St. Lawrence Island fossil ivory" turns up in a fantastic array of products in gift shops across Alaska—everything from belt buckles, earrings, and wall hangings to baskets full of polished ivory chips and walrus teeth selling for five dollars an ounce. Labels on these goods deliberately draw upon cultural tropes and the lure of the past, advertising them as "expressions from long lost millennia found in the frozen earth of ancient villages." At the same time, concerns among tourists and other consumers about animal rights and endangered species have inspired Alaskan retailers to promote goods made from old ivory as "*the* morally acceptable choice" since "no animals were killed to make this piece"! In reality this attitude subtly endorses subsistence digging and non-Native carvers, who can only work with old ivory, while maligning subsistence hunting and the work of Native ivory carvers. The irony is that old ivory and other materials from archaeological sources are equally endangered, even more finite, and nonrenewable.

Global production. Wholesale dealers sell old ivory for anywhere from U.S. $80 to $250 a pound to specialty carvers and to networks of distributors who use websites and mail-order businesses to supply craftspeople all over the world. Among the most dedicated consumers of old ivory are custom craftsmen who make scrimshaw, jewelry, knife and gun handles, and musical instruments.

Figure 5.5. Doll made by Beulah Oitillian of Gambell, showing the use of many different materials (Staff photographer, © 1995-96 The Trustees of Indiana University).

These artisans used to work with elephant ivory, sperm whale teeth, or newly harvested "white" walrus ivory, but various trade bans—the Marine Mammal Protection Act (MMPA), the Convention on International Trade in Endangered Species (CITES), and the global ban on elephant ivory—now restrict the use of these alternatives. As a result of these trade bans, the pressure on old ivory excavated from Native lands in the Bering Strait to serve as a legal substitute for other forms of ivory has definitely increased. Some countries regulate the import of old or new walrus ivory under CITES, but in many cases crossing

Figure 5.6. Old Bering Sea–style harpoon head made in Bali from old ivory (author's collection; photograph by the author).

borders requires some minimal paperwork and a permitting fee.[5] Whale bone is a different story; it is both less desired as an exotic material and subject to much more stringent import and export restrictions.

The outsourcing of old ivory and bone for overseas production is another global phenomenon associated with archaeological materials from St. Lawrence Island. Several dealers and manufacturers export archaeological walrus bone and old ivory to workshops in Indonesia and Hong Kong. For five dollars a day they employ displaced carvers who once specialized in elephant ivory to replicate carvings to their specifications, often using "Eskimo-style" designs (Melzer 1995). These products are imported back to Alaska, where they compete with Native-made work on gift shop shelves.[6] Some dealers use overseas labor for piecework, hiring carvers in Asian workshops to make hundreds of faces or hands for "Eskimo-style" figurines that will be assembled back in Alaska.

One day I found an intriguing example of global outsourcing of raw materials in an Anchorage gift shop owned by one of the large wholesalers of archaeological materials—an Old Bering Sea–style harpoon head like those used on St. Lawrence Island a thousand years ago (fig. 5.6). After several rounds of questioning, the clerk admitted that this was a replica, carved in Bali from old ivory, which had probably been purchased on St. Lawrence Island. I later took this piece to Savoonga and showed it to some diggers. Upon inspection, they soon realized it was recently made and voiced ample concern that inauthentic pieces like this could ruin the market for the real thing.

THE ARTIFACT MARKET

St. Lawrence Islanders find all kinds of artifacts along with old ivory when they dig. People save *any* artifact made from ivory, but diggers also collect any tools or other worked objects of bone, antler, wood, and slate in good, marketable condition. Whole, unbroken artifacts are difficult to find and also difficult to extract from the permafrost without breakage, but even fragments of artifacts are gathered and sold by the pound. On the island artifacts sell for anywhere from forty dollars a pound for wet and broken old tools to ten dollars apiece for small, undecorated objects, and up to sixty thousand dollars for a single exceptional piece. Some of the same wholesale dealers who handle bulk archaeological materials also buy artifacts. Other "artifact dealers" travel to the island specifically to purchase "old things."

With the exception of a few pieces each year that head straight for the art market, artifacts end up in shops in all the tourist centers of Alaska, selling as souvenirs and collectibles (fig. 5.7). Visitors to Juneau, Skagway, or Anchorage can hardly overlook the broken pieces glued onto three-by-five-inch cards, selling as "ancient Eskimo artifacts." Most gift shops or galleries have at least a display case with old tools and harpoon heads for sale. Some sell framed groupings known as "St. Lawrence Island Artifact Boards" that constitute a ready-made relic collection. Artifacts can also be "born again," fashioned into knife

Figure 5.7. Artifacts for sale in a Skagway shop (photograph by the author).

Figure 5.8. Old Bering Sea–style harpoon counterweight or "winged object" (Basha and Perry Lewis Collection; photograph by the author).

handles, worn as pendants, or used as a base for scrimshaw. Others end up sawn into pieces and made into jewelry. Interestingly, many people who see nothing wrong with selling *whole* artifacts draw the line here and consider it morally reprehensible to cut them into pieces.

High-End Artifacts and the Art Market

The segment of the market that typically receives the most attention includes the engraved, decorative Old Bering Sea-, Okvik-, and Punuk-style objects that fetch high prices on the global market for "tribal" or "primitive" art (fig. 5.8). Perhaps ten or twelve pieces out of the tons of marketable materials pulled from the ground in a year have qualities that make them desirable to art dealers and collectors. Any digger who finds an ivory animal, a human figure, a "winged object" (sometimes called a "butterfly"), or any decorated, unbroken object will save it to show to a high-end dealer. Some St. Lawrence Islanders send photos or even videos of objects to a small pool of potential buyers. These days diggers—familiar with the price estimates next to their pieces in auction and gallery catalogues—ask very high prices for particular pieces, often higher than any buyer is willing to pay. Setting a high price is one way St. Lawrence Islanders try to offset the limited access they have to buyers and other networks in the art market.

Over the past twenty years, just two or three art dealers have served as the direct links between diggers and the art world. They fly to the island near the end of the summer to see what has come out of the ground and meet with individual diggers to negotiate prices directly. After several weeks based in Nome, they return to Seattle or New York with a handful of objects, which they will selectively invite clients or other dealers to see.

Auctions function in the art world as channels for recirculating goods, and more importantly, as places where value and provenance are validated and become public record.[7] To date, the highest price paid at auction for a Bering Strait ivory is U.S. $216,000, but collectors pay even more in private transactions with dealers.[8] The best pieces found each year on St. Lawrence Island, however, *never* go straight to auction. Dealers always save them for the eyes of special, preferred clients. Nothing is more thrilling to many collectors than to have a dealer give them "first pick" of a newly excavated artifact, one never before seen by the art world and never "walked around" in public at an auction; that is, a "virgin" piece. The naming of objects as "ritual" or "shamanic," the association with "classical" forms (e.g., broken pieces become "torsos") and primitivist art, and their visual aesthetics and polymorphic qualities all enhance the value of these distinctive archaeological ivories from the Bering Strait.

As the diagram of the market in figure 5.2 indicates, the art world and its buyers exist in a niche of their own, far removed from the source community. Almost all of the objects that surface in the art market come from dealers or private collections and have been excavated since the 1970s, marking the moment when many Native lands in Alaska became private property and Bering Strait ivories began showing up in exhibition catalogues (see Collins 1973). Very few dealers and buyers have connections to materials, information, and people at both ends of the market chain.

Once in the art world, an object may be held for years in the hands of a dealer or collector, and then recycled back through the market, sometimes to the same dealers, ending up with a different collector. Provenance or history of ownership also enhances an artifact's social and economic value, especially in the context of an art or culture system that uses "old things" from distant times and exotic places as markers of taste, wealth, and status (Bourdieu 1984; Clifford 1988: 213). The social and geographic distance between the art world and the source community tends to erase the less palatable dynamics of cultural production, such as the damage done to the archaeological record and the everyday social and economic realities faced by St. Lawrence Island's subsistence diggers. Some of this will change as St. Lawrence Islanders begin to use the Internet, digital video, or other means to penetrate the boundaries of the art world.

In the case described here, the few high-end antiquities excavated on St. Lawrence Island that enter the art market are an extremely rare by-product of the search for old ivory and a range of other marketable things and are not the primary cause of site destruction or commercial digging. Studies that focus on objects surfacing in the high-end art market may capture only the tip of a much larger, more complex market system. Attempts to mitigate the negative effects of the antiquities market on the archaeological record will have a better chance of succeeding if they take the whole picture (the entire market) into account, particularly the economic situation of those at the source and the effects policies have on these source communities.

The Internet

The advent of the Internet has greatly facilitated access and networking among buyers and sellers of archaeological materials from St. Lawrence Island. Today there are hundreds of Internet sites where small businesses distribute old walrus ivory as a raw material or sell products fashioned from old ivory or bone. Many of these sites have web pages that attempt to explain the source of the materials and their legal status.

The best place to find artifacts for sale on the Internet is eBay. At any given moment, eBay has around a dozen or so lots of Bering Strait archaeological objects in its web auctions (<www.ebay.com>, "Eskimo ivory"). These have ranged in price from five dollars to nine hundred dollars, with only a few pieces listed for more than fifty dollars. Most artifacts on eBay are undecorated ivory or bone tools, but once in a while fragments show up that are fine enough to attract amateur relic collectors who have a special interest in "Eskimo" material. Sixty percent or more of the "Eskimo artifacts" found online come with a statement testifying that they were "legally excavated on St. Lawrence Island." A number of the Bering Strait artifacts found on eBay come from collections made in the first half of the century that have surfaced from attics and found their way into the hands of contemporary curio traders.

One major source on eBay for Bering Strait artifacts is "Big Al," a trader from Wisconsin who spends his summers in the Bering Strait purchasing artifacts directly from diggers. This Anchorage couple started making buying trips to St. Lawrence Island for bone, old ivory, and artifacts in 1996. They sell a range of archaeological goods out of a booth in the Anchorage Saturday market and through retail shops as well as on the Internet. St. Lawrence Islanders have not started selling their archaeological goods directly to buyers on eBay yet, but it is only a matter of time.

Fakes, Replicas, and Smuggling

Compared to other antiquities, very few Bering Strait ivories enter the market illegitimately, as fakes or smuggled goods. Infrequently, someone will carve a human figurine or some other highly valued form, use various staining techniques to make it look old, and try to pass it off as something new. This may work with a naïve buyer who arrives on the island or someone on the street in Nome, but seasoned dealers can usually spot a fake. It is difficult to tell just how much forgery occurs, but even minor incidents are remembered and talked about for years. Villagers and dealers alike discourage fakes and forgeries because they cast doubt on the authenticity of the entire genre and can easily hurt the market. One seller on eBay was recently cited to me as a source for forgeries of St. Lawrence Island artifacts.

No one on St. Lawrence Island currently carves replicas of the "old things" (though an ivory carver might do so by special request), partly because people worry that replicas can be artificially aged and mistaken for the real thing. On the Russian side of the strait, members of the carving studio in Uelen have experimented with making replicas of a few special objects from state-sponsored excavations using new white ivory. The results are difficult to market due to their high cost and because of Russian export restrictions on ivory.

A more common scenario than forgery occurs when an artifact excavated illegally from the vast state-owned lands in Alaska enters the market with claims that it came from a legal find spot or place of origin. Smuggling across the international border from Russia also occurs, especially since some very valuable Okvik- and Old Bering Sea–style artifacts and old ivory can be found on the Russian side of the strait. It is patently illegal to dig or sell archaeological objects anywhere in Russia without government permission, but desperate economic conditions in Chukotka make smuggling a tempting proposition. Since the Bering Strait reopened to travel in 1989, the opportunities for smuggling in connection with festivals, conferences, weddings, and evangelical meetings have continues to increase, and concomitantly, so has the undocumented digging in sites along the Russian coast.

A HISTORY OF MARKET DEMAND

Artifact markets are often treated as recent troublesome phenomena. A deeper look, however, reveals that they usually have long histories of commodification involving deep entanglements with global markets, state policies, and early practices of archaeologists. To understand the existence of and motivations for the market today, we need to understand its history.

The history of the trade in old walrus ivory probably goes back to at least the ninth century, when traders most likely carried old ivory found buried in riverbanks in eastern Russia to Persia, where it was a luxury good believed to have magical powers (Cammann 1954: 14–20). In the late 1800s, the trading ships that supplied store goods to whaling vessels and Inuit villages in the Bering Strait always paid more for old ivory than for new white tusks. Much of it went to San Francisco to be fashioned into specialty jewelry and cutlery handles. For many years the only artifacts that interested Native diggers were pieces they could reuse to carve into beads or curios.

The trade in *archaeological* "specimens," also called "relics" to distinguish them from newly made curios, grew out of the Victorian appetite for curios and the "salvage" collecting of the Museum Period (Cole 1985; Hollowell 2004: chap. 6; King and Little 1986; Ray 1966: 51–52). In Alaska by the 1890s, field collectors and tourists had already bought up most of the ethnographic goods that villagers were willing to part with (Cole 1985: 93–97). In the wake of this scarcity, people began taking objects from old sites and graves (graves in Alaska were often above ground) to sell as relics and curios (Cole 1985: 101; Krech 1989: 132). St. Lawrence Island was too remote to participate in this tourist trade or even to be much affected by the huge influx of people to northwestern Alaska for the Nome Gold Rush. Besides, the islanders had become relatively wealthy from the trade in whale baleen, used in corsets, hoop skirts, umbrellas, and buggy whips. By 1904 they were getting a whopping U.S. $7.50 a pound from whalers and traders for the lightweight springy substance.[9] But around 1910, with the invention of spring steel, automobiles, and new fashions, the global market for baleen crashed. In need of a substitute for baleen that people could use as credit, traders began accepting archaeological curios, along with old ivory and fox skins, as payment for store goods. Other ready markets for archaeological artifacts (as well as for newly made curios) included the crews of Coast Guard vessels and amateur collectors who visited the island while on official business.

Around the same time, popular and scientific interest grew in "Eskimo" relics as scientific "specimens" and "windows to the past," important clues in the puzzle of human development.[10] By the 1920s the search for the origin of peoples of the North, known as "the Eskimo problem" (Bandi 1969; Rudenko 1961), finally brought archaeologists and museum expeditions to the Bering Strait (Borden 1928; Jenness 1928; Mathiassen 1930). As soon as researchers saw the delicately engraved "specimens of a high fossil ivory culture" from Diomede and St. Lawrence islands (Hrdlicka 1930: 174, pl. 26), they purchased what they could for museums, and soon after, several returned with wheelbarrows and shovels. From 1927 to 1939, during a decade of seasonal excavations on St. Lawrence Island, archaeologists purchased hundreds of artifacts from villagers for ten to fifty cents each, often paying in store credit or trade goods like sugar, tea, ammunition, canned goods, and phonograph records. They supervised excavations with young diggers who received about thirty cents an hour, paid them for any artifacts they found, and let them keep unworked chunks of old ivory to carve for themselves.[11]

By 1935 the market for fox furs, which became an economic mainstay after the end of the whaling period, had crashed, and all the itinerant traders had left the Bering Strait. The Bureau of Indian Affairs, through the Alaska Native Service and its village teachers, set up a program to mass-market ivory carvings made in the Bering Strait as collectibles and tourist souvenirs as a way to invigorate village economies. This program, the Alaska Native Arts Clearinghouse, encouraged St. Lawrence Islanders to mine old ivory and use it in carvings or sell it to other ivory-carving villages. During the 1940s the Alaska Native Service also advertised archaeological artifacts as part of its sales inventory.

These federal programs saw archaeologists who excavated on St. Lawrence Island as competitors for old ivory and artifacts and wanted these materials to stay in the community for use as economic resources. This became more critical when the Bering Strait closed in 1948 due to the Cold War, cutting off the source of the finest old "fossil" walrus ivory (known as "Siberian" ivory) just when demand on the Alaskan tourist market for souvenir carvings was on the rise (Ray 1980: 31, 35). By 1950 the Department of the Interior added conditions to the federal excavation permits required of archaeologists, stating that all old ivory and any "broken or unneeded artifacts" must remain on St. Lawrence Island for local carvers.[12] In 1962 the new state of Alaska nominated the five "type" sites in Gambell as National Historic Landmarks, along with archaeological sites on the mainland at Wales and Point Hope, even though years of digging for old ivory had already disturbed a large percentage of the Gambell sites (Giddings 1967: 132).

Meanwhile, by the 1960s, Okvik-style figurines and Old Bering Sea–style carvings achieved recognition among museums and scholars in North America and Europe as important and distinctive examples of prehistoric art. This growing esteem, stimulated by the writings of archaeologists and art historians and the acceptance of "primitivist" aesthetics by the art world, reinscribed these archaeological specimens as valuable art (Collins 1959; Douglas and D'Harnoncourt 1941; Meldgaard 1960). The first Bering Strait ivories to surface in the art market probably came from museums that had purchased large private collections from Alaska and had then traded pieces to "primitive art" dealers, such as Julius Carlebach and J. J. Klejman in New York, or John Hewett in London, to recover some of their costs or to fill gaps in their collections. Collectors like Nelson Rockefeller and Lord Robert and Lisa Sainsbury, who had a penchant for primitive and primitivist art, were among the first to usher Bering Strait archaeological ivories into the art world.

Soon after St. Lawrence Island became private property in 1971, diggers from Savoonga, well aware of the rising value of "old things," began to approach museums with offers to sell figurines and other high-end objects that they had recently excavated. A turning point came in 1973 when an exhibition at the National Gallery of Art—The Far North: 2000 Years of American Eskimo and Indian Art—prominently featured Bering Strait archaeological ivories in its catalogue, including several of the recently excavated figurines museums had purchased from diggers (Collins 1973). That very year, two art dealers sent a "runner" to St. Lawrence Island, and he began supplying high-end objects to an elite cadre of primitive art collectors and dealers. By 1978 three art dealers were making annual buying trips to the island, and pieces had started showing up in London and New York art auctions, just in time for the art boom of the 1980s.

Museum exhibitions and scholarly writings have played a significant, if unwitting, role in creating art value, but my research indicates that art dealers, who see it as their *job* to create both supply and demand, play an even more critical role. Dealers have told me that if they did not supply a few new and exciting pieces each year, collectors would soon lose interest in Bering Strait ivories and turn their acquisitive eye to another genre.

Around the same time that the art world began to take note of Bering Strait ivories, the passage of international restrictions on trade in other kinds of ivory notably increased demand for "St. Lawrence Island fossil ivory" as a legal substitute. The steady growth of the Alaskan tourist trade, which utilizes archaeological materials in numerous products, has put additional pressure on these archaeological resources.

The Effects of a Legal Market

What effects does legality have on this blatant open market for archaeological goods? First, in comparison with *illicit* markets, these materials enter the market through more direct networks and through fewer middlemen than their illegal counterparts, since no bribery or laundering is necessary. Second, St. Lawrence Island artifacts come to buyers with more provenience information—usually the name of the archaeological site or village where the object was found, since this does not need to be kept secret. This contrasts with the "drifting provenience" information attributed to many antiquities excavated or exported under questionable legal circumstances (see Gill and Chippindale 1993). Having a known provenience or find spot adds to an object's authenticity and consequently increases its market value. Third, the people at the source—the diggers—ask for and receive a much higher percentage of the end-value of artifacts in their negotiations with art dealers (sometimes up to 70 percent). This arguably makes St. Lawrence Islanders the best-paid subsistence diggers in the world. Where else would an art dealer write a thirty-thousand-dollar check to a subsistence digger?[13]

The case of St. Lawrence Island, where legal artifact mining is a veritable cottage industry, also provides a test of the theory, advocated by several international art lawyers and studied by UNESCO, that an unregulated global free market in already excavated cultural property would be a better deterrent to site destruction than restrictive laws, which tend to stimulate a black market (Merryman 1994; O'Keefe 1997). This argument presumes that increasing the supply of legally available goods would have the effect of reducing demand.

But would it really work that way? It does not in the market for St. Lawrence Island's legal archaeological goods, where dealers simply continue to develop more and more niches and forms for marketing them. Diggers collect anything and everything they can sell. More artifacts are available to suit collectors at every price range. High-end art collectors, whose demands can *never* be satisfied because they are not based on utility, simply continue to compete for the rarest unique pieces available while tourists and souvenir seekers choose among an ever wider range of archaeological curios sold in retail shops.[14] Some of these trends may become visible only when one looks beyond the elite (and tiny) realm of the art market and finds that in many instances the assumption that greater supply decreases demand may well be inaccurate.

My research also offers empirical evidence that contradicts another argument sometimes used in support of a legal trade in antiquities—that laws restricting the circulation of antiquities naturally create higher market prices. Instead, the market values of legally owned and traded antiquities, such as St. Lawrence Island ivories or American Indian artifacts from private lands, have proportionately risen just as high over the past twenty years as have the values of illicit materials such as Pre-Columbian art (Gilgan 2001).

Nor does argument that a free trade in already excavated materials would reduce the demand for newly excavated goods appear to hold water. In the Bering Strait, where archaeological ivories have almost no trade restrictions, this freedom of movement (which in many cases translates to the power of wealthy collectors to hold particular objects *out* of circulation—see Belk 1995: 62) has certainly not slowed the digging, and the wealthiest collectors continue to prize newly excavated, never-before-seen artifacts just as much as those that have a renowned history of ownership or provenance.[15] The presence of a relatively lucrative legal artifact trade has also definitely incited illegal digging along the Russian coast and the smuggling of goods across the strait.

Due to rising ethical concerns about the relationship between the market and site destruction, in spite of the fact that the market is legal, few museums today will purchase Bering Strait archaeological ivories, and several even refuse or restrict their donation. This has the effect, however, of keeping more objects in private hands and potentially available to recirculate in the market. Perhaps archaeologists should direct more concern to things still in the ground than to objects in the market, which have already lost so much of their contextual information. In many cases, nationalist and retentionist cultural property debates swirling around high-profile unprovenienced antiquities tend to muddy the waters, overshadowing concerns for the archaeological record with nationalist desires to control cultural symbols.

These observations on the effects of a legal market are based on one case, and the issues raised here would benefit greatly from more comparative data. For example, to what extent do other antiquities markets have a low-end or a tiered or pyramidal structure, and to what degree might this be a phenomenon of a *legal* market? Mounting evidence, such as Blumt's (2002) description of the market for antiquities in Israel, suggests that other markets for archaeological goods, particularly in a legal or quasilegal environment, do encompass a broad low-end tier. It seems that people generally will gather anything that they can sell. In other places, local people ignore state-level prohibitions and recycle materials from archaeological sites for their own household use or for building construction, as in many cases they have done for centuries (Blumt 2002; Cacho and Sanjuan 2000; Karoma 1996; Padgett 1989; Paredes Maury 1998; K. D. Vitelli, pers. comm.).

Subsistence Diggers

Today subsistence digging is an integral part of economic and social life on St. Lawrence Island and certainly part of the heritage of the islanders. Older diggers are regarded as community historians; young people look forward to their first big sale. In Gambell, a third-grade primer portrayed children heading out to dig, and one woman's obituary noted: "She loved to dig for artifacts." When I asked a group of high-schoolers how many of them had dug for artifacts, every hand went up. Everyone wants to find an object worth a new boat, a four-wheeler, or a computer. Other people just need to pay their bills.

Yet on St. Lawrence Island there is a wide range of personal, sometimes conflicting, opinions about digging or selling "old things" that come from the ground. Some people dig for recreation, while others say they "don't have the patience." Some dig to pay the bills; others regard the artifact trade as a continuation of the pattern of white traders "ripping off" their cultural artifacts. People told me stories about voices that showed them where to dig or that warned them when to stop because an object did not want to be found. A couple of elders blamed all the social problems in the village on "those holes people dig out there." Almost everyone feels a sense of loss and concern that so many unique cultural objects leave the island, never to be seen again, and end up far away in unknown places and hands; yet the same people who work to establish a local museum might spend their free time digging.

The very act of digging connects people to the land and to the past, both considered inalienable. Archaeological objects, on the other hand, are alienable "gifts from ancestors" that help St. Lawrence Islanders survive in the present— an example of "keeping while giving" (Weiner 1992). The same sentiments arise in the way subsistence diggers in Belize refer to the artifacts they find as *semilla*, sacred seed scattered by the ancestors to help create the future (Matsuda 1998: 87–88).

Economically, diggers on St. Lawrence Island see little difference between what they do and how others extract nonrenewable resources like diamonds or oil or make a withdrawal from an inheritance or bank account. It is worth noting that when opportunities for a more reliable income exist, people *stop* digging. A few summers ago in Savoonga, many diggers took jobs installing the running water system, and dealers complained that it was a "bad" year, because no one was digging.

Politically, St. Lawrence Islanders are known for their independence and autonomy within the broad arenas of the Alaska Native community and the circumpolar region. They have rejected all offers from outsiders to lease, mine, or develop their natural resources, an indication of their intention to retain local control over their land and resources. Alaska Natives everywhere face intense challenges to subsistence rights from non-Native hunters, legislators, regulatory agencies, and developers. On St. Lawrence Island, the alignment of artifact digging with subsistence clearly marks it as an issue of cultural survival and self-determination. Though other indigenous groups may ascribe very different (noneconomic) values to archaeological materials, they appear to support the choices of the St. Lawrence Islanders, based on principles of sovereignty and self-determination.

HERITAGE ARCHAEOLOGY FOR WHOM?

Since 1973, when the art market started to escalate, the only archaeology projects on St. Lawrence Island have been construction-related monitoring, except for a 1984 survey of over fifty sites by the Smithsonian, conducted in hopes that the corporation might designate certain sites for conservation (Crowell 1985). No such plans have yet resulted. In 1987, when the National Park Service rescinded the National Historic Landmark status of the five old village sites in Gambell, based on continued reports of unabated commercial digging, no one in the village seemed to care.[16] The status had done nothing for them, and its unclear boundaries were interfering with plans to locate the new school. Off the island, however, the action generated a lot of press about local digging practices, with several archaeologists referring to St. Lawrence Islanders as "cultural cannibals"—not exactly good public relations.[17]

But perhaps a Western notion that venerates material culture as heritage is somewhat foreign to people who experience heritage as something inalienable, performed in daily practices like speaking Yupik, hunting, eating walrus meat, or drum-dancing (without tourists), in a place where people recognize their elders—rather than objects in a museum—as the real cultural treasures. NAGPRA and the symbolic power it accords to material objects may be changing some of these ideas. So far many human remains have been returned and reburied on the island, but the islanders have asked the museum in Fairbanks to store the artifacts for them because of the lack of a safe place for them on the island.

OKVIK, INC.

In July 1999 a full-page article written by St. Lawrence Islander and award-winning artist Susie Silook appeared in the Nome *Nugget* (July 22, p. 15) with the title "St. Lawrence Island 'Digs' Resource Management." It pictured a young boy shoulder-deep in a digging hole with a shovel and a caption reading: "Gambell archiologist [*sic*]." The article announced the formation by the island's two Native corporations of Okvik, Inc., a for-profit business to buy and sell archaeological goods, its objectives being to eliminate middlemen, gain more control over prices and supply, and retain more value locally from island resources. In 2001, Okvik started buying old ivory and bone from shareholders. Future plans include expanding to artifact and Internet sales, offering certificates of authenticity, training people in archaeology, and building a world-class museum.

This commercial approach to archaeological resources undoubtedly makes archaeologists cringe, but at the same time, in the long run, it addresses local concerns and has potential to benefit the community *and* the archaeological record. The outlook for Okvik is uncertain, however. In its first year the business used grant funds to amass a large inventory of old ivory and bone but had trouble finding buyers.

SUBSTITUTABILITY

This study of a legal market for archaeological goods indicates that the notion of substitutability—the ability to transfer demand to other goods—will play an important role in any consideration of how to remove archaeological goods from the commodity stream. In fact, a good portion of the market demand for old ivory today comes from its substitutability as a legal alternative in the face of policies that restrict the use of other kinds of ivory.

Substitutability is higher for goods nearer the base of the pyramid (fig. 5.3), where, for example, alternatives to bulk raw materials and to low-end souvenirs created from archaeological bone or ivory can more easily be found to satisfy the tastes of the tourist market. Even at the top of the pyramid, where no substitutes exist for one-of-a-kind art objects, undue scarcity of a genre often persuades collectors to substitute other art forms to satisfy the desire for acquisition.

St. Lawrence Islanders have, for now, made a conscious decision to prioritize the economic value of their unique cultural resources over the value of these as archaeological heritage. Artifact diggers are engaged and entangled in a global market that exploits cultural resources because it is one of the best economic options available. People on the island, as elsewhere in Alaska and all over the world, are likely to continue digging as long as a market for their archaeological goods exists, and until they have a viable economic substitute.

HOW CAN ARCHAEOLOGY PROCEED?

So, how can archaeology proceed under these conditions?

It cannot, if local people are forced to choose between selling excavated materials and doing scientific archaeology. It cannot, if archaeologists wait until the artifact market collapses or are unwilling to make some ethical compromises—compromises that in this case would involve working in a community where commercial digging is openly sanctioned and recognizing the corporation's legal right to sell artifacts after study (whether this happens or not). Dilemmas of this kind dare us to rethink whether archaeology is really about the objects or the knowledge.

This was brought home to me during my four seasons working as crew chief on excavations directed by Roger Harritt of the University of Alaska in the Bering Strait village of Wales, the northwesternmost point of the North American continent and once an important center for intercontinental trade. I signed on to the project because of my interest in the Wales Native Corporation's support of a scientific excavation in the midst of a small village where residents also openly dug for the market. The coexistence of diggers and archaeologists, awkward at times, fostered mutual respect and facilitated the exchange of all

Figure 5.9. Marie Ninglalook and Wes Komonaseak excavating on the Kurigitavik Mound in Wales, Alaska (photograph by the author).

kinds of knowledge and understanding. This does not mean that archaeologists converted anyone. On the weekend our local crew members sometimes went digging or made a few dollars driving a visiting dealer around (fig. 5.9). The artifacts and the piles of seal bones we excavated belong to the Wales Native Corporation. Though the project director has presented several curation options, the decision is theirs.

On St. Lawrence Island, things would be tougher because of the ubiquitous and high-stakes role that subsistence digging plays in the community, but if—I should say when—the Native corporation decides to set aside a site for scientific excavation, should archaeologists walk away, or should they work with local authorities to negotiate terms of stewardship and research that benefit both the community and the archaeological record?

ACKNOWLEDGMENTS

Portions of this manuscript appeared in Julie Zimmer (2003), "When Archaeological Artifacts are Commodities: Dilemmas Faced by Native Villages of Alaska's Bering Strait," in *Indigenous People and Archaeology*, edited by Trevor Peck, Evelyn Siegfried, and Gerald A. Oetelaar, pp. 298–312, and published by the Archaeological Association of the University of Calgary. Funding for this research has come from the Arctic Social Science Program of the National Science Foundation's Office of Polar Programs, the Phillips Fund for Native American Research of the American Philosophical Society, the Jacobs Research Fund of the Whatcom Museum, and at Indiana University, the Department of Anthropology's David K. Skomp Fund and the Research and University Graduate School. I also want to thank the people of St. Lawrence Island and Wales, Alaska, and the many others who have assisted and encouraged this work.

NOTES

1. Staley (1993: 348) and Matsuda (1998: 96) define a subsistence digger as a person who uses the proceeds from artifact digging to support a subsistence lifestyle.

2. For other discussions of subsistence digging on St. Lawrence Island, see Scott (1984) and Staley (1993).

3. I refer to the Wales Native Corporation, which, since the late 1970s, has excluded shareholders from digging on the Kurigitavik Mound site next to the present-day village.

4. This concept comes from Raymonde Moulin (1987: 139–43), who portrayed the French art market in a similar pyramidal fashion, with a broad base represented by large quantities of "junk art" consumed by the masses and one-of-a-kind goods consumed by an elite few at the pinnacle.

5. Information about restrictions on the import of these materials for several countries can be found in "A Customs Guide to Alaska Native Arts," website of the Alaska Division of Community Advocacy, Department of Community and Economic Development, <www.dced.state.ak.us/dca/nag/nativearts.htm>, accessed March 10, 2004.

6. This outsourcing of archaeological bone and ivory is part of a larger transnational cultural marketing phenomenon. Workshops in Bali also carve wooden replicas of Northwest Coast masks, rattles, and totems, among other things (Melzer 1995).

7. Dealers have cultivated many strategies for manipulating auctions to their advantage. Appadurai (1986: 21) briefly discusses art auctions as "tournaments of value," and Geismar (2001) looks in depth at the malleability of constructions of price and provenance in tribal art auctions.

8. The price was "set" in 2006 at Christie's for a pair of Punuk-style eyeshades from a private collection that had been illustrated in *National Geographic*'s September 2004 map of "North American Indian Cultures."

9. Journal of E. O. Campbell, teacher of the Government School in Gambell from 1902 to 1905, p. 91, in manuscript file 148, Journals from St. Lawrence Island, vol. 2, Archives of Alaska and Polar Regions, Rasmuson Library, University of Alaska, Fairbanks.

10. During the early part of the twentieth century, many people saw "the Eskimo" as a cultural relic who had survived outside of civilization whose existence raised questions about possible relationships with "stone age" cultures of Western Europe (see de Laguna 1932, 1933).

11. Otto Geist papers, sections 5 (St. Lawrence Island Papers) and 7 (Notebooks), Archives of Alaska and Polar Regions, Rasmuson Library, University of Alaska, Fairbanks.

12. These conditions are outlined in the letter of Assistant Secretary of the Interior William Warne to University of Alaska President Moore, May 16, 1950 (Papers of the Director's Office, F. G. Rainey, Box 4/5, Arctic: Bering Straits Expedition, University of Pennsylvania Museum Archives, Philadelphia).

13. In 1999 a New York dealer paid a Savoonga digger this much for a three-inch Okvik-style ivory head. In 2001 another digger received considerably more for an extraordinary ivory winged object and matching harpoon foreshaft.

14. Belk (1995) discusses various motivations behind acts of collecting, and Plattner (1998) examines some of the economic paradoxes that guide fine art collecting.

15. Provenience information about where and how an object was found and an illustrious provenance or history of ownership both serve to increase market value, the first because it validates an object's authenticity and the second because a renowned provenance increases the social capital associated with an object.

16. Proposal for Withdrawal of National Historic Landmark Designation, signed by Edwin Bearss (Chief Historian) and Bennie Keel (Assistant Director, Archeology) of the National Park Service, February 5, 1987; Files on "Gambell Sites," National Park Service, Alaska Region Office, Anchorage.

17. For references by archaeologists to digging on St. Lawrence Island as "cultural cannibalism," see Knecht in Perala 1989: G7; Morton in Eppenbach 1991: D6; Yesner 1989. For a counter-interpretation, see Crowell 1985: 26.

Bibliography

Ackerman, Robert E. "Settlements and Sea Mammal Hunting in the Bering-Chukchi Sea Region." *Arctic Anthropology* 25, no. 1 (1988): 52–79.

Appadurai, Arjun. "Introduction: Commodities and the Politics of Value." In *The Social Life of Things: Commodities in Cultural Perspective*, ed. Arjun Appadurai, 3–63. Cambridge, U.K.: Cambridge University Press, 1986.

Arnold, Robert D. *Alaska Native Land Claims*. Anchorage: Alaska Native Foundation, 1978.

Bandi, Hans-Georg. *Eskimo Prehistory*. Trans. Ann E. Keep. College, Alaska: University of Alaska Press, 1969.

Belk, Russell W. *Collecting in a Consumer Society*. London: Routledge, 1995.

Bureau of Indian Affairs. *Gambell: Its History, Population, and Economy.* Billings, Mont.: Planning Support Group, 1977.

Blum, Orly. "The Illicit Antiquities Trade: An Analysis of Current Antiquities Looting in Israel." *Culture without Context,* issue 11 (Autumn 2002): 20–23.

Borden, Mrs. John. *The Cruise of the "Northern Light."* New York: Macmillan, 1928.

Bourdieu, Pierre. *Distinction: A Social Critique of the Judgement of Taste.* Trans. Richard Nice. Cambridge, Mass.: Harvard University Press, 1984.

Bronshtein, Mikhail M. "Structural and Artistic Features of 'Winged Objects': The Discussion Continues." In *Archaeology in the Bering Strait Region: Research on Two Continents,* ed. D. E. Dumond and R. L. Bland. Eugene: Department of Anthropology and Museum of Natural History, University of Oregon, 2002.

Bronshtein, Mikhail M., and Patrick Plumet. "Ekven: L'art préhistorique béringian et l'approche russe de l'origine de la tradition culturelle esquimaude." *Études/Inuit/Studies* 19, no. 2 (1995): 5–59.

Cacho, Silvia Fernandez, and Leonardo Garcia Sanjuan. "Site Looting and the Illicit Trade of Archaeological Objects in Andalusia, Spain." *Culture without Context,* issue 7 (Autumn 2000): 17–23.

Cammann, Schuyler. "Carvings in Walrus Ivory." *University Museum Bulletin* 18, no. 3 (1954): 2–31.

Christie's. *American Indian Art, January 12, 2006.* New York: Christie's, 2006.

Clifford, James. *The Predicament of Culture: Twentieth-Century Ethnography, Literature, and Art.* Cambridge, Mass.: Harvard University Press, 1988.

Cole, Douglas. *Captured Heritage: The Scramble for Northwest Coast Artifacts.* Seattle: University of Washington Press, 1985.

Collins, Henry B. "Archaeology of St. Lawrence Island." *Smithsonian Miscellaneous Collections* 96, no. 1 (1937).

———. "Eskimo Cultures." *Encyclopedia of World Art,* vol. 5, 2–28. New York: McGraw-Hill, 1959.

———. "Eskimo Art." *The Far North: 2000 Years of American Eskimo and Indian Art,* ed. Henry Collins, Frederica de Laguna, Edmund Carpenter, and Peter Stone, 1–15. Bloomington: Indiana University Press, 1973.

Condon, Richard. "Modern Inuit Culture and Society." In *Arctic Life: Struggle to Survive,* ed. Martina M. Jacobs and James B. Richardson, 149–73. Pittsburgh, Pa.: Board of Trustees, Carnegie Institute, 1983.

Crowell, Aron. *Archaeological Survey and Site Condition Assessment of St. Lawrence Island, Alaska, 1984.* Washington, D.C.: Smithsonian Institution and Sivuqaq Native Corporation, 1985.

de Laguna, Frederica. "A Comparison of Eskimo and Palaeolithic Art." *American Journal of Archaeology* 36, no. 4 (1932): 477–551.

———. "A Comparison of Eskimo and Palaeolithic Art." *American Journal of Archaeology* 37, no. 1 (1933): 77–107.

Douglas, Frederic H., and Rene d'Harnoncourt. *Indian Art of the United States.* New York: Museum of Modern Art, 1941.

Dumond, Don E., and Richard L. Bland (eds.). *Archaeology in the Bering Strait Region: Research on Two Continents.* Eugene: Department of Anthropology and Museum of Natural History, University of Oregon, 2002.

Eppenbach, Sarah. "Thieves of Time: Looting of Archaeological Sites Is Threatening Alaska's Native Heritage." *Anchorage Daily News*, September 8, 1991, D6–7.

Fay, Frances. "Mass Natural Mortality of Walruses (*Odobeus rosmarus*) at St. Lawrence Island, Bering Sea, Autumn 1978." *Arctic* 33, no. 2 (1980): 226–45.

Fitzhugh, William W., and Susan A. Kaplan, eds. *Inua: Spirit World of the Bering Sea Eskimo.* Washington, D.C.: Smithsonian Institution Press, 1982.

Geismar, Haidy. "What's in a Price? An Ethnography of Tribal Art at Auction." *Journal of Material Culture* 6, no. 1 (2001): 25–47.

Geist, Otto W., and Froelich Rainey. "Archeological Excavations at Kukulik, St. Lawrence Island, Alaska." *Miscellaneous Publications of the University of Alaska*, vol. 2 (1936).

Gerlach, Craig, and Owen K. Mason "Calibrated Radiocarbon Dates and Cultural Interaction in the Western Arctic." *Arctic Anthropologist* 29, no. 1 (1992):54–81.

Giddings, J. L. *Alaska Aboriginal Culture: The National Survey of Historic Sites and Buildings. Special Study. Theme XVI: Indigenous Peoples and Culture.* Anchorage, Alaska: USDOI/NPS, 1967.

Gilgan, Elizabeth. "Looting and the Market for Maya Objects: A Belizean Perspective." In *Trade in Illicit Antiquities: The Destruction of the World's Archaeological Heritage*, ed. Neil Brodie, Jennifer Doole, and Colin Renfrew, 73–87. McDonald Institute Monograph. Cambridge, U.K.: McDonald Institute for Archaeological Research, 2001.

Gill, David W. J., and Christopher Chippindale. "Material and Intellectual Consequences of Esteem for Cycladic Figures." *American Journal of Archaeology* 97 (1993):601–59.

Hopkins, David M. *The Bering Land Bridge.* Stanford, Calif.: Stanford University Press, 1967.

Hollowell, Julia J. *"Old Things" on the Loose: The Legal Market for Archaeological Materials from Alaska's Bering Strait.* Ph.D. diss., Indiana University, 2004.

Hrdlicka, Ales. "Anthropological Survey in Alaska." *Annual Report of the Bureau of American Ethnology* 46 (1930): 29–374.

Jenness, Diamond. *Archaeological Investigations in Bering Strait.* National Museum of Canada, Annual Report for 1926. Vol. 50, 1928.

Jorgensen, Joseph. *Oil-Age Eskimos.* Berkeley: University of California Press, 1990.

Karoma, N. J. "The Deterioration and Destruction of Archaeological and Historical Sites in Tanzania." In *Plundering Africa's Past*, ed. Peter R. Schmidt and Roderick J. McIntosh, 191–200. Bloomington: Indiana University Press, 1996.

King, Eleanor M., and Little, Bruce P. "George Byron Gordon and the Early Development of the University Museum." In *Raven's Journey: The World of Alaska's Native People*, ed. Susan A. Kaplan and Kristin J. Barsness, 16–53. Philadelphia: The University Museum, University of Pennsylvania, 1956.

Krech, Shepard III. *A Victorian Earl in the Arctic: The Travels and Collections of the Fifth Earl of Lonsdale, 1888–89.* Seattle: University of Washington Press, 1989.

Krupnik, Igor. *Arctic Adaptations: Native Whalers and Reindeer Herders of Northern Eurasia.* Hanover, N.H.: University Press of New England, 1993.

Mason, Owen K. "Archaeological Rorshach in Delineating Ipiutak, Punuk and Birnirk in NW Alaska: Master, Slaves or Partners in Trade?" In *Identities and Cultural Contacts in the Arctic*, ed. Martin Appelt, J. Berglund, and Hans C. Gullov, 229–51. Copenhagen: Danish National Museum and Dansk Polar Center, 2000.

Mathiassen, Therkel. "The Question of the Origin of Eskimo Culture." *American Anthropologist* 32, no. 4 (1930): 591–607.

Matsuda, David J. "The Ethics of Archaeology, Subsistence Digging, and Artifact 'Looting' in Latin America: Point, Muted Counterpoint." *International Journal of Cultural Property* 7, no. 1 (1998): 87–97.

Meldgaard, Jorgen. *Eskimo Sculpture*. New York: Clarkson N. Potter, 1960.

Melzer, Barry. "Bali, Alaska." *Anchorage Daily News*, December 10, 1995, C1+.

Merryman, J. H. "A Licit International Traffic in Cultural Objects." In *The 5th Symposium on the Legal Aspects of International Trade in Art: Licit Trade in Works of Art*, 3–46. Vienna: Institute of International Business and Law, 1994.

Morphy, Howard. "Aboriginal Art in a Global Context." In *Worlds Apart: Modernity through the Prism of the Local*, ed. D. Miller, 211–39. London: Routledge, 1995.

Moulin, Raymonde. *The French Art Market: A Sociological View*. Trans. Arthur Goldhammer. New Brunswick, N.J.: Rutgers University Press, 1987.

Northern Resource Management and Yeti Map Studio. *Resource Inventory: Volume One*. Unalakleet, Alaska: Bering Straits Coastal Resources Service Area Board and Bering Straits Coastal Management Program, October 1984.

Nuttall, Mark. *Protecting the Arctic: Indigenous Peoples and Cultural Survival*. Netherlands: Harwood Academic Publishers, 1998.

O'Keefe, Patrick J. *Trade in Antiquities: Reducing Theft and Destruction*. London: Archetype Publications and UNESCO, 1997.

Padgett, Tim. "Walking on Ancestral Gods: Using Mayan Ruins for Patios and Pigstys." *Newsweek*, October 9, 1989, 83.

Paredes Maury, Sofia. *Surviving in the Rainforest: The Realities of Looting in the Rural Villages of El Peten, Guatemala*. Foundation for the Advancement of Meso-American Studies, August 1998, <www.famsi.org/spanish/reports/95096/section05.htm>, accessed February 20, 2004.

Perala, Andrew. "Pillaging the Past." *Anchorage Daily News*, June 25, 1989, Arts: G1, 3, 7.

Plattner, Stuart. "A Most Ingenious Paradox: The Market for Contemporary Fine Art." *American Anthropologist* 100, no. 2 (1998): 482–93.

Ray, Dorothy Jean. *Artists of the Tundra and the Sea*. Seattle: University of Washington Press, 1980.

Ray, Dorothy Jean (ed.). "The Eskimo of St. Michael and Vicinity as Related by H. M. W. Edmonds." *Anthropological Papers of the University of Alaska* 13 (1966): 2.

Rudenko, S. I. *The Ancient Culture of the Bering Sea and the Eskimo Problem*. Trans. Paul Tolstoy. Toronto: University of Toronto Press for the Arctic Institute of North America (1961 [1947]).

Scott, Stuart. "St. Lawrence Island: Archaeology of a Bering Sea Island." *Archaeology* 37, no. 1 (1984): 46–52.

Staley, David P. "St. Lawrence Island's Subsistence Diggers: A New Perspective on Human Effects on Archaeological Sites." *Journal of Field Archaeology* 20 (1993): 347–55.

Weiner, Annette B. *Inalienable Possessions: The Paradox of Keeping-While-Giving*. Berkeley: University of California Press, 1992.

Yesner, David R. "Looting Gravesites Is 'Cultural Cannibalism.'" *Anchorage Daily News*, December 21, 1989, Forum: C11.

6

A Model Investigative Protocol for Looting and Anti-Looting Educational Program

ROBERT D. HICKS

Archaeologists combat looting—the illegal removal of archaeological resources—through expert assistance in legal prosecutions and public education. Expert assistance in combating international looting relies on protocols that incorporate a universal code of archaeological ethics. In many countries, criminal investigations and prosecutions occur incident to the discovery of illegal trafficking long after the initial removal of artifacts from their original contexts. The local law enforcement agencies that are best poised to interdict looting, however, despite the existence of protective legislation, are frequently inexperienced in or ignorant of the appropriate investigative techniques. These local officers may not understand the role of an archaeologist in constructing a criminal case. While many countries have laws that forbid or control the removal of archaeological resources, and while the enforcement of laws may require the involvement of an archaeologist to evaluate an application for an export permit, most countries have not evolved a protocol for the investigation and documentation of *the original looting event*. Global efforts to reach consensus on the legal measures for reducing the illicit trade in artifacts have overlooked an essential component for making the system work. Mostly ignored have been the frontline law enforcement officers who must detect wrongdoing, respond to reports of wrongdoing, and document and present a criminal case for prosecution.

This chapter presents a model universal investigative protocol for looting based on the one required in the United States under the Archaeological Resources Protection Act (ARPA) and outlines roles for archaeologists and law enforcement officers. The model protocol is intended as a field checklist and as a means for archaeologists and law enforcement officers to understand and complement one another's roles at the looting scene. As cultural resource experts, archaeologists should expect to guide and educate local law enforcement officers in an investigation. As experts in investigation, law enforcement officers guide archaeologists in collecting evidence to support a prosecution. Checklists for law enforcement and for archaeologists are given in appendixes A and B to this volume.

In addition to the model investigative protocol, this chapter presents a model experiential anti-looting educational program that emulates an actual law enforcement investigation under ARPA. The investigative protocol is intended to aid a criminal investigation; the model educational program is designed to heighten citizens' knowledge of looting and its consequences.

ARPA requires collaboration between archaeologists and law enforcement officers in mounting a prosecution, and the law's prosecutorial history has created a solid technical protocol of crime scene investigation and the recovery of archaeological evidence. In justifying the adoption of the ARPA protocol into a universal checklist, I suggest that major international protocols to reduce looting and trafficking in illegally excavated artifacts mirror ARPA's protective ethic respecting archaeological resources. Therefore, sufficient consensus now exists through international protocols and legal precedent about the criminality of looting to define a universal code of investigative practices. These practices include standards of evidence gathering, reliance on probable cause for arrests and searches, and documentation for prosecution. In particular, the UNESCO Convention on the Means of Prohibiting and Preventing the Illicit Import, Export and Transfer of Ownership of Cultural Property of 1970 (UNESCO Convention), and the UNIDROIT Convention on Stolen or Illegally Exported Cultural Objects (UNIDROIT Convention) of 1995, promote legislative recommendations to signatory nations that are congruent with ARPA, although neither protocol is as specific or detailed as ARPA. ARPA's ideals and perspective of protecting archaeological resources reflect these conventions. The same ideals also inform model laws respecting the conduct of war in avoiding the destruction of cultural resources, as in the most important war-related criminal code of the International Criminal Court, the Rome Statute. Global trafficking protocols will have little practical effect if the investigation and documentation of criminal acts at the scene of illicit excavations of archaeological resources are deemed unreliable. Further, a successful investigation means that the participation and collaboration of an archaeologist is paramount.

While the investigative protocol is intended for multinational use, the anti-looting educational program is intended for North American audiences. Derived from many ARPA cases, the educational program presents a prototypical American looter with typical methods and tools. The looting episode does not address other cultural contexts or the subsistence digging of artifacts. The educational program affords citizens, whether school children or adults, a comparison between the rigor of archaeological methods for constructing the past and the legal necessity for this rigor to support a prosecution. Archaeologists have been successful in developing experiential learning programs to acquaint nonspecialists with the aims, methods, and ethics of archaeology, usually through fieldwork or laboratory analysis. Archaeologists have been less successful, however, in using the same experiential methods to communicate the fragility of our material heritage and the laws protecting cultural resources or in providing precise guidelines for observing and reporting criminality. The model educational program is intended to remedy this lack.

INTERNATIONAL CONVENTIONS AND THE MODEL INVESTIGATIVE PROTOCOL

The UNESCO Convention of 1970 has become the modern datum for international efforts aimed at reducing the illicit trafficking in archaeological finds and, indirectly, reducing the destruction of archaeological sites. For those nations that have not become signatories, 1970 remains a de facto datum to resolve disagreements about, for example, the repatriation of artifacts that left their countries of origin under suspicious circumstances (if illegality cannot be proven) or where the countries of origin, for reasons of national consciousness or other concerns, now want artifacts in foreign collections returned. My discussion of the UNESCO and UNIDROIT conventions is intended to show that their goals and recommended strategies for protecting cultural resources encourage signatory nations to adopt common mechanisms to reduce looting and its consequences. The conventions therefore promote, at least in spirit if not in detailed recommendations, local enforcement of protection laws pursuant to common investigative techniques. The model investigative protocol is intended to bolster the abilities of local law enforcement at the looting scene. If the spirit and goals of the international conventions parallel those of ARPA, then I suggest that ARPA's rigorous investigative protocol, the basis of this model, ought to be emulated by other countries.

The UNESCO Convention preamble states: "It is incumbent upon every State to protect the cultural property existing within its territory against the dangers of theft, clandestine excavation, and illicit export." The UNESCO Convention explicitly asks signatory nations to enact legislation not only to reduce illicit import, export, and trade but also to reduce illegal excavations at the origin of the export/import problem. "Cultural property" is defined to include, among "objects of ethnological interest" and "property of artistic interest," "products of archaeological excavations (including regular and clandestine) or of archaeological discoveries" (UNESCO Convention, article 1, definitions (f), (g), and (c), respectively). Little else in the UNESCO Convention, however, speaks to the initial criminal act and the scene of the act. The UNESCO Convention speaks, rather, to broad prohibitions, import/export controls, and protocols for reclaiming artifacts that were illegally exported. Recognizing the deleterious economic and cultural conditions that result from the illegal trafficking in cultural property, the UNESCO Convention observes "that the illicit import, export and transfer of ownership of cultural property is one of the main causes of the impoverishment of the cultural heritage of the countries of origin of such property," thus requiring international cooperation to protect resources (UNESCO Convention, article 2, paragraph 1). Broadly, too, the UNESCO Convention encourages signatory nations to set up oversight and enforcement mechanisms or "national services where such services do not already exist, for the protection of cultural heritage, with a qualified staff sufficient in number for the effective carrying out" of listed functions (UNESCO Convention, article 5). The listed functions relate primarily to archaeological and archival practices but include drafting legislation and undertaking educational measures (UNESCO Convention, article 5). Not mentioned is the creation of responsive and knowledgeable law enforcement resources. The UNESCO Convention, then, supports anti-looting measures by promoting legal and educational remedies but offers no specific guidance in preparing local law enforcement officials to handle looting. Not surprisingly, international police training and management courses and conferences rarely feature sessions on looting investigations, and when these sessions appear, they are limited to discussions of export/import inspections.

Some of UNESCO's language, particularly definitions of relevant terms or concepts, has begun to appear in the laws of United Nations member states. Similar language, for example, has appeared in United States law, most notably in ARPA. For instance, UNESCO lists categories of "cultural property" to include "antiquities more than one hundred years old," "objects of ethnological interest," or "products of archaeological excavations" (UNESCO Convention, article 1, definitions (e), (f), and (c)). Unlike UNESCO, ARPA specifically addresses the root of looting criminality as the illegal excavation or removal of protected artifacts. ARPA carefully circumscribes the elements of criminality and broadly outlaws not only the illegal removal and trafficking of artifacts but also the destruction of the context within which the artifacts were found. Similarly, other nations have begun, slowly, to enact protection laws based on the spirit of the UNESCO Convention.[1] Nevertheless, specific guidance for local law enforcement officers at the archaeological crime scenes in foreign countries has been lacking.

Although many countries have enacted archaeological protection laws and many observe strict controls on excavation and ownership permits, within the international diplomatic arena the discourse on the destruction of archaeological sites remains mostly focused on export/import controls, trafficking, and the means by which nations can make claims against other nations for the return of pillaged goods. The 1995 UNIDROIT Convention reflects a developing concern since 1970 for protecting archaeological resources in their countries of origin. The UNIDROIT Convention addresses "illicit trade" and its damage, "and in particular . . . the pillage of archaeological sites and the resulting loss of irreplaceable archaeological, historical and scientific information." The UNESCO Convention addresses the restitution and return of illegally removed and trafficked cultural objects. On the return of objects, the UNIDROIT Convention recognizes that the removal of archaeological resources impairs one or more of the following interests: the physical preservation of an object or its context, the preservation of historic or scientific information, "the integrity of a complex object," or an indigenous community's traditional or ritual use of an artifact (UNIDROIT Convention, chap. 3, Article 5, paragraph 3). The UNIDROIT Convention, then, is sensitive to archaeological resources in their contexts and the ideological value that archaeological resources may present. The UNIDROIT Convention, perhaps more specifically than the UNESCO Convention, strengthens the argument for a model investigative protocol.

The UNESCO Convention asks signatory nations to set up "national services" for the "protection of the cultural heritage, with a qualified staff sufficient in number for the effective carrying out" of specified functions (UNESCO Convention, Article 5). None of the specified functions includes law enforcement, but Article 5 calls upon signatory nations to draft appropriate laws with enforcement mechanisms. Wisely, if not yet widely practiced, Article 5 promotes the establishment of national inventories of protected property and the appropriate institutions to preserve and protect archaeological resources.

War, however, has proved to be a major stimulus to drafting international standards and codes of criminal law and criminal evidence. International agreements on the conduct of war have condemned looting by military forces and thus indirectly support the promotion of model law enforcement practices in combating archaeological crime. The International Criminal Court has enacted the most important war-related criminal code, known as the Rome Statute.[2] The recent war in Iraq has highlighted the need to protect archaeological resources from destruction by military forces, and the influence of the Rome Statute may consequently become strongly felt in strengthening anti-looting laws and trafficking protocols (for further discussion see Gerstenblith, chapter 3; Prott, chapter 1). Further, the Rome Statute echoes provisions of the Second Protocol to the Hague Convention of 1954 for the Protection of Cultural Property in the Event of Armed Conflict, which confers criminal responsibility on those who destroy cultural property (protected under the Hague Convention) or who commit "theft, pillage or . . . acts of vandalism" to cultural property (Second Protocol, chap. 4, Article 15). The Rome Statute concerns the conduct of signatory states in wartime and requires these states to develop protocols for recovering and arranging for the return of illegally exported cultural property: "The requesting Party shall furnish, at its expense, the documentation and other evidence necessary to establish its claim for recovery and return" (Rome Statute, Article 7(b)). Without a creditable law enforcement investigation at the source of the criminal act, this standard cannot be met.

Several observations can be made on the international agreements and protocols with respect to improving the response to looting by local law enforcement officials. First, despite the strong language on the need to protect archaeological resources from pillage, the principal legal concern is the restriction of imports and exports. To make a case for illegal export, however, a court must determine that the contraband artifact came from the source country. The issue of provenience, therefore, is paramount. If a country can document provenience through a local investigation at the looting source, then the investigators could claim an uncontaminated crime scene and therefore show the poisonous tree from the initial looting through export.[3] Second, all of the legal conventions discussed promote an ideology of arrests and searches based on probable cause and on thorough documentation of a crime scene, accompanied by rigid standards of evidence collection for prosecution. The UNIDROIT Convention's three-year statute of limitations on restitution cases highlights an imperative for a timely, reliable, documented criminal investigation, beginning at the source of the crime.

The international legal conventions outlined presume that nations will create the apparatus needed for internal enforcement. That the model investigative protocol promotes the involvement of an archaeologist reflects a similar concern of these protocols that local, regional, or national museum authorities can aid in verifying, validating, attesting, or witnessing criminality and may be responsible for storing evidence.

The role of museums—which is where most archaeologists outside the academy may be found—has been reinforced by the International Council of Museums (ICOM). ICOM has promoted a clear message in condemning the illicit trade in cultural objects: "Museums should recognize the destruction of human and natural environments and loss of knowledge that results from the illicit servicing of the marketplace. The museum professional must warrant that it is highly unethical for a museum to support the illicit market in any way, directly or indirectly."[4] In fact, ICOM has enacted memoranda of understanding with the World Customs Organization and Interpol to affirm a collaboration to reduce illicit trafficking of archaeological materials, both documents pledging collaboration with law enforcement agencies.[5]

The model investigative protocol at the back of the book is intended to place the country of origin in the strongest possible legal posture to prosecute looting and trafficking and to show good cause that the subject of an illegal export claim ought to be returned to the source country. The protocol borrows from ARPA in the United States and affirms the principles of the UNESCO and UNIDROIT conventions and the Rome Statute. The UNESCO and UNIDROIT protocols identify three forms of illicit trafficking. First, artifacts may be excavated illegally or clandestinely. Second, they may be stolen from their rightful owner before export. Third, they may have been illegally exported from the country of origin but perhaps not excavated illegally. These three forms are not neatly separable, but to demonstrate any of these three forms of trafficking, officials require documentation of the looting at its source. The two components to the model investigative protocol, one for law enforcement and one for archaeologists, are based largely on investigative experience in the United States and as taught in archaeological resources protection courses at the Federal Law Enforcement Training Center (FLETC) in Glynco, Georgia.

Standard texts in criminal investigation, widely used in the United States and abroad, now feature sections on archaeological crime, which have been incorporated into the investigative protocol.[6] Some components of the checklist are standard in any intensive criminal investigation; some components are unique to archaeological crime, such as the need for a damage assessment. Archaeologists who participate in ARPA investigations initially shy from assessing commercial estimates of value, important to the damage assessment; to a non-archaeological, legal world, however, the commercial value is the only value with universal meaning. Although ARPA requires the collaboration of an archaeologist with law enforcement for prosecution, a U.S. legal feature, this collaboration is essential for any investigation to succeed in prosecution in any country. No law enforcement agency can be expected to retain the expertise required to handle archaeological debris and damaged or displaced artifacts, or to identify them, or to provide an assessment of value.

The model investigative protocol is designed to be carried in the field by investigators and archaeologists (see checklists in appendixes A and B). Because looting cases require meticulous, informed management, it is essential that the investigator and the archaeologist thoroughly understand one another's roles. The archaeologist has a very specific, legal role; may handle artifacts in crime cases as evidence, not as lab specimens; may have to document his or her movement through a crime scene; and may have to testify in court later. When cases arise, the archaeologist and investigator must meet, plan a strategy, and employ the investigative protocol as self-checklists. The appendix A and B checklists themselves become part of the case file. Ideally, when a defendant's lawyer tries to assail the investigative method, the prosecution can offer a view that the protocols are in universal use and their validity has been affirmed through many investigations.

A MODEL ANTI-LOOTING EDUCATIONAL PROGRAM

Archaeology is a popular subject. It is one of the few academic disciplines to coexist with a huge avocational or hobby audience, to stimulate a news media appetite, and to lure financial backing based on the adrenaline surge of discovery. Avocational archaeologists in the United States who are not professional archaeologists may conduct field activities indistinguishable from those of professional archaeologists, while others may be relic collectors or pothunters (terms commonly used in the United States), those who dig artifacts on private lands with or without permission. Other relic collectors or pothunters may dig artifacts from public lands, which is almost always illegal. In any case, diggers who do not have the requisite permissions are looters. Some avocational archaeologists explicitly set aside academic codes of ethics and aims and conflate professional excavation techniques with a personal drive to handle, smell, savor, or own the past. And some of these avocational archaeologists break the law in pursuit of their interest in the past. Others break the law to further private or commercial interests.

While most formal public archaeology educational programs aim to allow the public to touch the past through a personal encounter with artifacts, these same programs encourage citizens to learn that touching should be scientific and that systematic exploration of the object may involve an analysis of its substance or components, patterns of wear or use, possible repairs, or reuse in another form. Exploration of the object may even involve ideological dimensions by considering the artifact's symbolic meaning to the user. Formal public archaeology programs teach that an artifact's context, its vertical and horizontal position within the landscape, can yield crucial information about how an artifact was used. Proper documentation of an artifact's context provides the scientific basis for interpreting its meaning.

Public archaeology programs in the United States usually include a small component on another aspect of encountering artifacts: the stewardship of archaeological resources. State support for archaeology exists in tandem with commercial interests in promoting growth, with the construction of roads and houses, and in the renewal of areas subject to abandonment or decay. Advice on the stewardship of archaeological resources, then, usually includes written or Internet-based resources such as guides to owners of historic properties, information on grant resources to restore historic structures, or other practical advice for keeping an old thing more or less intact. Some national programs mention site stewardship only rarely, if at all. The popular *Teaching with Historic Places* program of the National Park Service's National Register of Historic Places and the National Trust for Historic Preservation hardly mentions conservation and preservation issues. Nothing is said about looting or vandalism.

Most educational materials and programs for young people may mention stewardship but rarely mention looting and trafficking.[7] Occasionally, relic collecting or pothunting may be described and discouraged. For example, an Iowa booklet on archaeology for children includes a short essay, "Archaeological Ethics and the Law," which points out that legitimate archaeology is destructive, necessitating a reliance on scientific excavation methods in order to recover not artifacts but *information*, precisely the loss defined by ICOM's *Code of Ethics*. Knowledge of context is vital (Schermer 1992: 33). The Iowa document is careful to observe that the destruction of archaeological sites occurs for many reasons, including urban development, farming, and erosion. Among many recommendations on how children can exercise responsible citizenship by respecting archaeological resources, pothunters receive special mention. Children are discouraged from becoming pothunters and are encouraged to report finds to authorities and not to buy or sell prehistoric artifacts; and if they already have artifact collections, to identify and record provenience. The Iowa program may typify educational materials in most states by placing pothunting among many destructive activities and in not making too explicit the connection that pothunting may be looting, and therefore criminal, and looters may be subject to arrest and trial.

A national educational booklet for young people, produced by the Society for American Archaeology (SAA), makes a similar broad argument about site stewardship and the need to protect and conserve archaeological resources (Few and Smith n.d.). SAA promotes archaeology as an adventure, a mystery, a process that represents "a way to develop informed, thoughtful, and responsible behavior toward all cultural resources, which are nonrenewable and irreplaceable" (Few and Smith: 3). The SAA lesson plan on stewardship involves a group discussion exercise in which students review biographical sketches of people of different cultures with different perspectives on the meaning and value of preserving the past. Some of the biographical sketches include pothunters and subsistence diggers. Each biographical sketch presents a dilemma that must be discussed. The dilemma may, for example, involve a commercial search for artifacts when no other economic alternatives seem available in an impoverished region (subsistence digging).

The most innovative educational programs in public archaeology involve some simulation or form of role-play. Rarely, however, do these programs feature criminal prosecutions or examine the sordid facets of the relic trade. The

Iowa educational booklet includes a role-play exercise, "Archaeology and You," in which the instructor assigns students roles of landowner, professional archaeologist, construction worker, and politician, to decide how best to manage archaeological resources under threat by construction (Schermer 1992: 34). A similar national educational effort in archaeology has promoted a model lesson plan that has students role-playing archaeologists and officials to understand the difference between contract and salvage archaeology.[8] Students must prepare and present a preservation case to a town council.

Despite the promotion of role-playing and group discussion to focus on stewardship, conservation, and pothunting (and sometimes looting), simulations that examine the criminal nature of pothunting and its legal consequences are virtually absent. Further, role-play and group simulations are rarely conducted during public archaeological programs. In some respects, role-plays are daunting pedagogical tools: role-plays and simulations require facilitators who are competent to conduct them and who can manage unintended outcomes. Further, role-plays are most effective with older students and adults in fully exploring moral, ethical, and legal issues, a situation that heightens the need to manage the exercises competently. Multiple ambiguities inherent in the nature of looting and trafficking militate against the value of simple lesson plans yet render experiential teaching methods ideal for the topic. Role-playing thrives on complexity, multiple viewpoints, and outcomes that may not neatly resolve all questions. One national education program in archaeology has promoted the construction of a mock trial, a legal role-play, but relies on the teacher to locate a criminal case record, modify it into an educational program, and then conduct it (MacDonald 1995). The same program, possibly self-conscious that this recommendation will find no takers, offers limp and palliative methods of dealing with looting: find a guest speaker or show a film (in this case, *Silent Witness* by the National Park Service).

For teaching citizens about looting, does role-play represent a method that engages interest, reveals the ambiguities and complexities, and illuminates yet another value to archaeology by showing how artifacts deprived of context rob us of our understanding of our collective past? Law enforcement training has long used experiential methods precisely because of the ambiguous and complex nature of legal decisions. After all, training that simulates the actual circumstances in which officers find themselves and have to make legal decisions offers the best avenue for learning skills and exercising them safely. FLETC pioneered training in the enforcement of archaeological protection laws because of the criminal provisions of two federal laws, ARPA and the Native American Graves Protection and Repatriation Act. The course, which places archaeologists, prosecutors, and archaeologists in a team, includes a crime scene practicum in which teams observe a looting in progress, halt it, process the scene for evidence, interrogate the looter, and prepare the case for prosecution. Clearly, law enforcement officers are accustomed to experiential training techniques, which, in the case of archaeological crime, work well in simulating an actual criminal case.

A one-off teaching experiment intended to create a similar investigative experiential training session for students proved popular and furnished the basis for the model anti-looting educational program. A few years ago, staff at a historic site asked for a guest lecture on looting for a summer field school for high school students. Instead of the lecture, the students, with minimal preparation, were presented with a looting in progress. Students were told only that a crime had just occurred on the historic property involving digging for artifacts without permission. The students were enlisted to help investigate the matter: roles were assigned of police officers, crime scene technicians, reporters, and others, and using a version of the actual federal investigative protocol, students had to mimic a criminal case. The opportunity to investigate a crime invariably attracts interest; a criminal investigation offers the theatricality of excitement, a plot, an adventure, and an unknown outcome.

The conflation of a criminal investigation with an educational program in archaeology becomes a powerful pedagogical tool. A mock looting investigation does require some planning and investment in minimal tools, but the management of the exercise is less demanding than having students participate in an actual excavation or in lab processing and conservation (see appendix C for an outline of the practical exercise, instructions for role-playing, and all associated paperwork). Further, students see very clearly how archaeological methods parallel those of law enforcement when processing a crime scene: officers process a scene in order to tell a story in court. Archaeologists "process" a site in order to narrate the past. The damage done by looting through wanton excavation tells no story about the past. The careful documentation of an excavation, however, permits the archaeologist to tell the story, or multiple stories, about the past. The careful documentation of a looted site permits law enforcement officers to construct the story of a crime.

Historic sites have used innovative educational methods to promote new ways of engaging with the past. Archaeologists and educators in public archaeology might learn from the sophisticated educational programs now found at historic sites. In the United Kingdom, for instance, the National Trust inaugurated the Young National Trust Theatre in which students participate as actors in site-specific dramatizations of historical circumstances, and most of these programs require the student actors to use appropriate artifacts (Woodhead and Tinniswood 1996). The National Trust finds that theater-based education allows students to engage with the past with more intensity and perspicacity than with traditional classroom methods.

Although not a formal theater program, the simulated looting investigation initially developed as a result of an invitation from a Virginia historic site does incorporate the essential ethos and methods of the National Trust for Historic Preservation project. The model furnishes an unusual or at least untried experiential teaching method—role-plays or simulations—to use in field schools for younger students and adults alike. As shown, experiential methods are common and successful in law enforcement training.

The model anti-looting program has certain limitations and implicit assumptions. First, the simulated looting is based on hundreds of cases prosecuted through ARPA. As such, the model program reflects looting behavior in the United States. The circumstances of the looting may not obtain in other countries. Second, the model program reflects legal practices in the United States. Third, the looter in the simulation represents a composite of many ARPA defendants, including those prosecuted under individual state laws. That the looter drives a car to the scene of the digging, carries a relic price guide, and leaves debris at the crime scene are common characteristics of people who have been caught and prosecuted for theft of and vandalism to archaeological resources in the United States. The description of the looter may not apply to non-U.S. contexts. The looter in the model program reflects a contradictory self-perception common to many pothunters, who see themselves as generally law-abiding but see their collecting practices as involving only minor, insignificant, and harmless criminality. To apply in non-U.S. contexts, the model program would require substantial modification. Fourth, the program presumes that the looting has occurred at a managed historic site. Most of the requests for the anti-looting program have come from historic site managers, as these venues frequently feature public archaeology programs that can incorporate experiential projects for wide audiences. Fifth, the model program incorporates several discussion questions that are designed to make explicit the dissonance between scientific archaeology and the unscientific collecting of artifacts. Part of this dissonance is reflected in language—for example, the use of the term "relic" as opposed to "artifact." Sixth, although the model program involves a criminal case with a regimented and meticulous investigation, the discussion questions are intended to stimulate participants to consider how archaeology and crime scene processing follow similar methods for different ends, the distinctions between archaeology and relic hunting, and how best to conserve or become a responsible steward for archaeological resources.

CONCLUSION

This chapter offers two complementary guides for practice: an investigative protocol for archaeologists and law enforcement officers in handling looting cases, and a simulated looting investigation based on the investigative protocol, designed as an educational syllabus for citizens, children or adults. The investigative protocol is designed for universal law enforcement practice and recognizes the importance of processing and documentation of looting cases at their source. The model educational program, however, as it is based on ARPA cases, reflects North American looting practices and would require much modification for use abroad. The educational program is intended to demonstrate similarities and differences in the methods and ends of scientific archaeology, legal nonscientific collecting, and looting and to show the place of archaeology in criminal law and procedure. When citizens, archaeologists, and law enforcement officers share a common understanding of the damage done to archaeological resources through looting and the exacting legal requirements to be observed in reconstructing the crime and prosecuting the offenders, then the common understanding can translate into public policy. Above all, these audiences develop a heightened sensitivity to the value of archaeological resources in constructing our own stories. An informed interpretation of artifacts gives them a voice: they may tell us about our ancestors, or they may accuse looters in court.

NOTES

1. For example, the definitions of archaeological resources found in the UNESCO Convention and in ARPA have been mimicked by European Council Regulation No. 3911/92 of December 9, 1992 on the Export of Cultural Goods.

2. *Rome Statute of the International Criminal Court*, 2002.

3. For example, this poisonous tree documentation from looting to export existed for Peruvian antiquities from Sipán (see Alva 1995).

4. *ICOM Code of Ethics for Museums*, 2004.

5. ICOM 2000a; ICOM 2000b.

6. For example, see Swanson et al. 1992.

7. Examples of popular public archaeology guides that are typical in their brief treatment of site protection include Moe 2000, which suggests a fifteen-minute class on archaeological protection law as part of a two-day workshop; and the Archeological Society of Virginia 1991, which suggests that teachers feature a debate about vandalism.

8. "To Dig or Not to Dig," Lesson Plan 1995: 8–10.

BIBLIOGRAPHY

Alva, Walter. *Sipán: Descrubrimiento e Investigacíon*. Lima, Peru: Walter Alva, 1995.

Archaeological Resources Protection Act (ARPA), 16 U.S.C. §§ 470aa *et seq.*, 1979 (United States).

Archeological Society of Virginia. *Archeological Resources for the Classroom: A Guide for Teachers*, Special Publication no. 27. Falls Church, Va.: Archeological Society of Virginia, 1991.

Few, Joan, and K. C. Smith (eds.). *Teaching Archaeology: A Sampler for Grades 3 to 12*. Washington, D.C.: Public Education Committee, Society for American Archaeology, n.d.

International Council of Museums (ICOM). *Memorandum of Understanding between the World Customs Organization (WCO) and the International Council of Museums (ICOM) on Combating the Illicit Traffic in Cultural Property*. Brussels: ICOM, 2000 (2000a).

———. *Memorandum of Understanding between the International Criminal Police Organization (INTERPOL) and the International Council of Museums (ICOM) on Countering the Theft of and Trafficking in Cultural Property*. Paris: ICOM, 2000 (2000b).

———. *Code of Ethics for Museums*. 1986, as amended, 2004. Paris: ICOM, 2004.

International Institute for the Unification of Private Law (UNIDROIT). *UNIDROIT Convention on Stolen or Illegally Exported Cultural Objects*. Rome: UNIDROIT, 1995.

MacDonald, Cathy. "Learning the Law." *Archaeology and Public Education* 5, no. 4 (1995): 12–13.

Moe, Jeanne M. *Project Archaeology Primer: The Complete Guide for Creating a State or Regional Program*. Dolores, Colo.: Anasazi Heritage Center, 2000.

Rome Statute of the International Criminal Court. Document A/CONF.183/9, 17 July 1998, amended and enacted July 1, 2002. <www.un.org/law/icc/statute/romefra.htm> (Italy).

Schermer, Shirley J. *Discovering Archaeology: An Activity Guide for Educators*. Special Publication, Office of the State Archaeologist. Iowa City: University of Iowa, 1992.

Swanson, Charles R., Neil C. Chamelin, and Leonard Territo. *Criminal Investigation*, 5th ed. New York: McGraw-Hill, 1992.

"To Dig or Not to Dig," Lesson Plan, *Archaeology and Public Education* 5, no. 3 (Spring–Summer 1995): 8–10.

United Nations Educational, Scientific and Cultural Organization. *Convention on the Means of Prohibiting and Preventing the Illicit Import, Export and Transfer of Ownership of Cultural Property*. Paris: UNESCO, 1970.

———. *Second Protocol to the Hague Convention of 1954 for the Protection of Cultural Property in the Event of Armed Conflict*. Paris: UNESCO, 1999.

Woodhead, Sally, and Adrian Tinniswood (eds.). *"No Longer Dead to Me": Working with Schoolchildren in the Performing and Creative Arts*. London: National Trust, 1996.

7

The Plunder of the Ulúa Valley, Honduras, and a Market Analysis for Its Antiquities

CHRISTINA LUKE AND JOHN S. HENDERSON

By 1941 Doris Stone (1941) had documented at least several hundred mounds at the site of Travesía in the Lower Ulúa Valley. Today approximately twenty-five mounds remain, most riddled with large trenches. These looters' pits make it impossible to walk comfortably across the former downtown area of the site. Over the last fifty years Ulúa-style polychrome ceramics, jades, and—the most desired—marble vases have drawn local recreational treasure hunters, collectors, professional looters, and international dealers to the site and others in its vicinity. Many of these objects now reside in collections around the world, while their contexts have been completely lost. The destruction of this single site is symptomatic of a much larger, indeed global, problem of commercially motivated archaeological destruction.

This chapter uses data from the Lower Ulúa Valley of northwestern Honduras to address the global problem of pillage (map 7.1). Our goal is to explore how systematically collected archaeological data provide an invaluable tool for exploring the result of pillage on the landscape. In the first half of the chapter we summarize the findings of archaeological projects geared toward documenting the cultural history of the region to give readers a framework. Next, the correlation between intense looting, development, and the art market in Honduras is explored. Building on these data we examine the international art market for a specific object type, Ulúa marble vases, and the intensity and aim of looting activities for these vases.

BACKGROUND ON PRE-COLUMBIAN LOOTING

Many scholars argue for a direct relationship between the plunder of archaeological sites and the market for antiquities. A few excellent quantitative studies have shown a strong relationship between pillage and the art market for specific objects (Chippindale et al. 2001; Elia 2001; Gill and Chippindale 1993; Nørskov 2002). The market for Pre-Columbian antiquities is no exception (Coggins 1995, 1998; Gilgan 2001). While some studies have shown that in Central America extreme poverty alone may promote looting (Matsuda 1998; Paredes

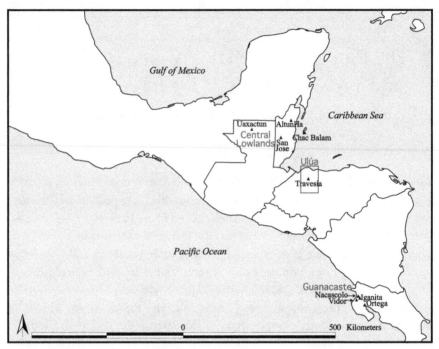

Map 7.1. The Ulúa Valley in greater Mesoamerica.

1998), others have argued convincingly that regardless of poverty levels, the antiquities market fuels looting simply because whatever their economic status, people know that collectors and dealers will pay a premium for fancy items and will risk breaking the law for potential monetary gain (Chase et al. 1996; Pendergast 1991; Pendergast and Graham 1983, 1989).

Certain areas in Mesoamerica have been and continue to be targeted for large-scale sculpture, jades, and fancy ceramics, particularly the central and southeastern Maya Lowlands (PAAG 1997; Quintaña et al. 1999; Reents-Budet 1994: 290–311). Correlations between media publication of spectacular finds and subsequent plunder, such as recent evidence of pillage at Copán and Dos Pilas, suggest that looters and those involved with trafficking and selling antiquities may follow media reports and gear their efforts accordingly.[1]

U.S. Legislation and Honduras

The 1972 Pre-Columbian Monumental or Architectural Sculpture and Murals Act (Public Law 92-587) provides one legislative tool to thwart the illicit traffic in large-scale objects into the United States. A second is the Cultural Property Implementation Act, implementing the 1970 UNESCO Convention in the United States, which has resulted in bilateral agreements with a number of

Central and South American countries (see Papa Sokal and Gerstenblith, this volume, for further discussion of the CPIA). These agreements place import restrictions on certain categories of materials and recognize the cultural property laws of the respective Latin American countries. An agreement with Honduras went into force on March 12, 2004. In addition to the CPIA, the National Stolen Property Act (NSPA) provides for protection of those trafficking in stolen materials. As the McClain and Schultz cases have shown, the NSPA recognizes national ownership laws of other countries, making it illegal to sell objects that have been stolen—from a museum or archaeological site—from their country of origin, provided that the country has a national ownership law.

Untrue statements on U.S. Customs declarations may also lead to confiscation of materials and to prosecution. During a U.S. Customs search in Miami in January 1998, 279 Pre-Columbian artifacts, subsequently determined to be from the Naco Valley of northwestern Honduras, were seized. Douglass Hall of Columbus, Ohio, was convicted in October 2002 of smuggling and making false declarations to U.S. Customs officials (Mayhood 2002). The artifacts were repatriated to Honduras in September 2003. At this time those responsible for helping to organize the transfer of these materials from Naco to Miami via the Bay Islands are being prosecuted in Honduras.

HONDURAN LEGISLATION

Formal protection of national patrimony in Honduras began in 1900 with Decree 127, making it illegal to export objects from Copán or other ruins in the republic but allowing for their exploration, excavation, and study for purposes of scholarship. Since then, Honduran law has become stronger (Agurcia 1984). In 1984 the Honduran Institute of Anthropology and History (Instituto Hondureño de Antropología e Historia, IHAH) became the executor of the Law for the Protection of Cultural Patrimony (the legislative decree *Decreto No. 81-84*). In 1997, Honduran Decree 220-97 clarified further that the state was the official owner of all cultural patrimony; the law is retroactive. And while objects may be held in existing private collections, upon the death of the collector all materials must be transferred to the state; they may not be inherited.[2] Under these various decrees, formal permission from the government has been required to excavate as well as export materials from the country since 1900.

CONTEXT: LOWER ULÚA VALLEY OF NORTHWESTERN HONDURAS

The fertile alluvium of the Lower Ulúa Valley (map 7.2) in northwestern Honduras supports a rich and varied flora and terrestrial and riverine fauna, including a range of large cats and monkeys as well as deer, tapir, and manatee. The

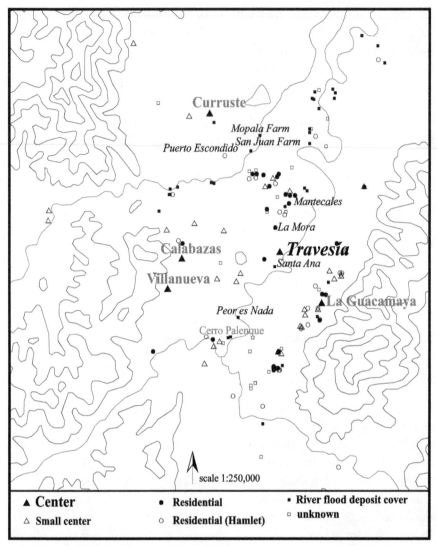

Map 7.2. Lower Ulúa Valley sites discussed in the text.

very size of the Lower Ulúa valley—some 2,400 square kilometers, embracing a substantial range of environmental conditions—highlights the importance of regional variability. At the time of the Spanish invasion, and probably in earlier times as well, valley societies were major producers of cacao. Shell and other marine resources are available in the north; nearby mountains are still home to the quetzal; there is a local obsidian source on the southwestern edge of the valley, and jade from the Motagua valley is only a little more distant. The Chamelecón, Ulúa, and Comayagua rivers that flow into the valley provide natural routes of communication to Copán (and the Maya highlands beyond) and to central, southern, and eastern Honduras and greater lower Central America. The Gulf of Honduras provides easy access to the central Maya Lowlands and on to the Yucatán Peninsula and the Gulf Coast of Mexico. It is not surprising that a region so favored by nature was the home of prosperous societies actively engaged with their neighbors.

HISTORY OF INVESTIGATIONS IN THE VALLEY

In 1979, IHAH, recognizing the need for an assessment of sites in the valley, initiated the Proyecto Arqueológico Sula (PAS) under the direction of John S. Henderson at Cornell University, later with the collaboration of Ricardo Agurcia. The goal of PAS was to compile a working inventory of sites in the valley to put IHAH in a position to manage them as cultural resources (Henderson 1984, 1988).

With active fieldwork from 1979 to 1988, PAS conducted a full survey of the valley using 1:20,000 scale stereoscopic air photos (Sheptak 1982) and on-the-ground survey of more than 15 percent of the 2,400-square-kilometer valley area. For the purposes of site registration and cultural resource management, heuristic sites were defined and numbered. These sites range in size from a single surface scatter of a few meters square to an area approximately one kilometer square covered by continuously distributed clusters of mounds that represent collapsed structures. Standard survey data included maps and surface collections for chronological assessment. Excavation provided the means to assess the occupational and depositional history of individual sites, including both deeply stratified sites and complex architectural centers.

Along with an inventory of archaeological resources in the valley, PAS developed a chronological framework based on seriation of ceramic complexes and external crossties, reinforced by radiocarbon dates (Beaudry-Corbett et al. 1993). Using the chronological control provided by this ceramic sequence, PAS produced the first systematic data relating to settlement patterns in the Ulúa Valley and documented the nature of its ancient environments and their impact on land use (Henderson 1988).

Building on the basis provided by PAS, the Proyecto Arqueológico Valle Inferior del Río Ulúa (PA-VIRU), initiated in 1992 under the direction of John S. Henderson and Rosemary A. Joyce, adopted a problem-oriented approach focusing on economic and social relations among sites located in the central floodplain of the valley. Excavations by PA-VIRU from 1992 to the present have extended our knowledge of the occupational history of the region back in time, while providing detailed information about social relations in the central valley and the northern shore of Lake Yojoa.

The documented occupational history of the valley now extends from Early Formative complexes represented at the site of Puerto Escondido, beginning before 1500 B.C., to the Colonial period (ca. A.D. 1521). Ties with communities along the Pacific Coast of Guatemala and Chiapas reflected in pottery are strong from the very beginning of the sequence, continuing through the late centuries between 1100 and 700 B.C., when valley communities were part of the greater Olmec world (Joyce and Henderson 2001).

During the centuries just before and after the time of Christ, valley communities increasingly constructed large platforms to support special buildings, a development that might be taken to reflect increasing societal complexity. Usulutan-style ceramics, a hallmark of this period, are produced throughout the region, and demonstrate ties with neighbors in El Salvador and Guatemala. The majority of excavated sites with visible surface architecture have occupations continuing through the Late Classic Ulúa phase.

The Ulúa phase (A.D. 500–850) saw the florescence of always prosperous Ulúa societies. It was a period of maximum population and maximum prosperity; communities were more closely spaced and more differentiated than ever before, and sites are found in all geomorphological zones. Our current understanding of the Late Classic settlement of the Lower Ulúa Valley is that it consisted of multiple communities, not united under a single political center (Henderson 1992b; Joyce 1991; Joyce and Hendon 2000). A handful of regional centers—Travesía, Currusté, la Guacamaya, Villaneuva—were spaced throughout the valley with smaller settlements, including rural farmsteads, perhaps homesteads of wealthy farmers, located in between these centers. The main center of Travesía boasted stone-faced public civic-ceremonial architecture, including a ballcourt, central plazas, and stelae surrounded by hundreds of smaller residential buildings (fig. 7.1; Joyce 1983, 1991; Stone 1941). A range of imported raw materials (shell, jade, and obsidian), imported pottery, and exported Ulúa pottery and stone vases—notably the wonderfully painted Ulúa polychrome ceramics and elaborately carved Ulúa marble vases (figs. 7.2, 7.3)—document valleywide social networks and external connections with more distant communities of lower Central America and the central Maya Lowlands (Henderson 1992a; Joyce 1986; Luke 2002a; Luke and Tykot 2002).

The ninth through twelfth centuries saw sweeping changes in the valley, as the social, economic, and political arrangements of the Late Classic period were replaced by new patterns in the Terminal Classic period, notably the rise of Cerro Palenque (Joyce 1991) as the valley's dominant center.

Few Postclassic (A.D. 1300–1521) settlements of any kind have been documented—in part because monumental architecture was rare; houses were often built directly on the ground, not elevated on platforms; and many sites

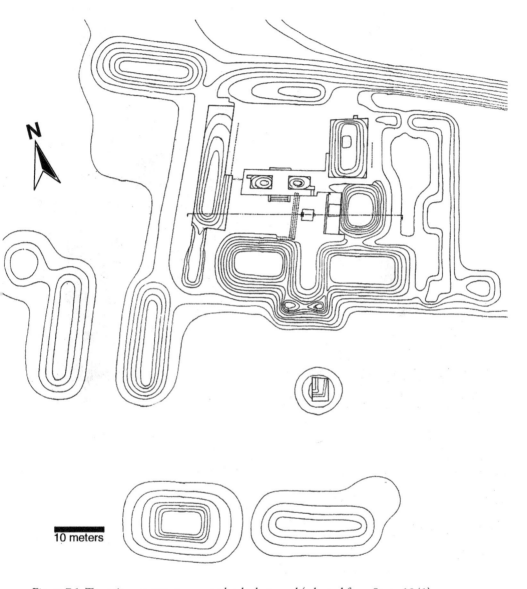

Figure 7.1. Travesía core area, now completely destroyed (adapted from Stone 1941).

have been buried by river alluvium or modern settlement—but all indications are that settlement hierarchies virtually disappeared during the eleventh and twelfth centuries. The archaeological record and ethnohistoric evidence demonstrate that substantial prosperous towns had reappeared in the Lower Ulúa region by the fifteenth century. In the sixteenth century, valley societies were linked to those of the Yucatán Peninsula by trade and other types of social ties

Figure 7.2. Ulúa marble vase, courtesy of the Middle American Research Institute, Tulane University (H.I.3 38.58: 18.8 cm H, 16.7 cm dia).

(Henderson 1979), and there were long-standing ties with the peoples to the south in lower Central America as well (Joyce 1986, 1993).

SITE DESTRUCTION

Pillage, increasingly compounded by development, has been endemic in most regions of central and western Honduras for decades. By the late 1970s site destruction in the Lower Ulúa Valley was accelerating, with especially intensive looting around Travesía (Agurcia 1984; Henderson et al. 1982).

Under Honduran law a cultural resource assessment must be carried out prior to the construction of buildings, roads, or other projects. However, the

Figure 7.3. Ulúa marble vase, Museo Etnografico Castello D'Albertis (15.4+ H, 16 cm dia; drawn by C. Luke).

possibility of uncovering salable antiquities from an ancient site scheduled for salvage excavations prior to development, along with the desire to avoid construction delays, anticipating lengthy and costly mitigation procedures, results in locals illicitly looting sites, often with heavy machinery. The focus of site destruction prior to development—the core area of mounds—demonstrates local familiarity with the archaeology of the region. This situation makes separating the results of development and systematic looting difficult.

Looting in the central valley was and remains highly organized, because so many sites in the region can be plundered for artifacts that command high prices on the antiquities market. In addition to the location of sites, test excavations, and artifact analyses, PAS recorded archaeological features at each site, including land use and site condition, such as the extent of alteration of the landscape from farming, construction, and pillage. The data collected by PAS indicate that some 60 percent of the more than 507 sites located in the valley show varying degrees of pillage; 15 percent have been completely destroyed (fig. 7.4). The majority of the undamaged sites survive intact only because they have been buried under alluvium. Some of the most horrid instances of plunder are from the sites of Travesía, Calabazas, and Gualjoquito. These examples served as a catalyst for site documentation and assessment and increased site protection, including implementation of the 1984 national legislation.

Reports from Travesía and the surrounding area in the 1970s and 1980s describe a highly developed system of looting. Farmers and their families, as well as professional looters and collectors, systematically (and not clandestinely) pros-

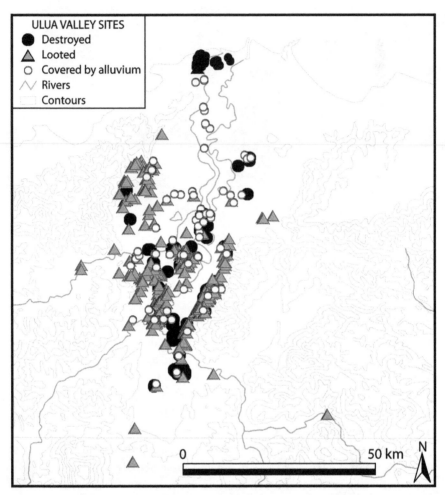

Figure 7.4. Percentage of pillaged sites in the valley.

pected for polychromes, marble vases, and jade. These activities demonstrate local knowledge of the market for antiquities from the Ulúa Valley. Looting and bulldozing to prepare the property for sugar cane production destroyed the civic core of monumental structures documented by Doris Stone in the 1940s along with most of the hundreds of surrounding residential structures. Today it is impossible to excavate a one meter by one meter excavation trench at the site without stumbling over a plundered area (fig. 7.5).

Calabazas, a major Classic period site, was almost entirely destroyed by construction of an industrial complex in the early 1980s, despite the fact that it had been added to IHAH's newly established list of protected sites (figs. 7.6, 7.7, and 7.8 depict the sequence of looting). The developers began to bulldoze the

Figure 7.5. Looted Travesía (photograph by the author).

property (reportedly at night, using floodlights) within hours of acquiring it from the previous owners. By the time IHAH officials arrived to stop the work (within days), all but one of the twenty large platform mounds had been leveled. Sanctions were limited to requiring the developer to finance salvage excavation of a few surviving small structures.

Gualjoquito, a large Classic period site in the middle drainage of the Ulúa River, was pillaged at about the same time. The landowner, an avid collector of Ulúa polychromes, employed heavy construction equipment to cut away the hearts of a series of large platform mounds (leaving the shells facing the access road, so that the mounds would appear undamaged to officials passing the site). Because the collector had taken archaeology courses from an archaeologist affiliated with IHAH, the government decided that the case was particularly egregious and sought the maximum sanctions, including confiscation of the part of the property containing the site, confiscation of the part of the collection that was then in Honduras, and heavy fines. Honduran courts eventually reduced the sanctions.

These examples document some of the most extreme cases of looting and confirm the drastic consequences of pillage. Pillage around these centers as well as in more remote areas of the valley continues today. The recent Ohio smuggling case already mentioned, continued looting at Tenampúa in the Comayagua region south of the Ulúa Valley, and incidents of looting at Copán demonstrate that the problem is not confined to the Ulúa region. Local IHAH officials do their best

Figure 7.6. Sequence of looting at Calabazas: mounds in plaza group (photograph by the author).

Figure 7.7. Sequence of looting at Calabazas: looting of mounds (photograph by the author).

Figure 7.8. Sequence of looting at Calabazas: final stages of site leveling (photograph by the author).

with their limited resources to educate local communities, particularly school children, and to thwart the widespread looting, but the market for Honduran antiquities in Europe and the United States creates a constant temptation.

MARKET FOR HONDURAN ANTIQUITIES

With an understanding of the cultural history, the condition of sites, and the focus of looting in the Ulúa valley, we now turn to the market for Honduran antiquities. Over the last thirty years a focus on "Maya" objects has driven the Central American antiquities market. Both sculpture and ceramics with hieroglyphic texts are among the highest-priced items, though fancy jades are also very desirable. The absence of written texts, in a narrow sense, in the Ulúa region—located on what is traditionally defined as the boundary between the Maya world and cultural groups placed in lower Central America—has given rise to the perception that it was peripheral to the Maya world, or "Mayoid" (Joyce 1993). Following this trend in scholarship, antiquities from the Ulúa Valley have usually commanded lower prices than those from the rest of the Maya World, although they are often labeled "Maya" by the trade.

As Gilgan (2001) notes in her research on the Belizean market, and as we have found in our study, provenience—the archaeological context—is notably absent for archaeological materials from Mesoamerica listed by Sotheby's. Gilgan's 2001 study included a broad survey of Sotheby's sales from 1971 to 1999. During this period, at least forty-four objects with a stated provenience of Honduras and 107 with a stated provenience of the Ulúa Valley were auctioned. Only Jaina

(451 objects), the Petén (120 objects), and the Maya Lowlands (177 objects) had greater numbers of auctioned artifacts, indicating that material from the Ulúa Valley is indeed desired by the high-end market. Our own research shows that the most sought-after materials from the valley are Ulúa-style polychromes and marble vases (Luke 2002b).

Marble vases provide the focus of this market analysis for several reasons. First, they are limited in number in the archaeological record, and their stylistic qualities make them easy to track on the antiquities market. Second, spatial distribution and chemical analyses indicate centralized production at one site, Travesía (Luke 2002a), which allows us to explore the correlation of marble vase sales and plunder of a specific region, if not site.

These Late Classic marble vases represent one of the few luxury goods produced in the valley that are restricted to high-status and/or special-purpose contexts (see Luke 2002a; Stone 1938). Based on marble vase, polychrome, and settlement data, the period of marble vase production corresponds to a particularly prosperous time at Travesía. Of the marble vases with known contexts, 20 percent are from Travesía and the neighboring site of Santa Ana, more than from any other single site or region. The distribution of marbles vases and the results of chemical analyses of the vases document centralized production at Travesía with a preferred procurement area located on the southeastern valley edge (Luke 2002a; Luke and Tykot 2002, 2001).

Ulúa-style marble vases are exquisitely carved from a single block of white marble with an exterior program sculpted in relief. This program almost always includes the hallmark scrolls, which often form the building blocks of profile and/or frontal figures framed by geometric borders. Most vases have two anthropomorphic handles placed opposite each other on the exterior of the vase and either tripod or ring supports (Luke 2002a; Schaffer 1992; Stone 1938). The known corpus of vases in museum and excavation collections in Central America, the United States, and Europe is approximately 130. Including those known to be in private collections in the United States and Central America, the number reaches almost two hundred.

Collecting of Ulúa marble vases began in the late nineteenth century. J. T. E. Hamy (1896), G. B. Gordon (1898, 1920, 1921), and E. G. Squier were among the earliest to recover Ulúa marble vases in Honduras. In the early twentieth century, Doris Stone (1938) excavated a large number in the central Ulúa Valley and from sites in Olancho and Costa Rica. These early collections were transported to museums and other institutions in Europe and the United States.[3] Over the last fifty years a number of vases from private collections, including museum collections, have circulated on the antiquities market. Professional excavations over the same period of time have recovered a limited number of fragments and a few isolated finds of whole vases; that is, these vases are extremely rare in the archaeological record, but more and more prevalent in the public marketplace.[4] We track the changes in marble sales, taking into consideration the year, price, and style.

There has been one museum exhibition devoted to the marbles: *On the Edge of the Maya World*—a 1992 show at the Museum of Fine Arts in Houston, Texas, by then curator Anne-Louise Schaffer (1992). Ninety-five whole vases from public institutions and private collections were exhibited.[5] A 1938 publication (Stone 1938) included the then known corpus of approximately twenty-five vases, and a more recent study (Luke 2002a, 2002b, 2003b) covers 155 vases, including those fragments known from excavations.

A review of Sotheby's auction catalogs from the 1970s and 1980s shows a limited number of vases in the Ulúa marble style.[6] It is during the 1990s and the last four years (2000–2004) that sales of marble vases have increased dramatically (see Aegean Antiquities 2002; Arte Primitivo 2002a, 2002b, 2003; Barakat Gallery 2002a, 2002b; Galerie Mermoz 2002; Harmer Rooke Galleries 1993; Sotheby's 1979, 1981, 1982, 1983, 1989, 1990, 1991a, 1991b, 1992a, 1992b, 1994a, 1994b, 1995, 1996, 1997a, 1997b, 1998a, 1998b, 1999a, 1999b, 2000a, 2000b, 2001, 2002). Marble vases have been auctioned forty-three times over the last thirty years.[7] Twenty-three have sold. Between 1972 and 1989 Sotheby's auctioned at least seven vases. Since 1990 Sotheby's has auctioned another twenty-three vases, other galleries at least eleven. The spring 2004 New York auction included two vases.[8] The vast majority of those auctioned have "surfaced" in the past decade.[9] Based on these numbers and museum accession archives of marble vase acquisitions, approximately 35 percent of the known corpus of marble vases in the Ulúa style has been traded in the very recent past.[10] And of those vases in museums with post-1950 accession dates, many have extravagant travel histories, usually including circulation to collectors and dealers in Europe, particularly Switzerland, Belgium, and France (Luke, archival and museum research, 1995 to present).

The data clearly show a growing trend in marble vase sales at public auction and in galleries and acquisitions by museums, particularly after 1992, the year of the MFA Houston exhibition. Prices paid range from U.S. $3,000 to $52,500, with an average of $15,000 and the median at $26,400. In 1972, one vase sold for $23,000, and this remained the price ceiling until an upswing in 1998; since then at least two vases have commanded prices in the $50,000 range, while the asking prices have been as high as $65,000.[11]

The vast majority of the other items from the region that are auctioned are Ulúa-style polychromes, which have traditionally sold for less than "Maya" polychromes.[12] This trend is slowly changing, particularly for certain types of Ulúa polychromes. Notably, in 2000 Sotheby's auctioned Red Class polychromes for U.S. $20,000–$30,000 and recent on-line prices for Red Class polychromes at Barakat have been as high as $35,000, almost seven times the normal price range for such material. This trend corresponds to increased scholarship, particularly published research linking Ulúa polychromes, in this case Red Class, to traditions in Belize, as referenced by Sotheby's, giving objects with a more direct link to the central Maya Lowlands greater monetary value.[13]

FAKING MARBLE VASES AND THE MARKET

The final aspect of looting and the antiquities trade for Ulúa-style marble vases is the increasing number of forgeries. Forgeries of Pre-Columbian material are not uncommon, and many date to the early 1900s, if not earlier (Pasztory 1982). The data on fakes of marble vases indicate a recent increase in forgery production and/or appearance on the market. Fakes are sold in private galleries, on-line, and at the major auction houses.

Those Ulúa-style marble vases in older museum and excavation collections fall nicely into five typological groups with at least two examples in each group or subgroup (Luke 2002a). If we include vases from private collections exhibited in the 1992 MFA Houston show, those held privately but on view for the public at museums, and recent acquisitions by museums, at least five other subgroups appear. In all cases, these vases were acquired from private collections. Furthermore, those auctioned in the last ten years rarely fit the established typology. Examples of these various new subgroups and unique vases are not found in excavated or older collections, particularly those established prior to 1950. Thus, either looters pillage areas with specific styles not represented in professionally excavated contexts or these new stylistic groups represent forgeries. Erroneous combinations of early border and support types with stylistically late iconographic programs as well as poor carving and sculpting of the imagery provide clear evidence for modern forgeries.[14]

One suspect class consists of vases with flat bases, a single row of scrolls, and a single bird handle. One of the best-known vases, from the collection at the University of Pennsylvania Museum of Archaeology and Anthropology, which was accessioned during the early 1900s, has a single feline handle, but none of the single-handled bird vases has the same fine carving. The crude blocklike carving style characteristic of so many of these single bird handles is unlike the fluid soft lines and almost butterlike carving on the handles of vases with provenience. Furthermore, the unusually large size of some of these vases also calls their antiquity into question. Many are attributed to "Costa Rica." While the region of Guanacaste was in close contact with the Ulúa Valley during the Classic period and marble vases are known from sites in the region, no professional excavation has ever recovered a vase with a single bird handle in Costa Rica or anywhere else (Luke 2002a).[15]

Other vases that have surfaced in the last ten years exhibit extremely rude blocklike or sloppy sculpting of the main program and handles, again not characteristic of the known vases from earlier collections or those with site provenience. There is also an abundance of vases on the market with composite feline handles and ring bases, which correspond to one of the five stylistic groups documented in the known corpus; apart from the one-handled examples, vases with bird handles are rare on the market. And, when not blocklike in carving style, many have the appearance of having been melted. Attention to the strict geometric program and careful proportions executed by Classic period Ulúa artisans is clearly not represented in this corpus.

DISCUSSION

Looting in the Lower Ulúa Valley continues at an astounding pace. San Pedro Sula has been a hub for foreign collectors with direct flights into Houston, Atlanta, New Orleans, and Miami, among other places. A direct boat between New Orleans and Puerto Cortes, Honduras, ferried much material out of the region over the years.[16] That is, getting material out of the Ulúa Valley was once relatively easy, given the bustling nature of the region and easy access to the United States. IHAH and local police now monitor the traffic as best they can, but the scale of the looting and market make it increasingly difficult.

What is clear from the market data is that material from the Ulúa Valley is among the most sought after on the Pre-Columbian antiquities market. The systematic looting at the site of Travesía and the neighboring vicinity, along with reports by locals of U.S. collectors making trips to El Porvenir and San Manuel (the nearest towns to Travesía) in the 1970s and 1980s specifically asking for marbles, provide evidence for a direct correlation between demand for marbles by museums and private collectors and the focus and scale of pillage. Looting at Travesía for marble vases increased dramatically during the period when more and more marble vases appeared in galleries and when they were stolen from well-known collections. Prices have continued to rise, and pillage continues. Looters know that marble vases fetch higher prices than other objects and have geared their digging accordingly over the years, in many cases selling to select dealers.[17]

Price increases for both marble vases and polychrome ceramics appear to be driven by museum exhibitions and academic publication.[18] Sales and prices of Ulúa material increased noticeably after Schaffer's 1992 exhibition and Reents-

Budet's 1994 stylistic link between the Ulúa region and Belize in her well-illustrated book *Painting the Maya Universe*. And since the early 1990s there has been a noticeable increase in the number of fake marble vases appearing on the market. The overall number of forgeries may be as high as half of the known corpus of two hundred.

Conclusion

Archaeological research in the region continues with foreign archaeologists and IHAH constantly working against the combined forces of development and pillage. The local IHAH office, located fifteen minutes from San Pedro Sula in La Lima, is charged with managing a research collection, working with foreign archaeological projects, conducting salvage operations in the valley, monitoring sites and the sale of antiquities, enforcing mitigation procedures, and implementing public education programs. With a staff of three and limited budgetary resources, the local IHAH office is overwhelmed by the current pace of development and looting.

As archaeology in Honduras becomes more contested as a reflection of national identity and an increasingly important tourism resource, local people do become more involved. Designated as the "periphery," Honduras constantly struggles with relating to its Maya past, most celebrated and promoted by Copán, just miles from the Guatemalan border. Honduras has much more to offer than just the Maya or Copán. Its multiethnic past with links to both the central Maya Lowlands and the regions of lower Central America make it unique. While many continue to focus on Copán with money for site development, museums, and site protection, other areas of Honduras receive little attention and little governmental or international tourism funding but remain a focus for looters. Clearly, the antiquities trade values items from the Ulúa Valley more and more. The potential for understanding its incredibly rich and complex past diminishes in proportion to the intensity of continued looting.

Acknowledgments

We would like to thank the Instituto Hondureño de Antropología e Historia for the opportunity to conduct this research in Honduras. We thank also the many organizations that have funded various aspects of work in the valley: the National Science Foundation, Foundation for the Advancement of Mesoamerican Studies, Geological Society of America, and departments, centers, and fellowships from Cornell University.

NOTES

1. In 1997 *National Geographic* (Stuart 1997) ran a special section on royal tombs at Copán. Several months later, the royal tombs were brutally looted (Agurcia 1998). In September 2002, a series of newspaper articles reported a splendid hieroglyphic stairway at Dos Pilas (Gugliotta 2002; Wilford 2002). In December 2002, sections of stairway were cut away using diamond saws and were illicitly exported out of the area (Ministerio de Cultura y Deportes de Guatemala, 2002).

2. This is one of the toughest national ownership laws in all of Central America. In Guatemala and El Salvador it is illegal to transport materials outside the national boundaries without permission from the government, but it is legal to transfer objects within the borders, provided that the collector notifies the government of the transfer and the current location of the antiquity. In both countries, antiquities may be inherited (see Guatemala decree 26-97 and El Salvador decree 513).

3. The Peabody Museum of Archaeology and Ethnology at Harvard University, the Middle American Research Institute at Tulane University, University of Pennsylvania Museum of Archaeology and Anthropology, the Museum of the American Indian, the American Museum of Natural History in New York, the Museum für Volkerkunde in Berlin, Germany, and the British Museum in London are among those institutions that currently hold these early collections.

4. Systematic professional excavations at the sites of Puerto Escondido, Mantecales, and Cerro Palenque have excavated one definite Ulúa-style marble vase fragment with three other marble and alabaster fragments suggestive of other stone vase carving traditions (Luke et al. 2003). Outside the valley, looting at the site of El Abra in La Florida valley included an Ulúa marble vase, and looting at the site of Tenampúa produced several extremely fine fragments of Ulúa-style marble vases; salvage excavations in Orica, Olancho, also included an Ulúa marble vase. In the central Maya lowlands, Ulúa marble vase fragments were recovered from Uaxactun, San José, and Altun Ha (see Luke 2002a). Dealers claim to have vases from the regions of El Salvador and Nicaragua, unsubstantiated by professional excavations.

5. A catalogue of the exhibition has never been published.

6. To ensure accuracy our data were compared with the data collected by Elizabeth Gilgan.

7. This includes several "repeat" vases. For example, the well-known Ulúa vase once in the Bliss collection at Dumbarton Oaks has been auctioned at least three times by Sotheby's.

8. The 2004 spring sale (Sotheby's 2004) included the ex-Bliss Collection vase (lot 197) as well as a "new" vase (lot 199). The ex–Bliss Collection vase was listed for U.S. $5,000–$7,000 and sold for $7,200. The other vase was listed at $8,000–$12,000 and sold for $8,400.

9. See Gill and Chippindale (1993) for a discussion of "surfacing."

10. Two dealers are noted most often in museum accession and auction records for selling Ulúa marble vases: Stendahl Galleries in Los Angeles and Throckmorton Fine Art

in New York City. Based on the records at the National Archives for Stendahl Galleries, Stendahl began seriously collecting Pre-Columbian antiquities in the late 1950s and early 1960s. The interest in marble vases increased in the late 1970s. It was during this period and the following decade that dealers made frequent trips to San Pedro Sula, Honduras (located in the heart of the Ulúa Valley), to purchase antiquities, including marble vases. Since the late 1980s Stendahl Galleries and Throckmorton Fine Art have turned away from dealing in Pre-Columbian materials.

Several Ulúa-style marble vases were stolen from the Middle American Research Institute at Tulane University in the early 1980s, again reflecting a growing interest in these items during the late 1970s and early 1980s (Guerra 1980). The FBI recovered the objects.

11. Elizabeth Gilgan's research accounts for price adjustment over time. A vase sold in 1979 for U.S. $20,000 would be worth $46,000 today.

12. The link between scholarly labels and market prices is real; they do correlate. In the Mediterranean and Central and South America, object types and styles described as rare or particularly fancy by archaeologists and art historians tend to sell for much higher prices at public auction; these do not include the much higher prices paid at private sales.

13. See Sotheby's (2000b: 94) for two Red Class polychromes with reference to Reents-Budet's (1994: 205) connection to the Holmul style of the central Maya Lowlands.

Several other Ulúa polychromes were also offered in this auction. One, a Black Class polychrome, was offered for substantially less money (Sotheby's 2000b: 99), and there is no reference linking it to the central Maya Lowlands.

14. A number of archaeologists working in museums with collections of marble vases recall visits from collectors during the 1980s with extremely suspect vases. The curators and directors believe that these visits were to test their responses to the style of the vases; that is, a test to see if those familiar with the vases suspected forgeries.

15. Archaeologists and dealers have speculated that items excavated in greater Mesoamerica are often laundered in Costa Rica for clean provenance. For many years Costa Rican cultural patrimony laws were among the most lax in all the Central American countries, making it a place where one could legally export archaeological material. Objects were often given a false provenience in Costa Rica in order to export them legally from Central America, and hence import them legally into the United States.

16. Archives at the Peabody Museum of Archaeology and Ethnology at Harvard University demonstrate the vibrant export of material from the Ulúa Valley and Copán area from the 1890s through the early 1940s. The vast majority of material was shipped from Puerto Cortes to New York and then on to Boston (see Luke 2006).

17. Based on conversations that I (Luke) had with locals in El Porvenir and San Manuel during January of 2000, people believe that most of the marble vases have now been found. In fact, when asked about local geologic sources of marble for a chemical characterization study of marble vase production and procurement, people said that all the marble was gone. That is, all the marble vases were gone!

18. Also see Caldararo (2000) for a discussion of publications of Olmec figures as templates for fakes. And see Eberl and Prager (2000) for a discussion of illustrations of inscriptions featured in *Blood of Kings* (Schele and Miller 1986) as templates for inscriptions on a fake Maya bone auctioned at Sotheby's in New York in 1999.

BIBLIOGRAPHY

Aegean Antiquities, item number PC-121. <http://www.aegeanantiquities.com/prc/prc. html>, accessed August 8, 2002.

Agurcia Fasquelle, Ricardo. "La Depredación del Patrimonio Cultural en Honduras: El Caso de la Arqueología." *Yaxkin* 8, no. 2 (1984): 83–96.

———. "Copan Honduras: Looting in the Margarita Structure." *Mexicon* 10, no. 4 (1998): 68.

Arte Primitivo. <http://www.arteprimitivo.com/scripts/detail.asp?LOT_NUM=101624>, accessed October 10, 2002 (2002a).

———. <http://www.arteprimitivo.com/scripts/detail.asp?LOT_NUM=101623>, accessed October 10, 2002 (2002b).

———. <http://www.arteprimitivo.com/scripts/detail.asp?LOT_NUM=105491>, accessed May 5, 2003.

Barakat Gallery. <http://www.barakatgallery.com, Lot number PF.6175>, accessed September 11, 2002 (2002a).

———. <http://www.barakatgallery.com, Lot number PF.6235a>, accessed September 11, 2002 (2002b).

Beaudry-Corbett, Marilyn, Pauline Caputi, John S. Henderson, Rosemary A. Joyce, Eugenia J. Robinson, and Anthony Wonderly. "Lower Ulúa Region." In *Pottery of Prehistoric Honduras: Regional Classification and Analysis*, ed. John S. Henderson and Marilyn Beaudry-Corbett, 65–135. Monograph 35. Los Angeles, Calif.: Institute of Archaeology, University of California, 1993.

Caldararo, Niccolo. "Fake or Transitional Form? Analysis of a Purported Pre-Columbian Olmec Artifact and Comparison with Similar Published Objects from Mesoamerica." *Mexicon* 22, no. 3 (2000): 58–63.

Chase, Arlen, Diane Z. Chase, and Harriot W. Topsey. "Archaeology and the Ethics of Collecting." In *Archaeological Ethics*, ed. Karen D. Vitelli, 30–38. Walnut Creek, Calif.: AltaMira, 1996.

Chippindale, Christopher, David Gill, Emily Salter, and Christian Hamilton. "Collecting the Classical World: First Steps in a Quantitative History." *International Journal of Cultural Property* 10, no. 1 (2001): 1–31.

Coggins, Clemency C. "Illicit International Traffic in Ancient Art: Let There Be Light!" *International Journal of Cultural Property* 4, no. 1 (1995): 61–79.

———. "United States Cultural Property Legislation: Observations of a Combatant." *International Journal of Cultural Property* 7, no. 1 (1998): 52–68.

Convention on the Cultural Property Implementation Act 19 U.S.C. §§ 2601 *et seq.* Public Law 97-446 [H.R. 4566], 96 Stat. 2329, approved January 12, 1983; as amended by

Public Law 100-204 [H.R. 1777], 101 Stat. 1331, approved December 22, 1987 (United States).

Decree 513 Ley Especial de Protección al Patrimonio Cultural de El Salvador, 1993 (El Salvador).

Decree Number 26-97, Law for the Protection of the Cultural Heritage of the Nation. Congress of the Republic of Guatemala, 1997 (Guatemala).

Decreto No. 127, 9 April 1900 Procctección de las Ruinas de Copán y otras ruinas del país, 1900 (Honduras).

Decreto No. 81-84 Ley para la Protección del Patroimonio Cultural de la Nación, 1984 (Honduras).

Decreto No. 220-97 Ley para la Protección del Patroimonio Cultural de la Nación, 1997 (Honduras).

Eberl, M., and C. Prager. "A Fake Maya Bone." Mexicon 22, no. 1 (2000): 5.

Elia, Ricardo. "Analysis of the Looting, Selling, and Collecting of Apulian Red-figure Vases: A Quantitative Approach." In Trade in Illicit Antiquities: The Destruction of the World's Archaeological Heritage, ed. Neil Brodie, Jennifer Doole, and Colin Renfrew, 145–53. McDonald Institute Monograph. Cambridge, U.K.: McDonald Institute for Archaeological Research, 2001.

Federal Register Notice 3853. Department of State, Notice of Meeting of the Cultural Property Advisory Committee, December 18, 2001, vol. 66 (243), 2001.

Galerie Mermoz. "Carved Cylindrical Vessel with Jaguar Shaped Handles." Item no. 258. Paris, France, 2002.

Gilgan, Elizabeth. "Looting and the Market for Maya Objects: A Belizean Perspective." In Trade in Illicit Antiquities: The Destruction of the World's Archaeological Heritage, ed. Neil Brodie, Jennifer Doole, and Colin Renfrew, 73–87. McDonald Institute Monograph. Cambridge, U.K.: McDonald Institute for Archaeological Research, 2001.

Gill, David W. J., and Christopher Chippindale. "Material and Intellectual Consequences of Esteem for Cycladic Figures. American Journal of Archaeology 97 (1993): 601–59.

Gordon, George B. Researches in the Uloa Valley, Honduras. Peabody Museum Memoirs 1, no. 4. Cambridge, Mass.: Peabody Museum, 1898.

———. "A Marble Vase from the Ulúa River, Honduras." Art and Archaeology 9 (1920): 141–45.

———. "The Ulúa Marble Vases." Museum Journal 12 (1921): 53–74.

Green, Eric. "Illegally Imported Mayan Artifacts Being Returned to Guatemala (Artifacts Undamaged from Attacks on New York's World Trade Center)." Washington File. Washington, D.C.: Bureau of the International Information Programs, U.S. Department of State, June 13, 2003.

Guatemala. Object ID: 1-03, 31 December 2002, Dos Pilas, Ministerio de Cultura y Deportes de Guatemala, 2002.

Guerra, Mary Ellen. "Marble Bowls Stolen from Tulane University." Journal of Field Archaeology 7 (1980): 446–47.

Gugliotta, Guy. "Stairs Lead to Change in Mayan Story." Washington Post, September 19, 2002, A03.

Hamy, J. T. E. "Etude sur les collections Américaines." *Journal de la Société de Américanistes de Paris* 1, no. 1 (1896): 1–31.

Harmer Rooke Galleries. *Absentee Auction 57*. New York, December 16, 1993.

Henderson, John S. "The Valle de Naco: Ethnohistory and Archaeology in Northwestern Honduras." *Ethnohistory* 24, no. 4 (1979): 363–77.

———. *Archaeology in Northwestern Honduras: Interim Reports of the Proyecto Arqueológico Sula*, vol 1. Ithaca, N.Y.: Archaeology and Latin American Studies Program, Cornell University, 1984.

———. "Investigaciones arqueológicas en el Valle de Sula." *Yaxkin* 11, no. 1 (1988): 5–30.

———. "Elites and Ethnicity along the Southeastern Fringe of Mesoamerica." In *Meso-american Elites: An Archaeological Assessment*, ed. D. Z. Chase and A. F. Chase, 155–68. Norman: University of Oklahoma Press, 1992a.

———. "Variations on a Theme: A Frontier View of Maya Civilization." In *New Themes on the Ancient Maya*, ed. E. C. Danien and R. J. Sharer, 161–71. Philadelphia: University of Pennsylvania Press, 1992b.

———. *World of the Ancient Maya*. Ithaca, N.Y.: Cornell University Press, 1997.

Henderson, John S., Ricardo Agurcia F., and Thomas A. Murray. "El Proyecto Arqueológi-co Sula: Metas, strategies y resultados preliminaries." *Yaxkin* 1 (1982): 82–95.

Joyce, Rosemary A. "Travesia (CR-35): Archaeological Investigations, 1983." *Report submitted to the Proyecto Arqueológico Sula of the Instituto Hondureño de Antropología e Historia*. Tegucigalpa, Honduras, 1983.

———. "Terminal Classic Interaction on the Southeast Maya Periphery." *American Antiquity* 51 no. 2 (1986): 313–29.

———. *Cerro Palenque: Power and Identity on the Maya Periphery*. Austin: University of Texas Press, 1991.

———. "The Construction of the Mesoamerican Frontier and the Mayoid Image of Honduran Polychromes." In *Reinterpreting Prehistory of Central America*, ed. Mark Miller Graham, 51–101. Niwot: University Press of Colorado, 1993.

Joyce, Rosemary A., and John S. Henderson. "Beginnings of Village Life in Eastern Meso-america." *Latin American Antiquity* 12, no. 1 (2001): 5–23.

Joyce, Rosemary A., and Julia A. Hendon. "Heterarchy, History, and Material Reality: 'Communities' in Late Classic Honduras." In *The Archaeology of Communities: A New World Perspective,* ed. Marcello-Andrea Canuto and Jason Yaeger, 143–60. London: Routledge, 2000.

Luke, Christina. "Ulúa-style Marble Vases." Ph.D. diss., Cornell University, 2002a.

———. Collecting the Pre-Columbian Past: Ulúa Style Marble Vases as a Test Case. Paper presented at the Annual Meeting of the American Anthropological Association, New Orleans, 2002b.

———. "La protección del acervo cultural de Guatemala y la venta de antigüedades pre-colombinas," *XVI Simposio de Investigaciones Arqueológicas en Guatemala*. Guatemala City: Instituto de Antropología e Historia de Guatemala/Asociación Tikal, 2003a.

———. Ulúa-Style Marble Vase Project: Dissemination of Results. Available from <http://www.famsi.org/reports/02081/index.html>. 2003b.

————. "Diplomats, Banana Cowboys, and Archaeologists in Western Honduras: A History of Trade in Pre-Columbian Materials." *International Journal of Cultural Property* 13, no. 1 (2006):25–57.

Luke, Christina, Rosemary A. Joyce, John S. Henderson, and Robert H. Tykot. "Marble Carving Traditions in Honduras: Formative through Terminal Classic." *ASMOSIA 6, Interdisciplinary Studies on Ancient Stone: Proceedings of the Sixth International Conference of the Association for the Study of Marble and Other Stones in Antiquity, Venice, June 15–18, 2000*, ed. L. Lazzarini. Padova: Bottega d'Erasmo, 2003.

Luke, Christina, and Robert H. Tykot. Craft Specialization in Late Classic Ulúan Communities: Ulúa-Style Marble Vases. Paper presented at the Annual Meeting of the Society for American Archaeology, New Orleans, 2001.

————. "Marble Sources and Artifacts from the Ulúa Valley, Honduras." *ASMOSIA 5, Interdisciplinary Studies on Ancient Stone: Proceedings of the Fifth International Conference of the Association for the Study of Marble and Other Stones in Antiquity, Museum of Fine Arts, Boston, June 11–15, 1998*, ed. J. Herrmann, N. Herz, and R. Newman. London: Archetype, 2002.

Matsuda, David J. "The Ethics of Archaeology, Subsistence Digging, and Artifact 'Looting' in Latin America: Point, Muted Counterpoint." *International Journal of Cultural Property* 7, no. 1 (1998): 87–97.

Mayhood, K. "Man Guilty of Smuggling Ancient Artifacts." *Columbus Dispatch*, October 23, 2002. <http://www.dispatch.com/>, accessed October 25, 2002.

Nørskov, Vinnie. *Greek Vases in New Contexts: The Collecting and Trading of Greek Vases—An Aspect of the Modern Reception of Antiquity*. Aarhus, Denmark: Aarhus University Press, 2002.

Proyecto Atlas Arqueológico de Guatemala (PAAG). "Complete Destruction of Archaeological Sites in the Southern Peten." *Mexicon* 19, no. 1 (1997): 3.

Paredes Maury, Sofia. *Surviving in the Rainforest: The Realities of Looting in the Rural Villages of El Peten, Guatemala*. Foundation for the Advancement of Meso-American Studies, (August) 1998. <www.famsi.org/spanish/reports/95096/section05.htm>, accessed October 1, 2003.

Parke-Bernet Galleries. *The Cranbrook Collections*. New York: Parke-Bernet Galleries, 1972a.

————. *Pre-Columbian Art Including Mexico, Central and South America*. Public auction May 5. New York: Parke-Bernet Galleries, 1972b.

Pasztory, Esther. "Three Aztec Masks of the God Xipe." In *Falsifications and Misreconstructions of Pre-Columbian Art: A Conference at Dumbarton Oaks, October 14th and 15th, 1978*, ed. Elizabeth Hill Boone, 77–106. Washington, D.C.: Dumbarton Oaks Research Library and Collection, 1982.

Pendergast, David M. "And the Looting Goes On: Winning Some Battles, But Not the War." *Journal of Field Archaeology* 18 (1991): 89–95.

Pendergast, David M., and Elizabeth Graham. "Fighting a Looting Battle: Xunantunich, Belize." *Archaeology* 34 no. 4 (1983): 12–19.

————. "The Battle for the Maya Past: The Effects of International Looting and Collecting in Belize." In *The Ethics of Collecting: Whose Culture? Cultural Property: Whose Prop-*

erty?, ed. Phyllis Mauch Messenger, 51–60. Albuquerque: University of New Mexico Press, 1989.

Pre-Columbian Monumental or Architectural Sculpture and Murals Act. 1972 Public Law 92-587 (United States).

Quintaña, Oscar, Stefanie Teufel, and Raúl Noriega. "The Destruction of the Archaeological Site of Naranjo, Peten, Guatemala." *Mexicon* 21, no. 1 (1999): 3–5.

Ramírez, A. "Rescate de piezas históricas fueron devueltas a Guatemala por autoridades aduaneras de Estados Unidos." *Prensa Libre* (Guatemala City), May 30, 2003.

Reents-Budet, Doris. *Painting the Maya Universe: Royal Ceramics of the Classic Period.* Durham, N.C.: Duke University Press, 1994.

Schaffer, Anne-Louise. "On the Edge of the Maya World." *Archaeology* March–April 1992, 50–53.

Schele, Linda, and Ellen Miller. *Blood of Kings: Dynasty and Ritual in Maya Art.* New York: George Braziller and Kimbell Art Museum, 1986.

Sheptak, Russell N. "Fotos aéreas y el partó n de asentamiento de la zona central del valley del Ulúa." *Yaxkin* 5, no. 2 (1982): 89–94.

Sotheby's Auction Catalog. *Pre-Columbian Art, New York Galleries, November.* Hong Kong: Sotheby's, 1979.

———. *Pre-Columbian Art, New York Galleries, November.* Hong Kong: Sotheby's, 1981.

———. *Pre-Columbian Art, New York Galleries, November.* Hong Kong: Sotheby's, 1982.

———. *Pre-Columbian Art, New York Galleries, May.* Hong Kong: Sotheby's, 1983.

———. *Pre-Columbian Art, New York Galleries, May.* Hong Kong: Sotheby's, 1989.

———. *Pre-Columbian Art, New York Galleries, May.* Hong Kong: Sotheby's, 1990.

———. *Pre-Columbian Art, New York Galleries, November.* Hong Kong: Sotheby's, 1991a.

———. *Pre-Columbian Art, New York Galleries, May.* Hong Kong: Sotheby's, 1991b.

———. *Pre-Columbian Art, New York Galleries, November.* Hong Kong: Sotheby's, 1992a.

———. *Pre-Columbian Art, New York Galleries, May.* Hong Kong: Sotheby's, 1992b.

———. *Pre-Columbian Art, New York Galleries, November.* Hong Kong: Sotheby's, 1994a.

———. *Pre-Columbian Art, New York Galleries, May.* Hong Kong: Sotheby's, 1994b.

———. *Pre-Columbian Art, New York Galleries, November.* Hong Kong: Sotheby's, 1995.

———. *Pre-Columbian Art, New York Galleries, May.* Hong Kong: Sotheby's, 1996.

———. *Pre-Columbian Art, New York Galleries, November.* Hong Kong: Sotheby's, 1997a.

———. *Pre-Columbian Art, New York Galleries, May.* Hong Kong: Sotheby's, 1997b.

———. *Pre-Columbian Art, New York Galleries, November.* Hong Kong: Sotheby's, 1998a.

———. *Pre-Columbian Art, New York Galleries, May.* Hong Kong: Sotheby's, 1998b.

———. *Pre-Columbian Art, New York Galleries, November.* Hong Kong: Sotheby's, 1999a.

———. *Pre-Columbian Art, New York Galleries, May.* Hong Kong: Sotheby's, 1999b.

———. *Arts of Africa, Oceania and the Americas, New York Galleries, November.* Hong Kong: Sotheby's, 2000a.

————. *Arts of Africa, Oceania and the Americas, New York Galleries, May.* Hong Kong: Sotheby's, 2000b.

————. *Arts of Africa, Oceania and the Americas, New York Galleries.* Hong Kong: Sotheby's, 2001.

————. *Arts of Africa, Oceania and the Americas, New York Galleries, May.* Hong Kong: Sotheby's, 2002.

————. *African, Oceanic and Pre-Columbian Art, New York Galleries.* Hong Kong: Sotheby's, 2004.

Stone, Doris Z. *Masters in Marble.* Middle American Research Series, Pub. 8, pt.1. New Orleans, La.: Middle American Research Institute, Tulane University, 1938.

————. *Archaeology of the North Coast of Honduras.* Peabody Museum Memoirs 9(1). Cambridge, Mass.: Peabody Museum Press, 1941.

Stuart, George. "The Royal Crypts of Copán." *National Geographic* 192, no. 6 (1997): 68–93.

United Nations Educational, Scientific and Cultural Organization. *Convention on the Means of Prohibiting and Preventing the Illicit Import, Export and Transfer of Ownership of Cultural Property.* Paris: UNESCO, 1970.

Wilford, John Noble. "Maya Carvings Tell of a War of 2 Superpowers." *New York Times,* September 19, 2002, A1.

8

Looting Lydia

The Destruction of an Archaeological Landscape in Western Turkey

CHRISTOPHER H. ROOSEVELT AND CHRISTINA LUKE

A fertile and resource-rich region of western Turkey, Lydia was once the domain of an independent dynasty of famously rich kings whose capital was Sardis (map 8.1). These kings and their elite successors left remnants of their greatness throughout the region. Some such remains were plundered as long ago as Roman times and others are still being looted today. The most famous case of looting in Lydia became well known through drawn-out and well-publicized legal battles between the Republic of Turkey and the Metropolitan Museum of Art in New York ("Collectors or Looters" 1987; Friendly 1970; Glueck 1987; Kaylan 1987; Özgen and Öztürk 1996; Rose and Acar 1996). That case concluded with the return to Turkey of the so-called Lydian Hoard for display in museums in Ankara and Uşak. The returned objects had been robbed in the 1960s from previously unexplored tombs concealed beneath large burial mounds, or tumuli—the most prestigious form of elite burial in the Lydian and Persian periods of the seventh through fourth centuries B.C. Groups of such burial mounds dot the Lydian landscape as conspicuous remnants of the Lydian and Persian period heritage of the region and were the focus of a recent survey. The primary goal of the survey and related research at regional museums was to improve our understanding of the relationship between Sardis and its hinterland by recording the regional distribution of archaeological sites indicative of general patterns of settlement. A secondary result of this research was the quantification of looting in the region. This chapter explores the looting of Lydia, and of tumuli in particular, and examines local and international responses to the destruction of an archaeological landscape.

THE LYDIAN HOARD CASE

It has been more than ten years since the Lydian Hoard was returned to Turkey, and thus a general review of the case and its implications on the trafficking of illegal antiquities from Turkey is appropriate here. Pillage of tumuli in the Güre-Uşak region of western Turkey between 1965 and 1968 produced what became

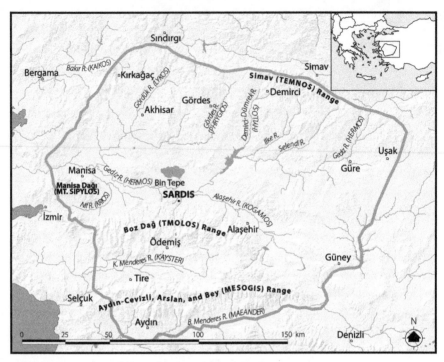

Map 8.1. Approximate limits of Lydia in western Turkey.

known as the Lydian Hoard—a vast assemblage of grave goods including items made of precious metals, ivory, wood, ceramics, and painted stone (Özgen and Öztürk 1996). The major part of the so-called hoard came from at least three tumuli in this region (Toptepe, İkiztepe, and Aktepe), and from at least one other tumulus located farther west in Kırkağaç-Manisa (Harta-Abidintepe).[1]

The objects made their way via İzmir and Switzerland to dealers in New York City and were eventually acquired by the Greek and Roman Department of the Metropolitan Museum of Art (Met). Following rare and brief displays of a few items from the assemblage over some thirteen years, the Met opened an exhibition in 1984 called the *East Greek Treasure* that included almost all of the items from the hoard, most of which had never before been put on display (Rose and Acar 1996: 74). The exhibition and its well-illustrated catalogue attracted the suspicion of the General Directorate of Antiquities and Museums in Ankara (now the General Directorate of Cultural Resources and Museums), which had claimed much earlier that the Met was in illegal possession of the material from Lydian tumuli ("Metropolitan Museum Queried" 1970). A formal investigation of the Met's acquisition of the materials began in 1987. After a failed attempt at claiming an expired statute of limitations, the Met argued that there was no evidence the material had been looted from Lydia, basing their case largely on the stylistic similarities of the items to those found across the Greek world, and especially in East Greece. Evidence provided by a team of art historians and archaeologists, internal acquisition documents from the Met, and especially the testimony of several of the original looters all suggested that the most likely sources of the material were the pillaged tumuli in Güre-Uşak. In 1993 the Met reached an agreement with the Republic of Turkey, and the material was returned with all expenses paid by the Met (see Özgen and Öztürk 1996).

The return of the material resulted in an excellent renovated display at the Uşak Museum, while a smaller collection of the pieces was put on permanent display in Ankara at the Museum of Anatolian Civilizations. The effect of the case and its publicity was to show that museums, even those as large and powerful as the Met, could be held responsible for the repatriation of materials with illegal provenance. The material was returned to the area from which it came and continues to be available to local communities, international tourists, and researchers. While such results are clearly positive and, one hopes, still reverberate throughout the world of archaeology and antiquities, we seem to have lost track of the original plunder and its most destructive effect: the loss of context. The tumuli from which the "hoard" or "treasure" of objects was looted were largely forgotten despite the continued intensive looting of such monuments in Lydia. What was the context of the Lydian Hoard, and why is it significant? How many other tumuli are there in Lydia, how many have been looted, and how are they significant?

REGIONAL CONTEXT

The primary focus of research in Lydia has been the excavation of its capital, Sardis. Following a Princeton University expedition in the early 1900s that was cut short due to the First World War and the Turkish War of Independence, a second expedition, sponsored primarily by Harvard and Cornell universities, first broke ground at the ancient capital in 1958. The ongoing investigations of the Sardis Expedition in and around the city site have documented a culture history of the area that spans Early Bronze Age to modern times with urban remains best preserved from the Lydian and Late Roman/Early Byzantine periods (Hanfmann 1983 and Greenewalt and Rautman 2000). The most famous period of the city belongs to the seventh- and sixth-century B.C. dynasty of Mermnad kings, beginning with Gyges and ending with Alyattes and Croesus. The brilliant wealth of the Mermnad kings was recorded in numerous contemporary and slightly later Greek sources, as was the spectacular fall of the kingdom to Persian forces under Cyrus in the mid-sixth century B.C. Sardis remained the seat of the Persian provincial governor, or satrap, until Alexander the Great freed the local populations from Persian hegemony in 334 B.C., and it remained a focal point of the region throughout its later history.

Lydian levels have been encountered in numerous exposures on the site, including discoveries of domestic areas (Cahill 2002), a gold refinery (Ramage and Craddock 2000), and a monumental fortification wall enclosing the urban center (Greenewalt and Rautman 2000). Besides a major destruction level associated with the Persian sack of the city, however, relatively few Persian-period occupation deposits have been uncovered (cf. Dusinberre 2003), and evidence for Persian-period activities is better sought in funerary remains.

In addition to more than a thousand chamber tombs excavated by the first expedition to Sardis in a necropolis near the city site, some forty tumuli of the Lydian and Persian periods have been investigated in the great burial mound cemetery of Bin Tepe, or "a thousand mounds." Located some eight kilometers north-northwest of Sardis across the Hermos (Gediz) River valley, Bin Tepe is a roughly 5.5 by 13-kilometer area stretching over the rolling hills of an elongated limestone ridge. It was presumably the royal burial grounds of the Mermnad kings, but only the monumental tumulus of king Alyattes may be securely identified today. Excavations since the 1960s have shown that the majority of the remaining one hundred or so tumuli in Bin Tepe probably date to the Persian period, like the tumuli in Güre-Uşak (Roosevelt 2003b).

Outside Sardis and Bin Tepe, little archaeological field research has focused on the rural countryside of Lydia, where the most easily recognizable ancient monuments are numerous tumuli. These vast earthen mounds remain one of the most conspicuous markers of Lydian- and Persian-period occupation. With the exception of a brief survey of regional tumuli in 1970 (Ramage and Ramage 1971) and other limited surveys (e.g., Dinç 1997; Meriç 1989), Lydian- and Persian-period settlements and tumuli in the region had never been systematically studied, nor had provenienced artifacts from the same periods housed in local museums.

REGIONAL RESEARCH PROJECT

In the absence of such fundamental research, and with the questions raised earlier in mind, a regional research project in Lydia commenced in 2000. The work began with almost a year of research in the Manisa and Uşak museums followed by a survey of tumuli in the spring of 2001. The primary goal was to establish patterns of settlement through examination of provenienced finds in local museum collections and through the accurate location of tumuli, with the underlying hypothesis that burial areas in Lydia are in some way indicative of settlement locations. By improving our understanding of Lydian settlement patterns, we hoped to understand better the relationship between the capital of Lydia at Sardis and settlements in its hinterland (see Roosevelt 2002, 2003a, 2003b).

The extensive survey method was based loosely on that of the one prior study of tumulus distribution in western Anatolia (Ramage and Ramage 1971): we traversed the area as thoroughly as possible and documented the locations of all sites encountered, with a special emphasis on tumuli. We accurately recorded the location and dimensions of each tumulus using a hand-held GPS receiver and a simple measuring tape. The range of ceramic types seen on the surface or in looters' trenches was noted, and particularly diagnostic pieces were photographed; nothing was removed from its context. The general setting of the tumulus was recorded, including description of the surrounding landscape, resources, access, and condition, especially noting on a diagram any signs of looting (fig. 8.1). Finally, if the burial complex itself was accessible, it was entered and fully documented with attention to its form, details of construction, general condition, and again, the effects of looting (fig. 8.2). We recorded a total of twenty-six such accessible burial complexes, adding an additional 30 percent to the previously known eighty-nine burial complexes (cf. McLauchlin 1985; Ratté 1989; Dinç 1993). A result of these findings is a fuller understanding of the rich diversity of tumulus burials in Lydia—including combinations of built

Figure 8.1. The Hacılı A (or "Tombaktepe") tumulus in central Lydia (diameter c. 70 m; preserved height c. 15 m).

Figure 8.2. The partially destroyed tomb chamber of the Çaldağ M (or "Musacalıtepe") tumulus in central Lydia (photograph by authors).

and rock-cut architectural tomb complexes, simple pits, and sarcophagi—and the variations of architectural tomb complexes, including such spatial units as chambers, antechambers, forecourts, porches, and *dromoi*, or entrance corridors, in varied arrangements (Roosevelt 2003b).

Through the course of the regional survey we personally inspected 397 tumuli that could be grouped into between 75 and 117 clusters based on statistical methods and natural topographic boundaries (map 8.2). Museum research and previous studies indicated the presence of 113 other Lydian and Persian period sites of varying types. Eighty-six, or over 75 percent, of these sites are located in close proximity to a tumulus group (five km.), suggesting that tumulus groups—such as the one in Güre-Uşak that produced the Lydian Hoard—are associated with and hence indicate the locations of settlement areas (Roosevelt 2003b).

For archaeological purposes, then, grave goods contained within tumulus burial complexes, such as those that compose the Lydian Hoard, are not the sole importance of tumuli. While the styles, types, and numbers of grave goods convey information on funerary beliefs, local wealth, craft production, and the degree of exterior communications via gift exchange, among other important societal indicators, the forms of burial complexes may show chronological

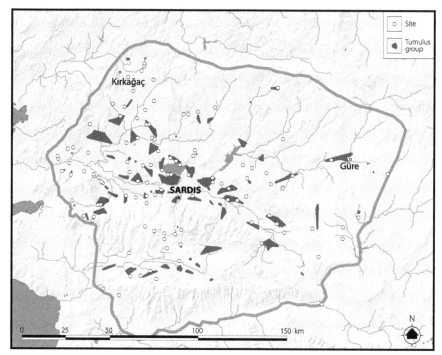

Map 8.2. Lydia, showing 75 tumulus groups and 113 Lydian and Persian period sites.

changes, local innovations, or formal similarities that point to a Lydian identity. Furthermore, tumuli themselves are important cultural monuments, and their very locations aid our understanding of settlement patterns. As we already know, unfortunately, grave goods are often looted, and both interior burial contexts and burial mounds themselves are often completely destroyed (Roosevelt 2003a, 2003b).

Of the 397 tumuli personally inspected, 357 or 90 percent showed signs of looting. Fifty-two of these had been completely destroyed, and an additional twenty located by the Ramages in 1970 had literally vanished by 2001 (cf. Ramage and Ramage 1971). A total of seventy-two or 18 percent of all tumuli in Lydia, then, have been completely destroyed. The survey also showed that the looting of Lydian tumuli is still quite active. In April of 2000 several gold jewelry items were looted from the Tilkitepe tumulus in the Kogamos (Alaşehir) River valley in central Lydia; fortunately, this grave assemblage was recovered and is now on display at the Uşak Museum with the Lydian Hoard returned by the Met. During our relatively short two-month survey, we caught looters in the act at one tumulus (Soyulan) and found a ladder, shovels, picks, and candles for nighttime looting in the freshly dug tunnels of another (Menye A, fig. 3). Both

Figure 8.3. Looters' tunnels and equipment in the Menye A tumulus in central Lydia (photograph by authors).

incidents were reported to local authorities, and the looting paraphernalia at the latter tumulus was confiscated. The archives at both the Manisa and Uşak museums are filled with numerous accounts of looting activities documented by museum staff who monitor the region. The records go back as far as the 1950s, in some cases, and are replete with information on various casts of looting characters and their techniques.

The Looting Culture

Looters in Lydia are generally members of rural agricultural communities who supplement the routine of their more relaxed winter schedules with the occupation of treasure hunting.[2] From our experience, looting in Lydia is a local, sometimes family-oriented activity that in rare cases also involves corrupt local officials and other institutions responsible for such public works as highway or forest management.[3] Using shovels, picks, tractors, plows, backhoes, bulldozers, and road graders, tumulus looters generally seek portable valuables, especially those made of precious metals, but have also been known to remove items with sculptural or painted decoration.

The incentive to loot appears to be at least twofold. The first stimulus is monetary gain: there is clear knowledge of the lucrative nature of the antiquities market even in the most remote rural areas. We learned of wealthy urbanites periodically patrolling rural villages in their fancy cars, looking for antiquities. Archives at the Manisa and Uşak museums refer also to looters who imitate Lydian-style wall paintings in tombs and then hack out their fresh renderings for sale to undiscriminating buyers: such is what occurred on the back wall of the Aktepe tumulus tomb chamber already mentioned.[4]

The second motivation is mysterious folklore. The mystical excitement derived from the search for forbidden treasures is evidenced in the local naming of such tumuli as "Treasure Hill," "The King's Grave," or "The Mound Where Money Was Found" and also in folklore surrounding one of the richer tumuli from which the Lydian Hoard was looted: İkiztepe. After a long period of illicit digging on this tumulus, the leader of the looters was said to have finally entered the tomb chamber at 6:00 a.m. on the sixth of June, 1966 (Kaylan 1987: 66). This mystical grouping of sixes was encountered again later when salvage excavations exposed the façade of the burial complex, measuring almost exactly six meters in length (K. Akbıyıkoğlu, director of the Uşak Museum, pers. comm.).

With such mystical or mythical occurrences inspiring looters, one can imagine the frustration of the looter who works tirelessly to access a tomb, only to find it previously looted or not quite as rich as hoped. Complete destruction of the interior tomb is the usual result. Some attribute such destruction also to a belief that precious metals, especially gold, lie hidden in tomb walls or beneath foundation stones. The result of looting Lydian tumuli, then, is not merely the loss of grave goods and their exact context but the partial or complete destruction of the tomb complex and its covering mound. Postinterment or secondary activities at the burial site are completely obscured, as are the construction of the mound itself, the burial form, its construction and decoration, and the relationship between and significance of all of these things: the deceased, the grave goods, and the burial form. As our survey has shown, the complete destruction of tumuli also obscures our understanding of settlement patterns and their significance for Lydian culture.

NATIONAL, LOCAL, AND INTERNATIONAL RESPONSES

Responses at the national and local levels to looting and destruction in Turkey are, in general, very strict. The first formal legislation to regulate cultural property in Turkey was put forth under Ottoman rule in 1869, after large quantities of material, if not entire monuments, were exported by French, German, and British scholarly expeditions (Leimenstoll 1989: 6–9). By 1884 an imperial decree stated clearly that Turkey was the sole owner of its cultural heritage, and amendments made to the decree by 1906 outlined registration, research, and export regulations (Leimenstoll 1989: 10–13). A series of legislative amendments continued to strengthen this decree over the following century and through the transition of rule from the Ottoman Empire to the modern Republic of Turkey. Law No. 2863 on the Protection of Cultural and Natural Assets was adopted in 1983, superseding all previous laws and regulations. It states clearly what is designated as cultural heritage; specifies how this heritage is managed, researched (including excavated), stored, and registered; and regulates also the sale, transfer, and export of both movable and immovable cultural property (Leimenstoll 1989: 16–19). Under the current law it is illegal to sell, transfer, or export cultural property without permission from the Ministry of Culture and Tourism. It is also illegal to excavate or conduct surveys without proper permits from the same ministry.

In order for sites of cultural heritage to be protected, however, they must be registered with the Ministry of Culture and Tourism as First Degree or Class One protection sites. These, then, can be carefully monitored and conserved as necessary (Leimenstoll 1989). On a local level, the responsibility of such registering and monitoring falls primarily to provincial museums in charge of the particular regions in which they are based. While *jandarma* (state police) stationed throughout the countryside report suspicious activities of any kind, the staff of museums are frequently occupied with cultural resource registering; monitoring all new development and construction activities; salvage excavations of accidentally discovered, high-risk, or already looted sites; and object acquisitions. For objects that have been accidentally unearthed in agricultural or other nonlooting activities, Turkish museums have a system of reimbursement for the purpose of keeping such objects at local museums rather than letting them enter the illegal international market. The system is commendable for the level of resources that Turkey commits to retaining such objects. In rare cases, however, it may create career looters (or "subsistence diggers") because an object's circumstance of discovery—by agricultural plow or by looter's spade—is nearly impossible to verify. Also, by providing any kind of market for antiquities, even one that is sanctioned, Turkish museums may themselves be unintentionally spurring on illicit trade.

Archaeological projects, too, have responsibilities to work in collaboration with local museums to educate people about local cultural heritage. At Sardis, the ancient capital of Lydia, tourist-oriented signage provides information about the archaeology and history of the site, and it is consistently stressed to members of the local community that protecting local archaeology is in their interest. Archaeological projects provide jobs and attract tourists: two positive economic stimuli in a country that has vast unemployment and rich archaeology. At the same time, archaeologists must be fully aware of the implications of their research. One of the looters of the Lydian Hoard is rumored to have learned his techniques from a local archaeological project (K. Akbıyıkoğlu, director of the Uşak Museum, pers. comm.).

On an international level, Turkey is party to a number of conventions that focus specifically on cultural property.[5] The problem for the cultural heritage of Turkey, however, is the way the rest of the world implements these various conventions, particularly the 1970 UNESCO Convention on the Means of Prohibiting and Preventing the Illicit Import, Export, and Transfer of Ownership of Cultural Property. The major market countries for items from Turkey include Switzerland (also a significant port of transfer), the United Kingdom, and Belgium. Until recently, none of these countries had ratified the Convention. At present, the United Kingdom has fully ratified the Convention as has Switzerland (see Gerstenblith, chapter 3). The United States is another major market, but although it has accepted the Convention, the implementation procedures under the Cultural Property Implementation Act (CPIA) require country-by-country consideration. A Memorandum of Understanding (MOU) with Turkey regarding cultural heritage under the CPIA does not exist at this time, but Turkey is in the process of preparing a formal request. Successful MOUs with Cyprus, Guatemala, Italy, and Peru, to name a few, provide models that indicate the potential benefit of such an agreement between Turkey and the United States (see Özgen 2001). Auctions at Christie's and Sotheby's in New York in recent years document a thriving trade in Classical antiquities. Material from western Anatolia and perhaps from Lydia continues to appear on the market in the United States and Europe, as evidenced by an assemblage of goods similar in composition to the Lydian Hoard that appeared in a gallery in Geneva in 2000 (K. Akbıyıkoğlu, director of the Uşak Museum, pers. comm.) and Achaemenid-type bowls recently offered by Sotheby's.[6] The difficulty in repatriating such items lies in proving their provenience and illegal provenance. When looted objects make it out of the country with the plundered site still unknown, it is impossible to claim a specific provenience. Even if detailed scientific study can show that an object was produced in a certain area, such items may have been exchanged over a wide area in antiquity and thus may have been recovered from nearly anywhere throughout the Near East and eastern Mediterranean. The Lydian Hoard case was successful in part because the original looters were able to give detailed information about the objects they plundered, and thus the original provenience of the artifacts was determined.

CONCLUSIONS

We know the significance of the Lydian Hoard case for the trafficking of antiquities and especially for that from Turkey, but what about its archaeological or contextual significance? Our research has suggested that tumulus groups like the one that produced the Lydian Hoard, and their associated settlement sites, probably represent extended estates of regional elites of the Lydian and Persian periods. Those based in Güre-Uşak may not have been of particular importance but were part of a system of distributed elite estates responsible to the capital for certain regional administrative duties, as the distribution of tumulus groups throughout the region and the derived settlement patterns would suggest. What more we might have learned from Lydian tumulus burial contexts we will never know due to the intensity of the looting of such monuments. Our research witnessed the continuing activities of looters in Lydia and the effects of their work—the destruction of an archaeological landscape specific to western Turkey and the irrecoverable loss of immeasurable knowledge.

A positive result of our research is that we have produced an inventory of the most conspicuous monuments on the Lydian landscape and recorded a baseline for the monitoring of their condition as regards looting.[7] All documentation was submitted to the Manisa and Uşak museums, and thus all such monuments can now be registered with the Ministry of Culture for their more effective protection. While we hope that this will help the problem, we must stress that pillage and archaeological destruction in Lydia are not restricted to tumuli. Museums are plagued by theft, and other sites and monuments in the rural countryside are often ransacked for archaeological goods or destroyed. Such continuing occurrences suggest a keen awareness of the illegal antiquities market, and while we can offer no ideal solution to the problem, we think that looting in Lydia will not be curtailed until the market for illegally excavated archaeological material is curtailed. We suggest that steps in the right direction would include a combination of local education, emphasizing the importance of cultural patrimony; involvement in cultural heritage preservation, on the part of archaeologists and museums; and a concomitant strengthening of both international antiquity trafficking legislation and the penalties for its contravention.

ACKNOWLEDGMENTS

For permissions and other assistance we would like to thank the General Directorate of Cultural Resources and Museums, Ministry of Culture and Tourism, Turkey, and its representative on the 2001 survey, Jale Dedeoğlu. We also thank the Archaeological Exploration of Sardis and, specifically, its director Crawford H. Greenewalt, Jr., for continuing support and encouragement; Kâzım Akbıyıkoğlu of the Uşak Museum; and Müyesser Tosunbaş of the Manisa Museum. This work was supported by the Olivia James Traveling Fellowship of the Archaeological Institute of America and the American Research Institute in Turkey.

NOTES

1. In addition to Toptepe (looted in 1965), İkiztepe (looted in 1966), and Aktepe (looted in 1967–68) in Güre-Uşak, the nearby Topçatepe tumulus, too, may have produced some items of the Lydian Hoard; it was looted in 1965. Wall paintings and *kline* (funerary couch) supports carved in the form of seated sphinxes from the Harta-Abidintepe tumulus in Kırkağaç-Manisa also formed part of the collection; these were looted in 1965–66 (Özgen and Öztürk 1996). For these and other details relating to klinai, see Baughan 2004.

2. Looting occurs at all times of the year but especially in winter and at times of extreme economic hardship (e.g., following the economic collapse of February 2001) or during periods of inefficient policing (e.g., following the physical isolation of Bin Tepe due to flooding in the Hermos (Gediz) River valley in the spring of 1966). As looting is primarily supplemental to other occupational means of support in the region of ancient Lydia, the term "looting" is preferable to "subsistence digging."

3. Manisa Museum archives reports 470-275/20.08.1969, 470-5199/17.12.1971, and 470-10576/16.12.1972 in binder 711.0 Saruhanlı.

4. Another example of this phenomenon is provided by a looter/artist who, having seen the wall paintings in the Harta-Abidintepe tumulus tomb chamber, broke into the previously looted chamber of the Yukarı Çobanisa B tumulus just east of Manisa. There, the looter/artist painted imitations of the Harta-Abidintepe paintings, intending to remove and sell them as originals. Local authorities apprehended the looter/artist before he could complete the task (Roosevelt and Luke, forthcoming).

5. Conventions to which Turkey is party include the following: the European Council/ European Cultural Convention, Strasbourg, 1954 (since 1957); the 1954 Hague Convention for the Protection of Cultural Heritage in the Event of Armed Conflict (since April 10, 1965); the 1970 UNESCO Convention on the Means of Prohibiting and Preventing the Illicit Import, Export, and Transfer of Ownership of Cultural Property (since July 21, 1981); the European Convention on Offenses (since September 26, 1985); and the 1992 European Convention on the Protection of Archaeological Heritage (since May 2000).

6. For examples of East Greek and/or Achaemenid wares (both commonly found in the tumuli of western Anatolia), see Sotheby's 2001: Lot 72 (A Silver Phiale, Achaemenid or East Greek, circa 5th Century B.C.); Lot 73 (A Silver Phiale Mesoamphalos, Achaemenid or East Greek, circa 6th/5th Century B.C.); Lot 74 (A Greek Silver Phiale Mesoamphalos, circa 4th Century B.C.).

7. For the reports of a recent project with the expressed purpose of recording such a baseline of the destruction of monuments all over Turkey, see Tanındı and Özbaşaran 2001 and Tanındı et al. 2003.

Bibliography

Acar, Özgen, and Melik Kaylan. "The Turkish Connection: An Investigative Report on the Smuggling of Classical Antiquities." *Connoisseur*, October 1990, 130–37.

Baughan, Elizabeth P. *Antolian Funerary Klinai: Tradition and Identity*. Ph.D. diss., University of California, Berkeley, Calif, 2004.

Cahill, Nicholas D. "Lydian Houses, Domestic Assemblages, and Household Size." In *Across the Anatolian Plateau: Readings in the Archaeology of Ancient Turkey*, ed. David C. Hopkins, 173–85. Annual of the American Schools of Oriental Research 57. Boston: American School of Oriental Research, 2002.

Christie's Auction Catalog. *Classical Antiquities, New York*. No. 84, June 11. New York: Christie's, 2003.

"Collectors or Looters." *Economist*, October 17, 1987, 117–18.

Dinç, Rafet. *Lidya Tümülüsleri*. Ph.D. diss., Ege University, İzmir, Turkey, 1993.

———. "Kulaksızlar mermer idol atölyesi ve çevre araştırmaları." *Arkeoloji Sonuçları Toplantısı* 14 (1997): 255–82.

Dusinberre, Elspeth R. M. *Aspects of Empire in Achaemenid Sardis*. Cambridge, U.K.: Cambridge University Press, 2003.

Friendly, Alfred. "Turks Warn of Bar to Archaeologists If U.S. Won't Aid Smuggling Fight." *New York Times*, November 3, 1970.

Glueck, Grace. "Met Files Motion to Retain Artifacts." *New York Times*, July 21, 1987.

Greenewalt, Crawford H., Jr., and Marcus L. Rautman. "The Sardis Campaigns of 1996, 1997, and 1998." *American Journal of Archaeology* 104 (2000): 643–81.

Hanfmann, George M. A. *Sardis from Prehistoric to Roman Times*. Cambridge, Mass.: Harvard University Press, 1983.

Kaylan, Melik. "Who Stole the Lydian Hoard? A Case History Involving the Hottest Issue Confronting American Museums Today." *Connoisseur*, July 1987, 66–73.

Leimenstoll, Jo Ramsay. *Historic Preservation in Other Countries, Vol. IV: Turkey*. Washington, D.C.: United States Committee of the International Council on Monuments and Sites (US/ICOMOS), 1989.

McLauchlin, Barbara K. *Lydian Graves and Burial Customs*. Ph.D. diss., University of California, Berkeley, 1985.

Meriç, Recep. "1988 yılı İzmir, Manisa illeri Arkeolojik yüzey araştırması." *Arkeoloji Sonuçları Toplantısı* 7 (1989): 361–66.

"Metropolitan Museum Queried by Turks on Smuggled Artifacts." *New York Times*, August 27, 1970.

Özel, Sibel. "Case Notes. The Basel Decisions: Recognition of the Blanket Legislation Vesting State Ownership over the Cultural Property Found within the Country of Origin." *International Journal of Cultural Property* 9, no. 2 (2000): 315–40.

Özgen, Engin. "Some Remarks on the Destruction of Turkey's Archaeological Heritage." In *Trade in Illicit Antiquities: The Destruction of the World's Archaeological Heritage*, ed.

Neil Brodie, Jennifer Doole, and Colin Renfrew, 119–20. McDonald Institute Monograph. Cambridge, U.K.: McDonald Institute for Archaeological Research, 2001.

Özgen, Ilknur, and Jean Öztürk. *Heritage Recovered: The Lydian Treasure*. Istanbul: General Directorate of Monuments and Museums, Ministry of Culture, Republic of Turkey, 1996.

Özsunay, Ergun. "Protection of Cultural Heritage in Turkish Private Law." *International Journal of Cultural Property* 6, no. 2 (1997): 278–90.

Prott, Lyndel V., and Patrick J. O'Keefe. "Turkey." In *Handbook of National Regulations Concerning the Export of Cultural Property*, 217–18. Paris: United Nations Educational, Scientific and Cultural Organization, 1988.

Ramage, Andrew, and Paul Craddock. *King Croesus' Gold: Excavations at Sardis and the History of Gold Refining*. Archaeological Exploration of Sardis, monograph 11. Cambridge, Mass.: Harvard University Press, 2000.

Ramage, Andrew, and Nancy Ramage. "The Siting of Lydian Burial Mounds." In *Studies Presented to George M. A. Hanfmann*, ed. David G. Mitten, John G. Pedley, and Jane A. Scott, 143–60. Mainz: Philipp von Zabern, 1971.

Ratté, Christopher J. *Lydian Masonry and Monumental Architecture at Sardis*. Ph.D. diss., University of California, Berkeley, 1989.

Republic of Turkey v. Metropolitan Museum of Art, 762 F. Supp. 44 (S.D.N.Y. 1990).

Roosevelt, Christopher H. Lydian and Persian Period Site Distribution in Lydia. Paper delivered at the Annual Meeting of the Archaeological Institute of America, Philadelphia, Pa., 2002.

———. Tumulus Tomb Complexes, Distribution, and Significance in Lydian and Persian Period Lydia. Paper presented at the Annual Meeting of the Archaeological Institute of America, New Orleans, La., 2003 (2003a).

———. *Lydian and Persian Period Settlement in Lydia*. Ph.D. diss., Cornell University, Ithaca, N.Y., 2003b.

Roosevelt, Christopher H., and Christina Luke. "Mysterious Shepherds and Hidden Treasures: The Culture of Looting in Lydia." *Journal of Field Archaeology*. Forthcoming.

Rose, Mark, and Özgen Acar. "Turkey's War on the Illicit Antiquities Trade." In *Archaeological Ethics*, ed. Karen D. Vitelli, 71–89. Walnut Creek, Calif.: AltaMira, 1996.

Sotheby's. *Classical Antiquities, New York*. New York: Sotheby's, 2001.

Swissinfo. "Swiss Deal Blow to Art Traffickers." *Swissinfo*. <http://www.swissinfo.org/sen/ Swissinfo.html?siteSect=105&sid=3957866>, accessed June 17, 2003.

Tanındı, Oğuz, and M. Özbaşaran. *Archaeological Destruction in Turkey—Year 2000 Preliminary Report: Marmara and Aegean regions, June–October 2000*. Trans. E. Tekin and B. Yazcıoğlu. Istanbul: TASK Foundation, 2001.

Tanındı, Oğuz, and Semiha Okan. *Archaeological Destruction in Turkey—Year 2002 Preliminary Report: Central Anatolia, June–October 2002*. Trans. E. Tekin. Istanbul: TASK Foundation, 2003.

United States Department of State. "Ancient Artifacts to Be Repatriated to Turkey." United States Department of State, Office of the Spokesman, Press Statement, February 28, 2000.

9

From the Ground to the Buyer

A Market Analysis of the Trade in Illegal Antiquities

MORAG M. KERSEL

Every day in shops, on the Internet, and in auction houses, people purchase archaeological artifacts. On Web sites such as eBay an individual can buy anything from a Folsom point to a Roman silver figure of Hermes to an Aztec water goddess wall plaque, paying from U.S. $2.99 to $29,000.[1] Archaeological material is readily available in the marketplace, but how does it get there? What kinds of conduits do these artifacts pass through on their way to the auction block? In an attempt to answer these questions, I set out a model of the trade in antiquities, highlighting its defining or unique features; provide concrete data illustrating the pathway of an artifact; and in light of this model, suggest some appropriate countermeasures for combating illegal trade.

The illegal excavation of archaeological sites is a global problem, and the attendant loss of cultural heritage is devastating. The assorted countermeasures imposed by various nations against illegal trade do not appear to be working, to some extent because the trade and the pathways that artifacts travel are poorly understood, and consequently the controls are inadequately targeted (Mackenzie 2002). Recent reports (Brodie et al. 2001; Brodie and Tubb 2002) indicate that archaeological sites are being looted at an alarming rate, and the looted material can be found in antiquities shops, at auction houses, and on eBay (Elia 2001). The amount of available archaeological resources is finite, and yet with myriad claims of provenance proffered by antiquities dealers—that the artifacts are from "old family collections" or "recent museum deaccessions"—there seems to be a never-ending legal supply.[2] Today's antiquities trade functions within the context of legal and illegal markets, high returns on investment, decreasing supply, and continued demand for cultural artifacts.

The illegal antiquities market is frequently compared to other major international criminal enterprises, especially drug trafficking and arms smuggling (Adler and Polk 2002; Bernick 1998; Borodkin 1995; Polk 1999, 2000). Although it shares many characteristics with other illegal markets, there is at least one fundamental difference: by passing through a series of markets or portals, as they are referred to by Polk (2000), the objects are transformed from illegal to legal; that is, in market parlance, they are laundered. Trafficking in antiquities blurs the lines between illegal and legal markets and between criminal and legitimate participants. Whereas the traffic in drugs is always illegal—meaning that the buyer is as culpable as the seller—in sharp contrast, the ultimate buyer of illegally excavated antiquities can often purchase them openly and legally, seemingly without engaging in illegal activity (Polk 2000: 83).

MODEL FOR THE TRADE IN ANTIQUITIES

The majority of markets consist of groups of intermediaries between the first seller and the final buyer of the commodity. Polk (2000: 84) asserts that what distinguishes the traffic in antiquities from other criminal markets is that most of the material must at some point enter the market as legitimate commodities in order for the goods to realize their full economic value. Savvy antiquities collectors understand the importance of provenience. This need for the assurance of good title (at least in appearance) has created specialized market nations, the main purpose of which is to act as a transit point from the archaeologically rich country to the buying country. In Argentina, Hong Kong, and Switzerland, for example, antiquities can pass through a market that imparts legitimacy to the goods being purchased (see Alder and Polk 2002; Kunitz 2001; Schávelzon 2002). The path of an illegal antiquity from its illegal excavation in the archaeologically rich country through the various transit points to its eventual exportation to and sale in the destination country can have many variations.[3] A simplified sequence is presented in figure 9.1. An important aspect of the

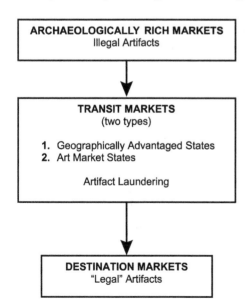

Figure 9.1. Market flow of the trade in illegal antiquities.

figure to be considered is that a sale of an archaeological artifact can occur at any time in the sequence if there is a willing buyer. An examination of the conduits through which illegally excavated antiquities are routed on their way to a "legitimate" home is critical to understanding the trade in antiquities and how countermeasures to looting may be developed.

Archaeologically Rich Market

The archaeologically rich market is based primarily on individuals, families, and organized bands of looters who supply antiquities for the more controlled components of the trade. Local people, in many cases subsistence diggers (Hollowell-Zimmer 2003; Matsuda 1998; Staley 1993), are usually responsible for the looting of archaeological sites, churches, and museums. This type of activity does not lead to great financial payoffs for the looters. They sell to middlemen, who take the goods to resell to the antiquities dealers at a hefty markup (Brodie 1998b). Typically, it is the middlemen who retain the majority of the profits, while the finders of the artifacts often receive less than 1 percent of the eventual retail value of their looted goods (Borodkin 1995: 377).

Once the items have been obtained from the looters, complex networks develop in order to handle the traffic in material. It is here that we see the emergence of organized criminal activity, given the need for movement on a regular and systematic basis (Freiberg 1997: 237). At this juncture the antiquity is still a stolen item, with no formal provenience, illegally acquired and illegally exported. It is usually smuggled out of the country of origin to a transit point via the airport in tourist luggage, on container ships, or in diplomatic pouches.[4]

In some cases, thefts are preordered by dealers and collectors. In China, for example, instances of "selling-to-order" have involved a looter showing photographs of art available in a poorly guarded museum to a prospective buyer, stealing the selected items, and arranging for their transport out of China (Adler and Polk 2002). Changes in supply can create new forms of demand—the market is intentionally flooded with a new genre in response to a newly created aesthetic fad. A current example is the demand for Spanish colonial art, which has caused a significant increase in the looting of churches in Central and South America for items to adorn homes in Spain and the United States (Luke 2003).

It is important to recognize that the various types of markets are not necessarily geographically separate and can in fact all occur within the same country or state. Archaeologically rich market countries can also serve as centers of demand, as in the trade in Native American artifacts in the United States. A good example is the case of the controversial ossuary that has recently been the focus of much attention (Gugliotta 2002; Legon 2002; Silberman and Goren 2003; Wilford 2002).[5] According to the purchaser, the ossuary was looted from a tomb near Jerusalem by local villagers (the archaeologically rich market) and then offered for sale in an antiquities shop in Jerusalem's Old City (the transit market). It was purchased by an Israeli collector (the destination market), who kept it in his home without realizing the significance of the inscription until it was pointed out by an expert epigrapher. Thus the entire process of the artifact's movement from the ground to the ultimate consumer took place in a single region. Further examples of geographically united markets include the case of the Salisbury Hoard in England (Stead 1998) and numerous instances in the American Southwest (Axtman 2002).

Transit Markets

A common feature of successful transit markets is the lack of concern regarding how the material reached the given jurisdiction (no questions asked), thus opening up a market that is focused on successfully exporting the objects. A key criterion for an effective transit point is the status of free port, where the laundering of the artifacts can occur and proper papers of exportation can be prepared (Polk 2000: 85).[6] Crucial to this stage is that when goods are imported into the destination market, they can be openly displayed in the most respectable establishments (like Sotheby's and Christie's). The situation is facilitated by the purchasers and the merchants, both of whom are either unaware of or choose not to question the origin of the goods being procured.

Prott and O'Keefe (1989: 532) state that there are two principal types of transit market countries: geographically advantaged states and art market states. The geographically advantaged states are those through which traders and smugglers must almost inevitably pass, if only briefly, because of their physical proximity to the archaeologically rich country(s) or their role as a regional hub. As a prime regional commercial area, Hong Kong is often cited as a major market and center of trade in antiquities (Lundén 2004). Evidence exists that antiquities looted from Angkor Wat in Cambodia are brought to Hong Kong (International Council of Museums 1997), "where the artifacts disappear into a semi-legitimate antiquities market that counts unwary international museums among its main customers" (Boyd 1994: 48). Israel is an excellent example of a geographically advantaged state due to its proximity to the Palestinian Authority (PA), where most of the looting in this region occurs.

Many of the geographically advantaged states, while conveniently located near archaeologically rich areas—such as the Gulf states, often a conduit for material leaving the Middle East—are not well positioned as shopping venues for dealers and collectors interested in purchasing archaeological artifacts. Art market states like Belgium, Germany, and Switzerland provide both a setting for artifact laundering and a desirable location for art fairs and auction houses.

The second type of transit market identified by Prott and O'Keefe (1989: 533) is the art market state, in which services such as auctions, valuation, and restoration are concentrated: "Traditionally, they [transit markets] have played a very important role in the movement of cultural property, even though the volume originating in different areas may have fluctuated widely." They cite the United Kingdom as an important transit state.

Licensing requirements under the Waverley system (*Committee on the Export of Works of Art, Waverley Report* 1952) make the United Kingdom an ideal transit market. Based on a system dating back to World War II, the Import, Export and Customs Powers (Defense) Act was enacted in 1939 to prevent the outflow of capital and to protect foreign exchange reserves. All export applications are reviewed by the Board of Trade pursuant to criteria recommended by the Waverley Committee (Brodie 2002). In their discussion of export licensing and the Waverley criteria, Maurice and Turnor (1992: 273) suggest that the review process could actually be used to create a provenance.

As a member of the European Union (EU), the United Kingdom is also bound by European Union Council Regulation No. 3911/92 and European Union Council Directive 93/7 (Brodie 1998a; O'Keefe 1997: 24–25). The former requires that export licenses be issued for taking EU cultural material outside the EU countries, while removing internal barriers, thus enabling the free movement of goods within the EU (Brodie 1998a). The latter provides for the recovery of "national treasures" illegally exported to other countries within the European Union. Scholars have commented on the ineffectiveness of the regulations in both instances due to their cumbersome paperwork requirements; and neither bars the issuing of U.K. or EU export licenses for artifacts from countries outside the EU (Brodie 1998a; O'Keefe 1997: 30; Palmer 1995).

While the United Kingdom has strict rules governing its own national treasures over fifty years old, export licenses are much more freely granted for foreign material that has been in England less than fifty years, allowing the British economy to benefit from the sale of the cultural heritage of other countries (Brodie 2002: 190). The U.K. restrictions on the export of antiquities are aimed at protecting its own cultural heritage rather than at curtailing the illegal trade in art (Prott and O'Keefe 1989: 502). On a more positive note, significant progress toward closing the loopholes in protecting the cultural heritage of other nations was made in 2002 when the United Kingdom ratified the 1970 UNESCO Convention. The British Parliament undertook further measures by enacting the Dealing in Cultural Objects (Offences) Act 2003 (for a detailed discussion, see Gerstenblith, chapter 3).

Switzerland's laws favoring the good faith purchaser, its proximity to archaeologically rich countries (Italy and the Balkans), and until recently, its general unwillingness to participate fully in or enforce international regulation of cultural property have created another ideal art transit state (see Watson, this chapter 4, for further discussion). Historically, the Swiss have been successful in promoting themselves as a conduit nation; the art trade industry in Switzerland was valued at over U.S. $2 billion nearly a decade ago (Greenfield 1996: 247). Launderers seek out those Swiss dealers who routinely look the other way and take great steps to conceal the illegal past of looted objects. Possessors of stolen items can store the works in private banks or at tax-free warehouses at Swiss airports and border crossings. After a statutory period and evidence of a good faith purchase, the stolen piece belongs to the purchaser (Prott and O'Keefe 1989: 384; Watson, chapter 4). In 2003 Switzerland also ratified the 1970 UNESCO Convention and enacted new legislation—the Federal Act on the International Transfer of Cultural Property—that may change Switzerland's historic role as a transit country.[7] While the enactment of this legislation is certainly a welcome step in the effort to prevent illegal dealing in stolen and illicitly excavated cultural objects, it remains to be seen whether the law will have a discernible impact on Switzerland's role as a transit market in the laundering of illegal antiquities.

It is in the transit market that the conversion from illegal to legal takes place. Once an export license is procured in those venues, the material can be successfully negotiated through customs, and retail functions can all be conducted openly and legally. By this time, the artifact has changed hands at least three times, making it much more difficult to prove exactly where the item came from, what borders it crossed, and how long it has been in circulation. Often there is an attempt to provide provenance in these locations by the use of well-known and thoroughly suspect euphemisms, such as "from the collection of a Swiss gentleman" or "a collection in Hong Kong" (Adler and Polk 2002).

Destination Market

Once the artifact has passed through the transit point and receives a "clean bill of sale," it can enter the marketplace as a legitimate antiquity. Despite evidence that a large proportion of material is illicitly traded and is directly connected with other illegal activities (clandestine excavation, theft, illegal drugs, terrorism, and possibly on occasion even murder), some participants in the sales and destination markets are indifferent to the origin of the goods being sold (Prott and O'Keefe 1989: 539).[8] These dealers, experts, collectors, and museums prefer to look the other way and not ask questions about provenance and authenticity. Furthermore, by not asking uncomfortable questions about where a piece originated and how it ended up on the market, legitimate dealers are acting in collusion with the illegitimate aspects of the market.

It is a fact that wealthy individuals, auction houses, and museums collect and buy stolen and illegally exported (or excavated) art and antiquities, whether knowingly or unknowingly. A remarkable characteristic of this market is pointed out by Bator (1988: 360):

> The most striking thing to a lawyer who comes upon the art work is how deep and uncritical is the assumption that transactions within it should normally be—are certainly entitled to be—secret.... No dealer or auction house will normally reveal the provenance of an object offered for sale; it is assumed that buyers and the public have no business knowing where and when and for how much the object was acquired.... Indeed the tradition is that such information is rarely even sought.... It is the propriety of secrecy which is assumed; and it is secrecy which enables persons, otherwise aspiring to the highest standards of personal probity, to become accomplices in the acquisition of looted masterpieces.

The trade's own unspoken etiquette upholds a façade of respectability that makes the provenance of a piece for sale a taboo subject (Renfrew 2000: 37). Client confidentiality is often cited as the chief reason why dealers and auction houses refuse to provide provenance. Auction houses on the whole are subject to little direct legal control of their activities. In the United Kingdom and in some U.S. states they are not required to guarantee title or to examine provenance and usually include in their conditions of sale an exclusion of responsibility for genuineness, authorship, provenance, etc. (Prott and O'Keefe 1989: 557).

Recently the prevailing sentiment at auction houses concerning the usefulness of provenance has begun to change. However, although collectors are increasingly requesting the pedigree of the objects they are buying, and although the pedigree is now included in most sale catalogues, the tacit agreement regarding secrecy remains. For some museums and collectors the familiar phrase "from the collection of a Swiss gentleman..." attached to the antiquity in question still suffices.

A CASE STUDY: COINS

I walked by Mohammed and his shoe-shine operation in Jerusalem every day for months, never suspecting that he also dealt in ancient coins until, in an interview with an archaeologist/coin collector, I was told that he purchased most of his coins from Mohammed.[9] I then began to track Mohammed's interactions with his various customers, with the local Palestinian women, and with a particular Israeli dealer who routinely visited him. The popular notion (rightly or wrongly) is that coins will increase in value, and one only needs to buy a few

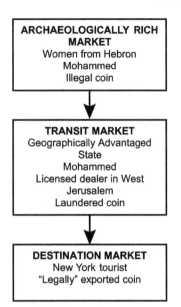

Figure 9.2. Pathway of a coin from Hebron to New York City.

to profit financially. The possibility that ancient coins in Israel and the PA may come from the temple from which Jesus drove the moneychangers (John 2:13–25) adds an extra dimension to their value. Coins are an integral part of daily life and are handled on a daily basis, which allows for easy concealment and transportation. The following relates how a coin travels from Hebron, a city in the PA, to New York City with few obstacles along the way (see fig. 9.2).

Introduction

Israel has a national patrimony law whereby the ownership of archaeological material is vested in the state. In Israel, it is legal to buy and sell artifacts from pre-1978 collections and inventories (that is, those predating the year of the national patrimony law). Currently there is a system of legally sanctioned dealers in antiquities who are allowed to request and provide export permits, issued by the Israel Antiquities Authority (IAA).[10] The PA is drafting new national patrimony legislation that will tackle the issue of legal sale of antiquities. Cultural heritage protection in the West Bank is presently governed by the Law of Antiquities Jordan, 1966, and in the Gaza Strip by the Antiquities Ordinance No. 51 of 1929, both laws being holdovers from the British Mandate period, when the sale of antiquities was permissible.

Recent research has shown that some of the material for sale in the legally sanctioned shops in Israel comes from looted sites in the PA (Blum 2001; Ilan et. al 1989; Kersel 2005; Keyser 2002), and licensed dealers are able to sell looted material by exchanging the registry numbers of items already sold with those of a similar description that have newly appeared on the market. For example, when a tourist purchases a Herodian oil lamp, registry number 147, from an officially sanctioned dealer, he or she receives a certificate of authenticity (supplied by the dealer) and an export license (but only if the tourist remembers to ask for one) issued by the IAA. Both a description of the item and the official registry number appear on the export license. If the tourist does not acquire an export license, the dealer can then reuse the registry number as there is no formal record of the sale. The dealer has another Herodian oil lamp in his stores very similar in size, color, and design to lamp number 147. He then assigns the second oil lamp the registry number 147 and places it among his inventory to be sold. This is common practice verified through a series of interviews with dealers, archaeologists, and representatives of the IAA.

While often proffered as a remedy for reducing the destruction and theft of archaeological artifacts, the licensing of dealers and the use of registry systems are often suspect. O'Keefe (1997: 31–32) states that "theoretically a register would allow acquisitions of artifacts to be traced and should dissuade dealers from acquiring those with dubious provenance. In practice their effectiveness is questionable."

Artifact Pathway

Archaeologically rich market. The village women in the Hebron area cultivate mint and herbs in their backyards for sale on the streets of East Jerusalem. Often while gathering produce for market, the women unearth ancient coins, and at times when economic circumstances are particularly tight, the local villagers dig for coins.[11] Once the village women arrive in Jerusalem, they sell the coins to Mohammed, one of the many shoe-shine operators who dot the streets of East Jerusalem and the Old City.[12] Mohammed's spoken English is fairly good, and he positions himself in an area of high tourist traffic. Many of his shoe-shine clientele are foreigners and he always offers to show them the coins in his pocket just in case they might like to buy a coin along with the shoe-shine. On a good day, Mohammed can make between U.S. $200 and $300 selling two or three coins to a foreigner. At this point, Mohammed, the middleman, is acting as a dealer of the coins; it is here in direct sales that his profit margin is at its highest.

Mohammed has been in the shoe-shine/coin business for a long time (some forty years) and has become quite knowledgeable about the coins sold to him. He can differentiate between the valuable, rarer pieces and the everyday run-of-the-mill coins. He sells the rarer coins to a licensed Israeli dealer from West Jerusalem who visits him regularly. He sells the more prosaic coins to less savvy foreigners, who may pay more than the estimated market value of the coin because they are unfamiliar with the market prices.

Transit market. Given the current disputed borders in Jerusalem, it is an ideal, geographically advantaged transit market. Licensed antiquities dealers from the Old City or West Jerusalem can easily meet with Mohammed and examine the coins coming in from the PA. Mohammed buys the coins from the village women for a set price and then sells them to licensed dealers for at least ten times what he paid for them.[13] The licensed dealer cleans the coins, provides each with a registry number as required by law (Antiquities Law 1978), and adds them to his shop inventory. It is in this transit market that the coins go from illegal to "legal" through the acquisition of a registry number, a pre-1978 provenance, and a certificate of authenticity, all made available by the licensed antiquities dealer.[14] An export license can now be issued by the IAA based on the falsified registry number.

Even if the IAA inspector pays an unannounced visit to the shop to check the inventory, nothing appears untoward since the coin now possesses a registry number that corresponds with the inventory description. The IAA would be able to confiscate the coin under the 1978 antiquities law only if it is unique or was a very rare example or if the IAA can prove the coin came from public land (which it generally cannot do). At this point, the coin has passed into the legitimate sales market for the unsuspecting tourist or collector to buy.

Destination market. The tourist from New York City ventures into the licensed antiquities shop in West Jerusalem looking for the perfect coin to complement his collection. The dealer offers Mohammed's coin to the innocent tourist for five times what he paid Mohammed.[15] Forewarned by the concierge at the hotel and in the guidebooks (Prag 2002: 26), the tourist is knowledgeable enough to ask for an export license, which he receives in due course. When he asks where the coin comes from, he is told that it was part of an old family collection from the Hebron area. Thus, satisfied that the coin is genuine and that he will not have a problem getting it out of the country, the tourist buys the coin.

At airport security the tourist is surprised that the security agents do not question him at all regarding the coin he is taking out of the country. They do not even ask him to produce the export certificate.

The PA Department of Antiquities and the IAA are both chronically underfunded and understaffed. Neither has the resources to monitor site looting, dealer inventories, or shop registries on a regular basis, nor does either have the financial resources to train customs agents and security personnel in archaeological resource protection. Political and economic instability in the region, a lack of effective law enforcement in the PA, and a unique legal market in Israel all create the perfect setting for looting and illegal excavation to occur and provide the market for the artifacts to be sold. Unfortunately, given the dire situation in the area, the illegal trade in antiquities is a low priority for both sides.

COUNTERMEASURES

The illegal trade in antiquities can be diminished only through appropriate countermeasures, such as the implementation of stricter national legislation enforcing the 1970 UNESCO Convention. In order to stem the flow of antiquities out of their countries, many archaeologically rich nations have instituted strict national patrimony laws that vest ownership of undiscovered antiquities in the nation and prohibit the export of archaeological and ethnological material (see the laws of Cambodia, Egypt, Honduras, Jordan, Mali, and Peru, to name but a few). The establishment of state ownership and the accompanying export regulations often rely on the willingness of market nations (mainly in the West) to recognize and enforce the claims of archaeologically rich nations requesting the return of their cultural patrimony, which is not always a realistic assumption.[16] Countries without national patrimony laws should be encouraged to implement such legislation. Nations should also be encouraged to acknowledge the import/export restrictions of other countries in order to seize and return illegally exported archaeological material. Increased intercountry memoranda of understanding with countries that focus on the protection of cultural property should be instituted as part of a global effort to prevent the illegal movement of goods.

At each stage along the pathway of an artifact, there needs to be greater enforcement of the existing laws to protect the cultural landscape. A starting point would be more financial resources for the on-the-ground protection of archaeological sites. Placing guards at sites that are routinely looted may act as a deterrent. Enhanced training of police, park rangers, and customs and border officials in the archaeologically rich transit and destination markets would aid in the monitoring of the international transport of illegal goods. These groups of officials should be able to recognize the types of antiquities they are protecting and should know how the laws in their regions work (O'Keefe 1997: 89).

Often foreign archaeological teams do not realize the ramifications of their projects on the local communities. In one sense the locals who are hired as laborers on archaeological excavations receive training in excavation techniques that they may then employ as looters (Kersel and Luke 2005). Greater effort to engage the local population with the project research objectives, the importance of their cultural heritage, and the long-term impact of looting should be an integral part of archaeological investigations (O'Keefe 1997: 90–91).

Providing alternative economic opportunities and financial incentives for those who engage in subsistence looting is another suggested countermeasure for combating illegal excavation in the archaeologically rich market (Mackenzie 2002). Unfortunately, demand is high, and local populations have become increasingly dedicated to the looting of archaeological sites, as Politis (2002) demonstrates in his research on the Ghor-es-Safi in Jordan. These villagers have honed their excavating skills and can distinguish between Byzantine period and Bronze Age materials (Politis 2002: 259). Local populations have now come to depend on the antiquities marketplace to such an extent that not only have they geared their excavations accordingly, but they have devoted time and effort to learning about the specific periods and artifacts in order to ensure the highest possible monetary payback. Changing this entrenched behavior would require viable economic alternatives for the local stakeholders. What is most relevant in the context of this chapter is that the market drove these individuals not only to loot but to learn how to loot in order to reap the greatest financial rewards.

Education, both formal and informal through the mass media, is a powerful tool that should be used in the fight against the plunder of antiquities. According to O'Keefe (1997: 89) "education and publicity must cover all States affected and all levels of society." Each of the stakeholder groups in this debate (dealers, museum professionals, collectors, archaeologists, and government representatives) has a code of ethics to which members should be held accountable. No single group should be omitted from the education process. Asking for provenance and assurance of good title should be second nature and an essential characteristic of the ethical standards of each of these parties. According to Herscher (1987: 213), "real progress in diminishing the illegal traffic in antiquities and the looting of archaeological sites will ultimately be accomplished not through law enforcement but through the ethical codes of the pertinent groups and the influence they exert on societal norms as a whole." There are no codes of ethics for individual private collectors—except the Swiss Association of Collectors (O'Keefe 1997: 44)—or tourists or local buyers, nor are there public education programs that depict the connection between the illegal excavation of archaeological sites and consumer demand. These should be highlighted in the public sphere. The market model implies that the illegal trade depends upon the willingness of consumers to purchase unprovenanced artifacts and upon a lack of awareness in the trade in general (Adler and Polk 2002: 48). "From the collection of a Swiss gentleman" or "from a collection in Hong Kong" should not be acknowledged and accepted forms of provenance. If collectors and museums refused to buy unprovenanced antiquities, and if the general populace could be made to understand the concomitant irretrievable loss of knowledge, the trade in antiquities would surely be diminished (Adler and Polk 2002; Gilgan 2001; Kersel and Luke 2003).

CONCLUSION

To address effectively the issues of how artifacts travel from the ground to the buyer, a concerted effort to integrate all aspects of the trade in antiquities must be made. The mechanisms currently in place to combat the illegal excavation of archaeological sites do not appear to be acting as deterrents. In order for the countermeasures to succeed, all of the various factions should be united. Education can only work if the laws underpinning the protection of cultural heritage provide policies, financial incentives, and oversight. There must be cooperation between the various stakeholders and greater disclosure of information. Emphasis on tighter legal measures, law enforcement, education, and a concerted effort by both archaeologically rich and market nations to lessen the demand for archaeological material in the marketplace are key to finding solutions to the loss of cultural heritage.

The essential goal is a situation in which consumers will not purchase objects that have been illegally removed from their original context. In terms of Israel and the PA, would Mohammed's coin have reached New York City without a registry number? Perhaps the coin would still be in New York, but certainly not with a legally provided export license and certificate of authenticity stating that the coin came from an old family collection from the Hebron area.

ACKNOWLEDGMENTS

I thank my many informants in the Middle East, without whom much of this research would be impossible. I would also like to thank Neil Brodie, Patty Gerstenblith, Christina Luke, Yorke Rowan, and Edna Sachar for insightful comments and editorial suggestions on earlier drafts of this chapter. This research was supported by the W. F. Albright Institute, Educational and Cultural Affairs Fellowship, the Palestinian American Research Center, Ridgeway-Venn Student Travel Scholarship, Tweedie Exploration Fund, and the University of Cambridge, Department of Archaeology. All errors and omissions are entirely my responsibility.

Notes

1. eBay website <http://listings.ebay.com/Antiquities-Classical-Amer_W0QQca-trefZC4QQfromZR10QQsacategoryZ37903QQsapricehiZQQsapriceloZQQsocmd-ZListingItemListQQsoloctogZ9QQsosortorderZ2QQsosortpropertyZ2>, accessed May 1, 2004.

2. The "provenance" (a term most often used by art historians) of an object includes the original location and context of the object as well as the history of ownership, a key part in the evaluation of its value. "Provenience" (the term most often used by anthropologists and archaeologists) means the archaeological find spot of an object.

3. For an interesting discussion of the chain of supply of an illicit antiquities market, see Mackenzie 2002.

4. A recent seizure of a shipping container at the port of Haifa in Israel revealed a large quantity of archaeological material destined for the United States (Archaeologist, Israel Antiquities Authority, interview by the author, May 4, 2004).

5. An ossuary is depository for bones, in this case a simple limestone box with a potentially history-making inscription if proven to be authentic, referring to James as the brother of Jesus (see Samuels 2004).

6. A free port is an international port at which cargo may be disembarked or unloaded, may remain, and may be transshipped without being subject to any customs charge or duties. Definition available from <http://www.eyefortransport.com/glossary/ef.shtml>, accessed September 12, 2004.

7. See Gerstenblith, chapter 3, for a detailed discussion of Switzerland's recent legislation and its potential impact on the trade in antiquities.

8. In his account of the intrigue surrounding the Sevso Treasure, journalist Peter Landesman suggests that Jozef Sumegh and two associates were murdered as a result of their involvement with the unearthing of the silver hoard (Landesman 2001: 68).

9. This case study is based on a series of interviews with Mohammed, a Palestinian shoe-shine operator; an Israeli dealer from West Jerusalem; an archaeologist/amateur collector; and a tourist. All participants agreed to be interviewed on condition of anonymity, and I have therefore changed their names. The interviews were conducted as part of my Ph.D. dissertation research on the legal trade in antiquities in Israel and the Palestinian Authority.

10. The IAA is charged with safeguarding the cultural heritage of Israel and enforcing the Israeli antiquities laws of 1978, 1989, and 2003. Further information is available at <http://www.israntique.org.il>.

11. For further information on the phenomenon of subsistence digging, see Hollowell-Zimmer 2003; Matsuda 1998; Staley 1993.

12. Under the current political conditions it is far easier for women than for men to travel between Hebron and Jerusalem.

13. No one interviewed would divulge the price paid for the coins.

14. For further discussion on the exchange of registry numbers as a common practice among licensed antiquities dealers, see Ilan et al. 1989; Kersel 2005.

15. If the price paid by Mohammed for the coins is U.S. $5, then the tourist is paying $250 for the same coin, fifty times the original price paid to the village women from Hebron. For further discussion of prices realized versus the original finder's price, see O'Keefe 1997: 19, n. 35.

16. For a detailed discussion of the issue of lack of enforcement of the import/export laws of foreign governments, see Gerstenblith, chapter 3, on the Schultz case.

BIBLIOGRAPHY

Alder, Christine, and Kenneth Polk. "Stopping This Awful Business: The Illicit Traffic in Antiquities Examined as a Criminal Market." *Art, Antiquity and Law* 7, no. 2 (2002): 35–53.

Antiquities Authority Law 5749-1989 (Israel).

Antiquities Authority Law Amendments-2003 (Israel).

Antiquities Law 5738-1978 (Israel).

Antiquities Ordinance No. 51, 1929 (Palestine).

Axtman, Kris. "Archaeological Looting: US Gets Tougher on Lucrative Crime." *Christina Science Monitor* <http://www.csmonitor.com/2002/0620/p02s02-usju.html>, accessed July 2, 2002.

Bator, Paul. *The International Trade in Art.* Chicago, Ill.: University of Chicago Press, 1988.

Bernick, Lauren. "Art and Antiquities Theft." *Transnational Organized Crime* 4, no. 2 (1998): 91–116.

Blum, Orly. *The Illicit Antiquities Trade: An Analysis of Current Antiquities Looting in Israel.* M.A. thesis, Sotheby's Institute, 2001.

Borodkin, Lisa. "The Economics of Antiquities Looting and a Proposed Legal Alternative." *Columbia Law Review* 95 (1995): 377–417.

Boyd, Alan. "The Raiders of Angkor Wat." *World Press Review* 41, no. 11 (1994): 48–56.

Brodie, Neil. "The Antiquities Trade in the United Kingdom: Recent Developments." Paper presented at the World Archaeological Congress Intercongress, Croatia, 1998a.

———. "Pity the Poor Middlemen." *Culture without Context*, issue 3 (Autumn 1998): 7–9 (1998b).

———. "Britannia Waives the Rules? Licensing of Archaeological Material for Export from the UK." In *Illicit Antiquities: The Theft of Culture and the Extinction of Archaeology*, ed. Neil Brodie and Kathryn Walker Tubb, 185–204. New York: Routledge, 2002.

Brodie, Neil, Jennifer Doole, and Colin Renfrew (eds.). *Trade in Illicit Antiquities: The Destruction of the World's Archaeological Heritage.* McDonald Institute Monograph. Cambridge, U.K.: McDonald Institute for Archaeological Research, 2001.

Brodie, Neil, and Kathryn Walker Tubb (eds.). *Illicit Antiquities: The Theft of Culture and the Extinction of Archaeology.* New York: Routledge, 2002.

Committee on the Export of Works of Art, Waverley Report (1952). The Export of Works of Art, etc. Report of a Committee appointed by the Chancellor of the Exchequer. London: HMSO (United Kingdom).

Dealing in Cultural Objects (Offences) Act 2003. Norwich, U. K.: Stationery Office Limited, 2003 (United Kingdom).

Elia, Ricardo. "Analysis of Looting, Selling and Collecting of Apulian Red-Figure Vases: A Quantitative Approach." In *Trade in Illicit Antiquities: The Destruction of the World's Archaeological Heritage,* ed. Neil Brodie, Jennifer Doole, and Colin Renfrew, 145–53. McDonald Institute Monograph. Cambridge, U.K.: McDonald Institute for Archaeological Research, 2001.

European Union Council Directive 93/7/EEC (Europe).

European Union Council Regulation No. 3911/92 (Europe).

Federal Assembly of the Swiss Confederation. *Federal Act on the International Transfer of Cultural Property.* Geneva: Switzerland, 2003 (Switzerland).

Freiberg, Arie. "Regulating Market for Stolen Property." *The Australian and New Zealand Journal of Criminology* 30 (1997): 237–58.

Gilgan, Elizabeth. "Looting and the Market for Maya Objects: A Belizean Perspective." In *Trade in Illicit Antiquities: The Destruction of the World's Archaeological Heritage,* ed. Neil Brodie, Jennifer Doole, and Colin Renfrew, 73–87. McDonald Institute Monograph. Cambridge, U.K.: McDonald Institute for Archaeological Research, 2001.

Greenfield, Jeanette. *The Return of Cultural Treasures.* Cambridge, U.K.: Cambridge University Press, 1996.

Gugliotta, Guy. "Stone Box May Be Oldest Link to Jesus." *Washington Post,* <http://www.washingtonpost . . . p-dyn/A61782-2002Oct21.html>, accessed October 22, 2002.

Herscher, Ellen. "Antiquities Market." *Journal of Field Archaeology* 14, no. 2 (1987): 213–23.

Hollowell-Zimmer, Julie. "Digging in the Dirt: Ethics and 'Low-End' Looting." In *Ethical Issues in Archaeology,* ed. Larry Zimmer, Karen D. Vitelli, and Julie Hollowell-Zimmer, 46–56. Walnut Creek, Calif.: AltaMira, 2003.

Ilan, David, Uzi Dahari, and Gideon Avni. "Plundered! The Rampant Rape of Israel's Archaeological Sites." *Biblical Archaeology Review,* March–April 1989), 38–41.

Import, Export and Customs Powers (Defense) Act, 1939 (United Kingdom).

International Council of Museums. *Looting in Angkor.* International Council of Museums, in collaboration with l'Ecole française d'Extrême-Orient. 2nd ed. Paris: ICOM, EFEO, 1997.

Kersel, Morag. "Archaeology's Well Kept Secret: The Managed Trade in Antiquities." In *SOMA 2003: Symposium on Mediterranean Archaeology, Proceedings of the Seventh Annual Meeting of Postgraduate Researchers,* ed. Camillia Briault, Jack Green, Anthi Kaldelis, and Anna Stellatou. British Archaeological Reports International Series, 79–83. Oxford: Archaeopress, 2005.

Kersel, Morag, and Christina Luke. "The Battle for the Past: Comment." *Culture without Context,* issue 12 (Autumn 2003): 28–30.

———. "Selling a Replicated Past: Power and Identity in Marketing Archaeological Replicas." *Anthropology in Action, Journal for Applied Anthropology in Policy and Practice* 11, nos. 2–3 (2005): 32–43.

Keyser, Jayson. "Holy Land's Ancient Sites Hit by Looting: Archaeologists Say Region's

Troubles Lead to Desperate Thefts." <http://www.msnbc.com.news/782447.asp?0si-&cp1=1>, accessed July 19, 2002.

Kunitz, Michelle. "Switzerland and the International Trade in Art and Antiquities." *Northwestern Journal of International Law and Business* 21 (2001): 519–43.

Landesman, Peter. "The Curse of Sevso Silver." *Atlantic Monthly*, November 2001, 62–89.

Law of Antiquities, Provisional Law No. 51, 1966 (Jordan).

Legon, James." Scholars: Oldest Evidence of Jesus?" <http://www.cnn.com/2002/TECH/science/10/21/jesus.box/index.html>, accessed October 22, 2002.

Luke, Christina. Colonial Art Research. On file with the U.S. Department of State Office of Cultural Property. 2003.

Lundén, Staffan. "The Scholar and the Art Market: Swedish Scholarly Contributions to the Destruction of the World's Archaeological Heritage." In *Swedish Archaeologists on Ethics*, ed. H. Karlsson, 197–247. Lindome: Bricoleur Press, 2004.

Mackenzie, Simon. "Regulating the Market in Illicit Antiquities." *Trends and Issues in Crime and Criminal Justice*, no. 239, Australian Institute of Criminology, Canberra. 2002.

Matsuda, David. "The Ethics of Archaeology, Subsistence Digging, and Artifact Looting in Latin America: Point, Muted Counterpoint." *International Journal of Cultural Property* 7, no. 1 (1998): 87–97.

Maurice, Clare, and Richard Turnor. "The Export Licensing Rules in the United Kingdom and the Waverley Criteria." *International Journal of Cultural Property* 1, no. 2 (1992): 273–95.

O'Keefe, Patrick. *Trade in Antiquities: Reducing Theft and Destruction*. London: Archetype, 1997.

Palmer, Norman. "Recovering Stolen Art." In *Antiquities Trade or Betrayed: Legal, Ethical, and Conservation Issues*, ed. Kathryn Walker Tubb, 1–38. London: Archetype, 1995.

Politis, Konstantinos. "Dealing with Dealers and Tomb Robbers: The Realities of the Archaeology of the Ghor es-Safi, Jordan." In *Illicit Antiquities: The Theft of Culture and the Extinction of Archaeology*, ed. Neil Brodie and Kathryn Walker Tubb, 256–67. New York: Routledge, 2002.

Polk, Kenneth. Illegal Property Markets. Paper presented at the 3rd National Outlook Symposium on Crime, Canberra, 1999.

———. "The Antiquities Market Viewed as a Criminal Market," *Hong Kong Lawyer*, September 2000, 82–91.

Prag, Kay. *The Blue Guide: Israel and the Palestinian Territories*. New York: W. W. Norton, 2002.

Prott, Lyndel, and Patrick O'Keefe. *Law and the Cultural Heritage*, vol. 3: *Movement*. London: Butterworths, 1989.

Renfrew, Colin. *Loot, Legitimacy and Ownership: The Ethical Crisis in Archaeology*. London: Duckworth, 2000.

Samuels, David. "Written in Stone." *New Yorker*, April 12, 2004, 48–59.

Schávelzon, Daniel. "What's Going on around the Corner: Illegal Trade of Antiquities in

Argentina." In *Illicit Antiquities: The Theft of Culture and the Extinction of Archaeology*, ed. Neil Brodie and Kathryn Walker Tubb, 228–34. New York: Routledge, 2002.

Silberman, Neil, and Yuval Goren. "Faking Biblical History." *Archaeology* 56, no. 2 (September–October 2003): 20–29.

Staley, David. "St. Lawrence Island's Subsistence Diggers: A New Perspective on Human Effects on Archaeological Sites." *Journal of Field Archaeology* 20, no. 3 (1993): 347–55.

Stead, Ian. *The Salisbury Hoard*. Stroud, U.K.: Tempus, 1998.

United Nations Educational, Scientific and Cultural Organization. *Convention on the Means of Prohibiting and Preventing the Illicit Import, Export and Transfer of Ownership of Cultural Property*. Paris: UNESCO, 1970.

Vogel, Carol. "Top Executives Quit Sotheby's as Art World Inquiry Widens." *New York Times*, February 22, 2000, C1; in LEXIS/NEXIS [database on-line], NEWS library, NY TIMES file; accessed October 23, 2002.

Wilford, John Noble. "'Jesus' Inscription on Stone May Be Earliest Ever Found." *New York Times*, October 22, 2002, <http://www.nytimes.com/2002/10/22/science/22JESU.html>, accessed October 22, 2002.

10

The Plunder of Iraq's Archaeological Heritage, 1991–2005, and the London Antiquities Trade

NEIL BRODIE

FROM THE 1991 GULF WAR TO THE 2003 IRAQ WAR

Before the 1991 Gulf War, Iraq's archaeological heritage was under the supervision and protection of a large, well-organized and professional Department of Antiquities and remained relatively free from theft and vandalism (Gibson 1997). In the aftermath of that war, however, as the country descended into chaos, between 1991 and 1994 eleven regional museums were broken into and approximately 3,000 artifacts and 484 manuscripts were stolen, of which only fifty-four items have been recovered (Lawler 2001a: 34; Schipper 2005: 252; Symposium 1994). By the mid-1990s, the organizational capabilities of the Department of Antiquities were deteriorating, and the focus of destruction shifted from museums to archaeological sites. Many Iraqis were reduced to destitution as massive inflation took hold in the wake of UN-imposed trade sanctions, and robbing archaeological sites became an attractive and viable economic option. Much of the looting appears to have been orchestrated by Saddam Hussein's brother-in-law Arshad Yasin (Garen 2004: 30).

In the north, Assyrian palaces at Nineveh and Nimrud were attacked. At least fourteen relief slabs from Sennacherib's palace at Nineveh were broken up, and pieces were discovered on the market (Russell 1997a, 1997b). Often these fragments had been reworked to alter the original design orientation, or roughly squared off, both strategies intended to disguise their origin and make it harder for them to be recognized. The storeroom at Nimrud was broken into and bas-reliefs from the palaces of Ashurnasirpal II and Tiglathpileser III were stolen (Paley 2003; Russell 1997a, 1997b). In the south, tell sites were targeted—for example, it was reported that hundreds of armed looters had descended on Umma and dug up a cuneiform archive (Symposium 1994). During this chaotic period, at least one guard and one looter were shot dead.

In response to this plunder, British, U.S., and Japanese academics prepared three fascicles of *Lost Heritage: Antiquities Stolen from Iraq's Regional Museums*, listing objects taken from regional museums, with an illustration, description, and Iraq Museum (IM) number provided for each object (Baker et al. 1993; Fujii and Oguchi 1996; Gibson and McMahon 1992). These fascicles are now available on-line and can be downloaded from the University of Chicago's Oriental Institute.[1]

Things improved toward the end of the 1990s when Saddam Hussein began to take a personal interest in Iraq's archaeology and formed a new State Board of Antiquities with an increased budget and better-paid staff to replace the by then ineffective Department of Antiquities. Official excavations started again at several sites around the country, and foreign archaeologists were encouraged to return (Lawler 2001b, 2001c). Harsh penalties were introduced for those caught digging illegally (Lawler 2001a: 35), although the vicious face of this new regime was revealed in 1997 when ten people were executed for stealing the head from a human-headed bull at Khorsabad.

Despite the fact that under the 1990 UN Security Council Resolution (UNSCR) 661 trade in cultural material from Iraq was illegal, the plunder of archaeological sites and museums attracted little or no media attention or political action in Europe or North America. In 2001, Andrew Lawler felt it necessary to write in *Science* that an "extensive crisis has been unfolding for the past decade with barely a murmur of protest from the international community" (Lawler 2001a: 32). The international community was about to be rudely awakened.

APRIL 2003

By early 2003, it was clear that another war was imminent. U.S. forces had been criticized after the 1991 Gulf War for damaging archaeological sites in Iraq (Zimansky and Stone 1992), and so on January 24, 2003, McGuire Gibson of the Oriental Institute at the University of Chicago accompanied a delegation from the American Council for Cultural Policy to the Department of Defense and provided the locations of four thousand (later increased to five thousand) archaeological sites that should be protected from military action in the event of war.[2] He also emphasized that looting would probably break out afterward (Gibson 2003a: 109; Lawler 2003: 583). Similar moves were afoot in the United Kingdom (Renfrew 2003; Stone 2005). The Department of Defense stressed that U.S. troops were already under orders not to damage archaeological and other cultural sites, and according to Gibson they made an effort not to do so (Gibson 2003b: 20), but the Department of Defense also maintained that stopping Iraqi civilians from looting was not their business. Nevertheless, by March 2003 the National Museum of Iraq was in second place behind the Central Bank on a list compiled by the Pentagon's Office of Reconstruction and Humanitarian Assistance of places to be secured by U.S. forces to forestall looting, although this list was for guidance only and had no command function (Lawler 2003: 583; Renfrew 2003: 323).

In the event, looting was widespread. No sooner had the fighting reached Baghdad in April 2003 than many of Iraq's cultural institutions, including the Iraq National Library and Archives, the National Museum, the Museum of Fine Art, and the Saddam House of Manuscripts (now the Iraq House of Manuscripts) were ransacked and in some cases burned. Initial reports were confusing, and damage assessments were nothing more than guesses. In the weeks and months that followed, Iraqi and U.S. investigators endeavored to discover what had happened, and two officially sanctioned reports were prepared (Bogdanos 2005; Deeb et al. 2003).

The Central Library of the Ministry of Endowments and Religious Affairs (Awqaf Library) is the oldest cultural institution in Iraq, and before the 2003 war it contained about 6,500 manuscripts and almost 60,000 books (al-Naqshbandi 2004). It was attacked on April 14 and burned to the ground. Journalist Robert Fisk alerted U.S. forces to the attack but there was no response. About 5,000 manuscripts had been moved to secure storage before war began, and are safe, but the remainder were stolen by the arsonists. Most of the books perished in the flames (al-Naqshbandi 2004; al-Tikriti 2003).

The National Library and Archives was burned and looted twice in April, with upward of 1,200,000 books destroyed (Bouchenaki 2003: 133; Gibson 2003a: 108, 110). In June 2004, a U.S. investigation reported that most of what had been lost had been archives relating to post-1977 Iraq and that the fires had been deliberately started to destroy records of Saddam Hussein's regime. All microfilms of newspapers and other archival sources were also destroyed (Deeb et al. 2003). Between attacks, about 200,000 items of the library's holdings were removed to a local mosque for protection, and these have since been returned intact to the library. Another 40,000 books and documents, many pertaining to the British colonial, Hashemite, and Ottoman periods, taken for safekeeping to the basement of the State Board of Tourism, also survived the looting but were then inundated in July 2003 when the basement flooded. The documents were moved to a dry environment above ground, but by the time they were taken to the Senior Officers' Club in October they were badly affected by mold and needed to be placed in freezers to prevent further damage. The documents were still frozen in June 2004, waiting for allocation of the resources and expertise necessary to thaw and conserve them (al-Tikriti 2003; Bahrani 2004; Deeb et al. 2003).

The collection of the Saddam House of Manuscripts, about 50,000 items in total, was removed to a climate-controlled bomb shelter before war broke out. The bunker was protected by local residents, who repeatedly chased off looters, and the collection is safe (al-Tikriti 2003; Deeb et al. 2003).[3] Although the damage caused to libraries and archives was serious, most public and professional outrage was directed toward the ransacking of the National Museum. The Iraq National Museum was founded in 1923 and moved to its present location in 1966. It was enlarged in 1986. Before the 1991 Gulf War, close to 10,000 artifacts from prehistoric through Islamic periods were on display, though this constituted less than 5 percent of the museum's total holdings (Ghaidan and Peolini 2003: 98). The National Museum and its collections survived the Gulf War intact, although the building suffered some damage from nearby bomb impacts. Unfortunately, flooding damaged many objects that had been packed away at that time for safekeeping in vaults of the Central Bank. When the museum reopened in April 2000, water damage was apparent on hundreds of objects, particularly ivories (Bailey 2004; Ghaidan and Peolini 2003: 99). By this time, the National Museum also contained material that had been moved there for safekeeping from the more vulnerable regional museums (Schipper 2005: 253). In March 2003, the museum closed once more to prepare for the imminent war.

Once it became clear that war was unavoidable, museum staff moved to offer the collections what protection they could. Some material was still in storage at the Central Bank, where it had been since 1991. A further 8,366 objects were moved from display cabinets to a secret underground storage facility, and large or fragile pieces that could not be moved were protected by foam-rubber padding and sand bags. Padding was also placed in front of Assyrian stone reliefs and on the floors of storerooms (al-Radi 2003: 103; Bogdanos 2003; Gibson 2003a: 110). Eventually, as the fighting closed in on Baghdad, staff were forced to evacuate the museum on April 8, 2003, when Iraqi soldiers moved in and took up positions in the museum compound.

The Iraqis soon became embroiled in heavy fighting with advancing U.S. troops, during which time the museum was left unprotected. The first break-in occurred on Thursday, April 10, and looters had the run of the museum until returning museum staff chased them off on April 12 (by which time the Iraqi troops had left). Staff repeatedly asked U.S. forces on the ground to provide some protection for the museum, but the local commander was not prepared to detach any troops or tanks without orders. On April 12 the then director of research at the museum, Donny George, visited the U.S. Marines' headquarters and was promised help, but none materialized. It was not until April 16 that four tanks finally arrived (Atwood 2003a; Lawler 2003: 584; Tubb 2003: 23).

The first journalists and television crews managed to arrive at the museum on April 11, five days before the tanks, and the tanks' late arrival has proved to be controversial. The reluctance of U.S. troops on the ground to move without orders while fighting continued is understandable, but what is harder for many Iraqis to understand is why it took so long for orders to be issued. It is conceivable that orders were not forthcoming because the situation was confused, or because there were more urgent military priorities, and in any case the dangers of urban warfare should not be underestimated (Bogdanos 2005: 503–7). Nevertheless, to some, it smacks of a high-level conspiracy designed to leave the museum unguarded for the purpose of allowing looters to fulfil "orders" placed by rich U.S. collectors and, at first, helped sour relations between the museum's staff and U.S. authorities. One immediate effect of this breakdown in trust, and one that was to have regrettable consequences, was that museum staff kept secret from U.S. forces and foreign journalists that they had moved 8,366 displayed objects into safe storage several weeks earlier. This fact was not discovered until early June 2003, and in the meantime the items were presumed stolen (Bogdanos 2005: 490).

In the immediate aftermath of the museum's looting, the world's media demanded facts and figures, but in the confusion there were few forthcoming. Wild estimates began to circulate of how many artifacts might have been stolen, anything up to 170,000, and although this figure of 170,000 seems to have been conjured up by an ex-employee of the museum with no direct knowledge of the situation, it was seized upon by many reporters as an actual fact. Once staff and military investigators gained access to the museum more sober assessments of the damage began to circulate, but unfortunately by then a reaction to the early sensationalist reporting had set in, as Kathryn Tubb reports in chapter 16. At a press briefing on May 20, U.S. Secretary of Defense Donald Rumsfeld—keen to downplay U.S. culpability—announced that the theft at the National Museum was probably an inside job and that only an estimated thirty-eight objects were confirmed as missing (U.S. Department of Defense 2003).

The most reliable assessment of what really happened at the National Museum has been provided by Colonel Matthew Bogdanos, a U.S. Marine reservist and New York City district attorney, who led the official U.S. government investigation into the plunder. Bogdanos and his team arrived on April 21. He immediately declared a local amnesty for anyone returning objects and later discovered that the 8,366 artifacts hidden by staff but feared missing were in fact safe. At a U.S. Defense Department briefing on September 10, 2003, he revealed that at least 13,515 objects had been stolen, of which 3,500 had been recovered—over 1,700 returned under the amnesty and 900 through raids within Iraq. A further 750 had been recovered abroad. He also presented a detailed summary of his team's findings and discussed the nature of the looting (Bogdanos 2003). His final report was published in 2005, by which time he estimated that as of January 2005, more than 13,864 objects had been stolen, with 1,935 returned under amnesty and 3,424 seized in Iraq and abroad (Bogdanos 2005: 515).

The museum offices and laboratories were thoroughly ransacked, with equipment stolen or destroyed and safes emptied. Computers, cameras, telephones, air conditioners and office furniture were taken, together with a fleet of about forty cars (Tubb 2003). Files had been scattered but were recoverable. Abandoned ammunition and army uniforms confirmed that Iraqi fighters had taken positions in the museum during the fighting (Bogdanos 2003).

Forty good quality objects were stolen from the exhibition galleries and a further sixteen were damaged. There are indications that the thieves were knowledgeable, as only the most valuable objects were stolen—copies and less valuable pieces were left untouched. Perhaps the thieves came armed with a copy of Basmachi's 1976 catalogue *Treasures of the Iraq Museum*, as they ignored a stela not listed there (al-Gailani 2004: 13). Fifteen of these display pieces had been recovered by January 2005, including the 3000 B.C. white alabaster Warka vase (IM19606), which was returned voluntarily in June 2003 under the amnesty. Later, in September 2003, the 3000 B.C. white marble Warka head (IM45434) was found buried in a field, and in November the 2200 B.C. bronze Bassetki statue base and lower torso was discovered smeared in grease in a cesspit.

A minimum of 3,138 objects were stolen from restoration and above-ground storage rooms, of which 3,037 had been recovered by January 2004. In these rooms genuine objects had sometimes been ignored and copies were taken by mistake, which suggests that the thieves had no real knowledge of what they were taking. Most pieces were handed back soon afterward as part of the local amnesty program, and the looting in this part of the museum seems to have been by local people acting opportunistically.

Thieves also broke into a small storage room in the basement. The museum basement consists of four rooms; the intruders left three rooms untouched but entered the fourth. It contained collections of small and valuable—and thus portable and saleable—cylinder seals, coins, and jewelry. Investigators discovered the keys to thirty storage cabinets in this room; the keys had been dropped by looters and lost in the dark, leaving the cabinets' contents safe. However, 103 small plastic storage boxes had been emptied and 10,686 pieces stolen, including 5,144 cylinder seals. By January 2005, 2,307 pieces had been recovered. This part of the break-in was obviously planned with the open market in mind. It was carried out by thieves who knew in advance what material was easy to move and sell and where it was stored. They had even taken the time to locate a set of keys. Bogdanos (2005: 511) suggests that it might have been an "inside job."

The cylinder seals that were stolen are particularly important as most were derived from archaeological excavations, unlike collections in many other museums that have been bought on the market (Biggs 2003). Thus they have good documented contexts and are guaranteed to be free of fakes (Muscarella 2000: 28, n. 12). Cylinder seals are also quite valuable. At an auction held at Christie's London on May 13, 2003, one month after the break-in at the National Museum, twenty-one cylinder seals were sold (obviously none from the museum), with prices ranging from about U.S. $400 up to $4,000, on average about $1,000. At the same time, seals were being offered on the Internet for an average price of $700. Trade sources suggest lower prices, between $200 and $500 each (Eisenberg 2004a), but even if the stolen cylinder seals appeared on the London or New York markets at the rock-bottom price of $200 apiece, the haul of 5,144 cylinder seals removed from the museum basement would fetch more than $1 million, and potentially much more.

Although at first there was suspicion in some quarters that Iraqi staff had been involved in at least some of the incidents, most have since been exonerated of all blame. It is now clear that the staff of the museums and libraries acted throughout the crisis in a highly professional manner, despite the very difficult and sometimes life-threatening circumstances. Without their foresight and initiative, the damage caused to the museums and libraries would have been far greater.

FROM MAY 2003 TO MAY 2005

In the immediate aftermath of the 2003 war, surveys of archaeological sites and cultural institutions in Iraq were carried out by the National Geographic in May (Wright et al. 2003) and UNESCO in June (UNESCO 2003), and some individual sites were visited by reporters.

In northern Iraq, the Mosul Museum was looted at the same time as the Baghdad institutions. At least thirty-four objects were taken from the main display galleries and two storage rooms were broken into, although most important objects had already been moved out of the museum to Baghdad before the war started (Atwood 2003b). Twenty books were stolen from the museum's library, which was otherwise left intact. The books stolen were the most valuable in the library's collection, which again argues that someone with knowledge of the market had deliberately targeted them. The overall situation in the north was that archaeological sites had suffered minimal war damage or were threatened by urban or agricultural development, but although there had been some thefts and illegal excavation, looting was not severe. At Nimrud, for example, two stone reliefs had been stolen, and the site had suffered some damage during a gun battle that had broken out between site guards and looters. U.S. troops arrived to guard the site in May 2003 (Atwood 2003c; Paley 2003).

In the south of the country, looting was widespread, though patchy, but in some cases quite severe. A few large sites seemed to have escaped reasonably lightly. Coalition military camps were established at large, well-known sites such as Ur, Babylon, and Hatra to frighten off would-be looters, though defensive foxholes and heavy traffic caused some damage. Uruk was safe under the protection of a local Bedouin family (Schwartz 2003). At some other sites, the position was dire. There had been extensive recent looting at Larsa, and hundreds of looters were reported at work at Adab, Umma, and Isin; other sites, too, had been badly damaged. U.S. marines arrested one hundred looters at Umma in May 2003, and it was estimated that 30–50 percent of Isin had been destroyed by illicit digging; there were holes 2–3 meters in diameter and 5–7 meters deep. The situation had obviously deteriorated in the time between the National Geographic and UNESCO surveys. Thus in mid-May the National Geographic team reported that although there were some looters' holes at Nippur, guards were present and the site was secure. By the time the UNESCO team arrived in early July, however, there was no longer a guard at the site, and looting had started in earnest. The team observed fifty to a hundred recent holes.

As the security situation in Iraq deteriorated through into 2004, media attention drifted away from archaeology. It has, in consequence, become harder to obtain reliable information, but eyewitnesses report massive looting still in the south, on a scale much larger than during the 1990s. In April 2004 heavily armed gangs chased Iraqi archaeologists off Umma (Garen 2004: 31), while similar gangs moving in all-terrain vehicles were working at other southern sites (Banerjee and Garen 2004).

Coalition patrolling of archaeological sites seems to have been sporadic and largely ineffective, with the exception of Italian *carabinieri* based in the area of Nasiriya since autumn 2003. The carabinieri are trained to deal with looting on sites in Italy and were patrolling the area by helicopter and on the ground (Garen 2004: 28–29), but their activities were curtailed toward the end of 2003 as fighting escalated between the local Shiite militia and coalition troops (Farchakh 2004). Twelve carabinieri were killed in November 2003 (Bogdanos 2005: 501). By the end of 2004 the State Board of Antiquities had 1,750 recruits for its newly constituted Facilities Protection Service to patrol and to guard archaeological sites, but the service was still not fully outfitted with vehicles, weapons, and communication equipment (Kaufman 2005).

At Babylon, the U.S. company Kellogg Brown and Root, a subsidiary of Halliburton, badly damaged the site of Babylon while extending a military base there, and coalition forces subsequently relocated in January 2005 (Bahrani 2004; Bailey 2005; Curtis 2005).

By April 2005, four thousand objects had been returned to the National Museum from within Iraq, and a few thousand more had been seized in countries around the world and were awaiting return. Major hauls were just over a thousand in Jordan and more than six hundred in the United States. Material had also been seized in Italy, Kuwait, Saudi Arabia, Syria, and Turkey (Bogdanos 2005: 514).

At the outbreak of the 2003 Iraq War neither the United States nor Britain had ratified the 1954 Hague Convention for the Protection of Cultural Property in the Event of Armed Conflict or its two protocols, but an alternative protective strategy emerged when UN trade sanctions were targeted specifically at cultural heritage. Trade sanctions had originally been placed on Iraq in August 1990 by UNSCR 661, which banned any country from importing commodities exported from Iraq after that date. It did not make special provision for cultural heritage, which was subsumed within the term "commodities." On May 22, 2003, UNSCR 1483 lifted general trade sanctions. The resolution specified that states should take appropriate steps to facilitate the return of all cultural objects illegally removed from Iraq since the date of UNSCR 661 (August 6, 1990) and that trade in Iraqi cultural objects should be prohibited when there is reasonable suspicion that they have been illegally removed.

The United States responded to UNSCR 1483 by lifting general sanctions but leaving them in place for cultural objects, and then in December 2004, as noted by Patty Gerstenblith in chapter 3, a new law was passed empowering the president to impose import restrictions unilaterally on archaeological material of Iraqi origin, although by April 2005 this had not happened.

In the United Kingdom, UNSCR 1483 was implemented in June 2003 by Statutory Instrument 1519, The Iraq (United Nations Sanctions) Order (SI 1519). This legislation has proved controversial, as it is not necessary to prove guilty intent, which inverts the burden of proof that normally applies in a criminal prosecution. Whereas UNSCR 1483 asks that trade in objects should be prohibited when there is reasonable suspicion that they have been illegally removed, SI 1519 prohibits trade unless it is known that the objects left Iraq before August 1990. In effect, under SI 1519, an object is not treated as "innocent" until proven "guilty," as is usual, but "guilty" if there is nothing to indicate otherwise. This interpretation of UNSCR 1483 has been criticized as contravening the European Convention on Human Rights, which enshrines the principle of "innocent until proven guilty" (Chamberlain 2003: 361).

The London Antiquities Market

Throughout the 1990s there were persistent rumors that Iraqi material was being moved through Jordan to Amman and thence to London. In 1994 the British Department of Customs and Excise intercepted a shipment of Iraqi antiquities at Heathrow airport addressed to a Jordanian woman living in London. The shipment of four boxes contained cuneiform tablets, pottery, and some Aramaic incantation bowls, but the woman to whom it was addressed claimed that it was an unsolicited delivery and she could not, therefore, be prosecuted (Hunter 1997). In 1996 a department of University College London obtained on loan from the Norwegian collector Martin Schøyen 650 Aramaic incantation bowls that, by the department's own admission, had been "collected" from archaeological sites (Geller n.d.), probably in Iraq and exported through Jordan (Alberge 2005).[4] By 1997 it was reported that enough antiquities had been seized at Iraq's border with Jordan to form an exhibition at Baghdad's National Museum (Gibson 1997: 7), and cuneiform tablets, cylinder seals, and other small antiquities were on open sale in London ("Short Notes" 1997: 22; Gibson 1997: 7). Two years later in 1999, a further thousand artifacts were returned to Iraq by Jordan (Doole 1999: 8).

In 2001 two significant pieces of stone relief sculpture were returned to Iraq from London. The first was a stone relief head from Hatra, which had been smuggled out through Jordan and seized by Scotland Yard from a London antiquities dealer (Doole 2001: 15); the second was a fragment from the Sennacherib palace that the London collector Shlomo Moussaieff had bought in good faith in 1994 in Geneva Freeport from the Brussels-based Lebanese dealer Nabil Asfar (Gottlieb and Meier 2003). Since then, there have been two other seizures in London: a relief from the Nimrud palace of Ashurnasirpal II in 2002, and in 2003 an eleventh-century A.D. book that had been stolen in 1995 from the Awqaf Library in Mosul was brought to Christie's London auction house, which handed it over to the police. In September 2003 it was reported that the first seizures of material stolen from the National Museum had been made in New York and Rome, after having first passed through London (Bailey 2003: 1). The most important recovery was of just over six hundred small objects at a New York airport, including many cylinder seals stolen from the National Museum's basement storeroom in April 2003.

Further insights into the London market for Iraqi antiquities are provided by the analysis of a diachronic series of auction sales. Figures 10.1 and 10.2 show the numbers of Mesopotamian cylinder seals offered for sale each year at the major London auction houses from 1980 to 2005. Although some cylinder seals may be found in countries adjacent to Iraq, and some have been found as far afield as Greece, the vast majority are recovered from archaeological sites in Iraq itself. There is no real evidence that the UN trade sanctions introduced in August 1990 by UNSCR 661 made any impact on sales, despite cautionary notices that were included at that time in auction catalogues. Figures 10.1 and 10.2 also

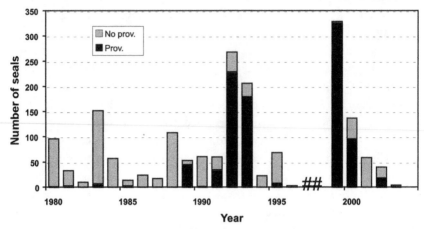

Figure 10.1. Number of cylinder seals offered for sale annually in London at Sotheby's (1980–96) and Bonhams (1999–2004) excluding single-owner sales. (## = no data available.)

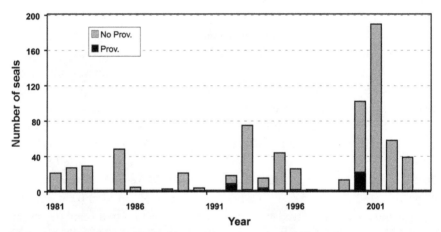

Figure 10.2. Number of cylinder seals offered for sale annually in London at Christie's (1981–2004) excluding single-owner sales.

show, however, that the major auction houses were not selling increased quantities of unprovenanced material through the 1990s into the 2000s, as might have been expected in the presence of the Amman-London nexus. But, as Watson (chapter 4) and Hollowell (chapter 5) point out, auction data cannot be taken at face value as an indicator of market shape or size. In the long term, the number of seals offered each year for auction has remained within certain limits, probably because the auction houses themselves have an interest in not selling too many at any one time for fear of causing a glut in the market and then losing commission on the falling prices that would ensue.

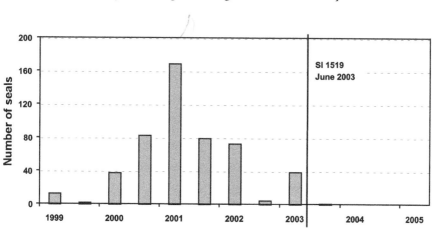

Figure 10.3. Combined number of unprovenanced cylinder seals offered in London at Christie's and Bonhams spring and fall sales. The vertical black line marks the U.K. implementation of SI 1519 in June 2003 and shows the complete fall-off in seals offered after that date .

However, the questionable character of the unprovenanced seals sold at auction remains an issue. There are no indications of ownership history provided for them in auction catalogue descriptions, which leaves open the possibility that they had been moved only recently out of Iraq. On the other hand, it might equally suggest that the consignors wished to remain anonymous. It is surely significant, though, that the quantities of unprovenanced seals offered for auction dropped off to nothing immediately after the implementation of SI 1519. An obvious explanation for this plummet, which is shown in figure 10.3, is that it is not possible to demonstrate with any degree of certainty what unprovenanced seals may have moved out of Iraq since August 1990, and either the auction houses will not handle them or vendors are not consigning them for fear of contravening SI 1519. This explanation seems to be confirmed by a report from Christie's London that far fewer cylinder seals and cuneiform tablets without provenance have been offered to them since April 2003 than they would normally expect (Eisenberg 2004a), and this implies that many of the unprovenanced seals previously offered for sale by auction really were of unknown pedigree and may therefore have been moved out of Iraq illegally.

Another independent line of evidence strongly suggests that many, if not most, unprovenanced antiquities from Iraq that appear on the market have only recently been dug up. Large numbers of cuneiform tablets and other objects have been offered for sale over the past ten years or so with a certificate of authenticity and translation provided by Wilfred Lambert, emeritus professor of Assyriology at Britain's Birmingham University. Presumably, if a tablet needs authenticating and translating in this way, it is because it has not previously come to the attention of the scholarly community. The alternative explanation that large numbers of previously unseen tablets have begun to surface from forgotten collections is possible but hardly credible. Lambert has said as much himself. When interviewed by the *New York Times* in April 2003, he was quoted as saying that when he authenticates an object he does not necessarily know its origin, and he suspects that often the dealers themselves do not know either (Gottlieb and Meier 2003).

In April 2003, shortly after the break-in at the National Museum, the websites of four United Kingdom–based companies, all members of the Antiquities Dealers Association (ADA), or claiming to adhere to the ADA's code of ethics, had on offer between them twenty-nine cuneiform tablets for sale. By October 2003 one website had disappeared, while the other three offered only five tablets. By August 2004 the missing website had reappeared, and on all four sites together there were four cuneiform tablets for sale. Three of the companies had on offer in total only four antiquities that might have been Iraqi in origin (although there were suspiciously large quantities of "Sassanian" material or items "from Iran" available). However, the fourth company had something like sixty-four objects on sale that might have come from Iraq, including eleven cylinder seals. None of the seals had any provenance; five had been authenticated by Wilfred Lambert and a further five by "a former curator of Egyptian and Near Eastern Art" at the Boston Museum of Fine Arts. Previously, the same company in October 2003 had offered for sale seventeen cylinder seals, again with no provenance, and with fourteen authenticated by Lambert. All but one of these seals had been sold by August 2004, so presumably more might have been offered and sold over the intervening period. All objects were priced in U.S. dollars with an eye on the export market.

Thus there is strong evidence to suggest that many if not the majority of unprovenanced Iraqi antiquities that have been traded in Britain since the Gulf War have been from illegal excavations and that this trade has dropped off sharply since the implementation of SI 1519. Yet this trade in illegally acquired antiquities through the 1990s carried on despite codes of ethics formulated by trade associations, which, they claim, are designed to guard against just such an eventuality.

For example, Article 2 of the Antiquities Dealers Association's Code of Ethics states: "The members of ADA undertake not to purchase or sell objects until they have established to the best of their ability that such objects were not stolen from excavations, architectural monuments, public institutions or private property." Article 2 of the Code of Ethics of the International Association of Dealers in Ancient Art (IADAA) is identical.

Unfortunately, the wording of this article is ambiguous and is open to at least two different interpretations. One reading appears obvious—members undertake, to the best of their ability, not to sell material that has been stolen or illegally excavated. But an alternative reading is possible and is flagged by the use of the term "private property." British and American antiquities dealers have long objected to foreign patrimony laws—such as Iraq's—that vest ownership of unexcavated antiquities in the state; they favor instead common law regimes that vest ownership in the landowner. In that case unexcavated antiquities are private property and can be dug up by the landowner and disposed of—sold—like any other legally owned possession. Thus it is possible to read Article 2 as stating that dealers are happy to trade in material that has been dug up by a landowner from his or her own land (i.e., not stolen from private property), even if the subsequent sale or export was illegal within the jurisdiction of the country of discovery. It is significant that there is no clear and unambiguous statement that members will not deal in stolen public property or in illegally exported cultural objects.

Antiquities dealers are not particularly open about their business, and indeed there is no legal reason why they should be. But their stance toward Iraq might be gauged from that of Jerome M. Eisenberg, who is a leading antiquities dealer with galleries in London and New York and proprietor of the trade magazine *Minerva*, through which he is able to voice his opinion. He is hardly a shady character, and cannot be accused of operating a seedy little smuggling business out of a Geneva warehouse, but would like to see himself and is regarded by others as part of the "reputable" or "legitimate" trade. As such, his published opinions and arguments deserve close scrutiny for what they may reveal about trade attitudes more generally.

The first issue of *Minerva* to appear after the National Museum was looted helpfully provided illustrations of three hundred objects, which at the time were thought to be missing (Eisenberg 2003a). In the editorial of the same issue, however, Eisenberg lost no time in castigating the "usual cadre of posturing, often 'born-again,' academics" (Eisenberg 2003b: 2) for making exaggerated claims about the size of the antiquities trade, and their propensity to "finger unscrupulous dealers as being at the heart of the world's ills." It was time for "cooler hearts and wiser heads" to prevail and to consider the truth. At that time, while noting the uncertainties that still prevailed, the truth for Eisenberg was that thirty-eight valuable pieces were officially listed as stolen, with another 2,000–3,000 objects missing. Curiously, the editorial then went on to accuse the academics responsible for the compilation and production of the three fascicles of *Lost Heritage: Antiquities Stolen from Iraq's Regional Museums* after the 1991 Gulf War of "ineptitude" for not ensuring that they reached the appropriate dealers and academics: "*Minerva* was unaware of the series until recently and finally obtained copies (the originals are long out of print) only in the past few weeks. Certainly, if made aware of these publications, *Minerva* would have allocated ample space to publicising the losses" (Eisenberg 2003b: 3).

It is true that the distribution of the fascicles could have been wider; for example, the major art museum bookshops that sell *Minerva* and other glossy publications could have taken it upon themselves to stock copies. But it is not true, as Eisenberg claimed, that *Minerva* was unaware of them. In the May–June 1997 issue they had been clearly mentioned in an article by John Russell on the looting of Sennacherib's palace, in which he noted that the fascicles were available free of charge by writing to the publisher of each, and he provided addresses (Russell 1997a: 19–20). Russell mentioned the fascicles again in a similar article published in the first issue of *Culture without Context*, also in 1997 (Russell 1997b). This issue of *Culture without Context* received a full-page review from Eisenberg, who had obviously read it carefully, though not carefully enough, it seems, to have noticed the existence of the fascicles. Of Russell's article, he asked: "Is this repetition really necessary?" (Eisenberg 1998: 6). Clearly, in Eisenberg's case, it was necessary but a waste of time.

Minerva's September–October 2003 editorial, written in light of the Bogdanos briefing and National Geographic report, gave a balanced overview of the situation in Iraq though the writer still felt the need to lash out at academics (Eisenberg 2003c). Unfortunately, this balance was undermined by another piece in the same issue reviewing the spring 2003 antiquities auctions, the last auctions to be held in London before the implementation of SI 1519 (Eisenberg 2003d). Favorable mentions were made of record prices fetched by a first-millennium B.C. Egyptian wooden coffin sold at Christie's and a silver cup from Iran sold at Bonhams, before the review ended on an upbeat note that "the antiquities market is unusually robust in times of economic uncertainties" (Eisenberg 2003d: 33). Eisenberg lost his opportunity to take a last look at unprovenanced objects appearing for sale before SI 1519 hit home. He might have questioned, for example, the histories of at least sixteen lots of probable Iraqi origin that Christie's had offered without provenance, including cuneiform tablets and cylinder seals, and an unusual inscribed stone door socket dating to about 2000 B.C. from the site of Isin. Offered with an estimate of U.S. $4,075 to $5,705 it sold for U.S. $22,983 (Christie's 2003: 31, lot 46).

The January–February 2004 issue of *Minerva* again presented a balanced report on what was missing and recovered from the National Museum, based largely on Bogdanos, but passed over in silence the ongoing site looting (Eisenberg 2004b). Finally, in the July–August 2004 issue, Eisenberg published a historical review of the trade in Iraqi antiquities (Eisenberg 2004c). Mention was made of early twentieth-century collectors and dealers, notably the American Edgar J. Banks, and of sales by auction of known collections through the 1980s and 1990s. No explanation was offered for the continuing sale of unprovenanced objects over the same period, nor was there any discussion of major new collectors—Jonathan Rosen, for example, who is rumored to have accumulated thousands of cuneiform tablets and cylinder seals over the last couple of decades, many of which he has donated to educational institutions within the United States (D'Arcy 2003).

Eisenberg also noted that since April 2003 most antiquities dealers have stopped trading in unprovenanced material from Iraq (Eisenberg 2004c: 43), which is in accord with evidence provided here. After this highly selective review he stated that "it seems apparent, therefore, that if any quantity of material has been smuggled out of Iraq since 1990, little if any has surfaced on the legitimate market" (Eisenberg 2004c: 43), although he had offered no evidence to substantiate this view. He went on to recommend that there was little need to send any cuneiform tablets or cylinder seals back to Iraq unless they were demonstrably stolen from a museum, because in its present state Iraq's National Museum would not be able to cope with the necessary conservation and recording.

Eisenberg's strategy is clear. Any adverse information about antiquities trading and collecting that is already in the public domain is deployed in such a way as to hide what is not public, or at least to veil information that is not well known. If an episode of antiquities looting or theft is firmly established, beyond doubt, it is denounced loudly; if not, no notice is given. Thus in 1997 the looting of Sennacherib's palace was highlighted and denounced because it was by then well known. The fascicles of *Lost Heritage*, which could have received equal publicity, were quietly overlooked, despite later protestations of ignorance. Similarly, the April 2003 ransack of the National Museum was headlined and condemned, but although the ongoing plunder of archaeological sites was noted when it was first reported by the National Geographic, since then it has not been mentioned. Early twentieth-century dealers and collectors are openly discussed, but the sources of contemporary collections are not considered. While it is interesting to know that from 1915 to the mid-1930s Edgar J. Banks is said to have brought into the United States a minimum of 11,000 cuneiform tablets, and possibly many more, it would be more useful to learn about the pedigree of Rosen's collection. It is encouraging to be told that the trade in Iraqi antiquities has gone dead since April 2003, but it is disappointing not to hear why it did not happen thirteen years earlier when United Nations sanctions were first imposed. This strategy of argumentation is duplicitous, and while it might convince *Minerva* readers, it raises serious doubts about the sincerity of the self-styled "legitimate" trade.

It is impossible for an outsider to penetrate the inner workings of the antiquities trade, and antiquities dealers are not inclined to help. Yet from the scattered clues gathered together here a consistent picture begins to emerge. Behind the rhetoric, Eisenberg's reporting on the thefts from the National Museum has been consistent, honest, and in accordance with Article 2 of the ADA/IADAA Code of Ethics, which calls on dealers not to sell objects that have been stolen from excavations or public institutions. He has been much quieter about the looting of archaeological sites, perhaps due to a belief consistent with the reading of Article 2 offered here: that publicly owned or illegally exported property should not be subject to trade restrictions. This seems to be a belief adhered to by other parts of the London trade, at least during the 1990s, although it is counter to U.S. and U.K. criminal law, as the convictions of Frederick Schultz and Jonathan Tokeley-Parry have now confirmed. But perhaps this explanation is too elaborate, and perhaps dealers have simply disregarded their own ethical codes. Either way, there is a problem. Codes of ethics constitute the trade's mechanism of self-regulation, and if they are ignored, self-regulation has failed. But equally, if ethical codes are weaker than the law, then self-regulation does not exist. The only real ameliorating effect exerted on the London trade in Iraqi antiquities has been the statutory one of SI 1519 and its threat of criminal prosecution. If (when) it is repealed, the trade will no doubt bounce back with a vengeance.

NOTES

The report of the official U.S. investigation into the sack of the National Museum was published while this chapter was in press (Bogdanos 2005). It was not possible to take full account of the report, but it was used to ensure factual accuracy. There are several sources of information on the Internet that are continually updated and that should be consulted for news of more recent developments. The Oriental Institute of the University of Chicago hosts a web resource entitled Lost Treasures from Iraq at <http://oi.uchicago.edu/OI/IRAQ/iraq.html>. It contains an illustrated and searchable database of the National Museum collections (still under construction), bibliographies documenting the contents of Iraq's museums and libraries, the archives of the IraqCrisis moderated Internet discussion list, and images and descriptions of archaeological sites damaged by looting. The Oriental Institute also hosts the website of the Middle East Librarians Association, which contains links and information concerning Iraq's libraries and manuscript collections, at <http://oi.uchicago.edu/OI/IRAQ/mela/melairaq.html>. The site also contains an on-line copy of Nabil al-Tikriti's (2003) report on Iraq's libraries and archives. The website of archaeologist Francis Deblauwe contains a complete archive of news reports from Iraq together with comment dating back to March 2003 and is continuously updated. It can be found at <http://iwa.univie.ac.at>.

In 2003 the International Council of Museums launched their Emergency Red List of Iraqi Antiquities at Risk. Rather than present images or descriptions of objects known to have been stolen from museums, it illustrates and describes the types of objects that are under threat of looting, noting that anything with Aramaic of cuneiform script is suspicious, and also illustrating what an IM number looks like. The Red List is available on-line in English, French, and Arabic versions at <http://icom.museum/redlist/irak/en/index. html>.

1. Available on-line at <http://oi.uchicago.edu/OI/IRAQ/lh.html>.

2. An organization representing the interests of private collectors and some museum curators.

3. The fates of other archives and libraries in Iraq are discussed by al-Tikriti (2003).

4. The department in question was not the Institute of Archaeology at University College London, which adopted a policy in 1999 adhering to the *ICOM Code of Ethics for Museums* (see Tubb 2002, 288–89, for Institute policy; and see Brodie, introduction to this volume, for the ICOM ethical code).

BIBLIOGRAPHY

Alberge, Dalya. "Museum Inquiry into 'Smuggling' of Ancient Bowls." *Times*, April 22, 2005.

Al-Gailani, Lamia. "Notes on the Looting in Iraq." In *Not For Sale: A Swiss-British Conference on the Traffic in Artifacts from Iraq, Afghanistan and Beyond*, ed. Matt Kimmich, 13–14. Geneva: British Council, 2004.

Al-Naqshbandi, Zain. Report on the Central Awqaf Library. <http://oi.uchicago.edu/OI/IRAQ/zan.html>, accessed October 14, 2004.

Al-Radi, Selma. "The Destruction of the Iraq National Museum." *Museum International* 219–20 (2003): 103–7.

Al-Tikriti, Nabil. "Iraq Manuscript Collections, Archives and Libraries Situation Report. June 8, 2003." <http://oi.uchicago.edu/OI/IRAQ/docs/nat.html>, accessed August 12, 2004.

Atwood, Roger. "Inside Iraq's National Museum." OpinionJournal, July 17. <http://www.opinionjournal.com/la/?id=110003754>, accessed October 14, 2003 (2003a).

———. "In the North of Iraq: Mosul's Museum, Hatra and Nimrud." Archaeology on-line features, June 4. <http://www.archaeology.org/online/features/iraq/mosul.html> accessed October 14, 2003 (2003b).

———. "Day of the Vulture." MotherJones.com, September–October. <http://www.motherjones.com/news/outfront/2003/09/ma_505_01.html>, accessed October 14, 2003 (2003c).

Bahrani, Zainab. "Days of Plunder." *Guardian*, August 31, 2004.

Bailey, Martin. "Seized: Over 600 Objects Looted from Iraq." *Art Newspaper*, no. 139 (2003): 1, 3.

———. "The Steady Deterioration of Iraq's Great Nimrud Ivories." *Art Newspaper*, no. 146 (2004): 27.

———. "US Base Has Caused 'Shocking' Damage to Babylon." *Art Newspaper*, no. 155 (2005): 1, 4.

Baker, H. D., Roger J. Matthews, and J. Nicholas Postgate. *Lost Heritage: Antiquities Stolen from Iraq's Regional Museums*, fascicle 2. London: British School of Archaeology in Iraq, 1993.

Banerjee, N., and M. Garen. "Saving Iraq's Archaeological Past from Thieves Remains an Uphill Battle." *New York Times*, April 4, 2004.

Biggs, Robert. "Cuneiform Inscriptions in the Looted Iraq Museum." *IFAR Journal* 6, nos. 1–2, <http://www.ifar.org/cuneiform.htm>, accessed August 14 2004 (2003).

Bogdanos, Matthew. Iraq Museum Investigation: April 22–September 8, 2003. <http://www.defenselink.mil/news/Sep2003/d20030922fr.pdf>, accessed October 14, 2004 (2003).

———. "The Casualties of War: The Truth about the Iraq Museum." *American Journal of Archaeology* 109 (2005): 477–526.

Bouchenaki, Mounir. "Setting up the International Collaborative Framework." *Museum International* 219–20 (2003): 126–37.

Chamberlain, Kevin. "The Iraq (United Nations Sanctions) Order 2003: Is It Human Rights Act Compatible?" *Art, Antiquity and Law* 8 (2003): 357–68.

Christie's Auction Catalog. *Antiquities: Including an English Private Collection of Ancient Gems*, pt. 1. London: Christie's South Kensington, 2003.

Curtis, John. Report on Meeting at Babylon 11–13 December 2004. <http://www.thebritishmuseum.ac.uk/news/babylon.html>, accessed May 25, 2005 (2005).

D'Arcy, David. "Collector Gets Tax Break for Donating Cylinder Seals to University." *Art Newspaper*, no. 139 (2003): 5.

Deeb, Mary-Jane, Michael Albin, and Alan Haley. The Library of Congress and the U.S. Department of State Mission to Baghdad. Report on the National Library and the House of Manuscripts. October 27–November 3, 2003. <http://www.loc.gov/rr/amed/iraqreport/iraqreport.html#top> (2003).

Doole, Jennifer. "In the News." *Culture without Context*, issue 5 (Autumn 1999): 5–11.

———. "In the News." *Culture without Context*, issue 8 (Spring 2001): 7–17.

Eisenberg, Jerome M. "And Now for Something Completely Different: The Illicit Antiquities Research Centre." *Minerva*, January–February 1998, 6.

———. "Mesopotamia: Masterworks and Minor Works from the Iraq Museum." *Minerva*, July–August 2003, 9–40 (2003a).

———. "The Looting of the National Museum of Iraq, April 2003: The Present Held Hostage to the Past" (editorial). *Minerva*, July–August 2003, 2–3 (2003b).

———. "The Looting of Iraq's Cultural Heritage: An Up-Date" (editorial). *Minerva*, September–October 2003, 2 (2003c).

———. "The Spring 2003 Antiquities Sales." *Minerva*, September–October 2003, 27–33 (2003d).

———. "Media Exaggeration of Illicit Antiquities Trade" (editorial). *Minerva*, March–April 2004, 2 (2004a).

———. "The National Museum of Iraq: Looting and Recovery." *Minerva*, January–February 2004, 33–35 (2004b).

———. "The Mesopotamian Antiquities Trade and the Looting of Iraq." *Minerva*, July–August 2004, 41–44 (2004c).

Farchakh, Joanne. "The Massacre of Mesopotamian Archaeology: Looting in Iraq Is out of Control." *Daily Star*, September 21, 2004.

Fujii, Hideo, and Kazumi Oguchi. *Lost Heritage: Antiquities Stolen from Iraq's Regional Museums*, fascicle 3. Tokyo: Institute for Cultural Studies of Ancient Iraq, Kokushikan University, 1996.

Garen, Micah. "The War within the War." *Archaeology*, July–August 2004, 28–30.

Geller, Mark. "From the Director of the IJS: Spies, Thieves and Cultural Heritage." <http://www.ucl.ac.uk/hebrew-jewish/ijs/news.htm>, accessed June 1, 2005.

Ghaidan, Usam, and Anna Peolini. "A Short History of the Iraq National Museum." *Museum International* 219–20 (2003): 97–102.

Gibson, McGuire. "The Loss of Archaeological Context and the Illegal Trade in Mesopotamian Antiquities." *Culture without Context*, issue 1 (Autumn 1997): 6–8.

———. "From the Prevention Measures to the Fact-Finding Mission." *Museum International* 219–20 (2003): 108–17 (2003a).

———. "Where Civilisation Began." *Archaeology*, July–August 2003, 20–21 (2003b).

Gibson, McGuire, and Augusta McMahon. *Lost Heritage: Antiquities Stolen from Iraq's Regional Museums*, fascicle 1. Chicago: American Association for Research in Baghdad, 1992.

Gottlieb, Martin, and Barry Meier. "Of 2,000 Treasures Stolen in Gulf War of 1991, Only 12 Have Been Recovered." *New York Times*, April 30, 2003.

Hunter, Erica C. D. "Returned Antiquities: A Case for Changing Legislation." *Culture without Context*, issue 1 (Autumn 1997): 21–22.

Kaufman, Jason E. "Museums Closed and Looting Rampant." *Art Newspaper*, no. 155 (2005): 4.

Lawler, Andrew. "Destruction in Mesopotamia." *Science* 293 (2001): 32–35 (2001a).

———. "New Digs Draw Applause and Concern." *Science* 293 (2001): 38–41 (2001b).

———. "Iraq Opening Sets Off Scramble for Sites." *Science* 293 (2001): 36–38 (2001c).

———. "Mayhem in Mesopotamia." *Science* 301 (2003): 582–88.

Muscarella, Oscar White. *The Lie Became Great: The Forgery of Ancient Near Eastern Cultures*. Groningen, Netherlands: Styx, 2000.

Paley, Samuel M. "Nimrud, the War, and the Antiquities Markets." *IFAR Journal* 6, nos. 1–2, <http://www.ifar.org/nimrud.htm>, accessed 14 August 2004 (2003).

Renfrew, Colin. "Reflections on the Looting of the Iraqi National Museum in Baghdad." In *The Iraq War and Its Consequences: Thoughts of Nobel Peace Laureates and Eminent Scholars*, ed. Irwin Abrams and Wang Gungwu, 319–35. River Edge, N. J.: World Scientific, 2003.

Russell, John Malcolm. "Looted Sculptures from Nineveh." *Minerva*, May–June 1997, 16–26 (1997a).

———. "The Modern Sack of Nineveh and Nimrud." *Culture without Context*, issue 1 (Autumn 1997): 6–20 (1997b).

Schipper, Friedrich T. "The Protection and Preservation of Iraq's Archaeological Heritage, Spring 1999–2003." *American Journal of Archaeology* 109 (2005): 251–72.

Schwartz, Gary. "Dutch Help Bedouins Guard the Sumerian Site of Uruk." *Art Newspaper*, no. 141 (2003): 10.

"Short Notes." *Culture without Context*, issue 1 (Autumn 1997): 22–23.

Stone, Peter. "The Identification and Protection of Cultural Heritage During the Iraq Conflict: A Peculiarly English Tale," *Antiquity* 79 (2005): 933–43.

Symposium 1994. "Final report." The International Symposium on the Looted Antiquities from Iraq during the War of 1991. Baghdad, 10–12, December 1994.

Tubb, Kathryn W. "Point, Counterpoint." In *Illicit Antiquities: The Theft of Culture and the Extinction of Archaeology*, ed. Neil Brodie and Kathryn W. Tubb, 280–300. London: Routledge, 2002.

———. "Iraq: The Evolution of a Response to Disaster." *Conservation News*, no. 85 (2003): 22–25.

United Nations Educational, Scientific and Cultural Organization. "UNESCO Second Assessment Mission to Iraq, June 28–July 7, 2003." <http://portal.unesco.org/culture/en/ev.php-URL_ID=14658&URL_DO=DO_TOPIC&URL_SECTION=201.html>, accessed August 13, 2004 (2003).

U.S. Department of Defense. "DoD News Briefing: Secretary Rumsfeld and General Myers." <http://www.defenselink.mil/transcripts/2003/tr20030520-secdef0207.html>, accessed August 14, 2004 (2003).

Wright, Henry T., T. J. Wilkinson, and McGuire Gibson. "The National Geographic Society's Cultural Assessment." <http://news.nationalgeographic.com/news/2003/06/0611_030611_iraqlootingreport.html>, accessed August 13, 2004 (2003).

Zimansky, Paul, and Elizabeth C. Stone. "Mesopotamia in the Aftermath of the Gulf War." *Archaeology*, May–June (1992): 24.

11

Afghanistan's Cultural Heritage

An Exceptional Case?

JULIETTE VAN KRIEKEN-PIETERS

The fate of Afghanistan's cultural heritage since 1993 has been quite extraordinary. Not only has the country been deprived of a large part of its movable heritage, but also its most significant immovable heritage has fallen victim to an act of willful destruction. This unfortunate fate provides a starting point for many archaeological, legal, ethical, and political debates. Several aspects of these debates are highlighted in this chapter.

First, an outline of Afghanistan's intriguing history is given. Second, the initial efforts of the Society for the Protection of Afghanistan's Cultural Heritage (SPACH) to preserve what was possible are described. Third, the following five aspects of the present situation in Afghanistan are examined in greater detail:

- The importance of archaeology for understanding Afghanistan's history.
- The plundering of the National Museum of Afghanistan in Kabul.
- The illegal excavation and looting of archaeological sites.
- The willful destruction of the Bamiyan Buddhas and figures from the National Museum.
- Material that has survived the war.

Finally, I argue that the lessons learned from the recent history of Afghanistan could be applied beneficially in other situations.

HISTORICAL OUTLINE

The Afghan region has a long and rich history from prehistoric times. From the earlier periods there are many important finds, which include sculpture, pottery, and golden objects from the third to second millennium B.C. at Aq Kupruk, Mundigak, and Tepe Fullol. In the fourth century B.C., Alexander the Great marched through the region and founded several "Alexandrias"—Greek towns in which a genuine Greek way of life was maintained for several centuries. The Hellenistic cultural influence of these towns was subsequently of the utmost importance for the development of Buddhism, which was introduced by Ashoka in the third century B.C. However, it was not until the second-century A.D. reign of Kanishka, who wanted to unite his large kingdom by promoting a single religion, that Buddhism became properly established. The Hellenistic tradition of depicting gods and goddesses in human form coincided with the development of Mahayana Buddhism and resulted in the first appearance of the Buddha image in human form. Before this time the Buddha had been represented only by symbols. These new images, on coins, in sculptures, paintings, and so forth, were traded along the Silk Road and helped spread Buddhism to China, Korea, Japan, and the Himalayas. During the early centuries of the first millennium A.D. the Afghan area was one of the main centers of the Buddhist world.

Huns from Central Asia destroyed most of the Buddhist monasteries during the fifth century A.D., although some Buddhist sites, particularly those located in remote areas such as the Bamiyan Valley, survived until as late as the ninth century. Then, with the introduction of Islam, Buddhism vanished completely. During the eleventh and twelfth centuries, the great Ghaznavid Empire ruled the Afghan area from its capital Ghazni, until, together with the Ghorid culture, it was almost completely destroyed by Ghengis Khan and his troops in 1221. Only a few monuments, such as the mysterious minaret of Jam, now in the center of Afghanistan, and the Bamiyan Buddhas, survived this destruction.

During the fifteenth century, the Timurids (descendants of Timur Lenk/Tamerlane) managed to establish a flourishing civilization distinguished for its architecture, poetry, and numerous famous manuscripts. The beautiful blue-tiled monuments in Herat and Balkh bear witness to this time. Finally, Babur, the founder of the Great Mogul Empire—which stretched far into India—was buried in his beloved Kabul, in the Babur Gardens that are now in the process of being restored.

The Society for the Preservation of Afghanistan's Cultural Heritage (SPACH)

In 1989, after the Russians ended their ten-year occupation of Afghanistan, a devastating civil war between various Afghan factions broke out. In 1992 the puppet-president Najibullah, who had been installed by the Russians, was overthrown. Until 1993 the National Museum of Afghanistan in Kabul was left untouched, as both the Russians and the Afghans considered the museum to be of great value. However, in the summer of 1993, it was accidentally bombed. The real target had been the Ministry of Defense on the opposite side of the road, but from that moment on, the museum was open to looters, and during the months that followed it was systematically plundered. The various warring factions did not permit museum staff to enter the area until the autumn of 1993, by which time most of the museum's artifacts had been either looted or damaged. An estimated 70 percent of the collection was missing, including Buddhist statues and reliefs, the world-famous Begram ivories, Greek and Roman sculptures, and valuable coins from the time of Alexander the Great onward (Dupree 1996, 1998).

As a lawyer and art historian specializing in the protection of cultural heritage, I became involved in the foundation of the Society for the Preservation of Afghanistan's Cultural Heritage (SPACH), which was established in September 1994. Its main goal during that period was to draw up an inventory of what remained in the museum. Carla Grissmann, SPACH's liaison officer in Kabul at the time, worked for two years under harsh circumstances to compile the inventory. The next step was to transport the remaining pieces, mostly fragments, to a safe place inside Kabul. Initially, France was also considered as a possible place of refuge for the collection. By the summer of 1996 most of the materials had been moved to Kabul Hotel, although some pieces, mostly intact but too heavy to transport, remained in the museum.

SPACH was also concerned in 1994 with the illegal excavation of archaeological sites, the subsequent trade in archaeological material, and the threat of destruction that was facing the Bamiyan Buddhas. SPACH undertook several initiatives aimed at encouraging both the authorities and local inhabitants to adopt a more positive attitude toward protecting their own cultural heritage. For example, SPACH suggested that the BBC should refer to cultural heritage in a popular radio soap series that was broadcast in several local languages. This initiative made an impact on some local leaders.

In September 1996 the Taliban took control of Kabul and moved the materials from Kabul Hotel to the Ministry of Information and Culture. At the same time they banned depictions of the human form and destroyed ornaments on buildings, ripped up photographs, and closed the cinema. Nevertheless, the pieces in the museum, including a Buddha image and a torso of Kanishka, were not touched.

The Present Situation

Importance of Archaeology for Understanding Afghanistan

Afghanistan has a rich oral tradition, and for this reason written sources of its history are quite limited. A few references exist in Persian and Greek chronicles, and several Chinese Buddhists provided valuable descriptions, but on the whole early written records are poor. Therefore archaeological excavation is of the utmost importance for our understanding of the history of Afghanistan and its region. Systematic excavations were started in Afghanistan in the 1920s by the Délégation Archéologique Française en Afghanistan, and in 1922 an agreement was signed between France and the Afghan king Amanulah that gave the French the exclusive right to excavate in Afghanistan for thirty years. The excavated objects were divided equally between Afghanistan and France, and for that reason the Musée Guimet, the museum for Asian art in Paris, now owns an unparalleled collection of Afghan material. Now that the National Museum in Kabul has been looted, the Musée Guimet houses the world's largest collection of Afghanistan's art.

Plundering of the National Museum of Afghanistan

During the civil war (1993–2001), many museum pieces were stolen and left the country illegally. Rumors spread that pieces were on sale at the Peshawar market in Pakistan. In view of this, in 1994, SPACH agreed upon a very controversial course of action. After much internal discussion the organization decided to purchase objects at the market, provided that they could be identified as having come from the National Museum and if it were financially possible. SPACH bought several minor items, two Bronze Age seals, two small ivories from Aï Khanoum, Roman plasters, and a dozen Buddha heads. Currently the objects are kept in a secret location awaiting their return to the National Museum when conditions permit. However, it seems likely that most pieces never appeared in Peshawar because they went directly to dealers and private collectors abroad.

After the destruction of the Bamiyan Buddhas and other artifacts in March 2001, UNESCO made special agreements with SPACH and two other institutions, recognizing the right of these institutions to retain Afghan objects in secure custody until such time as it becomes safe to return them to Afghanistan. SPACH's objects were sent to the Musée Guimet for safekeeping. The other institutions are the "Afghan Museum in Exile" in Bubendorf, Switzerland, and the Hirayama Foundation in Japan. The Swiss museum was founded by Paul Bucherer-Dietschi in the autumn of 2000 at the request of Afghans from different factions (from both mujahideen and Taliban). The pieces at the museum have all been donated; none was purchased (Romey 2002).

In early 2003 Afghanistan declared that the situation was "under control" and asked for the return of stored objects. However, UNESCO—the organization responsible for overseeing the return—did not agree. As long as the National Museum is structurally unsound and security remains an issue, the basic conditions for return of the artifacts have not been met, and thus the objects have not yet been repatriated.

Illegal Excavation and Looting of Archaeological Sites

The most important problem at present is the indiscriminate plundering of both known and unknown archaeological sites. Complete sites have been dug up using shovels and bulldozers. At Aï Khanoum, a Greek town probably founded by Alexander the Great, traces of a theatre, gymnasium, and mosaics were discovered. All that is left today is a field that is fit only for growing crops. Other examples of sites that have fallen victim to illegal diggers working for unscrupulous dealers are the numerous Buddhist sites of Hadda and the golden mounds of Tellya Tepe. It is impossible to protect sites in a country that is still subject to latent war and where it is too dangerous to start official excavations. The ultimate threat is consumer demand for Afghan artifacts. Thus the damage to sites will continue unless the importing countries take steps to discourage the trade through which demand is satisfied. An international ban on trade in Afghan artifacts can be the only solution. However, at this point they are being offered openly on the Internet, even by London art dealers. Unfortunately, Afghanistan has not ratified the 1970 UNESCO Convention on the Means of Prohibiting and Preventing the Illicit Import, Export and Transfer of Ownership of Cultural Property.

It is incredible that people are still buying items to keep for themselves, even though it must be presumed that those with an interest in the area know the fate of Afghanistan's cultural heritage full well. For example, Martin Schøyen, a wealthy Norwegian collector, bought a rare early collection of Buddhist manuscripts in London during the mid-1990s (Braarvig 2004). He claimed they were from a monastery in the Bamiyan Valley. Schøyen made them available to scholars and placed them on the Internet—all very commendable, but one may doubt whether he is the rightful owner of the manuscripts. It could be argued that someone who bought unknown Afghan manuscripts during the mid-1990s did not act in good faith. At the end of 2002, Norway ratified the 1995 UNIDROIT Convention on Stolen or Illegally Exported Cultural Objects, which is aimed at protecting the rightful owners of stolen artifacts. Although the Convention is not retroactive, and its ratification does not threaten Schøyen's ownership, it does indicate that the Norwegian government has decided against the morality of such purchases. Yet Schøyen offered to sell his collection for several million U.S. dollars, and in Norway a discussion arose about whether the Norwegian state should buy it; clearly, the right hand does not always know what the left hand is doing (Omland and Prescott 2002; Prescott and Omland 2003). In September 2004 a Norwegian television program revealed that none of the manuscripts in Schøyen's collection was actually from Bamiyan; they were from other sites in Afghanistan and Pakistan. Some of his manuscript fragments were from the National Museum (Lundén 2005).

It is interesting that under the Taliban regime (1996–2001), severe penalties were introduced for the illegal excavation and looting of cultural heritage, and the destruction of archaeological sites diminished sharply. However, once the Taliban were overthrown, the looting resumed and continues.

Willful Destruction of the Bamiyan Buddhas and Kabul Figures

In March 2001 the already war-torn country was confronted with yet another major tragedy when the famous Buddhas of Bamiyan were blown up with explosives by the Taliban militia. This barbaric destruction of the Bamiyan Buddhas came as a shock but was not a complete surprise for SPACH and other people involved in the protection of cultural heritage. Since the mid-1990s, SPACH had been especially worried about the fate of the large Buddha, as the space between its feet had been used as an ammunition dump by one of the warring factions long before the Taliban seized control of the Bamiyan Valley. SPACH was eventually successful in securing the removal of the ammunition. Once the valley was taken by the Taliban in 1998, one commander in particular was keen to destroy the Buddhas. He blew off the head of the small Buddha in 1998 and was in the process of doing the same to the large Buddha when he was stopped by the local Taliban governor. In July 1999 the Taliban leader Mullah Omar issued two decrees: (a) Concerning the Protection of Cultural Heritage, and (b) Concerning the Preservation of Historic Relics in Afghanistan. The latter decree stated: "The Taliban Government states that Bamiyan shall not be destroyed but protected." Special emphasis was placed upon the importance of the Buddhas, including the fact that they had been constructed before the emergence of Islam (and therefore should be respected, according to the Koran), and it was noted that there are no Buddhists to worship the statues in the country.

And yet, although the decision to destroy the Buddhas was not totally unexpected, at the time what had happened within the Taliban to precipitate this decision was a mystery. As became clear after the attacks on the World Trade Center in New York in September 2001, the Taliban had fallen under the influence of foreign ideologies (Al Qaeda, following the strict Wahabi Islam, which tolerates no depictions of human beings whatsoever). As a consequence, not only were the Bamiyan Buddhas brutally destroyed, but many of the remaining artifacts in the museum were also smashed to pieces.

Since then, there have been some proposals to rebuild the Buddhas. Apart from the feasibility of reconstructing them, the form that the restoration should take also raises dilemmas. Should they be rebuilt in their original form, with gold and other ornaments; as they were in 1998, before the first damage by the Taliban; or in their condition on the eve of the demolition in March 2001? Moreover, it could be argued that Buddhist tradition would counsel against any restoration. The aim of Buddhism is total detachment, both material and spiritual. According to that line of thinking, their loss should be accepted and people should move on. From the Buddhist point of view, every construction includes destruction, every destruction construction. Of course, others argue that the country needs improved infrastructure and security more than it needs rebuilt statues. Yet the Afghans themselves seem to regard the rebuilding of the Buddhas as being a step of the utmost importance toward restoring a sense of history and national pride.

Material That Has Survived the War

In 1993 the fate of the National Museum collections was totally unclear. It was not known which pieces had been damaged by the bombing, which ones had been stolen, and which had left the country. All kinds of rumors were making the rounds. Was it true that Najibullah, the last pro-Russian president, had ordered that the most valuable items, like the Tellya Tepe Hoard, should be packed away beforehand? Over the years things have become somewhat clearer. Objects (with the exception of the Tellya Tepe Hoard) appeared on the market, mainly in Pakistan, Western Europe, the United States, and Japan. SPACH and other organizations acquired pieces when and where they could, with the intention of returning them to National Museum in due course. Even private collectors are sometimes willing to return pieces voluntarily. In this way a number of pieces have been saved for a future National Museum of Afghanistan in Kabul. It is not impossible that some institutions that have acquired Afghan material since 1993 may be willing to follow suit.

The best news for a long time about Afghanistan's cultural heritage was released in the autumn of 2003 and concerned the Tellya Tepe Hoard. This hoard was excavated by a Russian-Afghan team in 1978–79 and consists of twenty thousand extraordinary gold objects and ornaments, from around the beginning of the first millennium A.D. It seems that in 1992 Najibullah asked at least one Westerner to evacuate the collection of the museum, because he felt then that everything was about to get out of hand. For reasons that are not known the request was not met, and a few months later almost everything in the museum was thought to have been damaged or looted. However, the most precious objects, the Tellya Tepe Hoard, had indeed been put in trunks and stored in the National Bank vaults of the presidential palace. In the autumn of 2003 these bank vaults were opened, and it was revealed that the Tellya Tepe gold had survived the war. Then, in 2004, it was revealed that a further two thousand pieces from the National Museum had been discovered in the vaults. It is now estimated that 90 percent of the objects that were on display in the 1980s have survived intact (Kaufman 2004). Still, where and how these treasures will be kept safe has to be considered. It would be unforgivable to the community as a whole if these items were now to be stolen.

Conclusion

The destruction of Afghanistan's cultural heritage is exceptional because this heritage fell victim both to extensive looting and to religiously inspired iconoclasm. However, it could, and in my opinion should, serve as a case study to illustrate the types of threats that need to be guarded against in the future and to indicate what might constitute appropriate preventive action or countermeasures.

During World War II, material from European museums was evacuated into bunkers and caves. It is now clear that material from the National Museum was likewise placed in safe storage, but obviously not enough was done. In the future, there should be more preparation for the temporary evacuation of movable cultural heritage. Preventive evacuation could take place either in or outside the country and could be nationally and/or internationally organized. As we have seen in the case of Afghanistan, specially designated safe havens could provide temporary refuge.

After the most tragic destruction of the Bamiyan Buddhas and the demolition of what remained in the National Museum, the idea of temporary evacuation should be strongly advocated. Let us hope that the world will not forget these tragic disasters in Afghanistan (and Iraq for that matter) too soon and that attitudes and laws can be changed so that the evacuation concept becomes a reality whereby we can do the utmost to protect what we cherish.

Bibliography

Braarvig, Jens. "The Case of Ancient Buddhist Manuscripts from Afghanistan." In *Not For Sale: A Swiss-British Conference on the Traffic in Artefacts from Iraq, Afghanistan and Beyond*, ed. by Matt Kimmich, 35–37. Geneva: British Council, 2004.

Dupree, Nancy H. "Museum under Siege." *Archaeology*, March–April 1996, 42–51.

———. "The Plunder Continues." *Archaeology online*. <http://www.archaeology.org/online/features/afghan/update.html>, accessed October 10, 2004 (1998).

International Institute for the Unification of Private Law (UNIDROIT). *UNIDROIT Convention on Stolen or Illegally Exported Cultural Objects*. Rome: UNIDROIT, 1995.

Kaufman, Jason E. "National Museum Treasures Found Intact." *Art Newspaper*, no. 153 (2004): 6.

Lundén, Staffan. "Skriftsamleren (The Manuscript Collector)." *Culture without Context*, issue 16 (Spring 2005): 3–11.

Omland, Atle, and Christopher Prescott. "Afghanistan's Cultural Heritage in Norwegian Museums?" *Culture without Context*, issue 11 (Autumn 2002): 4–7.

Prescott, Christopher, and Atle Omland. "The Schøyen Collection in Norway: Demand for the Return of Objects and Questions about Iraq." *Culture without Context*, issue 13 (Autumn 2003): 8–11.

Romey, Kristin M. "The Race to Save Afghan Culture." *Archaeology*, May–June 2002, 18–25.

United Nations Educational, Scientific and Cultural Organization. *Convention on the Means of Prohibiting and Preventing the Illicit Import, Export and Transfer of Ownership of Cultural Property*. Paris: UNESCO, 1970.

12

Illicit Trafficking and Trade in Indian Antiquities

Renewed Efforts to Save and Preserve India's Heritage

S. K. PACHAURI

Article 49 of the Constitution of India states: "It shall be the obligation of the State to protect every monument or place or object of artistic or historic interest, declared by or under law made by Parliament to be of national importance, from spoliation, disfigurement, destruction, removal, disposal or export, as the case may be." Article 51A states: "It shall be the duty of every citizen of India to value and preserve the rich heritage of our composite culture." While allowing for private ownership, national Indian legislation requires that the central government give permission for the exportation of cultural artifacts. The relevant laws are the 1972 Antiquities and Art Treasures Act, 1947 Antiquities (Export Control) Act, and Customs Acts of 1961 and 1962. Still artifacts are leaving the country and are for sale in the auction houses and sales rooms of the world (see Peter Watson's exposé of Sotheby's and Indian artifacts for further discussion; Watson 1997).

The Archaeological Survey of India (ASI) is the chief custodian of India's archaeological heritage. It protects more than five thousand monuments of national importance and sixteen World Heritage sites, including the Taj Mahal and Ajanta Allora. The ASI also has thirty-three museums located at sites of cultural or archaeological importance. Apart from these centrally protected monuments, there are more than four thousand monuments throughout the country that fall under the jurisdiction of state archaeological departments, and yet there are still thousands of buildings of historical importance that are in private ownership and unprotected from the constant threats of vandalism and theft. However, due to increased security, thefts are gradually lessening.

The severity of the problem of the theft of cultural material can be gauged from statistics provided by the National Crime Records Bureau of India in the state of Andhra Pradesh, one of the major states and one with a rich heritage and an abundance of archaeological sites and museums. The total value of reported and discovered thefts from 1998 to 2003 was 291,092,000 rupees (Rs.), equivalent to U.S. $6,295,253, and the value of items recovered is Rs. 5,099,050

($110,275). Recoveries are few and far between. Two recent cases at Kanuparthy and Chandavaram illustrate the nature of the problem (National Crime Records Bureau 2005).

The site museum at Kanuparthy was broken into during the night of May 1, 2002. The thieves stole two small idols: a stone sculpture of Nagadevatha, the serpent deity (49 cm × 43 cm), and a limestone pillar on which a half *padem* (footprint) was depicted (0.40 cm × 0.32 cm). The case is under investigation, and the stolen objects have not yet been recovered.

The second case involved the theft of sculptured panels from the site museum at Chandavaram, a theft that took place in three episodes. The first was on October 9, 2000, when two relief panels were removed; a further three panels were taken on February 2, 2001; and finally on March 23, 2001, three limestone *silpas* (birds) and a limestone pillar were stolen. Four of the nine objects were recovered on October 11, 2001; however, the case is still under investigation.

Outside Andhra Pradesh, an investigation by the Central Bureau of Investigation (CBI) and ASI recently revealed a typical case of smuggling in New Delhi. On November 8, 2002, a CBI raid recovered four bronze statues of the fourteenth-century Chandela dynasty from a house in the New Friends Colony area of New Delhi. The four figures—two of Lord Shiva, one of Parvati, and one of Lord Rama—would be valued at more than Rs. 1 *crore* (one crore equals 10 million rupees, or U.S. $216,310) on the international market. Officials said that the statues were intended for shipment to Sydney, Australia, where the owner of the raided house resides. "An application had been placed with the ASI asking for a certificate proving that the statues were non-antiques," said a CBI official, but the request was turned down, and instead the applicants were asked to register the statues with the ASI.[1] However, the owner refused to register the statues, and although they were kept in an unlit dungeonlike room, the CBI team, acting on intelligence received, was able to locate them. A CBI official suggested that it was likely the statues had been transported from South India. A case has been registered under the Antiquities and Art Treasures Act against the owner of the house. "We will try to convince him to come to India for questioning but in case he does not come, we will try other means to get him here," said a CBI official.

The severity of the problem can also be gauged from a simple list of important recoveries made in India of stolen objects between 1999 and 2002:

1. A Holy Quran written in Persian dating to the reign of Emperor Aurangzeb. The book was given by Aurangzeb to one of the local chieftains of Chittoor in reward for services rendered during the emperor's southern campaigns. The book was seized while it was being sold for a record amount of Rs. 45 *lakhs* (U.S. $97,323; one lakh equals 100,000 rupees).

2. A Dashbuja Ganesh figure in red stone performing a dance.
3. A Buddha.
4. More than thirty stone sculptures.
5. Panch Loha (five metals) figures of Goddesses Bhu Devi, Sri Devi, and Lord Vishnu.
6. Ashtdhatu (eight elements) figurine of Goddess Aradhkali.
7. Ganesh figures in various forms, including the dancing Ganesh.
8. A large number of terra-cotta items relating to Kala Bhairav (one of Shiva's many forms), Goddess Laxmi, Goddess Saraswati, and Lord Vishnu.
9. Bronze idols of Shiva, Shiva in Tandav Mudra, Rama, and Parvati.
10. Paintings or other illustrated material.

This list is far from comprehensive, and it must also be assumed that many pieces were exported illegally (for further examples see Deb 2005).

THE NEW PROBLEM OF CYBER-CRIME

A new problem is the sale of antiquities on the Internet, where ancient statues, figures, stones, coins, or jewelry can all be showcased and sold. All it takes is a website and an e-mail address to work out a deal. The problem of Internet sales is growing more serious with time and thus far no cases have been prosecuted. This situation shows no sign of improvement. CBI officials maintain that although they constantly monitor Internet auction sites, they have found little evidence to suggest that smugglers are making use of the sites. Experts in "cyber-law" are of the opinion that smugglers prefer to make use of temporary websites that can easily disappear, so that keeping track of them is a difficult proposition. The existing law on antiquities pertains to the terrestrial world and cannot cope with cyberspace. India's Information Technology Act of 2000 is also silent on the subject. There is a definite need to strengthen existing laws and make the on-line trade in antiquities illegal. Until then, antiquities will continue to fall victim to the World Wide Web.

PREVENTION OF CRIME AGAINST WRITTEN HERITAGE

The National Archives of India was first established in March 1891 at Calcutta as the Imperial Record Department, before moving to New Delhi in 1912 following the transfer there of the capital. It has one regional office at Bhopal and three record centers at Jaipur, Bhubaneshwar, and Pondicherry. The National Archives of India is custodian of the public records of the government and has a large holding of records occupying thirty kilometers of linear shelf space. Besides English materials, there are records in Arabic, Hindi, Persian, Sanskrit, Urdu, and many other languages. An annex was constructed in 1991 with an additional forty kilometers of linear shelf space to meet the growing demands of the department.

The archives contain some remarkable and unique documents, from papers that may in the future decide the fate of the Kohinoor diamond to scriptures of religious importance. For example, the *sanad* (document) related to the transfer of Kohinoor is displayed at the National Archives Museum. It was issued by the East India Company to Maharaja Dalip Singh on "confiscation of his rights and privileges and presentation of the diamond by the Maharaja as nazr [offering] to the Queen of England on March 28, 1849."

The Indian government has recognized the importance of the archives and has ordered that the documents in its custody should be microfilmed and copies should be stored at a different location—Bhopal—in case of theft or a more serious man-made or natural disaster at its Delhi headquarters. This is a standard security practice worldwide, which ensures the survival of records in the event of a loss at the main storage facility.

RECOVERY OF ARCHAEOLOGICAL HERITAGE ILLEGALLY REMOVED FROM INDIA

Indian heritage has been illegally removed from India in two distinct periods: before and after the passing of the Antiquities (Export Control) Act of 1947. The removal of cultural objects from India before this act came into force cannot be claimed to have violated the law, and so claims for restitution depend for their success on the goodwill of the individuals or institutions concerned. India, however, is raising its voice through international conventions and forums for repatriation of cultural heritage that was taken clandestinely after 1947, and particularly after the implementation of the 1972 Antiquities and Art Treasures Act in 1976. Unlicensed export of archaeological objects is an offense under section 25 of the act, although the punishment prescribed is weak and does not serve as a deterrent. There are no restrictions on the export of replicas, nor are any guidelines offered in the act for the production of replicas.

Several obstacles confront India in the restitution of cultural heritage to its place of origin:

1. Nonrecognition by affluent countries of foreign export controls on cultural heritage.
2. Nonratification by many of the affluent countries of the 1970 UNESCO Convention on the Means of Prohibiting and Preventing the Illicit Im-

port, Export and Transfer of Ownership of Cultural Property, though this situation is changing (see Gerstenblith, chapter 3).[2]

3. The need to pay compensation to "an innocent purchaser or to a person who has the valid title to that property" as defined in the Article 7(b) (ii) of the 1970 UNESCO Convention.

4. Expensive and time-consuming civil litigation.

Nevertheless, despite these obstacles, India has successfully retrieved objects that had been taken out of the country surreptitiously. For example, the ASI has recently recovered three pieces of sculpture from the United States. They had been stolen from different parts of India and exported clandestinely before being acquired by museums and private collectors in the United States. It is notable that the restitution of these sculptures was achieved without payment of any compensation.

THE BODH GAYA BUDDHA

This eighth-century stone image of Buddha, measuring 122 × 50 cm, disappeared sometime between February 1987 and March 1989 from Bodh Gaya, Bihar. Dr. D. Mitra, former director-general of the ASI, had seen this sculpture on the premises of a *math* (monastery) sometime in February 1987, but on a subsequent visit in March 1989 she found it to be missing. Mitra also ascertained in 1989 that neither the local authorities nor the police had been notified of its disappearance.

A few years later, one of Mitra's colleagues drew her attention to an image of a standing Buddha shown in the exhibition catalogue *The Lotus Transcendent: Indian and Southeast Asian Sculpture from the Samuel Eilenberg Collection* (Lerner and Kossak 1991: fig. 30, accession no. 1990.115). Mitra realized that it was the missing Bodh Gaya Buddha, and in 1996 she brought it to the attention of the ASI. The ASI discovered that the statue had been registered in 1976, and the director of the Patna department of archaeology confirmed its subsequent disappearance.

The Indian Embassy in New York raised the matter with the Metropolitan Museum of Art and provided copies of the ASI registration certificate as proof of identity and origin. After prolonged discussions, the Metropolitan agreed to return the Buddha to India without recompense. ASI's director of antiquities on behalf of the government of India received the sculpture in March 1999 in New York from the museum and returned with it to India.

THE SCULPTURE OF LAKULISA

The sculpture of Lakulisa (a Shiva cult image) was in the collection of James and Marilynn Alsdorf of Chicago. A large part of the Alsdorf collection, including the Lakulisa, was exhibited at the Art Institute of Chicago in 1997. The Lakulisa was listed in the exhibition catalogue as AL. 126 Buddha (Jina?), India, Uttar Pradesh, Almora/Jageswar, 10/11th century, 57 × 33 × 14 cm. However, while preparing for the exhibition, Marilynn Alsdorf learned that the image of Lakulisa had already been referred to in the publication *The Archaeology of Kumaon* (Nautiyal 1969: 142–44, fig. 54), which led her to suspect that it had been removed illegally from India. She discussed the matter with the Consulate General of India in Chicago and disclosed that the sculpture had been in the possession of the Alsdorfs since early 1970.

The Consulate conveyed this information to the ASI, which discovered that the sculpture had been photographed and documented in 1957 but subsequently stolen from Dandesvar Temple in the Jageswar group of shrines, Jageswar, District Almora in Uttar Pradesh, sometime in 1967. On September 8, 1999, the Consulate General of India in Chicago was instructed to take up the matter with Mrs. Alsdorf, and after a short period of negotiation she agreed to return the sculpture without receiving any compensation in return. It reached India on October 29, 2000.

THE SCULPTURE OF KRISHNAJANMA

An image of Krishnajanma (a ritual image of the baby Krishna) was stolen from Dhubela Museum, District Chhatarpur in Madhya Pradesh, on March 8, 1968, along with seven other objects. Notice of the theft was lodged on the same day with the local police authority. The sculpture passed from view for nearly a decade until it was purchased in London by John D. Rockefeller III, who subsequently donated it to the Asia Society in 1978. In December 1988 the government of Madhya Pradesh requested the Indian Department of Culture to approach the Asia Society through the Consulate-General of India in New York for its retrieval. The Consulate-General took up the case with the Asia Society in 1999. After discussions, the Asia Society handed over the image of Krishnajanma to the Consulate-General on April 29, 1999, without compensation, and it returned to Madhya Pradesh on May 7, 1999 (Dobrzynski 1999).

CONCLUSION

Cultural and natural heritage are irreplaceable, not only for each nation but for humanity as a whole. Loss through deterioration or disappearance is an impoverishment of the heritage of all the peoples of the world. Parts of that heritage, because of their exceptional qualities, can be considered to be of outstanding universal value and as such are worthy of special protection against the dangers that increasingly threaten them.

One new aspect of the trade is that the national government's policy of opening the Indian market and making its economy more internationally responsive has brought about new threats to the Indian subcontinent. As more and more tourists visit India, with their foreign exchange that helps boost the economy, the danger to cultural heritage has increased, as there are many who would like to acquire cultural objects at any price, whether legally or illegally. Another factor is that the new symbols of our age are the cell phone and the computer. These two technological innovations have improved communication and, without doubt, have facilitated the work of those who indulge in the antiquities trade. Cyber-crime is on the increase, and no solution has so far been found.

In India a holistic approach has been adopted to check the illicit trafficking of antiquities. The agencies involved are the Customs Department, CBI, ASI, and the police and archaeological departments of the state and provincial governments. One possible solution may be to make replicas more readily available. However, it is already the case that many genuine antiquities are being exported under the guise of handicrafts or replicas. It is essential that proper training should be provided for police officers and customs officials to discriminate between handicrafts and genuine antiquities. Public awareness can be raised and a new consciousness developed by print and electronic media. Museums can also help to increase awareness. Of late there have been exchanges of heritage objects between India and other countries enabling the display of Indian heritage abroad and of the cultural patrimony of other nations in India. Some authorities have suggested that the demand for illicit antiquities might be assuaged in the short term by increasing the market supply of artifacts with good provenance, while in the long term programs of public education might help to reduce demand. This suggestion remains untested but has thus far not been accepted with any enthusiasm.

The consequence of the illicit trade is the spoliation of India's monuments and archaeological sites, many of which form part of continuing, living secular and religious traditions. Clearly, greed plays a part in this. Perhaps, then, in this context, it is worth pausing to reflect on some of the advice in the *Bhagwad Gita*, the holy scripture of India and one of Hinduism's most authoritative sources of both doctrine and ethics.

For example, it is said: *Pravrttim ca nivrttim ca jana na vidur asurah! na saucam na' pica' caro na satyam tesu vidyate*, which means "The demoniac know not what to do and what to refrain from: neither purity nor right conduct nor truth is found in them." Commendable acts are those that are conducive to general human welfare; they are designated as *dharma*. Prohibited acts are those that make people depraved and ruin careers. They are condemned as *adharma*. The good always conform to *dharma*. People of the *Asura* or demoniacal type are impure in thoughts and deeds. Their utterances are said to be distorted, diabolical, and devoid of truth. Their personalities are entirely polluted.

It is said about a person who has succumbed to the overwhelming force of greed: *Idam adya maya labdham idam prapsye manoratham! idam asti dam api me bhavisyati punar dhanam* and *Adhyo bhijanavan asmi ko nyo sti sadrso maya! yaksye dasyami modisya ity ajnanavimohitah*, which means "This today has been gained by me; this desire I shall fulfill; this is mine, and this wealth also shall be mine in future. I am rich and well-born. Who else is equal to me? I will sacrifice, I will give alms, I will rejoice." However, the scripture judges such people as "thus deluded by ignorance." *Aneka citta vibhranta moha jala samavrtah! prasaktah kamabhogesu patanti narake sucau*: "Bewildered by many a fancy, enmeshed in the snare of delusion, addicted to the gratification of lust, they fall into a foul hell."

The *Gita* advocates the following qualities: *abhayam sattvasamsuddhir jnanayoga vyavasthitih! danam damas ca yajnas ca svadhyayas tapa arjavam—* "fearlessness, purity of heart, steadfastness in knowledge and yoga, alms giving, control of the senses, Yajna [the offering of food], study of the scriptures, austerity and straightforwardness." Another stanza adds "*Ahimsa satyam akrodhas tyagah santir apaisunam! daya bhutesv aloluptvam mardavam hrir acapalam*, which means "Non-injury, truth, absence of anger, renunciation, serenity, absence of calumny, compassion to beings, uncovetousness, gentleness, modesty, absence of fickleness." These are the positive qualities that have to be inculcated in all humanity. This consciousness is the kind that has to be created to make the world a safer place, not only for the survival of humanity but for the survival of our priceless heritage.

To conclude, in the end we have a collective responsibility to safeguard our common human heritage. It is a responsibility furthermore that links past, present, and future generations in a chain of reciprocity and care. Saving our heritage is like saving the life blood essential for the survival of humanity and of our planet. Thus, a metamorphosis in thinking and a radical change in attitude have to be achieved if the heritage is to be saved.

ACKNOWLEDGMENTS

I would like to thank Neil Brodie and Kathy Tubb for all their encouragement, patience, and constant interaction all through the years.

NOTES

1. A recent article by Gitanjali Deb (2005: 41–42) discusses the practice of smuggling real artifacts out of the country among modern forgeries.

2. India ratified the 1970 UNESCO Convention in 1997.

BIBLIOGRAPHY

Antiquities and Art Treasures Act, 1972.

Antiquities (Export Control) Act, 1947.

Customs Act, 1961.

Customs Act, 1962.

Deb, Gitanjali. "Stealing Gods: Illegal Trade in Indian Antiquities." *Art Antiquity and Law* 10, no. 1 (2005): 29–62.

Dobrzynski, Judith. "Asia Society to Return Sculpture, Once Stolen to India." *New York Times*, February 24, 1999, E1, E5.

Information Technology Act, 2000.

Lerner, Martin, and Steven M. Kossak. *The Lotus Transcendent: Indian and Southeast Asian Sculpture from the Samuel Eilenberg Collection.* New Haven, Conn.: Yale University Press, 1991.

National Crime Records Bureau. *Crime in India 2003.* <http://ncrb.nic.in/crime2003/cii.html>, accessed June 5, 2005 (2005).

Nautiyal, Kanti Prasad. *The Archaeology of Kumaon, Including Dehradun: A Comprehensive Account of the Cultural Heritage of Modern Garhwal and Kumaon Divisions.* Varanasi, India: Chowkhamba Sanskrit Series Office, 1969.

United Nations Educational, Scientific and Cultural Organization. *Convention on the Means of Prohibiting and Preventing the Illicit Import, Export and Transfer of Ownership of Cultural Property.* Paris: UNESCO, 1970.

Watson, Peter. *Sotheby's: The Inside Story.* London: Bloomsbury, 1997.

13

Museum Acquisitions

Responsibilities for the Illicit Traffic in Antiquities

COLIN RENFREW

The disaster that befell the Iraqi National Museum immediately after the co-alition occupation of Baghdad in 2003 reminds us again of the widespread practice of looting, both adventitious and organized, both of existing museum collections and of still unexcavated areas of archaeological sites. The looters are financed, whether before or more often after the event, by collectors. But I argue that the climate of opinion is to a large extent set by museum curators. For it is the content of public exhibitions that establishes the conventions in this matter, and it is the acquisitions of museums, as often by gift or bequest as by purchase, that sets the tone. I argue, moreover, that what is shown in a major museum on temporary loan is as relevant as the permanent acquisition. Very few museums exercise the same degree of due diligence in this area as they do for permanent acquisitions. And some museums consider it one of the criteria for acquisition that an unprovenanced piece has already been publicly exhibited and published in a major museum exhibition. I argue that "reputation laundering by public exhibition" is the up-market version of money laundering in the traffic of drugs.

Adverse reference is made to the Boston Museum of Fine Arts and the Metropolitan Museum of Art in this context, and a statement of their acquisitions policy is requested. Favorable reference is made to the published acquisitions policies of the University of Pennsylvania Museum of Archaeology and Anthropology, the British Museum, and the new Code of Deontology of the International Council of Museums (ICOM).

As a case study, reference is made to acquisitions of Cycladic antiquities by the Badisches Landesmuseum in Karlsruhe during the 1970s and to the unfortunate episode of the so-called Keros Hoard, which first surfaced in the Erlenmeyer Collection around that time and which must have been illegally excavated and illegally exported from Greece in the preceding years.

My intention is not to inquire tiresomely into history but to make explicit certain principles and to invite museum curators and directors to acknowledge these and to follow them.

The Problem of the Illicit Market

The looting of the Iraqi National Museum in Baghdad was foreseeable and fore-seen (Renfrew 2003). It has again thrown into prominence the international market in illicit and unprovenanced antiquities and its destructive effects. Even more damaging to the potential for understanding the past is the destruction of archaeological sites to provide antiquities for the market. This, as is widely recognized, destroys the contexts in which finds are made and hence the pos-sibility of using the work to add to our understanding of the sites in question. For it is almost exclusively through the excavations of archaeological contexts in their entirety and their systematic publication that our knowledge of the early human past is founded. This point is recognized by all serious archaeologists (see Renfrew 2000). It is a principle embodied in the 1970 UNESCO Conven-tion on the Means of Prohibiting and Preventing the Illicit Import, Export and Transfer of Ownership of Cultural Property. This was clearly recognized in the Berlin Declaration of 1988 (Heilmeyer and Eule 2004: 227).

Since the Berlin Declaration there has been significant progress in some respects. The International Council of Museums has revised its Code of De-ontology, and has been active, through its One Hundred Missing Objects se-ries, in making the nature of the problem more widely known. UNESCO has been active in a number of ways. And the 1995 UNIDROIT Convention on the International Return of Stolen or Illegally Exported Cultural Objects has set new standards, although it has not yet been as widely adopted as the 1970 UNESCO Convention.

Restitution as a Different Issue

So far as possible I wish to separate the issue under discussion from that of the restitution of antiquities that left their country of origin many years ago—for instance, more than thirty to fifty years ago. There are legitimate issues concern-ing restitution. But my main concern is to stop the ongoing looting now. Thus I shall deal with antiquities that have been illicitly excavated recently—since 1970.

The Spectrum of Museum Ethics

I want to share my growing conviction that currently it is a group of prominent museum directors who must take the main blame for the continuing scale of looting. Let me say at once that some museum directors are above reproach. There is a spectrum here between the meticulous and careful, on the one hand,

and the irresponsible, on the other. I do not claim that the looting of archaeological sites would stop if no museums were to accept looted material into their collections. But I do think that the ethos of collecting looted antiquities and presenting this as acceptable is fostered by some of the world's major museums, which would wish to be thought of as among the world's respectable museums.

THE NUB: "DUE DILIGENCE"

Most of the world's museums are members of the International Council of Museums (although probably not one of the most dubious in its acquisitions activity, the Miho Museum) and so are supposed to subscribe to the ICOM Code of Ethics, including its section on collection policies (Renfrew 2000: 121). ICOM is of course against looting and against the acquisition of looted antiquities, and it has recently revised its code. So how is it that museums still acquire and exhibit loot?

The answer lies in due diligence. No museums will admit to the offense of knowingly buying looted antiquities. But until recently, few have had an acquisitions policy that firmly prevents the purchase of unprovenanced and therefore possibly looted pieces. It seems that to this day, the Metropolitan Museum of Art in New York has no written and published policy on acquisitions.

One of the first to adopt a clear policy preventing such acquisitions was the University of Pennsylvania Museum of Archaeology and Anthropology. To quote from the Philadelphia Declaration of 1970 (see Renfrew 2000: 118): "The curatorial faculty of the University [of Pennsylvania] Museum today reached the unanimous conclusion that they would purchase no more art objects or antiquities for the Museum unless the objects are accompanied by a pedigree—that is information about the different owners of the objects, place of origin, legality of export, and other data useful in each individual case. The information will be made public."

The British Museum now has a policy, which prevents the acquisition of recently looted objects, although it does not extend the protection back prior to 1970. To quote from the 1998 statement by the trustees of the British Museum on the acquisition of antiquities (see Renfrew 2000: 124): "Wherever possible the Trustees will only acquire those objects that have documentation to show that they were exported from their country of origin prior to 1970 and this policy will apply to all objects of major importance."

The point here is the crucial one that it is not enough to avoid acquiring objects that are known to have been illegally excavated or illegally exported from the country of origin. The onus of responsibility must be more extensive: it is necessary to be able to prove, through appropriate documentation, that an object has *not* been illegally excavated or illegally exported. In the Philadelphia case, the object requires a full pedigree documenting its legal origins. In the British Museum case, proof is needed that the object in question had left its country of origin prior to 1970 (unless there is a full pedigree available for an object legally exported after that date). This practice means in effect that the object must already have been documented in some form, preferably by photography, prior to 1970 (and that the documentation remains currently available). Clearly no object illegally excavated after 1970 could be accompanied by such documentation, and the British Museum is thus protected by its policy against purchasing such an object.

So the nub of the matter is one of the criteria of due diligence, and the proof of the pudding lies in the documentation. Of course some dealers will say that their clients often find antiquities in their grandmothers' attics, items that have been out of their country of origin for many decades but have somehow escaped documentation. Today, I am afraid, there can be only one ethical answer: no documentation, no acquisition.

Changing Moralities

Although a chapter like this must inevitably take a moral tone, my purpose here is not to be unduly censorious. For those museums that have already adopted a firm acquisitions policy, it is perhaps possible to be more flexible concerning earlier acquisitions that would not have conformed to the newly adopted policy. But it cannot be acceptable in this day and age that any museum should lack a clear policy in relation to acquisitions. Museums like the Boston Museum of Fine Arts or the Badisches Landesmuseum in Karlsruhe must come under public scrutiny, because it is their lack of an ethical acquisitions policy that legitimizes (in some eyes) the illicit traffic in antiquities and hence the looting of archaeological sites. Their trustees have a lot to answer for.

Proposed Resolutions

In the light of these considerations, it seemed appropriate to propose to the Conference on the Illicit Traffic in Antiquities held in Berlin in May 2003 (Renfrew 2004a: 66) that all museum directors and all museum boards of trustees should be invited to reflect upon their responsibilities in these matters. For that reason it seemed appropriate to propose the following three resolutions (with one clarifying supplementary statement).

That It Be Resolved:

To call upon the Board of Trustees and the Director of each Museum:

I To formulate and then to make publicly known a specific acquisition policy in relation to antiquities, and specifically in relation to cultural property without documented provenance.

II To apply their acquisition policy for antiquities to gifts and to bequests as well as to purchases, and to apply the policy with equal force also for the acceptance of objects on loan or for conservation.

III To frame their acquisition policy for antiquities so that the Museum will acquire only those objects which have documentation to show that they were excavated and known prior to 1970 or such earlier date as determined by the legislation of their country of origin.

Note that these resolutions in effect express the position reached in 1998 by the trustees of the British Museum, following the early lead given by the University of Pennsylvania Museum of Archaeology and Anthropology.

There is, however, one complicating factor for which allowance must be made if museums are to be able to follow these resolutions to the full: the question of antiquities that are illicitly excavated and that come to light (or are seized) within their country of origin. The resolution of the British Museum trustees makes allowance for this factor as follows (Renfrew 2000: 125): "The Trustees recognise the principle that regional and national museums must sometimes act as repositories of last resort for antiquities originating within their areas of responsibility, and they will on occasion approve the acquisition of antiquities without documented provenance where it can reliably be inferred that they originated within the United Kingdom, and where such payment as may be made is not likely to encourage illicit excavation." It follows here that the notion of a "repository of last resort" can only apply to a location situated within the territory of the nation where the antiquities in question are discovered. It is conceivable, however, that UNESCO might in some cases be willing to approve the temporary location of such a repository outside the nation of origin until such time as stable conditions can be established in that nation. This indeed happened in 2002, when UNESCO approved the location in Switzerland of such a temporary repository for antiquities originating in Afghanistan and exported during the times of the depredations there and the systematic destruction of antiquities organized by the Taliban.

These considerations give rise to a fourth resolution:

IV To recognise the principle that a museum of last resort can be designated for each region or nation to serve as a legal destination for illicitly excavated antiquities found within the territory of that region or nation and only within such territory.

A Few Examples

In my book *Loot, Legitimacy and Ownership: The Ethical Crisis in Archaeology* (2000), I set out some of the most scandalous recent examples of the public exhibition of objects that are likely to have been looted—illegally excavated and illegally exported from their country of origin. Of course, without categorical evidence it is difficult to be certain in every case. But certainly the following examples would fail to conform to the criteria established by the University of Pennsylvania Museum of Archaeology and Anthropology or the British Museum.

- The Weary Herakles in the Boston Museum of Fine Arts consists of the upper part of a marble statue of Herakles, of which the lower half is in the Archaeological Museum in Antalya, originally looted from at the classical site of Perge. It is widely believed, but cannot be documented, that the upper part was discovered and illegally exported around 1980 (Renfrew 2000: pl. 4). The Boston MFA currently declines to return the upper part of the statue to rejoin the lower half in Antalya.
- The exhibition of the Ortiz Collection in the Royal Academy in London caused widespread criticism. The catalogue (Ortiz 1994) included many pieces without adequate provenance, many of them recent acquisitions.
- The acquisition of the Fleischmann Collection by the Getty Museum in 1995 involved many antiquities without provenance, which had likewise been recently acquired for the collection. It is difficult to see how the acquisition of the collection involved any form of due diligence. Moreover the Italian government has since recovered some of the pieces, which seem to have been looted from Italy, and has taken legal steps to recover more (Felch and Frammolino 2005).
- A purchase by the Louvre Musée des Arts Premiers involved two looted heads, one of the Nok culture, from Nigeria. A request from the Nigerian government for restitution was circumvented, following the personal intervention of President Jacques Chirac.
- A substantial part of the collection of the Musée Barbier-Mueller of Geneva involves recently acquired antiquities lacking adequate provenance. This is exemplified by their collection of Early Cycladic antiquities (Zimmerman 1993).

My argument is that glamour receptions and public openings of such exhibitions or in celebration of new acquisitions are enterprises that reinforce in the private collector the notion that "anything goes." How can we expect the private amateur to show a more carefully thought-out and ethical collecting policy than the professional curator? One notes the collusion between museums of this category and less ethical collectors who obtain tax benefits from their subsequent donations or bequests of looted antiquities. Many of us remember the embarrassing case of Dr. J. Frel, some years ago a curator at the Getty Museum in Malibu, who encouraged charitable (and tax-deductible) benefactions from donors by deliberately inflating the valuations he assigned to the donated pieces. In this way donors sometimes obtained a tax deduction greater in scale than the price they originally paid for the piece donated.

But I want to focus instead on an exhibition held in 1976, which I now believe served to legitimize the looting of Early Cycladic antiquities, and which was not subjected at the time to the criticism it merited. Had it been, the museum in question would have been spared the embarrassment it suffered three years ago through its public exhibition of looted material.

THE BADISCHES LANDESMUSEUM IN KARLSRUHE

I refer to the Badisches Landesmuseum, and the 1976 exhibition in question was entitled *Art and Culture of the Cyclades*. The Greek government wisely decided not to lend any material at all from Greece. Close to 50 percent of the pieces exhibited were previously unpublished, the great majority of which (if one excludes some fakes) must have been looted over the previous two decades.

The objection underlying this criticism is that the Badisches Landesmuseum in the three or four years prior to the exhibition had purchased Early Cycladic antiquities without the adequate exercise of due diligence. The pieces were previously unknown to scholarship and unpublished, and therefore almost certainly derived from illegal excavations undertaken within the Cycladic Islands. They must then have been illegally exported from Greece, since there is no record of export permits for such important pieces. The site of Dhaskalio Kavos provides clear evidence of the devastation that this process caused at one particular site of which I have knowledge.

It is unfortunate that I must quote from the introduction to the exhibition catalogue a statement by the then director, Ernst Petrasch. No doubt he was a scholar of good intentions, but by allowing the State of Baden-Württemberg to spend public money upon looted antiquities without the exercise of due diligence, he was conniving at the looting further discussed later. He said: "An important law, enacted in 1958 by the legislative assembly of Baden-Württemberg, assures the museums under its administration of adequate funds for the acquisition of important works of art. This has enabled our Museum to build up its collections during the past eight years. By intense and careful planning, the antiquities department has been able to add to the basic collection of Cycladic art inherited from the nineteenth century by purchasing a number of objects of which several are exceptional" (Thimme 1976: x).

Among these acquisitions were several of evident importance yet completely without published provenance. The inference must surely be that they had been recently purchased, following illegal excavation in Greece and subsequent export without license. I have no means of documenting either the circumstances of excavation or of export of each piece. But the absence of any documentation or provenance for these pieces must give rise to the surmise that they had recently appeared on the antiquities market, since such pieces would not long remain unknown. The inference must therefore be that they had been looted. The three most prominent of these pieces are the Syrinx player (Thimme 1976: no. 256, Tafel VI); the "frying pan" of chlorite schist (Thimme 1976: no. 364, Tafel III), published for the first time in the 1976 catalogue; and the large folded-arm figure (89 cm), then the second largest complete figure known (Thimme 1976, 259, no. 151), published for the first time the previous year (Thimme 1975).

Some of the leading scholars of the day in the field of Aegean prehistory were invited to contribute to the 1976 exhibition catalogue—although they were not consulted in advance about the inclusion in the exhibition of unpublished and looted antiquities. I was myself one of their number. When I visited the exhibition I was perplexed to see the large numbers of unpublished works; clearly some of them had been recently looted. But, regrettably as it now seems, like other scholars, I made no formal protest at the time. With the wisdom of hindsight it can now be recognized that the 1976 Karlsruhe exhibition with its wealth of looted material, some purchased by the Landesmuseum itself, was an affront to archaeological decency.

Also included in the catalogue—rather unusually—were advertisements from dealers: Uraeus and Simon de Monbrison (Paris), Elie Borowski (Basel), Robin Symes and Bruce McAlpine (London), N. Koutoulakis (Paris and Geneva), and so on.

Moreover the catalogue contained a very strange photograph of a large group of 140 broken Early Cycladic figures then part of the Erlenmeyer Collection in Basel (Thimme 1976, 87). The photograph had also been published the previous year by the museum's curator of antiquities, Jürgen Thimme, in the *Jahrbuch der Staatlichen Kunstsammlungen in Baden-Württemberg* (Thimme 1975). It could reasonably be said to be an assemblage of illicit Cycladic antiquities apparently fresh from the looting. Several pieces from this assemblage were on view in Karlsruhe. They were reported in the catalogue to come from the Cycladic island of Keros.

Before continuing, it is appropriate to state my feeling that the scholars who participated in the catalogue, without knowing in advance of the inclusion of so many looted pieces in the exhibition, were in a sense made unwittingly part of a great laundering exercise. In retrospect, we should have protested against the inclusion of these probably illegal and looted pieces in what purported to be a respectable display. To do so even today may hold some useful purpose. For the failure of the Greek government to lodge a protest at the time against the flagrant breach of its legislation relating to antiquities had important and unfortunate consequences when the Erlenmeyer Collection was later offered for sale at auction in the notorious series of antiquities sales that Sotheby's were then conducting in London.

DESTRUCTION ON KEROS

The circumstances of the looting of the site of Dhaskalio Kavos on Keros are now known in outline (Doumas 1964; Renfrew 1984; Zapheiropoulou 1967, 1968a, 1968b). The site was ransacked by looters during the 1950s and early 1960s. It was not until 1963 that it was first visited by professional archaeologists (including myself) and that steps were taken to recover the remaining fragmentary material strewn upon the surface. The attribution of the Erlenmeyer pieces to Keros has been discussed by Getz-Preziosi (1982).

The complete destruction of what had undoubtedly been the richest site, by an order of magnitude, in the Cycladic Islands during the Early Bronze Age is now well documented (Broodbank 2000).

It was in 1990 that pieces from the Erlenmeyer Collection were offered for public sale at the London auction house Sotheby's (Sotheby's 1990a, 1990b). They included many marble figurine fragments from the so-called Keros Hoard, including pieces that appeared in the original photograph mentioned earlier.

The Greek Embassy was notified of this public sale of looted material and applied promptly through the London court for an injunction against the sale of its looted antiquities. A temporary injunction was indeed granted. But it was set aside when lawyers on behalf of Sotheby's pointed out that many of these objects had been first exhibited publicly in Karlsruhe in 1976 and that the Greek government had made no protest at that time. The sale consequently went ahead, and the collection was dispersed. Several pieces were, however, returned to Greece following their acquisition by the N. P. Goulandris Foundation.

Assigning Responsibilities

When individuals and institutions mend their ways it is appropriate to welcome this. It is not appropriate then to be censorious over past sins. But when the sins continue and their effects multiply, it is time to speak out.

My own conclusion is that 1976 was a parting of the ways. Of course much of the looting had taken place by then—certainly at Dhaskalio Kavos the site had already been ransacked. But that was the year that the academic world and the Greek government failed to condemn the Badisches Landesmuseum for its illegal and foolish purchases and for its shameless display of obviously looted material. Scholars and the Greek authorities both failed in 1976 to object to the legitimization of such dirty trading by the inclusion of unprovenanced antiquities in this major exhibition and in its imposing catalogue, published with the participation of so many scholars.

This opened the way to further such exhibitions and to the continuing acquisition of looted Cycladic antiquities by private collectors, who then in some cases donated or bequeathed them to leading museums, mainly in the United States. It led the way to further prestigious publications in which looted antiquities were mixed promiscuously with those of more legitimate provenance. It led the way to the outrageous Erlenmeyer sale, ostensibly in favor of some environmental charity, and to the failure of the Greek government to stop it, despite their best if belated efforts.

Karlsruhe 2001

The events of 1976 can now be seen to have led on naturally to the international embarrassment occasioned by the Karlsruhe exhibition of 2001. This was a major display of Minoan antiquities, again at the Badisches Landesmuseum, under the title *Im Labyrinth des Minos* (Karlsruhe 2001). Along with many fine Minoan pieces from Greek and other museums, the exhibition and the catalogue once again included two important groups of antiquities that were all labeled "unpublished" in the catalogue and carried the by-line "Jerusalem, Collection of Batya and Elie Borowski." If the name Elie Borowski looks familiar, it is because he was one of those dealers advertising in the *Kunst und Kultur der Kykladen* catalogue of twenty-four years earlier.

The first group was a series of gold beads of Late Minoan or Late Helladic III date, which need not concern us here, although their provenance does indeed remain unpublished and therefore a matter of concern. It is difficult to avoid the suspicion that important antiquities coming onto the market without provenance are the product of looting. The second was a group of Kamares vases of Middle Minoan II date, all complete, which have indeed generated some predictable and well-warranted controversy. They could only have come from a tomb, probably located in central Crete and perhaps not far from one of the great palace centers. In Crete it is said to be common knowledge which tomb was looted. I therefore have to indicate that in the considered view of many Greek archaeologists, these objects had been illegally excavated in Crete and illegally exported from Greece in recent years. It is scandalous that the Borowskis should purchase such material without the exercise of due diligence. And it is doubly scandalous that the authorities of the Badisches Landesmuseum should once again allow such looted materials to be exhibited. For in doing so they were, in effect, legitimizing the looting process, by performing a kind of antiquity laundering in which unprovenanced and presumably plundered antiquities acquire a catalogue entry for an exhibition at a well-respected institution and hence gain the beginning of a pedigree of a kind. The practice of antiquity laundering has recently been the subject of criticism in relation to several Swiss museums (Renfrew 2004b).

Of course, it is because the events of 1976 did not immediately have the serious consequences they amply merited that these things could still be happening once again so flagrantly twenty-five years later. As a result there has been a well-merited furore in the Greek press. This has been particularly strident since the president of the Greek Republic, Konstantinos Stephanopoulos (along with the Ministerpräsident des Landes Baden-Württemberg), had been invited to perform the opening ceremony and indeed did so. The head of state was thus unknowingly involved in the legitimizing of the looting process by which the archaeological heritage of Crete is being destroyed.

My conclusion is that it was the Karlsruhe Museum authorities who had the primary responsibility in this matter and that they failed significantly to observe the necessary professional standards, such as those promulgated by ICOM. That they could do so in this public manner was in part the legacy of the unfortunate *Kunst und Kultur der Kykladen* exhibition of 1976.

I am happy to say that the law recently enacted in the British Parliament—the Dealing in Cultural Object (Offences) Act (2003)—has made it a criminal offense knowingly to deal in illicitly excavated or looted antiquities. If a collector in Britain were to add to his collection in the future in such a way as we have seen, he might find himself the subject of a criminal prosecution. So might the curatorial staff or indeed the trustees of a museum so unwise as to exhibit illicit material excavated after the enactment of the legislation. It is to be hoped that other countries will follow this legislation, which has the merit of applying to illegally excavated antiquities originating in any part of the world, not simply from British soil.

IRAQ 2003

To return to the issue of the recent looting in Iraq: the mentality we have been reviewing is the mentality that connives in the looting of Iraqi antiquities. I would ask the reader most seriously to consider the resolutions presented in this chapter—perhaps they are phrased in more diplomatic language than some of the foregoing remarks. They were discussed at the final session at the Berlin meeting in May 2003, and I am happy to say that they were approved (Heilmeyer and Eule 2004: 236–38)

I would summarize by arguing that it is the major museums of the world that establish the ethos for the private collector. Those museums at the wrong end of the ethical spectrum, like some of those I have mentioned, are in my view the principal obstacles to progress in this area.

BIBLIOGRAPHY

Broodbank, Cyprian. *An Island Archaeology of the Early Cyclades*. Cambridge, U.K.: Cambridge University Press, 2000.

Dealing in Cultural Objects (Offences) Act 2003. Norwich, U.K.: Stationery Office Limited, 2003 (United Kingdom).

Doumas, Christos. "Archaiotites kai mnimeia Kykladon," *Archaiologikon Deltion* (Chronika) 19 (1964): 409–12.

Felch, Jason, and Ralph Frammolino. "Getty Had Signs It Was Acquiring Possibly Looted Art, Documents Show" *Los Angeles Times* September 25, 2005, p. A1.

Getz-Preziosi, Patricia. "The 'Keros Hoard': Introduction to an Early Cycladic Enigma." In *Antidoron: Festschrift für Jürgen Thimme*, ed. D. Metzler and B. Otto, 37–44. Karlsruhe: C. G. Müller, 1982.

Heilmeyer, Wolf-Dieter, and J. Cordelia Eule (eds.). *Illegale Archäologie?* Berlin: Weissensee Verlag, 2004.

International Institute for the Unification of Private Law (UNIDROIT). *UNIDROIT Convention on Stolen or Illegally Exported Cultural Objects*. Rome: UNIDROIT, 1995. <www.unidroit.org/english/conventions/c-cult.htm>, accessed May 23, 2003.

Karlsruhe. *Im Labyrinth des Minos, Kreta: Die erste Europäische Hochkultur*. München: Biering und Bruhm Verlag, 2001.

Ortiz, George. *In Pursuit of the Absolute: Art of the Ancient World—from the George Ortiz Collection*. Catalogue of Exhibition held at the Royal Academy of Art, London, January 20–April 6, 1994. London: Royal Academy of Arts, 1994.

Renfrew, Colin. "Speculations on the Use of Early Cycladic Sculpture." In *Cycladica: Studies in Memory of N. P. Goulandris*, ed. J. L. Fitton, 24–30. London: British Museum Publications, 1984.

———. *Loot, Legitimacy and Ownership: The Ethical Crisis in Archaeology*. London: Duckworth, 2000.

———. "Reflections on the Looting of the Iraqi National Museum in Baghdad." In *The Iraq War and Its Consequences: Thoughts of Nobel Peace Laureates and Eminent Scholars*, ed. Irwin Abrams and Wang Gungwu, 319–35. River Edge, N.J.: World Scientific, 2003.

———. "Ankäufe durch Museen: Verantwortung für den illegalen Handeln mit Antiken." In *Illegale Archäologie?*, ed. Wolf-Dieter Heilmeyer and J. Cordelia Eule, 61–75. Berlin: Weissensee Verlag, 2004 (2004a).

———. "Thoughts on the Impact of the Swiss Accession to the 1970 UNESCO Convention." In *Not for Sale: A Swiss-British Conference on the Traffic in Artefacts from Iraq, Afghanistan and Beyond*, ed. Matt Kimmich, 8–10. Geneva: British Council, 2004 (2004b).

Sotheby's Auction Catalog. *Cycladic and Classical Antiquities from the Erlenmeyer Collection, the Property of the Erlenmeyer Stiftung (a Foundation for Animal Welfare), 9th July 1990*. London: Sotheby's, 1990 (1990a).

———. *Sotheby's Antiquities, London, 13th and 14th December 1990*. London: Sotheby's, 1990 (1990b).

Thimme J., "Ein monumentales Kykladenidol," *Karlsruhe, Jahrbuch der Staatlichen Kunstsammlungen in Baden-Württemberg* 12 (1975): 7–20.

———. *Kunst und Kultur der Kykladen im 3. Jahrtausend v. Chr.* Karlsruhe: Badisches Landesmuseum, 1976.

True, Marion, and Kenneth Hamma. *A Passion for Antiquities: Ancient Art from the Collection of Barbara and Lawrence Fleischman*. Malibu, Calif.: J. Paul Getty Museum, 1994.

United Nations Educational, Scientific and Cultural Organization. *Convention on the Means of Prohibiting and Preventing the Illicit Import, Export and Transfer of Ownership of Cultural Property*. Paris: UNESCO, 1970.

Zapheiropoulou, P. "Archaiotites kai mnimeia Samou kai Kykladon: Keros," *Archaiologikon Deltion* (Chronika) 22 (1967): 466.

———. "Kyklades: Anaskaphikai erevnai—periodeiai: Keros," *Archaiologikon Deltion* (Chronika) 23 (1968): 381–83 (1968a).

———. "Cycladic Finds from Keros." *Athens Annals of Archaeology* 1 (1968): 97–100 (1968b).

Zimmerman J.-L. *Poèmes de marbre: Sculptures cycladiques du Musée Barbier-Mueller*. Geneva: Musée Barbier-Mueller, 1993.

14

Structural Complexity and Social Conflict in Managing the Past at Copán, Honduras

LENA MORTENSEN

In the field of cultural patrimony protection, academics and practitioners face increasing challenges in developing long-term strategies for the care of archaeological sites. Now more than ever, a growing number of audiences find relevance in the past: descendant groups, local and national governments, academics, local communities, tourists, collectors, museum and heritage professionals, and many others.[1] The diversity of these groups is matched by the divergence of their interests in the past and by the range of approaches they follow to stake their claim on its material and ideological legacy.

Archaeological sites operating as heritage tourism centers are especially complex kinds of resources given that they often combine the interests of the scientific and preservationist communities, national and local identity movements, and local and regional economies. Accepted wisdom dictates that caring for such places requires acknowledging competing interested parties as legitimate stakeholders and involving as many as possible in developing management structures. While this ideal is certainly commendable, it is also, in most cases, extremely difficult to achieve. This is especially the case for prominent sites such as the ancient Maya city of Copán in Honduras, the subject of this chapter, where daily operations involve negotiating a shifting mix of local politics, national bureaucracy, foreign experts, and international norms. In this chapter, from my standpoint as an ethnographer studying this process, I discuss some of the social complexity inherent in managing Copán. In order to illustrate some of the stakeholder positions involved, and their implications for the long-term care of this site, I focus on the recent process of crafting a new management plan for Copán, which took place during 2000 and 2001.

Located less than a dozen miles from the border of Guatemala, Copán is situated on the margins of the territorial state, but it is at the center of the cultural patrimony and recent tourism initiatives in Honduras. It is an internationally known archaeological park crafted from the ruins of an ancient Maya city that flourished during that culture's Classic period (approximately A.D. 250–900). Replete with reconstructed temples, intricately sculpted stelae, and an impressive hieroglyphic stairway, Copán is often featured in *National Geographic, Ar-*

chaeology magazine, documentary features, and other media. For the past nearly thirty years, Copán has been the subject of ongoing investigations that have generated a wealth of data about the site, building on a history of interest that dates back nearly 150 years.

Copán is many things at once. In 1980 it was inscribed on UNESCO's list of World Heritage sites, making it the first and thus far only cultural site of World Heritage in Honduras (Veliz et al. 1984). The Honduran state recognizes Copán as a National Monument and has declared its interests in the site through evolving legislation beginning in 1845. For many, Copán is a familiar archaeological park, a travel destination for over 120,000 national and international visitors per year. In addition to these formal designations, Copán has numerous other identities. The site's international stature and scientific importance also make Copán a great source of pride for Honduran citizens. As the most salient physical manifestation of the ancient Maya past in Honduras, Copán plays an integral role in nationalist campaigns that underwrite the modern *mestizo* identity with the perceived splendor of the indigenous Maya past (Euraque 1998; Joyce 2003; Mortensen 2001). Mayanist archaeologists consider Copán one of the most significant sites in the region, making it a key location for fostering successful academic careers. Numerous prominent and upcoming scholars have invested significant time and energy working at Copán, even becoming fixtures in the local scene.

Copán straddles the geographical overlap between the boundaries of the modern Honduran nation-state and the ancient Maya cultural region (as traditionally defined by Mayanist scholars), sitting ironically at the margins of each. For many archaeologists, Copán marks the southeastern extension of the major cities of the Classic Maya period. The territorial boundaries of modern Honduras circumscribe a region with a complex and multicultural prehistoric past, in which the ancient Maya were but one of many cultural influences. However, the Copán site has played a central role in the development of Maya archaeology and Honduran archaeology in general (e.g., Agurcia Fasquelle 1989; Veliz 1983), leading to a disproportionate emphasis on the Maya in the modern presentation of Honduran prehistory and an academic and popular bias that tends to gloss all other archaeological cultures in Honduras as "non-Maya" (e.g., Henderson and Joyce 2002).

Locally, the Copán site is an important source of income for residents who live in the neighboring town of Copán Ruinas and surrounding communities in the Copán Valley. Once dominated by tobacco farming, agricultural production in the Copán Valley is rapidly being supplanted by tourism-related activities that center on the archaeological park (Loker 2005). For the modern descendants of the ancient Maya, Copán is a sacred site, a legacy of their ancestors, and increasingly a focal point for ongoing struggles to achieve greater economic and social justice. It is also, of course, a beloved site for many tourists who have long engaged with popular images of the ancient Maya that circulate through different media channels.

In addition to its many official and socially defined identities, Copán also falls into the category of "Protected Areas." This aligns Copán with other kinds of restricted public spaces such as biological corridors, wildlife areas, nature reserves, and others. Like most other Protected Areas, Copán has its own management plan, a holistic document consisting of a series of standardized components that outline initial conditions, management objectives, zones and use areas, and management activities (see Ledec 1992). The first plan was created in 1984 by a group of international experts and planners together with key Honduran individuals and institutions (Barborak et al. 1984). Composing the plan was one of the first steps in fulfilling the site's numerous obligations as a newly designated UNESCO World Heritage site (Veliz et al. 1984). The original document, now two decades old, proved useful for developing Copán as a modern tourism destination. Unlike the situation with many management plans for similar kinds of resources, most of the recommendations in Copán's original plan were implemented, making it an effective management tool. However, as is to be expected with evolving international norms and rapid local growth, conditions have changed at Copán, and the original management plan has long since exceeded its shelf-life.

Planning for Copán

In 1999 Honduras received a U.S. $6.2 million loan from the World Bank for the Interactive Learning and Science Promotion Project.[2] A portion of these funds was designated for updating the Copán management plan, a long overdue priority. At this point the Wildlife Conservation Society (WCS), a U.S.-based non-governmental organization (NGO) tasked with protecting wildlife and wild lands, entered the story. This organization was selected to update the management plan based on its proposal to use an international team of experts in Protected Areas, including some of the consultants who worked on the original management plan. Following international norms for this kind of work, the proposal included an integrated and highly ambitious mandate to "develop a clear vision and mission for the monument, with a definition of the general goals, management strategies, and management program for the site."

WCS proposed to "identify a legal and institutional framework, a financial strategy, a revision of the boundaries and the division of the monument into management zones" and to "make recommendations about the growing challenge of assuring harmonization between the development of the protected area, the use of the adjacent lands, and the landscape of the Copán Valley." They would accomplish this multidimensional program through the use of "best practices" (a term typically left undefined in development rhetoric) to ensure efficiency and broad-based participation by local and other stakeholders, and it would all be completed within six months. It was, by design, a monumental task.

WCS approached this task by combining a locally based skeleton staff, responsible for nearly all the legwork and social negotiation, with a wider team of expert consultants in a range of management and design fields. This team was slated to work hand in hand with both foreign and national archaeologists, relevant government officials, and local leaders. The highlights of the planning process were two high-budget, intensive plenary workshops. These workshops were designed to bring together as many participants as possible to take part in a series of prescribed activities common to popular international management workshop formats (e.g., brainstorming, guided analysis, breakout sessions, and small group discussion). Through these activities, which were compressed into a rapid-pace two-day agenda, participants ideally would collaboratively frame, discuss, and eventually draft the final document.

Any project, whether it is focused research or a massive multilateral aid program, enters a series of ongoing social conversations already well under way. The team of consultants about to embark on revising the Copán management plan was in just such a situation, needing to learn quickly how to navigate the long and complicated histories of relationships and the shifting points of conflict and alliances that make up the social context of Copán. Understanding the field of power, and where different actors were positioned within it, was a crucial step for moving forward with such an ambitious task, especially given the complexity of the structural dynamics in play at the time.

STRUCTURES OF INTEREST

By law, Copán is managed by the Honduran Institute of Anthropology and History (Instituto Hondureño de Antropología e Historía, IHAH), the government institution responsible for the care and protection of all the cultural patrimony of Honduras. This makes IHAH the most critical agency concerned with the day-to-day operations of the site. However, it is not alone. The Ministry of Tourism also has an intimate relationship with Copán as it is the second largest tourist destination in Honduras. The Ministry of Tourism and IHAH do not always share goals and priorities for the site, although they are both concerned with its long-term care. The central offices of both IHAH and the Ministry of

Tourism are located some six hours' drive away from Copán in Tegucigalpa, the capital of Honduras, and many Copán residents regularly accuse both agencies of not investing enough resources in Copán and of ignoring local concerns.

Archaeological research at Copán is funded and carried out by a patchwork of different universities, foundations, and institutions from around the world, including the Honduran government but also international organizations like UNESCO and the World Bank. The articulation among these entities has ranged over time from highly collaborative to extremely competitive, at times creating a tense and difficult working environment. Most of the scientific projects at Copán have been directed by foreign academics, whose investment in academic research agendas sometimes conflicts with the priorities of the Honduran government. For example, research questions that may gain funding, intellectual accolades, and even media attention tend to be governed by academic and popular trends in Maya archaeology that highlight excavation of monumental architecture and royal tombs. IHAH, on the other hand, must always balance the prestige of high-profile excavation with the high costs of essential but less glamorous work in conservation.

The town of Copán Ruinas, with a population of approximately seven thousand, lies a kilometer away from the Copán park entrance. Since the mid-nineteenth century when Euro-American explorers first drew attention to Copán, the history of the small town has been intertwined with the development of archaeological research and archaeological tourism at the neighboring site (Mortensen 2001). As the importance of the site has grown, local business leaders and municipal government representatives have become increasingly interested in the management of the park and in benefiting more directly from the proceeds. Since 1994 the municipal government has lobbied to receive a percentage of the park entrance fees, arguing that the town bears the structural burden of tourism to the site without receiving the necessary resources to support it. Local government officials have also begun to criticize management decisions that IHAH has taken on a range of issues at Copán. The opposing political affiliations of the local mayor and the head of IHAH have contributed to the growing antagonism between the two entities.

Tourism to Copán has increased dramatically in the past decade, growing from approximately 51,000 in 1991 to over 120,000 in 2001 (including Hondurans and foreigners).[3] Consequently, many local residents have shifted their fortunes from the declining tobacco and coffee industries to the tourism service sector. In 2001 alone, the rate at which new hotels, restaurants, or souvenir stores opened up averaged one per month. Many of the people who now work as guides or other service sector employees have previously worked in some capacity on local archaeological projects, which has provided these individuals with a more intimate perspective on the management issues at Copán.

Residents of Copán Ruinas are by no means unified in their perspectives toward or interests in the Copán park. Although the town is home to a few powerful and influential families, the municipality of Copán includes communities with some of the highest levels of poverty in the country (United Nations Development Programme 2002). Copán is also home to a significant number of expatriates, most of whom operate tourism-related businesses, as well as to representatives of a growing number of local and international aid organizations.

The Maya Chortí, a politically organized group of indigenous descendants, live primarily in small communities on the hillsides throughout the Copán Valley and the surrounding region of western Honduras and eastern Guatemala. Building on political activity to lobby the government for more land, the Chortí have also recently articulated their claims to greater involvement in and benefit from the Copán site through means of legal solicitation and formal protests. In 1998, and again in 2000, thousands of Maya Chortí from the region created international headlines by blocking access to the Copán park over multiple days to draw attention to their ongoing claims.[4]

Relationships within and among these various interest groups, and others, have passed through shifting periods of cooperation and alliance as well as heated competition and open conflict. When the WCS team began its work on the Copán management plan, conditions at the site had reached one of the tensest points in its modern history. The confluence of several factors—including the increasing economic importance of the site, several high-profile cases of structural damage and loss, and a series of personal feuds and political struggles between powerful actors—created a situation in which almost everyone was suspicious of or at odds with almost everyone else. Above all, it was an election year.

"Local Participation"

Today, most multilateral aid and development organizations recognize that successful management of successful projects requires "local participation." However, defining what constitutes both "local" and "participation" is not a simple task. "Local" is always a relative term and usually refers to people who live in the immediate vicinity of a resource or project area. But a working concept of being "local" is not necessarily limited by a geographical referent. In a sense, nearly all the players outlined previously are local in that they have some sort of vested interest and typically long-term involvement in the locality of the ruins. The WCS team, which included numerous North American consultants, considered their own local component to be the several consultants from Central America, and especially the two from Honduras, who made up their Copán-based staff. But none of these people was from the Copán region, nor an expert on the site, nor someone with ongoing experience there, which made them nonlocals in the eyes of practically every other participant in the management plan process.

Most of the drafting process took place over a six-month period from October 2000 through April of 2001, as WCS had promised. During that time the WCS team organized two intensive workshops that brought together selected paid consultants, other "experts," and as many representatives of stakeholder groups as they could manage, including the desired, but undefined, "locals." Not only was it confusing to determine who was local; the locality of the ruins themselves was a subject of ongoing dispute. This situation was reflected most tangibly by the absence of a governmental decree marking the official park boundaries, which has carried over into a current legal dispute between IHAH and the owners of adjoining properties.

In a breakout session during the second workshop, a small group of participants was charged with addressing the issue of zoning; that is, defining the limits and nature of different use areas. When the group returned to present their conclusions to the entire workshop, they also proposed changing Copán's current designation from Monumento Nacional las Ruinas de Copán (Copán Ruins National Monument) to Parque Arqueológico Copán (Copán Archaeological Park). The group reasoned that this new title better reflected the public perception of Copán and that this name had long been in public use. Fixing this title, however, caused immediate concern among the larger audience and generated an additional half hour of discussion. The positions that different parties adopted, based in part on separate rhetorical traditions, reflected both varying conceptions of the site and their respective visions for its future. The long discussion also showed that the central question of *what* exactly was to be managed was itself difficult to pin down.

Several long-term employees of IHAH argued for maintaining the element of "monument" in Copán's title because the term carried legal national stature. As representatives of the government institution, the IHAH employees were well versed in the importance of Copán as a national cultural monument and saw changing this particular designation as a potential threat to the site's official stature. A number of archaeologists raised the issue that "monument" was a confusing term, particularly because they use it to refer to individual site features, such as altars, stelae, and buildings. Protected Areas specialists countered with a discussion of international conventions and a thirty-year precedent in Latin America that designates Protected Areas like Copán as "cultural monuments." Some felt that the title "monument" made the area sound unappealing to visitors, off-limits, not for public consumption. Others felt that the term "park" debased the importance of the site, undermined the principle of conservation, and made Copán indistinguishable from other places to picnic and play.

The WCS team had already put forth a concerted democratic effort to assemble the participants for the workshop and create a "collaborative" plan. So, in the interests of maintaining this spirit, the group took a vote. Following this democratic convention, the leader of the WCS team accepted the majority vote for Parque Arqueológico Copán, but with the recommendation that the additional status and title "UNESCO Cultural World Heritage Site" be used as often as possible. The title was accepted, but no one was fully satisfied with the designation, in part because the different perspectives on the site were aired but never reconciled. While the group defined the "ruins" in the short term, at least for the superficial purpose of the document, naming the entity did not really succeed in locating it, nor in bringing it under control.

According to Ledec (1992) management plans exist ostensibly to ensure adequate management and to minimize potential conflicts among different users of a resource. The goal of the management plan team at Copán was to unite all of the disparate interests and achieve some sort of ideal democratic document, balancing all interests for the "good of the ruins." The management plan began with the archaeological resource, which by the WCS definition is inseparable from its physical environment. The site and its physical environment are of course also inseparable from the social environment, which taken together implied an almost limitless set of issues to consider. The undefined nature of the subject and therefore potentially boundless reach of the task at hand was reflected in the extreme range of individuals and institutions called upon to "participate" in managing it.

The entity in control of the process, and therefore deciding who should take part, was WCS, the only group consisting primarily of nonlocals. Who should participate? WCS answered this question by extending their roster of participants, targeting various kinds of locals. They adopted a strategy of ad hoc inclusion, officially inviting nearly a hundred individuals and extending invitations to almost anyone who expressed an interest. Others answered this question with strategies of selected engagement and disengagement with the planning process. Some key players, including municipal representatives and political candidates, refused to attend any meeting or presentation during the entire six-month planning process, despite phone calls, official letters, reminder memos, and repeated personal visits from the WCS team. Other individuals dominated meetings, meanwhile running disinformation campaigns about the process. Who should participate? Everyone agreed that the most important category of individuals who should were the ever-present and ever-ambiguous locals and that, in the end, not enough locals did participate.

This scenario brings us back to the well-traveled question of "who is local?" Defining this category requires making explicit both the logic of inclusion (in other words, on what basis do people stake their interest?) and the object of interest—the multivalent site of Copán. Planners, managers, and international organizations typically consider a singular document, a management plan, to be the solution to account for the multiple dimensions at play in a complex resource. However, the singular and authoritative control implied by the term "management" does not seem to fit well with the complicated social realities of this site, especially given the many entities that participate in its daily operations. Additionally, the success or failure of such a document, and consequently the prospects for long-term care of a site, rely in part on the ability of the document to address the specific context of fundamental differences in defining a resource and on distinguishing the interests that various stakeholder groups bring. In this case, it would seem, these conditions were not met. In fact, three years after the management plan was supposed to be completed, there was still no official document.

CONCLUSION

The task of reconciling the disparate interests of Copán's many stakeholders was further complicated by the politics and pressures of other factors that influence Copán's development. For instance, the Copán site has guaranteed the inclusion of Honduras in the five-nation tourism consortium project called the Mundo Maya, the original goals of which include promoting the natural and cultural resources of its member countries (Garrett 1989). The Mundo Maya project effectively remaps a contemporary vision of the ancient Maya homeland over the current political borders of five Central American states for the purposes of creating a tourist megazone, based on the popular fascination with both Maya archaeology and adventure or ecotourism. This tourism is fueled in large part by the continuous production of archaeological research on the ancient Maya, funneled to the public through popular media like *National Geographic* and the Discovery Channel and more recently through public conferences like the "UCLA Maya Weekend" that feature Mayanist archaeologists, epigraphers, and art historians. There is now a significant subset of the tourism market devoted exclusively to archaeological tourism in the Maya world and elsewhere. Copán is a favorite destination in the Mundo Maya and allows Honduras continued access to and participation in this increasingly lucrative project.

Member states in the Mundo Maya are rhetorically committed to facilitating regional travel, improving tourism infrastructure, and conserving the major archaeological and ecological resources in an effort to generate greater economic development. Yet planning in the Mundo Maya rarely involves local actors, even at a superficial level, resulting in an influx of uncoordinated tourism initiatives that neither take into account the local concerns of individual sites nor directly benefit local populations. In this way, planning in the Mundo Maya suffers from some of the same structural problems as planning at Copán.

The growing popularity of Copán as a Maya tourism destination has also increased its vulnerability. In February of 1998 an important early Classic tomb in the center of the site was looted. Blame and suspicion were intense in the following days, heightening tension among the Copán Ruinas municipality, IHAH officials, park employees, and foreign archaeologists. Items stolen during the robbery have not yet been recovered, and the circumstances of the robbery itself remain unclear despite substantial investigation. Local groups, including the Copán park's employee union and the local Maya Chortí organization, have also used the site as a backdrop for political protest, blocking entrance to the park to pressure the government to attend to their concerns. Copán's growing international profile makes these events particularly dramatic and disruptive to the ongoing management of the site.

One of the major challenges in protecting the past is learning how different stakeholder groups understand the past. For instance, the concept of World Heritage gives a site international recognition but may hold little meaning for a local employee who survives on the income from a job maintaining that World Heritage Site. The politics of Maya archaeological research may condition the kinds of projects that take place at Copán, but they do not necessarily influence how a Maya Chortí descendant decides what is important about the Maya past. Many local residents who depend on tourism revenue for their businesses lament IHAH's necessary constraints on excavation projects in the site core of Copán. For these business owners, new discoveries mean continued tourism interest in the site. For IHAH, too much excavation in Copán's site core poses risks to its long-term conservation, an important and overriding goal for Copán as a national monument, World Heritage Site, and tourism destination.

The situation described is certainly not unique. Although the details may differ, the development of long-term management plans, or the efforts to develop even informal management structures involving a variety of interested groups, are typically underscored by politics and positioning. The ways in which management functions reflect the relative power of the individuals and groups and their ability to shift those positions in respect to the resource in question. Structural overlap and social complexity are inherent in the specific contexts of nearly every heritage center, nearly every concept of "the past." At Copán, the ultimate responsibility and burden for the care of the site lie with the state agency, IHAH. Yet this obligation is challenged by volatile local conditions and the strains of international interests and expectations. Although the official responsibility lies with this institution, the realities of daily operations take place at different levels and in multiple frames that resist control by a single entity. Crafting a management plan attempts to resolve this tension by means of broad-based inclusion. But of course this document and its formation are also subject to the very politics the plan seeks to manage.

Is there a way out of these conundrums? Regardless of whether a document acknowledges the role of competing interests or establishes a framework for negotiating among them, one thing is clear: various stakeholder groups have the power to define themselves through their ability to disrupt the daily operations of places like Copán. A document like a management plan, while important, is merely a starting point for ensuring the long-term care of heritage centers and can only be successful when the invested parties acknowledge its power to guide.

NOTES

1. There is a large and growing literature demonstrating the varied interests in the publicly presented past and the complexity of managing it. Some recent volumes include Little 2002; McManamon and Hatton 2000; Nicholas and Andrews 1997; Swidler et al. 1997; Zimmerman et al. 2003.

2. See World Bank Project Information Document (PID) for Honduras: Interactive Environmental Learning and Science Promotion Project #P057350.

3. Visitor statistics are taken from "Copán Informe Anual," 1991 and 2001, Oscar Cruz M., Monumento Cultural las Ruinas de Copán, IHAH.

4. See, for example, newspaper articles in the Honduran press: *La Tribuna*, September 8, 2000; *El Tiempo*, September 9, 2000; *La Prensa* October 22 and 24, 1998, September 6 and 9, 2000.

BIBLIOGRAPHY

Agurcia Fasquelle, Ricardo. "Síntesis de la arqueología de Honduras." *Yaxkín* 12, no. 1 (1989): 5–38.

Barborak, James, Roger Morales, and Craig MacFarland. *Plan de Manejo y Desarrollo del Monumento Nacional Ruinas de Copán, Sitio de Patrimonio Cultural Mundial.* Turrialba, Costa Rica: IHAH, CATIE, 1984.

Euraque, Darío. "Antropólogos, arqueólogos, imperialismo y la Mayanización de Honduras: 1980–1940." *Yaxkín* 17, no. 1 (1998): 85–103.

Garrett, William E. "La Ruta Maya." *National Geographic* 176, no. 4 (1989): 424–79.

Henderson, John S., and Rosemary A. Joyce. "Who Do We Work for Now? Imperialism, Nationalism, Globalism: Archaeology in Honduras 1839–2002." Paper presented at the 67th annual meeting of the Society for American Archaeology, Denver, 2002.

Joyce, Rosemary A. "Archaeology and Nation Building: A View from Central America." In *The Politics of Archaeology and Identity in a Global Context*, ed. Susan Kane, 79–100. Boston: Archaeological Institute of America, 2003.

Ledec, George. "Guidelines for Preparing Management Plans for National Parks and Other Protected Areas." Paper presented at the IV World Congress on National Parks and Protected Areas, Caracas, Venezuela, February 10–21, 1992.

Little, Barbara (ed.). *Public Benefits of Archaeology*. Gainesville: University Press of Florida, 2002.

Loker, William M. "The Rise and Fall of Flue-Cured Tobacco in the Copán Valley and Its Environmental and Social Consequences." *Human Ecology* 33, no. 3 (2005): 299–327.

McManamon, Francis, and Alf Hatton (eds.). *Cultural Resource Management in Contemporary Society: Perspectives on Managing and Presenting the Past*. New York: Routledge, 2000.

Mortensen, Lena. Las dinámicas locales de un patrimonio global: Arqueoturismo en Copán, Honduras. *Mesoamérica* 42, December 2001, 104–34.

Nicholas, George P., and Thomas D. Andrews. *At the Crossroads: Archaeology and First Peoples in Canada*. Burnaby, B.C.: Archaeology Press, Simon Fraser University, 1997.

Swidler, Nina, Kurt Dongoske, Roger Anyon, and Alan S. Downer (eds.). *Native Americans and Archaeologists: Stepping Stones to Common Ground*. Walnut Creek, Calif.: AltaMira, 1997.

United Nations Development Programme. *Informe sobre Desarrollo Humano: Honduras* <http://www.undp.un.hn/IDH2002.htm>, 2002.

Veliz, Vito. "Síntesis histórica de la arqueología en Honduras." *Yaxkín* 6, nos. 1–2 (1983): 1–9.

Veliz, Vito, John Bright, and James Barborak. "Planning and Managing Honduras' Copán Ruins World Heritage Site: The Role of Cultural Parks in Contributing to Education and Economic Development." In *International Perspectives on Cultural Parks: Proceedings of the First World Conference*, 55–62. Mesa Verde National Park, Colo: U.S. National Park Service, Colorado Historical Society, 1984.

Zimmerman, Larry J., Karen D. Vitelli, and Julie Hollowell-Zimmer (eds.). *Ethical Issues in Archaeology*. Walnut Creek, Calif.: AltaMira, 2003.

15

Supporting and Promoting the Idea of a Shared Cultural Patrimony

PAULA KAY LAZRUS

Damage to cultural property belonging to any people whatsoever means damage to the cultural heritage of all mankind, since each people makes its contribution to the culture of the world.

Preamble to the 1954 Hague Convention for the Protection of Cultural Property in the Event of Armed Conflict.

Rule 6: Remember that cultural objects are not only for you but also for your children and grandchildren and for all humanity.

Basic Rules on Cultural Property, Albania and Serbia

The concept of the interconnectedness of humanity whereby all humans share a deep and complex cultural heritage is important in archaeology, although it is not necessarily shared by people outside the discipline. The diverse stakeholders in cultural heritage take various stands both in terms of how this heritage is to be preserved (or not) for the future and in terms of how it is to be interpreted. From their different viewpoints academics and other professionals, lay people, tourists, collectors, and indigenous populations may see cultural remains as national or public property, belonging to a particular place and people, or conversely as belonging to no one at all and thus subject to rules of private ownership as a treasure trove available for salvage. Some constituencies are opposed to the idea of a nation assuming a sovereign and exclusive right to the ownership of all cultural resources found within its soil, while others object to "outsiders" viewing, touching, or interpreting what they consider their own history. Still others see cultural heritage as a vanishing and nonrenewable resource that will require initiatives of global character.

To those who question whether the concept of a shared cultural heritage is solely a Western one, it is worthwhile noting that the statements quoted at the start of this chapter do not reflect the particular and proprietary worldviews of an academic discipline; rather they are extracted from the preamble to the 1954 Hague Convention for the Protection of Cultural Property in the Event of Armed Conflict and from a rule sheet distributed to communities in order to assist them with understanding and implementing that convention. These documents were drafted by an international group of concerned scholars, lawyers, and diplomats from across disciplines seeking the preservation of the world's cultural patrimony. Thus the people framing these documents and those who have chosen to accept them are by no means exclusively from the Western world. On the contrary, many of the individuals who are most resistant to this concept are from Western countries that have, in consequence, been among the most reluctant to join other nations in preserving the cultural expressions of previous generations.

At a time when there is ongoing discussion about the world becoming smaller and more interconnected, societies may find themselves faced with situations and experiences that are apparently quite contrary to the idea of a shared cultural patrimony. Some social groups, including ethnic and religious communities, large and small, are increasingly concerned that they will lose themselves in the culturally homogenizing world of global commerce. This has led them to adopt a variety of political and social attitudes, and ideologies, that reinforce their real or perceived individual identities and thus help to keep the world at bay (Meskell 1998; Togola 2002). The destruction of the Bamiyan Buddhas or the library at Sarajevo can be considered in this regard as attacks on opposing ethnic or cultural identities; similarly, some Native American groups are concerned that the concept of "shared" patrimony merely perpetuates the loss of control over their past already suffered at the hands of those with a Western or imperialist perspective. In Honduras, for example, there are indigenous Maya who feel that the idea of a global patrimony is a very Western one, promoting current political boundaries and regimes that ignore their historical and political experience, and who thus consider the idea contrary to their modern needs (Joyce 2003: 82).

The concept of a global cultural patrimony has been around for some time now, as can be seen from UNESCO's numerous documents addressing the need for education and the protection of cultural resources.[1] And yet among members of the general public, in the United States at least, it is an idea much less easily understood or accepted than that of a shared environment. The fact that the idea of a shared cultural heritage is not well developed may not seem all that pressing, but it can still shape the attitudes people adopt toward the past and the physical remains of the past. These attitudes in turn can contribute to the pervasive acceptance of the trade in illicit antiquities, which directly contributes to the destruction of cultural heritage worldwide.

Professionals whose disciplines, like archaeology, focus on art, history, and culture in antiquity may be unaware of the views regarding cultural resources in other academic fields or among the general public. Despite efforts at education and outreach by professionals in archaeology, many members of the general public are confused about the issues at stake, except where there are clear-cut images of destruction, as was the case with the Bamiyan Buddhas or since 2003 with the looting in Iraq. In an informal survey conducted over several years with students taking classes in the Program in the Arts at New York University's School of Continuing and Professional Education, as well as with members of the public who are not directly involved in the field but are interested in the arts (such as music and dance, for example), the question of whether cultural patrimony is something that can or should be shared elicited some unexpected responses. The answers indicate that many people find this notion to be challenging, disturbing, disconcerting, and potentially unacceptable, a range of negative responses not usually linked to related questions about natural resources. In the United States, for example, students in arts administration or in appraisal studies classes—(who are mostly individuals interested in a change of career and hence lacking an anthropology, archaeology, or art history background)—have commented that it may be unreasonable to expect people to "understand" that an object or a space important to one culture does not necessarily belong to that culture alone. The concept of a cross-cultural interest in the archaeological remains of past peoples, an interest beyond the aesthetic appreciation of an object to encompass an understanding of the culture or society that produced it, may be alien to them. For the most part, their main node of concern is not for the protection of important foreign or culturally alien archaeological remains but about how should such a thing should be financed. Why should people be called upon to protect something they do not own? What are the costs to those who do pay for upkeep? Why should and how can people ensure the safety of works they may never see? I believe that this unfamiliarity with the concept of shared cultural heritage stems from the fact that many of these students in the United States are not exposed to ongoing manifestations in their own culture that involve sacred spaces or respected sites and works of art, and they thus find it difficult to understand why others can feel so deeply attached to these things.

In seeming contradiction to these attitudes, however, there are new organizations springing up in response to the looting and destruction of cultural resources in Afghanistan and Iraq and other countries. Their existence reflects a rising consciousness among some members of the public in the United States and abroad that the desire to own pieces of the past actually contributes to the destruction of the world's cultural resources and results in the general impoverishment of the wider public. One such group is Saving Antiquities for Everyone (SAFE). It was founded in 2003 by individuals from the communications, media, and advertising industries who wanted to respond to the looting they saw reported in the papers and on television. SAFE's founders felt that they lacked the intellectual background to support their campaign, and so they solicited input from academics to define problems and suggest solutions. Although SAFE is based in the United States, it intends to be international in scope and it now has members from a number of countries. SAFE's mission is to bring the current epidemic of looting to public attention and thus to stimulate discussion and change. The organization supports the idea that it is in everyone's best interest, as well as being everyone's responsibility, to protect cultural resources globally.[2] SAFE is a sure sign that the idea of shared cultural heritage is beginning to take root in the United States.

The issue of sharing cultural heritage is not simply one of ownership but also one of access. In the United States, for example, many people outside archaeology do not consider the beautiful objects and monuments they see in magazines, museums, and private collections, or on their travels, as representative of our understanding of a group of people and their way of life. They view monuments and artifacts for their aesthetic value either as fine art or as decorative art, or as a manifestation of the technologies an object embodies, but they rarely establish a holistic connection with the people or societies that produced and used the objects. As discussed in the introduction and conclusion to this book, the ways in which collectors and museums view and present ancient artifacts have made an indelible impact on the perceptions of the general public. While archaeologists see the physical remains of the past as a historical resource—not something to be owned but something to be discovered, analyzed, and understood for the lessons it can impart about the past—others see these remains solely as commodities and objects for aesthetic enjoyment. This tension between ownership of the past and stewardship of the past has come increasingly to the fore (Messenger 1999: 1–25, 253–74).

Today the problem is further complicated by the way things are displayed and discussed, whether in a museum or in the media. Sometimes single objects or tomb groups are presented in such a way as to imply that it is known exactly why and how they were used or constituted. At other times objects that belong together are displayed separately as individual items and not as part of a related group. For example, in the recent exhibition *China: Dawn of a Golden Age 200–750 A.D.* (October 12, 2004–January 23, 2005) at the Metropolitan Museum of Art, panels of a Sui dynasty sarcophagus from an excavated tomb were displayed with a drawing that illustrated just how the panels fit together, but they were displayed separately in a space that failed to recreate either their formal order and relationships or the shape of the original sarcophagus. Thus a great opportunity to display the object as a whole was lost, and instead each panel appeared as a single entity and commodity.

Contextual information is not always made easily accessible to the viewer, even when the contexts of displayed objects are known. In the Guggenheim Museum's exhibition of material from Mexican museums, *The Aztec Empire* (October 15, 2004–February 13, 2005), there was almost no descriptive information visible about the individual items on display. Despite the fact that there was a clear provenience for many of the pieces, and many of them had been found together in single contexts, they were displayed separately as works of fine art rather than as complete assemblages. Additional information was available in slim volumes attached to the walls of resting areas between galleries, but there was only one of these volumes per area, making it hard to have access, and of course it was impossible to consult the book when considering an object. In another instance, a panel in one gallery gave useful information about the Tempio Major, its multiple buildings, and how items were given as tribute over a period of time, but all the items were displayed without any reference to the building from which they came or to the ruler with whom they were associated. Again, a valuable opportunity to share with the public the use of these items and their actual meaning to the people who created them was lost. Instead, the objects were reduced to magnificent commodities, creating an incentive to acquire them and thus spurring the looting of yet more unknown sites in Mexico and elsewhere in the Pre-Columbian world. The kind of information provided in museums or the descriptions we find about archaeological remains in books and magazines, or on display boards at sites of archaeological interest (see also Lundén 2004), can have a substantial impact on how people view these items and whether they are seen to represent shared cultural heritage or as commodities to be acquired. The way in which the past (in terms of objects and people) is portrayed on television and on the Internet has a similar effect (Brodie 2002).

Whereas special exhibitions often excel at putting the objects displayed into context with panels that provide information about provenience and find circumstances, and that describe their historical or sociocultural significance (although the preceding two examples show that this is not always the case), permanent exhibitions often fail in this regard, as do many sites and monuments. Art museums, like the Metropolitan Museum of Art, provide vague labels for many of their antiquities—"Roman Head, 2nd century," or "Female dancer, Western Han dynasty (206 B.C.–A.D. 9)." Where is the information about the actual provenience of the piece? Or why is there none? What about the object's original use or the context of its discovery? How is the visitor to understand whether a statue, for example, was used in a private home, a public space, or a funerary context? Many visitors, perhaps most, do not feel that they are missing anything. Yet once people are aware of what else there is to know, they are often astonished about the lack of information provided by museums and begin to miss it when it is not offered.

SAFE has recently instituted museum tours (of the Metropolitan and the Boston Museum of Fine Arts) to alert people to what they are missing and to point out objects of dubious or unknown provenance. Roger Atwood (2004) gave several tours recently to interested members of the public, who seemed shocked and dismayed by what they learned. In tours that I have guided over the years to illustrate what can and cannot be learned from objects displayed with or without context, I have also found that unless it is explained otherwise, people never seem to realize that there is anything to be learned from ancient objects aside from their being old and attractive. This issue of communication is a critical aspect of the problem, and it appears to have been overlooked by scholars, who continue to talk in general terms about helping people understand cultures of the past. Yet although in academic discourse the focus might be upon a culture or a society as represented by the objects and architecture that have been discovered and preserved over the years, emphasizing what these features tell us about a society's social, political, ideological, technological, and/or artistic solutions to life, the focus in exhibition displays and popular writing is more often restricted to the aesthetic.

One may counter that this is the purpose of an art museum. Its mission is to support conservation, preservation, connoisseurship, and so forth—art museums are not ethnographic museums (Boyd 1999). Although this is true, it is difficult to wrest ancient art from its original contexts of use and production. Most of the time the objects displayed were not created simply as works of art. The aesthetic qualities are part of their larger significance. To some degree an item's status as art is also dependent upon the changing tastes and values of those living in generations far removed from the societies that created the item on display. We categorize ancient objects in this way as art, in part because the items are so often known to us only out of context (as a result of looting) but also because ancient objects have become an important part of our own contemporary aesthetic (see also Lundén 2004).

While it is important to stress the place of an object within the society that produced it, it is also worth informing the public that suppressed proveniences offer openings for those who create "new" antiquities for the market. Without proper understanding and documentation of the background of displayed items, we are often unable to judge what is fake and what is real, and many collections, private and otherwise, are surely filled with forgeries. Those who create these fake works are becoming increasingly sophisticated. Italia Brontesi has reported that a forger from Cerveteri was found to have created fake kylikes (stemmed drinking cups) and other works of such quality that they passed the review of an expert at the British Museum and fooled thermoluminescence dating by using radiation of the sort that is usually used in cancer treatment. The *carabinieri* exposed the artisan and the clinic in Brescia that allowed the use of its equipment (Brontesi 2005: 6).

In order to think in terms of cultural heritage, however, it is imperative to express how particular monuments, sites, sacred places, simple homes, and objects are interrelated—in other words, an object should be presented within its social and historical contexts rather than simply as a solitary piece of art. It is necessary to illuminate the story of how humanity has developed the means to create and to survive, and how cultures have interacted and influenced one another, and it must be done in an engaging manner. This would represent one concrete way to help our increasingly interconnected world come to a greater understanding of how humanity has evolved in its many cultural forms, and why some of our cultural differences may have developed in the ways in which they did.

What we have to say about the objects we display often indicates how the museum has come by the objects themselves. This opens numerous questions about the responsibilities of curators and writers with regard to the legitimacy of how the artifacts themselves have come to be known or displayed (for further discussion of museums and responsibility, see Renfrew, chapter 13). It may also raise questions about the appropriateness of some objects for display and description, taking into account how much information a particular descendant group may feel it is possible to share with an outside public (Barker 2003). It may be true that many of our most important art museums were not established with the goal of teaching about those who created the cultural resources we value, but rather to display those resources (although these are by no means mutually exclusive goals, as many excellent exhibitions have shown). However, when the focus is on ancient artifacts, it is impossible to move forward with discussions of how important context is, or with curbing the traffic in antiquities, unless people are convinced of the benefits of knowing versus not knowing.

On the other hand, there are groups worldwide whose understanding of the past emphasizes that the interconnectedness of communities is either contrary to their worldview or interferes with whatever political or social agenda they happen to adhere to (Boylan 2002; Kane 2003; Meskell 1998). Clearly, there is a conflict of interest here. While many may consider universal access and preservation to be necessary for the understanding of our collective past and for the sake of the future, others do not agree with that position. Some Native American groups, for example, feel strongly about their right to conserve, share, or if necessary destroy particular objects if it is warranted, not only on the basis of their religious beliefs but also in light of their worldview and history (Watkins

2003). A dialogue between these opposed visions of the past must be kept open and should be addressed repeatedly if we are to make any progress toward mutual understanding.

One way in which many students in the United States may find themselves at odds with their contemporaries elsewhere in the world derives from their seeming lack of personal connectedness to objects from the past, whether buildings or pots. One of the more difficult notions for some students to accept is that other citizens around the world feel profoundly attached to the material expressions of their culture—landscapes, historical buildings, and individual artifacts. Perhaps this is because so many people in the United States see their family history as rooted abroad (McManamon 2003). This may cause them to have ambivalent feelings about the protection of local cultural heritage in the United States and may confuse their attitudes toward heritage abroad. The majority of students appear to start out believing it is conceivable that within the United States anything is for sale, for a price—from the Statue of Liberty to the Declaration of Independence—to say nothing of individual colonial artifacts and buildings or archaeological remains that predate contemporary Native American tribes (Janeway and Szántó 2001).

The question for archaeologists is how to promote the idea that a shared global cultural patrimony exists and that it is in everyone's best interest to preserve it for the future. Why should wealthier nations help preserve cultural remains within the jurisdictions of less wealthy nations? What is worth preserving and what is not? The 1972 UNESCO Convention Concerning the Protection of the World Cultural and Natural Heritage and its associated World Heritage List put the responsibility squarely on the country in which the monuments, sites, and objects in question are situated. But what happens when a country cannot or will not acquiesce? The world has always known changing boundaries, and the current occupants of a given territory may not feel much connection with previous inhabitants of the recent or distant past. They may want to eradicate heritage or simply let it deteriorate through neglect. Economic development or urban expansion may generate competing priorities. It has become imperative to propose solutions for these scenarios and, at the very least, to open up a constructive discussion of the problem.

The first step is to increase our efforts to convince the public about the importance of our shared cultural resources. Discussion with nonprofessionals concerning the recent destruction of libraries, archives, monuments, and objects as attempts to eradicate cultural identities often provokes a shocked reaction. "I never thought of it that way" is the common response. Our rhetoric about educating the public—the consumers of what will be preserved—is useful; but it is critical to be more compelling about why this should be done, what there is to learn, and most crucially, what there is to lose. Talk of context, a fundamental concept for archaeologists, is often not comprehensible to nonarchaeologists. One must also acknowledge that at present, professionals in the United States who teach nontraditional students (i.e., nonmajors) often receive little support or recognition for these activities, and that must change in order to reach a broader audience, an imperative if we really wish to preserve the world's cultural patrimony.

In an interesting statement made at a conference at New York University addressing some of these issues (The Certainty of Uncertainty: Preserving Art and Culture in the 21st Century, June 5–7, 2003), Brian Michael Jenkins pointed out that perceptions of what is "worth saving" change quickly. If scholars fight for the preservation of the petroglyphs in Portugal or the Bamiyan Buddhas in Afghanistan, why, he asked the audience, are we not upset by the toppling of the statue of Saddam Hussein in Baghdad by local citizens and U.S. coalition military? Is it because we see that statue as "simply contemporary propaganda" (Jenkins 2003)? Certainly there is much ancient art that was originally created for propagandistic purposes, and we have learned much from knowing about it. The question he poses is worth thinking about when discussing the preservation of sites and monuments in areas of conflict.

One area of critical importance concerns the difficulties inherent in protecting monuments or entire cultural complexes that have yet to be discovered. Material derived from such sites often finds its way into the illicit antiquities market, which flourishes in consequence. The exhumation of objects from sites and contexts as yet unknown is particularly damaging to our understanding of diverse cultures around the world. The search continues for ways to stop the traffic in antiquities. Demand, like that for most illegal things, is the font of our troubles. Experience has taught us that despite many years of law making, laws alone have had only limited success. Aside from doing more to enforce existing laws, one potentially effective line of action is to make the collection of illicit antiquities and the destruction of cultural resources socially unacceptable. This can be encouraged through continued educational outreach, community involvement, and by getting our word out to the media (Lazrus 1999: 83–90). This is something the community has the power to combat and change, and it must be pursued. Additionally, we need to strengthen and connect the various existing archaeological inventory databases, and create new ones where they do not yet exist, making them truly relational. These data sets represent our most reliable information about objects, monuments, and sites. This should be viewed as critically important in contributing to our ability to curb the trade in illicit antiquities, while also helping us avoid corrupting the corpus of known materials with fakes. Connecting these inventories (on secured systems) will allow academics, researchers, museum staff, and law enforcement officials to state simply that if items are not listed, they are unequivocally illicit by default.

One attempt to address the issues just discussed can be found in the work of University of Gothenburg graduate student Staffan Lundén, who worked with a Swedish television station on the production of an episode of their news/exposé series *Striptease* in 2000. This program, based on Lundén's work, explored the web of misinformation and lies that continues to permeate the antiquities trade and to infiltrate the world of legitimate auction houses, museums, galleries, and private collections, and it brought the situation to the attention of the Swedish public (Brånstad and Råstam 2000). Several of Sweden's museums and galleries were exposed as complicit in the acquisition and distribution of illicit antiquities. The Swedish ambassador to Peru was interviewed denying the purchase and sale of illicit antiquities, while museums and galleries that had acquired objects from him showed record upon record confirming that they must have known the items to be illegal. Gallery owners were caught boasting of smuggling materials from South America and East Asia, and monks from Thailand were interviewed trying to understand why Westerners would want to purchase objects that "can have no meaning to them" (Brånstad and Råstam 2000).

Since this program was aired, Lundén has continued to press for action and change at all levels. Among the results one can point to codes of conduct that have been drafted by some Swedish museums. In 2003 Sweden finally signed the 1970 UNESCO Convention on the Means of Prohibiting and Preventing the Illicit Import, Export and Transfer of Ownership of Cultural Property, although it should be noted that Sweden has enacted no implementing legislation, and hence its internal laws have not changed (Lundén 2004). As a result of this continued pressure, one auction house in Sweden now says it does not accept unprovenanced archaeological objects and appears to abide by this policy. Two other Swedish auction houses continue to sell unprovenanced objects, but at the latest auction over half of the objects remained unsold (Lundén 2004). Prior to this, Peter Watson's 1997 exposé of a British auction house led to an internal inquiry and later to the closure of its classical antiquities department in Britain—unfortunately simply transferring sales to New York (Doole 2000: Watson 1997). Nevertheless, on the whole, these are welcome events and demonstrate that the media can be used to our benefit if we take the initiative.

That said, in many countries the problem continues unabated, while nationally and internationally governments continue in their attempts to fight the problem. In 2005 China petitioned the U.S. Cultural Property Advisory Committee to ban the importation of illicit Chinese antiquities. Italian newspapers have recently announced that Italy recovered 28,021 stolen works of art in 2004, of which 16,941 were from illicit archaeological excavations; also "recovered" were 2,374 fake items. One hundred and fifteen people were arrested (Morosetti 2005: 11). In addition, Luca Liverani reports that 3,500 archaeological artifacts, ranging from Greek and Roman amphorae, cups, lamps, and plates to a Roman column capital and an Etruscan bucchero ware, were sequestered by a Roman tribunal investigating the dealer Giacomo Medici, exposed during the Watson investigation already mentioned (see Watson, chapter 4). Medici was found guilty in criminal court and sentenced to ten years in prison, a fine of 16,000 euros, and 500,000 euros in court costs. He was also required to pay anticipated indemnification costs of 10 million euros toward the upcoming civil proceedings. The large sums of money reflect the estimated market value of the items found in his possession (Liverani 2005: 12), which included a fragment of a vase by Euphronios thought to fit the vase returned to Italy by the Getty Museum in the late 1990s (Maestosi 2005a: 1). If we consider that this is a single individual from an archaeologically rich "supplier" country, it becomes all the more apparent how illicit archaeology continues to be a major business, with such deep pockets that curtailing the problem requires ever more sophisticated means.

The disdain that many collectors and politicians feel toward what they see as the "protectionist" views of countries that wish to protect their cultural resources is particularly upsetting to many archaeologists. Here the lack of comprehension regarding what historical and cultural items can mean to a particular community is enormous, and the challenge to help individuals understand how cultural items can still have a living meaning becomes an imperative. Scholars must continue to be conscious of who is benefiting from archaeological sites and the knowledge and meaning they represent. But aside from the cultural benefits, the important economic potential of archaeological sites also needs to be recognized. If economic benefits do not accrue in some measure to local communities, it will be difficult to engage them in preservation efforts.

Archaeologists and associated professionals tend to avoid becoming embroiled in combating pseudoscience and pseudohistory as they appear in the media, but it is crucial to face this issue if the public is to understand the true value of what we are fighting to preserve. The difference between fact and fiction needs to be identified publicly. It is not obvious to many students nor to the broader public that the protection of the world's cultural heritage is of concern and value to humanity as a whole. Information about the past (and how and why we know it) needs to be moved into the general public domain, through skillful use of the media, including the Internet, through new teaching strategies, and by the introduction of this information into primary and secondary school curricula.

Cultural resources are irreplaceable and nonrenewable, and as a result archaeologists must continually strive to help people understand why context can say something exciting and astonishing about history and about who we are today. We cannot afford to look like petty professionals conducting turf wars, which is how many of our detractors portray us. As the world becomes more interconnected, we can be at the forefront in helping individuals understand how different social groups have come to be what they are today. Here in the United States, for example, it remains troubling that government officials and the press can continue to talk about Iraq as the cradle of civilization (in the broadest sense) but then totally abstract that concept and ignore the implication that we are thus connected through descent. Our different nations draw on cultural trajectories that can be traced back to the dawn of urbanization. There is often a failure to acknowledge that modern societies have roots reaching across modern political boundaries to bind people with vastly different worldviews. This is especially applicable, as already mentioned, where ethnic and religious groups are custodians and stewards of a past to which they feel no connection. Archaeologists must help people see this integrated and changing web of relations in order to promote the preservation of the fragile and increasingly threatened remains of our past and to build a more cohesive and understanding future.

NOTES

1. UNESCO legal instruments related to culture are available at: <http://portal.unesco.org/culture/en/ev.php@URL_ID=2187&URL_DO=DO_TOPIC&URL_SECTION=-471.html>.

2. See the SAFE website, <http://www.savingantiquities.org>.

BIBLIOGRAPHY

Atwood, Roger. *Stealing History: Tomb Raiders, Smugglers, and the Looting of the Ancient World*. New York: St. Martin's Press, 2004.

Barker, Alex W. "Archaeological Ethics: Museums and Collections." In *Ethical Issues in Archaeology*, ed. L. Zimmerman, K. D. Vitelli, and J. Hollowell-Zimmer, 71–83. Walnut Creek, Calif.: AltaMira, 2003.

Boyd, Willard L. "Museums as Centers of Controversy." *Proceedings of the American Academy of Arts and Sciences* 128, no. 3 (1999): 185–228.

Boylan, Patrick. "The Concept of Cultural Protection in Times of Armed Conflict: From the Crusades to the New Millennium." In *Illicit Antiquities: The Theft of Culture and the Extinction of Archaeology*, ed. N. Brodie and K. W. Tubb, 43–108. New York: Routledge, 2002.

Brånstad, J., and H. Råstam. *I gravplundrarnas spår* (On the trail of the tomb robbers). English title: *Heritage for Sale*. SVT, Channel 2. February 29, 2000.

Brodie, Neil. "Introduction." In *Illicit Antiquities: The Theft of Culture and the Extinction of Archaeology*, ed. N. Brodie and K. W. Tubb, 1–22. New York: Routledge, 2002.

Brontesi, Itali. "Falsifacano vasi antichi con I raggi anticancro." *Il Giorno*, January 4, 2005, 6.

Doole, Jennifer. "TV Review: On the Trail of the Tomb Robbers." *Culture without Context*, issue 7 (Autumn 2000): 24–27.

Janeway, Michael, and Andras Szántó (eds.). *Who Owns Culture? Cultural Property and Patrimony Disputes in an Age without Borders*. New York: National Arts Journalism Program, Columbia University, 2001.

Jenkins, Brian Michael. Preserving the Past, Protecting the Present, Ensuring the Futures: Culture as a Target. Paper presented at the New York University conference The Certainty of Uncertainty: Preserving Art and Culture in the 21st Century, June 5–7, 2003.

Joyce, Rosemary A. "Archaeology and Nation Building: A View from Central America." In *The Politics of Archaeology and Identity in a Global Context*, ed. Susan Kane, 79–100. Boston: Archaeological Institute of America, 2003.

Kane, Susan (ed.). *The Politics of Archaeology and Identity in a Global Context*. Boston: Archaeological Institute of America, 2003.

Lazrus, Paula Kay. "Taking Action: Local Initiatives for Global Understanding and Protection of Cultural Resources." In *Heritage, Tourism and Local Communities*, ed. Wiendu Nurayanti, 83–90. Yogyakarta, Indonesia: Gadjah Mada University Press, 1999.

Liverani, Luca. "Maxi-Sequestro di Reperti Archeologici." *Avvenire* January 15, 2005, 12.

Lundén, Staffan. "The Scholar and the Market: Swedish Scholarly Contributions to the Destruction of the World's Archaeological Heritage." In *Swedish Archaeologists on Ethics*, ed. H. Karlsson, 197–247. Lindome: Bricoleur Press 2004.

Maestosi, Danillo. "Scacco matto ai tombaroli." *Messaggero*, January 15, 2005, 1 (2005a).

———. "Vaso del celebre artista tra le opera salvate dai caribinieri l'euphronio ritrovato." *Messaggero*, January 15, 2005, 1 (2005b).

McManamon, Francis. "Archaeology, Nationalism, and Ancient America." In *The Politics of Archaeology and Identity in a Global Context*, ed. Susan Kane, 115–37. Boston: Archaeological Institute of America, 2003.

Meskell, Lynn. "Introduction: Archaeology Matters." In *Archaeology under Fire*, ed. Lynn Meskell, 1–12. New York: Routledge, 1998.

Messenger, Phyllis Mauch (ed.). *The Ethics of Collecting Cultural Property: Whose Culture? Whose Property?* Rev. ed. Albuquerque: University of New Mexico Press, 1999.

Morosetti, Gerardo. "Furti d'arte, 28 mila opera recuperate l'anno passato." *Gazzetta del Sud*, January 15, 2005, 11.

Togola, Tereba. "The Rape of Mali's Only Resource." In *Illicit Antiquities: The Theft of Culture and the Extinction of Archaeology*, ed. N. Brodie and K. W. Tubb, 250–66. New York: Routledge, 2002.

United Nations Educational, Scientific and Cultural Organization. *Convention Concerning the Protection of the World Cultural and Natural Heritage*. Paris: UNESCO, 1972.

———. *Convention on the Means of Prohibiting and Preventing the Illicit Import, Export and Transfer of Ownership of Cultural Property*. Paris: UNESCO, 1970.

———. *Hague Convention on the Protection of Cultural Property in the Event of Armed Conflict*. Paris: UNESCO, 1954.

Watson, Peter. *Sotheby's: The Inside Story*. London: Bloomsbury, 1997.

Watkins, Joe. "Archaeological Ethics and American Indians." In *Ethical Issues in Archaeology*, ed. Larry Zimmerman, Karen D. Vitelli, and Julie Hollowell-Zimmer, 129–41. Walnut Creek, Calif.: AltaMira, 2003.

16

Artifacts and Emotion

KATHRYN WALKER TUBB

The discussion surrounding the trade in antiquities is heated and highly politicized. That much is plain to anyone who ventures into this field. It is also obvious that the arguments are polarized with entrenched positions that appear to be intractable. And yet it is clear that destruction of archaeological sites and monuments, which all parties profess to deplore, continues at an unabated rate. Cultural heritage is not being served by those who purport to be interested in it. Some common ground needs to be identified and acknowledged in order for the dialogue to continue with the hope of an outcome that may enhance the protection and preservation of this resource.

The subject of contention is the artifact, and all that is attached to it by adherents of the opposing camps. One of the most salient features of the engagement is the emotional involvement of the participants. The power of the sentiment suggests that an acceptance of this passionate attachment might serve as a point of agreement and a basis for renewed debate. Ultimately the hope, currently so forlorn, must be that some form of reconciliation can be discovered before the archaeological resource is exploited to the point of extinction.

Little would seem to have been written about emotion in the context of archaeologists, archaeological conservators and scientists, curators, and dealers. This is certainly not true when it comes to collectors and collecting, where the motivations driving such activity have been scrutinized from many different perspectives, all of which acknowledge feeling as a constituent impulse. The emotional content ranges from the visceral to the cerebral. For example, Ruth Formanek (1996: 335) concludes, from analysis of a questionnaire put to collectors from a psychoanalytic approach and designed to assess the motivations for collecting, that "what is common to all motivations to collect, and what appears to be the collector's defining characteristic, is a passion for the particular things collected." Souren Melikian, arts correspondent for the *International Herald Tribune* and private collector, has written eloquently and with considerable feeling of the extreme pleasure to be derived from living with an object: "Collecting alone can preserve the intimate knowledge of art that living with it generates. It is the basis of connoisseurship, and visual knowledge is as essential as the conceptual approach of academe.... Private connoisseurship is the crucial element that paradoxically guarantees the freedom of looking at art other than by institutional decree, in an environment, lighting and presentation included, that is not predetermined" (Melikian 1998).

Insights into the motivations of private collectors can also be gleaned from exhibition catalogues. One such example concerns the Fleischmans, who gathered together objects of Greek, Etruscan, and Roman origin for their home and who allowed their collection to be exhibited at the J. Paul Getty Museum and the Cleveland Museum of Art. True and Kozloff write that "for the Fleischmans, collecting is not an act of accumulating trophies or private treasures. It is also neither complicated nor scientific. They collect on the basis of instantaneous emotional response to the object's aesthetic appeal and its historic interest for them" (True and Kozloff 1994: 7). In an exhibition catalogue written to accompany a display of some of his collection of antiquities and ethnographic objects that was held at the Royal Academy of Arts in London, George Ortiz includes an essay in which he muses about his motivation for collecting, stating: "The vision of certain objects struck me viscerally, then they came to fascinate and move me, I let them speak to me, I let their content and spirit nourish me" (Ortiz 1994: 6).

Curators involved in acquisition may display obsessive tendencies that are more usually associated with private collectors in pursuit of a particular object. See, for example, Thomas Hoving's (1981) *King of the Confessors*, chronicling his quest as a young assistant curator at the Metropolitan Museum of Art in New York for a mediaeval ivory cross; it was written much later in the style of a "boys' own" adventure story. Dealers, too, may enjoy the excitement involved in such transactions. Felicity Nicholson, former director of Sotheby's Antiquities Department in London, is reported as having professed in an internal memorandum that she found "the shady side of the antiquities market not uncongenial" (Farrell and Alberge 1997). As a further example, this time in the fine art branch of the trade, Philip Mould's (1995) *Sleepers* addresses the rediscovery of lost Old Masters; as noted on the dust jacket, "he describes the high-risk, high-stakes game of art dealing—a game of hair-trigger intuition, of poker nerves and pumping adrenalin, of fierce rivalry and ruthless competition."

Much of the archaeological community regards its endeavors as being largely scientific in nature; the rational is prized, and emotion is eschewed as compromising the objective interpretation of evidence. Professionalization has required the "idealization of rationality and the correlative demonization of emotions" (Stocker 2002: 67). However, this dualist conception of emotion and reason has been challenged by neurologists and cognitive psychologists. For example, it is the neurophysiologist Antonio Damasio (2000: xii) who, based on observations of neurological disease, has come to the conclusion "that emotions and feelings may not be intruders in the bastion of reason," espousing rather "that certain aspects of the process of emotion and feeling are indispensable for rationality" (Damasio 2000: xiii). Observations of individuals whose capacity to feel emotion has been impaired (for example, as a result of injury), and of the subsequent catastrophic impairment of their ability to lead their lives, have led to the realization that the rational and emotional must operate together, affecting a balance, for normal functioning to be possible. The notion that emotions and actions arising from them are inferior to reason has been challenged further by such authors as Daniel Goleman (1996) in *Emotional Intelligence*. This volume brings together much of the research exposing the inadequacies of an overreliance on intelligence (IQ) tests as predictors of success in life. Peter Salovey identified emotional intelligence and analyzed it by splitting it into five subsets. Three of these involve self-awareness, self-control to ensure that the emotional response correlates with the stimulus, and empathic awareness of others (Salovey and Mayer 1990: 185–211).

Of course, the intimate conjunction of emotion and reason seems to be so compelling as to be blindingly obvious, but it runs counter to much classical philosophical and scientific thinking. It is perhaps not so new to archaeology when couched in terms of objectivity versus subjectivity. In this latter context, it is now commonly acknowledged that the subjective in terms of the individual archaeologist and his or her contemporary sociocultural context cannot be separated from the interpretation of evidence. This awareness does not relieve the individual from evaluating and analyzing the accumulated data and presenting data and methodology to facilitate future reinterpretation. Rather it compels investigators to scrutinize themselves for limitations and biases in the anticipation that they can be kept to a minimum and exposed in light of future developments. Here, as in the emotion-reason discourse, the tidiness and tension of the oppositional model is exposed as artificial, part of an impulse to categorize and classify that, ironically, produces obscurity through oversimplification.

The development of a theory of emotion is bedeviled by attempts to define terms and isolate constituents. Efforts to grapple with this subject abound in many different disciplines, such as psychology, neurology, philosophy, art, and anthropology. Emotions are categorized as basic, innate, and universal or as secondary and culturally specific.

Many of these terms are used pretty much interchangeably in ordinary conversation, but academic efforts to develop agreed-upon, universally accepted definitions have proved to be unsuccessful. The complexity of the subject and the interdependence of emotional response and personal experience make the deconstruction of emotion difficult and unsatisfactory. There is perhaps an innate difficulty in trying to analyze and intellectualize this aspect of the self.

Often, emotions are categorized at their most basic as responses associated with physical alterations in the individual organism, evinced externally by facial expression and internally by changes in respiration, heart rate, circulation, and hormonal levels. These responses are linked to the organism's ability to survive. Charles Darwin (1897: 12) used these biological manifestations to further his contention that humans are not distinct from other animals when in *The Expression of the Emotions in Man and Animals* he wrote: "The community of certain expressions in distinct though allied species . . . is rendered somewhat more intelligible, if we believe in their descent from a common progenitor." He also concludes that these expressions are universal, since they are interpretable cross-culturally, and he devotes individual chapters to joy, grief, hatred and anger, disgust, surprise and fear, and blushing. Damasio suggests using the term "feeling" when referring to "experienced components" of emotion rather than those that are "expressive." Often "emotion" and "feeling" are used synonymously. The real digression in deconstructing emotion arises, understandably, as the intellectual/cognitive content of the experience increases.

Dylan Evans, a research fellow in philosophy at King's College, London, in his eminently readable *Emotion: The Science of Sentiment*, suggests that the word "sentiment" as employed by philosophers of the Enlightenment might serve as a convenient term (2001: xi–xii). "Sentiment" in this sense has been defined as "a thought or body of thought tinged with or influenced by emotion; an opinion, attitude or judgment" (Chambers Dictionary 1994: 1572) and as "a mental attitude, thought, or judgment permeated or prompted by feeling; . . . a complex organization of ideas and instincts built up in the course of the individual's experience" (Webster's Dictionary 1942: 2280). The difficulty in resorting to the use of the term "sentiment" is that it is defined in all three dictionaries that were consulted (the Oxford English Dictionary is not quoted here) in numerous ways; for example, Webster's Dictionary gives nine definitions, and the Oxford English Dictionary gives ten (1979: 2730). Also, in common parlance, emotion and feeling have supplanted it for the most part, except when the intention to connote mawkishness is desired, especially in its adjectival form. Consequently, "sentiment" has not been adopted as the word of choice in the following discussion.

There are basic emotions that can be argued to be universal, such as fear, anger, and disgust. But the triggers of an emotional response may be culturally, temporally, and personally specific. Additionally, more cerebral or conceptual thinking is infused with emotion that is based on personal experience, that is therefore individual per se, and that is resistant to being picked apart without the loss of something essential. Selfhood arises out of the neural plasticity of the brain and its adaptability to accommodate each person's individual experience.

For the purposes of this chapter, emotion and reason are accepted as a dynamic entity in which the prevalence of one or the other is dependent on context at any given moment. For example, the construction of values and morality, of ethics and judgment, is common to all and is intimately and inextricably bound up with reason and the rational—with what might be associated with "disinterested" science. At the same time, violation of such values often triggers a visceral, physical response associated with emotion.

Investment of self in the past satisfies a desire for rootedness, connectedness, and identity that is experienced, not uncommonly, by many people. Deprivation of such links can be profoundly disturbing both for individuals, where ignorance of biological parents can be traumatic, and for societies and/or cultures, where loss of the past can lead to a breakdown in cohesion and loss of tradition to the detriment of the group as a whole. In the discussion that follows, the exploration of emotional involvement in the past is via the tangible medium of the artifact, in the particular context of the trade in antiquities.

A sustained effort in communicating archaeological, conservation, and heritage concerns about the looting of sites throughout the world has certainly begun to produce some tangible results, at least to a limited degree. One obvious indication is the renewed interest in the 1970 UNESCO Convention on the Means of Prohibiting and Preventing the Illicit Import, Export and Transfer of Ownership of Cultural Property, which has recently attracted signatories from among the art and antiquities importing and trading nations, such as France, Japan, the United Kingdom, and Switzerland. From this we can perceive that the message of how damaging the illicit trade in antiquities is has been communicated fairly effectively.

However, from listening to comments and conversations at various conferences, it is also apparent that the advent of the 1995 UNIDROIT Convention on Stolen or Illegally Exported Cultural Objects—drafted to facilitate return of stolen cultural material by hammering out a compromise between legal systems that privilege the victims of theft over good-faith purchasers and vice versa, and thus serving as a corrective to a loophole left open by the 1970 UNESCO Convention—has been perceived as threatening to the trade, which has reacted to it negatively. Perhaps the key reason for this is that article 3.2 states: "For the purposes of this Convention, a cultural object which has been unlawfully excavated or lawfully excavated and unlawfully retained shall be considered stolen, when consistent with the law of the State where excavation took place" (Askerud and Clément 1997: 16). In this way, the particular problem of antiquities looted from archaeological sites is addressed, and the primacy of source country legislation is affirmed.

Article 4.1 supports this by requiring that the possessor of an object being claimed should be able to demonstrate that due diligence had been exercised in investigating the provenance of the piece prior to its acquisition. Article 4.4 fleshes out the concept of due diligence. The threat to the trade then arises since the bulk of the antiquities on the market are without provenance. Consequently many dealers, feeling increasingly pressurized by the criticism being directed at them, and apparently acknowledging that doing nothing was no longer an option, chose to support the 1970 UNESCO Convention as the lesser of two evils.

Unfortunately, the process of persuasion and education proceeds at a snail's pace, and taking one's eye off the ball, even for a moment, creates the risk of countervailing arguments regaining the ascendancy. Some museum curators seem to be attached to the old paradigm of unfettered collecting and have a hankering for the days when they could cozy up to dealers and hobnob with collectors without fear of any opprobrium being attached to their actions. Sadly, it seems inevitable, at least for the foreseeable future, that such relationships must remain strained, given the scale of the ransacking of sites for artifacts to sell and the burgeoning of a market stocked with a seemingly inexhaustible number of unprovenanced artifacts.

Some archaeologists are postulating that the current focus on preservation is unrealistic, compulsive, and driven by a Western obsession with the material past, along with concepts arising from that (see, for example, Holtorf 2001). The extent to which this framing of the endeavor to save the archaeological resource for future generations ought to be seen from such a social constructivist perspective is questionable. After all, the 1970 UNESCO Convention owes its existence at least in part to the formerly colonized, newly independent nations that went to UNESCO seeking a vehicle to redress escalating losses of their cultural patrimony. A history of which countries became States Parties to the Convention, and when, sheds some light on this.[1]

Despite some signs indicating that optimism is in order, the actual looting of sites is unhappily continuing unabated, seemingly unphased by changing attitudes at governmental level, possibly because this does not extend to adequate on-the-ground enforcement of existing legislation, often because of inadequate resources. Cognizance of the shift in attitude does exist among dealers and has impelled some of them to market their wares by advising customers to purchase now, before the supply of antiquities is cut off by regulation.

It is stating the obvious to reassert that the discourse among dealers, collectors, and heritage professionals is polarized and often rebarbative. From this, a question of great urgency arises: does any common ground exist among these

groups, and if so, can this common ground be used to promote greater understanding, an understanding that might lead to reduced pressure on tangible
heritage in general and on archaeological sites in particular?

As mentioned earlier, there is emotional engagement; there is a shared interest in artifacts. Values are ascribed to them. These values may be economic,
aesthetic, auratic, or evidential. They can be elaborated and ascribed to artifacts by the various concerned groups, in one form or another. They are heavily
invested with emotion. People engaged in trading and collecting antiquities,
whether licit or illicit, are passionate in that engagement, as already discussed.
While it may seem from reading academic books and journal articles written by
heritage professionals that all feeling has been expunged from the subject, consideration of advertisements for positions in museums and archaeological units
amply demonstrates that the financial remuneration cannot be the motivating
factor behind seeking employment in these fields. The aridity of the publications belies the fascination and enormous satisfaction derived by archaeologists,
conservators, and curators from reconstructing the past. Salaries tend to be low
and career structures are limited. The *Penguin Careers Guide* (Alston and Daniel 1996: 322) lists "patience for waiting for the right job and for promotion" as
one of the personal attributes needed by those contemplating a career in museums and art galleries.

Thus it is easily demonstrated that artifacts arouse emotion, but whether that
emotion can be harnessed to effect enhanced protection of the archaeological
heritage is another matter. It is plain that dialogue is essential and that it must be
accompanied on both sides by an acknowledgment of the emotional investment
felt by all participants and a determination to listen attentively, at least, and
empathetically if at all possible. However, such a rapprochement is not easily
achieved. An examination of events in Iraq demonstrates just how difficult an
endeavor this may prove to be. It also provides a graphic example of the consequences of being unable to work in concert.

In the buildup to war, large numbers of people protested against a preemp-
tive strike justified, in part, by a dossier of largely plagiarized material related
to an Iraq of some thirteen years ago. At the forefront of people's minds was
the threat to civilian and military life and limb. Concern also existed for Iraq's
cultural heritage, for its sites, monuments, and museums, in accordance with
the laws of war and particularly the 1954 Hague Convention on the Protection of Cultural Property in the Event of Armed Conflict.[2] This concern was
signaled to the U.S. and U.K. governments, with special emphasis on the danger
of looting in the wake of war, a credible threat fully warranted by events in the
immediate aftermath of the 1991 Gulf War.

Distressingly, the perceived threat became actual disaster, and as news of the ransacking of the National Museum of Iraq in Baghdad began breaking, the public outcry was immediate and global. The museum offices had been broken into, equipment was stolen, and files were scattered. The museum was without electricity. The collections inventory was retrievable but only with time. At this juncture, it is important to bear in mind that prior to 1990 Iraq's archaeological sites and collections had not been subjected to pillage to any appreciable degree. However, with the imposition of sanctions following the Gulf War, extreme poverty drove people to begin mining sites for their salable antiquities. These found ready buyers in the West throughout the 1990s. See, for example, a cuneiform tablet and copper alloy bowls as featured in the "Homes and Gardens" section of the *Guardian* (Murphy 1996) and Mesopotamian spearheads, daggers, beads, cuneiform tablets, figurines, and inscribed cone mosaics in a dealer's sales catalogues (see fig. 16.1).

Perhaps the acme of this process is best illustrated by the sale of antiquities from Iraq, and many other source countries, out of the Gift Department of Fortnum and Mason in London in 2000. Cleverly marketing the items as the "Millennia Collections," the dealer–department store partnership produced a glossy sales brochure that featured Mesopotamian artifacts, among others, and that incorporated on its penultimate page a rationale for the sale of such material. Please note that in the case of the particular examples cited, it cannot be said that these specific objects were looted. Rather they serve to illustrate the abundance of these types of artifacts on the market at the time, a time when sites in Iraq were being pillaged.

A recent example concerns 650 incantation bowls of unknown provenance that "were borrowed from Mr. Schøyen [a Norwegian private collector of inscribed materials] in 1996 by Professor Mark Geller of UCL's Institute of Jewish Studies for translation, interpretation and cataloging" (Bailey 2005). University College London is investigating claims that the bowls were looted from Iraq, allegations made "in an award-winning documentary by the Norwegian Broadcasting Corporation (NRK) in 2004 by David Hebditch, a British documentary-maker" (Smallman 2005).[3] Geller asserts that "within the past decade, hundreds of Aramaic incantation bowls have appeared on the antiquities market, collected from archaeological sites; there is no evidence that these objects have been stolen from a museum. As such, there is no identifiable owner" (Geller 2005). He does not dispute their country of origin and dates such bowls to A.D. 400–700. If the incantation bowls were exported following the First Gulf War, as might be assumed in this case, then their export will have been in violation of UN sanctions legislation. In any case, Iraqi antiquities legislation prior to 1990 prohibited possession of, trade in, and export of antiquities, antiquities being defined as more than two hundred years old (Prott and O'Keefe 1988:

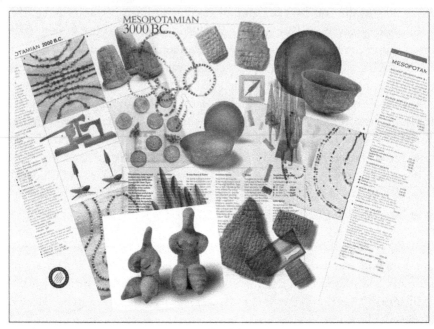

Figure 16.1. Mesopotamian antiquities offered for sale in 1990s catalogues (photograph courtesy of S. Laidlaw, Institute of Archaeology, University College London).

109). The presence of all these Mesopotamian objects is relevant, since it might demonstrate that Iraq has had established smuggling routes out of the country for many years. As a result, exportation from Iraq of artifacts looted in the aftermath of the war was capable of being accomplished easily and effectively.

In an effort to curtail the dispersal of this material through the markets, both the *Art Newspaper* and the Oriental Institute of the University of Chicago responded immediately by creating databases of stolen Mesopotamian antiquities; anyone encountering a suspect piece could freely consult the data. This is a heartening example of a unified response from both the academic and commercially oriented communities.

As reported in the press, the convergence of voices seemed pretty much universal at this stage, with headlines such as "Pillagers Strip Iraqi Museum of Its Treasure" in the *New York Times* (Burns 2003) and "A Civilisation Torn to Pieces" in the *Independent* (Fisk 2003).

However, dissonance began resurrecting itself as early as April 29, at a meeting held in London by UNESCO and the British Museum to coordinate international support for Iraq's museums. At this meeting, Lord Renfrew stressed the need for a UN resolution that would protect Iraq's cultural property before the lifting of sanctions. He argued further for the imposition of a moratorium on the sale or purchase of and traffic in undocumented artifacts from the region. A London antiquities dealer also attending the meeting, objected to the moratorium on the basis that it would be impossible to distinguish between legitimate and looted objects, and a moratorium would thus make trade in any Mesopotamian material unworkable.

On May 6, 2003, a report in the *Denver Post* by Kyle MacMillan raised the question of a moratorium under the banner headline: "Questions abound on losses from Iraq museum." The article cited Robert Haber, a New York antiquities dealer, who "said that such a moratorium would only make things worse, ensuring the trade would move underground without any of the checks that legitimate dealers can provide." Perhaps the key word here is "can," since Haber was himself the dealer who acted as middleman for Steinhardt, a New York financier, and Veres, a Hungarian dealer based in Switzerland, in the purchase of the Achyris phiale (Slayman 1998: 39). This gold libation bowl, thought to have originated in one of the Greek colonies of Sicily, was seized by U.S. Customs, and in the ensuing court case Haber elected to remain silent on the grounds that he might incriminate himself (Slayman 1998: 40). In the event, the phiale was returned to Italy. This begs the question as to what happened concerning "the checks that legitimate dealers can provide." In the *Denver Post* article, Haber is further said to have advocated "the careful regulation of imports and exports of these other kinds of antiquities, an approach that would still allow the normal and necessary flow of ideas between cultures." He is directly quoted as saying: "There is always a hunger for people to know their past." It is telling that knowledge of the past and the flow of ideas between cultures seem in this dealer's opinion to necessitate a transfer of ownership. Haber concludes by saying, "There have been people collecting ideas and objects and literatures of cultures since the beginning of man, and the idea that you can all of [a] sudden stop a spigot of some kind of reflection of man's intellect is an absurdity." This unwillingness to react positively to such an extreme situation is ominous, intimating that dialogue here would be doomed from the outset.

On May 7, 2003, Souren Melikian's review of the Metropolitan Museum of Art's exhibition *Art of the First Cities: The Third Millennium B.C. from the Mediterranean to the Indus* appeared in the *International Herald Tribune*. In it he stated: "Unfortunately, the likelihood of such discoveries [namely, what mankind owes the Sumerians] is receding by the day with the accelerating loot in the East, with or without wars. This dooms us only to have scraps of knowledge." He went on to say: "Some of the greatest masterpieces of the Ancient Near East in the show have no ID papers. . . . As the show unfolds, the extent of our ignorance, largely resulting from the commercial devastation becomes oppressive and embarrassing. . . . Non-specialists visiting the show will barely be aware that much of what they read is hypothesis. Disguised by the scholarly apparatus in heavily footnoted entries, the guesswork is taken for straightforward information. The destruction of mankind's buried cultural treasure thus becomes compounded by the dissemination of pseudo-knowledge." These observations are both perspicacious and alarming but sadly, not surprising. It had been remarked that the Metropolitan's exhibition had been drawing huge crowds as a result of the war and its aftermath. Certainly, the potential damage and loss arising from the impact of disasters such as war, fire, flood, and earthquake on a particular geographical area are graphically demonstrated by what is happening in Iraq, but that is not to say that advocating some dispersal of collections need be achieved by a change in ownership of the material concerned. The negotiation of long-term loans, for example, might be a possible alternative.

Reports in the press in June, and on television (in the United Kingdom), noted a lower level of loss from the National Museum of Iraq collections than had previously been feared. Extraordinarily, the predominant reaction to this news was outrage rather than relief. At this stage, the presumption was made that senior staff members of the Iraq museum had lied about the loss in order to dupe the press and world. One of the worst of these reports was a BBC history program titled "Return to Baghdad" by Dan Cruickshank, an expert in architectural and historic buildings. He had visited sites in Iraq that were thought to be vulnerable shortly before the war. He confined his postwar visit to the Iraq museum. Cruickshank seemed to feel that answers to his questions, and unrestricted access anywhere and everywhere, were his due. His utter lack of understanding and empathy was most disturbing. The entire program and the written account that stands as a companion piece to it were filled with damaging innuendo and slurs. A quote from his conclusion provides something of the flavor of the piece when he states that "the British government, the British Museum and UNESCO are all now offering help to the Iraq Museum. . . . The museum is too important to the Iraqi people—to us all—to be left in the hands of people whose past is murky and mysterious" (Cruickshank 2003).

Such reports were characterized by impatience at the unavailability of reliable figures of losses to the collections. This betrayed lamentable ignorance of the need to proceed carefully, if recovery was not to compound the initial damage. The authors also did not seem to have considered how these systematic and controlled procedures could possibly operate where electrical supplies had only recently been restored but remained unreliable. The fact that staff members had not been paid for months was also not acknowledged, nor indeed was the fact that they had survived a punishing and terrifying onslaught by an invading army and were being scrutinized at that time as part of the U.S. de-Ba'athification decree.

David Aaronovitch (2003), writer for the *Guardian* newspaper in London, began his piece with a series of highly emotive quotes by academics confronted with breaking news of the looting of the Iraq museum. He went on to say: "So, there's the picture: 100,000-plus priceless items looted either under the very noses of the Yanks, or by the Yanks themselves. And the only problem is that it's nonsense. It isn't true. It's made up. It's bollocks." Consumed with self-ascribed fury, he condemned "the credulousness of many western academics and others who cannot conceive that a plausible and intelligent fellow-professional might have been an apparatchik of a fascist regime and a propagandist for his own past." These are strong statements. But was the article based on reliable evidence? It seems possible that he might have been guilty of credulousness himself.

Among the most vitriolic of all the pieces to be cited representing this shift in reportage was an article written by Charles Krauthammer for *Buffalo News*. A selection of two quotes from it reflects this. In the first of these, he said: "Turns out the Iraqi National Museum lost not 170,000 treasures, but 33." His explanation for this deception (in his opinion) was that the "museum officials who wept on camera were Ba'ath Party appointees, and the media, Western and Arab, desperate to highlight the dark side of the liberation of Iraq, bought their deceptions without an ounce of skepticism. It played on front pages everywhere and allowed for some deeply satisfying antiwar preening." The rabidity of this tirade discloses a fury so consuming that arguments countering the prejudices inherent in the article would be unlikely to be heard. For example, while trumpeting the liberation of the Iraqi people from an oppressive regime, he ignores the fact that the museum and Department of Antiquities staff would have had to be Ba'ath Party members if they were to remain in Iraq and survive and continue the struggle to preserve their rich past, for which the world might have been expected to be grateful. Clearly, emotion of this intensity does not serve to foster understanding.

Responses from academics, such as Eleanor Robson of All Souls College, Oxford, and a council member of the British School of Archaeology in Iraq, and from John Russell, then a senior advisor with the Coalition Provisional Authority, brought much needed thoughtfulness back to the debate. Robson's (2003) article begins with the question: "What is the true extent of the losses to the Iraq Museum—170,000 objects or only 33?" She went on to state that "the arguments have raged these past two weeks as accusations of corruption, incompetence and cover-ups have flown around. . . . The truth is less colourful."

John Russell stated: "Most people I know share my relief that so much of the collection survived, yet many also feel manipulated not only to produce shock and grief at a loss of such unprecedented magnitude but also to provoke rage at the cultural callousness of the United States in failing to prevent this predictable tragedy" (2003). He acknowledged the sense of betrayal that many felt upon discovering that the losses from the museum were far fewer than originally reported but concluded by referring to the looting of the archaeological sites, still ongoing, when he wrote: "If we were outraged by what we thought was the looting of Iraqi heritage, we should still be, because it is happening still and on a phenomenal scale" (Russell 2003). But the splintering of the united response—splintering that began with the dealers' opposition to a moratorium on trafficking in Mesopotamian antiquities and progressed into dismissal of the losses as negligible by a number of very vocal journalists—eclipsed, at least in part, the kind of response that might have been expected to looting of the great archaeological sites throughout the country.

This has proved exceedingly difficult to monitor given the lack of security in the country, its size, and the remoteness of many of the sites. At a conference in Geneva in early February 2004, titled Not for Sale: Swiss-British Conference on the Traffic in Artefacts from Iraq Afghanistan and Beyond, Mario Bondioli-Osio, formerly a cultural adviser to the Coalition Provisional Authority, presented a paper outlining damage to archaeological sites and describing a pilot scheme to try to regain control of the areas to protect them. This was based on a helicopter investigatory expedition, and the assembled delegates were shown aerial views of site after site all devastated by looters' pits (fig. 16.2). It was reported that the looters were so heavily armed that the planned Archaeological Site Protection Police Force would need not only vehicles to access sites but also guns and radios with which to summon military support whenever pillagers were encountered.

It is interesting to note that within the archaeological community, the views regarding how to protect sites have been passionately framed, and diametrically opposed stances have been adopted. One of the two extremes is characterized by Elizabeth Stone, an American professor of archaeology, who was quoted in the *Telegraph* as having declared that she "would like to see helicopters flying over there shooting bullets so that people know there is a real price to looting this stuff. . . . You have got to kill some people to stop this" (Bennett 2003). The other is an avowal by Francis Deblauwe, an independent scholar who has maintained an extraordinarily comprehensive website devoted to Iraq's cultural heritage and the situation there as it has unfolded. In his introduction to the website he states that "no epic Sumerian cuneiform tablet, majestic Neo-Assyrian lamassu sculpture or any other Mesopotamian artifact is worth a human life, be it Iraqi, American, British or other" (2003).[4]

On May 22, 2003, the Security Council adopted UN Security Council Resolution 1483 ending international sanctions that had been imposed on Iraq fol-

Figure 16.2. The looted Sumerian city site of Umma (Tell Jokha) in December 2003 (photograph courtesy of Comando Carabinieri Tutela Patrimonio Culturale).

lowing the First Gulf War. However, in recognition of the need to continue conferring protection on Iraq's cultural heritage, paragraph 7 had been drafted, prohibiting "trade in or transfer of" Iraqi cultural property that is suspected of having been illegally removed since August 6, 1990, when sanctions were imposed. It also directed member states to facilitate the safe return of this material to Iraq. This was a chapter 7 resolution and as such should have been mandatory for all UN members. Unfortunately, it was not self-executing. The United Kingdom enacted implementing legislation very swiftly, which seems to have been encountering some difficulty in its enforcement. But as attested to by Patty Gerstenblith, implementing legislation in the United States was held up, not only by the dealing and collecting fraternity but also by U.S. museum associations (see Gerstenblith, chapter 3). None of the clauses in UN Security Council Resolution 1546 that concerns the handover of sovereignty to the interim Iraqi Council on June 30, 2004, relates specifically to heritage. Such reference is limited to the preamble, merely "stressing the need for all parties to respect and protect Iraq's archaeological, historical, cultural, and religious heritage" but not then following through with a clause reaffirming paragraph 7 in Resolution 1483.

The potential for a concerted and unified effort to protect the cultural patrimony of Iraq has failed to materialize in a substantial and effective manner. Indeed, those values that archaeology invests in the artifact as a bearer of knowledge have not prevailed. The value of the artifact as a commodity has triumphed. Consequently, the evidential attributes of the artifact are being lost. Knowledge that might have been obtained by utilizing archaeological objects as tools to help in the reconstruction of past societies, contexts, and technologies has vanished as sites are ransacked.

Aesthetic and auratic values ascribed by collectors feature comparatively rarely in archaeological discourse. It is difficult to imagine how archaeology might relinquish the notion of the "artifact in context." Most artifacts recovered from sites are not pleasing enough in appearance to provoke an emotional response without interpretation, rather like abstract art. Archaeology seeks to recover something of the social, political, and cultural contexts of artifacts. The aim is to develop a deeper understanding of the past to help enhance the ability to create links in contemporary minds with individuals from a remote past. In a sense, it is social construction based on material and human remains, where there is no possible recourse to living representatives, in an attempt to recreate the emotional and rational landscapes of our forebears. The destruction of sites for short-term gain is therefore often met emotionally with anger, frustration, and disgust, since it thwarts archaeologists' rational goals.

Territoriality on individual/personal and group/professional levels is evident. Iraq experienced through the prism of personal experience, where primacy of the self is operating, coexists with Iraq experienced through adherence to a particular group or community. However, individuals usually have little influence on actual events, and the identities of groups within the heritage sphere have been demonstrated to be loosely drawn and of divergent views, diminishing their effectiveness in eliciting a consensual response and reducing their powers of persuasion. Reactions are emotional and rational, acting conjointly, with the preponderance of one over the other altering according to the specific situation. Discussion is hampered by too much emotion, and yet acknowledgment of the existence of strong feelings and an exploration of them may facilitate further communication when conceptual thinking is predominant. If feeling is ignored, participants in the debate fail to address a crucial and intrinsic part of the problem. To quote Mourid Barghouti (2004: 43), it is essential to accept "the difference between 'facts' and that 'reality' which includes all the emotions of people and their positions." Nafziger (2004: 13) argues for a less adversarial, more collaborative approach in the development of cultural heritage law and argues that "greater priority" be given "to information exchange, consultation, consensus-building, and sharing of material." He suggests that "it may be advisable . . . to rely more heavily on such alternatives as mediation and arbitration" (Nafziger 2004: 4). The skills of an experienced mediator might prove invaluable, provided that cooperation and compromise are perceived by all parties to be essential. Ultimately, it is possible that the opposing views may remain intractable and irreconcilable, with unknown and unknowable consequences.

Currently, the prognosis for the survival of archaeological sites, and the potential knowledge of the past that they hold, is grim. In the absence of any common ground to defuse the polarization of the illicit trade discourse, it remains incumbent on archaeologists and archaeological conservators to continue persuading and alerting the general public to the threat that illicit trade poses to archaeology. To quote Souren Melikian (2003) again: "Something is wrong, dangerously so. We had better wake up. So much is being lost."

NOTES

1. One hundred and three countries have adopted the 1970 UNESCO Convention between the years 1971 and 2003. They are listed by date of deposit at <http://erc.unesco. org/cp/convention.asp?KO=13039&language=E>. The first nine States Parties are Ecuador, Bulgaria, Nigeria, Central African Republic, Cameroon, Kuwait, Cambodia, Mexico, and Niger; the last nine States Parties are the United Kingdom of Great Britain and Northern Ireland, Japan, Bhutan, Sweden, Morocco, Denmark, Gabon, Switzerland, and South Africa. The list of countries to have adopted the 1995 UNIDROIT Convention is presented differently, citing initially the countries to have signed the Convention, a step available for a limited period after the final document has been agreed, which needs ratification by the government concerned, often but not invariably necessitating new national legislation to make implementation possible. The second list consists of the countries to have ratified the Convention, and the third list is of those States that have acceded to it. The first nine countries taken from both the second and third lists and cited together by date of adoption are Lithuania, China, Paraguay, Ecuador, Romania, Peru, Hungary, Brazil, and Bolivia. The full list can be accessed at <http://www.unidroit.org/english/ implement/I-95.html>. While it is obvious that many complex reasons must lie behind each country's decision to adopt these conventions, it is possible to argue that these lists can be interpreted as indicating that concern for cultural property is not necessarily the exclusive preserve of the West. It can seem to be a sort of inverse arrogance to suggest that such concerns have been imposed and are therefore invalid. Rather the early signatories are predominantly those nations whose cultural property has been threatened by the acquisitive nature of the wealthy art-transit and art-importing countries.

2. To mark the sixtieth anniversary of the 1954 Hague Convention, in a news release issued on May 14, 2004, by the Department of Culture, Media and Sport, the United Kingdom government announced its intention to ratify the Convention and its First and Second protocols.

3. For further information on this case see Alberge 2005 and the press release issued by University College London, May 16, 2005. It is interesting to note that the issue of unprovenanced antiquities is now under consideration by UCL as a whole, rather than by its

department of archaeology, the Institute of Archaeology. The latter's history of grappling with this issue is briefly outlined in "Point, Counterpoint" (Tubb 2002). See especially pages 287–89 and the appendixes, the first of which is an Institute document, dated 1990, stipulating that the acceptance of objects and material for treatment and examination be restricted to those of known, documented origin. This document related to a "services division" that was, in fact, stillborn because of the stringency of the policy. The second appendix consists of the Institute's policy statement regarding the illicit trade in antiquities, which fleshes out the services division document in appendix 1, substantially changing it and extending it to all staff members, affecting all their academic activities. It was adopted without objection at a staff meeting in December 1999.

4. This view is expanded upon by Yannis Hamilakis (2003), in an impassioned paper.

BIBLIOGRAPHY

Aaronovitch, David. "Lost from the Baghdad Museum: Truth." *Guardian*, June 10, 2003.

Alberge, Dalya. "Museum Inquiry into 'Smuggling' of Ancient Bowls." *Times*, April 22, 2005.

Alston, Anna, and Anne David. *The Penguin Careers Guide*. London: Penguin Books, 1996.

Askerud, Pernille, and Etienne Clément. *Preventing the Illicit Traffic in Cultural Property: A Resource Handbook for the Implementation of the 1970 UNESCO Convention*. Paris: UNESCO, 1997.

Bailey, Martin. "To Study or Not to Study?" *The Art Newspaper* 159 (June 2005).

Barghouti, Mourid. *I Saw Ramallah*. Trans. Ahdaf Soueif. London: Bloomsbury, 2004.

Bennett, Will. "Professor Calls for Looters to Be Shot." *Daily Telegraph*, <http://www.portal.telegraph.co.uk/news/main.jhtml?xml=/news/2003/07/09/wloot09.xml&sSheet=/news/2003/07/09/ixworld.html>, accessed July 9, 2003.

Bondioli Osio, Mario. "The Archaeological Site Protection Project: Progress and Problems." In *Not For Sale: A Swiss-British Conference on the Traffic in Artefacts from Iraq, Afghanistan and Beyond*, ed. Matt Kimmich, 16. Geneva: British Council, 2004.

Burns, John. "Pillagers Strip Iraqi Museum of Its Treasure." *New York Times*, April 13, 2003.

Cruickshank, Dan. "Return to Baghdad." *BBCi History*. <www.bbc.co.uk/history/war/iraq/iraq after the war 01. shtml>, accessed June 11, 2003.

Damasio, Antonio R. *Descartes' Error: Emotion, Reason, and the Human Brain*. New York: Quill, 2000.

Darwin, Charles. *The Expression of the Emotions in Man and Animals*. New York: Appletons, 1897.

Deblauwe, Francis. "Introduction." The 2003 Iraq War and Archaeology, <http://iwa.univie.ac.at/index.html>, accessed June 14, 2004.

Evans, Dylan. *Emotion: The Science of Sentiment*. Oxford: Oxford University Press, 2001.

Farrell, Stephen, and Dalya Alberge. "Italian Police Seek to Question Ex-Sotheby's Staff." *Times*, February 27, 1997.

Fisk, Robert. "A Civilisation Torn to Pieces." *Independent*, April 13, 2003.

Formanek, Ruth. "Why They Collect: Collectors Reveal Their Motivations." In *Interpreting Objects and Collections*, ed. Susan M. Pearce, 327–35. London: Routledge, 1996.

Fortnum and Mason with Ancient Art. *The Millennia Collections (March 20–April 22, 2000)* (brochure). London: Colournet, 2000.

Geller, Mark. "From the Director of the IJS: Spies, Thieves and Cultural Heritage." <http://www.ucl.ac.uk/hebrew-jewish/ijs/news.htm>, accessed June 1, 2005.

Goleman, Daniel. *Emotional Intelligence: Why It Can Matter More than IQ*. London: Bloomsbury, 1996.

Hamilakis, Yannis. "Iraq, Stewardship and 'The Record': An Ethical Crisis for Archaeology." *Public Archaeology* 3 (2003): 104–11.

Holtorf, Cornelius. "Is the Past a Non-Renewable Resource?" In *Destruction and Conservation of Cultural Property*, ed. Robert Layton, Peter G. Stone, and Julian Thomas, 286–97. London: Routledge, 2001.

Hoving, Thomas. *King of the Confessors: The Quest for the Bury St. Edmunds Cross*. London: Hamish Hamilton, 1981.

Krauthammer, Charles. "The Left Simply Changes the Subject." *Buffalo News*, June 13, 2003.

MacMillan, Kyle. "Questions Abound on Losses from Iraq Museum." *Denver Post*, May 6, 2003.

Melikian, Souren. "On the Eve of Destruction? Some Solutions to the Looting of Cultures," *International Herald Tribune*, January 17, 1998.

———. "Magnificent Treasures of a Vanishing World." *International Herald Tribune*, May 7, 2003.

Mould, Philip. *Sleepers: In Search of Lost Old Masters*. London: Fourth Estate, 1995.

Murphy, F. "Sale of the Centuries." *Guardian*, November 2, 1996.

Nafziger, James A. R. "A Blueprint for Avoiding and Resolving Cultural Heritage Disputes." *Art, Antiquity and Law* 9, no. 1, (2004): 3–20.

Ortiz, George. *In Pursuit of the Absolute: Art of the Ancient World—from the George Ortiz Collection*. Catalogue of Exhibition held at the Royal Academy of Art, London, January 20–April 6, 1994. London: Royal Academy of Arts, 1994.

Prott, Lyndel, and Patrick O'Keefe. *Handbook of National Regulations Concerning the Export of Cultural Property*. Paris: UNESCO, 1988.

Robson, Eleanor. "Iraq's Museums: What Really Happened." *Guardian*, June 18, 2003.

Russell, John Malcolm. "We're Still Missing the Looting Picture." *Washington Post*, June 15, 2003.

Salovey, Peter, and John D. Mayer. "Emotional Intelligence." *Imagination, Cognition, and Personality* 9 (1990): 185–211.

Slayman, Andrew L. "Case of the Golden Phiale." *Archaeology* 51, no. 3 (1998): 36–41.

Smallman, Lawrence, "UK University Reviews Artefact Loan," May 20, 2005. <http://english.aljazeera.net/NR/exeres/786A252E-B572-4CE4-AF9A-BD8ADFC63434.htm>, accessed May 23, 2005.

Stocker, Michael. "Some Ways to Value Emotions." In *Understanding Emotions: Mind and Morals*, ed. Peter Goldie, 65–79. Aldershot: Ashgate, 2002.

True, Marion, and Arielle Kozloff. "Barbara and Lawrence Fleischman: Guardians of the Past." In *A Passion for Antiquities: Ancient Art from the Collection of Barbara and Lawrence Fleischman,* ed. Marion True and Kenneth Hanna, 1–8. Malibu, Calif: J. Paul Getty Museum, 1994.

Tubb, Kathryn W. "Point, Counterpoint." In *Illicit Antiquities: The Theft of Culture and the Extinction of Archaeology,* ed. Neil Brodie and Kathryn W. Tubb, 280–300. London: Routledge, 2002.

University College London. "UCL Establishes Committee of Enquiry into Provenance of Incantation Bowls" (press release), available at <http://www.ucl.ac.uk/media/archive/archive-release/?bowls>, accessed May 16, 2005.

17

Conclusion

The Social and Cultural Contexts of Collecting

NEIL BRODIE AND CHRISTINA LUKE

The themes expressed in most chapters of this book are remarkably similar: the pillage of archaeological sites and cultural institutions continues, and the antiquities market thrives. On the ground, data from field surveys clearly point to a growing problem of plunder, and the type of material appearing on the open art market correlates to the regions, even sites, that are consistently targeted. Our authors tease out the differences between looting and subsistence digging; the roles of source, transit, and market countries in the trade; the impacts of war, political agendas, and tourist development on cultural heritage; and the effectiveness of legislation in thwarting pillage and the illicit traffic of archaeological material. What most authors have been reluctant to explore is the root cause of exactly *why* pillage occurs. It is now more than thirty years since the world-awakening 1970 UNESCO Convention, and still the problem persists, and even grows worse. As a concluding chapter, we turn to the why question in order to investigate some of the complex issues that are critical for understanding and resolving the problem. Our analysis concentrates in particular on the ways in which collectors use archaeological heritage as symbolic capital to gain social status and prestige.

THE PRIVATE COLLECTOR

A growing body of literature examines the social and psychological motivations of collecting, though little has been written that is specific to antiquities collecting, and it is always difficult to distinguish what truly motivates from what merely justifies. Most definitions of collecting emphasize that the activity is not directed toward monetary gain (Belk 1995: 67), and although some antiquities collections are assembled simply as investments—most obviously by the British Rail Pension Fund in the 1970s—it is probably true that many antiquities collectors are not motivated by profit. This pecuniary indifference is easily demonstrated by the fact that many antiquities collections are donated to museums as gifts or bequests. Indeed, Norton Simon even had to buy his own museum, Pasadena, to house his collection of Asian antiquities. Some authors have imputed psychological motives to wealthy art collectors and suggested that collecting allows an exercise of power. Acquisition of rare pieces on the auction floor or through other means is a form of competitive display (Baekeland 1994: 206), and the possibility of defining a new aesthetic category through ownership and display allows for the "imposition of taste" (Price 2001: 106). Graepler (1993) has pointed out that the collector's own self-image might prove an important stimulus if the collector is thought to be engaged upon an altruistic campaign that is of benefit to the public or to posterity. Shelby White, for example, a leading U.S. collector of Classical antiquities, believes that she is "preserving and expanding knowledge of the past" (White 1998: 170). Antiquities collecting may also be prompted by a search for personal discovery or fulfillment. Switzerland-based collector George Ortiz's quest for the spirit of Greek humanism (Ortiz 1996) is paralleled by the spiritualism of many collectors of South and East Asian antiquities (Barnard 2002: 50; Kossak 1984: 7).

In many societies, skilled crafting and the production of art are thought to reveal a natural order and are thus considered to be a sign of moral goodness (Helms 1993). Similarly, in the Western tradition, there has usually been a sense transcending genres that artistic production constitutes an engagement with personal or natural truth. By the eighteenth century the capacity to recognize and appreciate art was seen to be a moral quality, so that good taste became a sign of good character and ultimately of good breeding. Although Bourdieu has exposed the "misrecognition" of socioeconomic relations that this view of innate good taste presupposes (Bourdieu 1984: 54, 68), it remains the case that in Western society the appreciation of beauty, particularly as realized in art, is a sign of moral propriety. For a person considered to be of coarse character and rude taste, art provides one route to personal transfiguration and entry into polite society. Most, if not all, antiquities collectors consider themselves to be art collectors, and indeed many have a passion for other categories of art, and this is probably the fundamental motivation for much antiquities collecting: to facilitate entry into social circles that would otherwise be out of reach; or, in Bourdieu's terminology, to exchange economic capital for cultural capital (Bourdieu 1984).

Collecting antiquities certainly brings the collector into contact with what might be perceived as part of the cultural elite: the museum curators and academics who identify, authenticate, describe, discuss, and even desire the antiquities and who, in so doing, validate collecting as a socially useful and culturally important activity. U.S. Classical antiquities collectors Barbara and Lawrence Fleischman believe that what makes collecting antiquities so stimulating is "meeting so many talented people, all of whom enrich our lives" (Fleischman and Fleischman 1994: ix), and most collectors are quick to acknowledge a long list of scholarly "experts" from whose help, and always friendship, they have benefited.

But if antiquities are collected for reasons that are external to the objects themselves—for personal redemption or to provide a passport into polite society—this moves the focus of argument away from the collection as an end in itself and on to the collection as a means to an end. Clifford suggests that in the West the structured accumulation of possessions that collecting entails provides a culturally intelligible strategy of identity formation or transformation; he contrasts this activity with that of the Melanesian "big men," whose aim is to accumulate goods only to gain prestige by giving them away (Clifford 1994: 259–60). However, a more complex relationship is suggested here, whereby reputation is gained initially through the acquisition of antiquities, and the entry into social networks that collecting both allows and entails, and reputation is then secured or fixed for posterity by an act of largesse—by giving away the "valuables" much as a Melanesian big man might do, a gift imbued with the spirit and expectation of reciprocity (Mauss 1954).

Our analysis implies an interesting distinction between the fate of old and new collections. Antiquities dealers are fond of claiming that their stock is derived from an old country house or an established family collection, and perhaps in a sense they are right. New collections accumulated by an active collector with a personal or social goal in mind are likely to end up in museums. Owners who inherit collections may view the antiquities merely as heirlooms, with a sentimental value perhaps but with a market value too, and may be more likely to sell them. Nørskov, in her study of private collections of Greek vases, notes just such a phenomenon: "most first-generation collectors—in order to keep their collections intact and thereby preserve an immortal memorial—present their collections to museums or even found their own museums. Heirs, on the contrary, are more inclined to sell on the free market" (Nørskov 2002: 271). She points out, however, that there may also be financial considerations; "in some countries, like the U.S., it may be more profitable to donate objects to a museum and benefit from the tax deductions" (Nørskov 2002: 271). The objects donated under this system and awarded a deduction by the Art Advisory Panel of the U.S. Internal Revenue Service are mainly ethnographic and archaeological (as opposed to Western paintings and sculpture; Atwood 2004: 142), and the system is open to abuse by both patrons and staff. Thomas Hoving, former director of the Metropolitan Museum of Art in New York, records that between 1973 and 1985 the J. Paul Getty Museum pulled in more than U.S. $14 million worth of gifts, a huge figure even by the Metropolitan's standards. Hoving discovered that the pieces had been valued at way over their true market value to ensure that tax deductions would be far in excess of the purchase price of the piece (Hoving 1996: 286–87). In 1984 the Getty fired the curator responsible for this particular piece of chicanery.

The arguments developed here about why collectors collect have firmly separated an object-bound justification from socially grounded motivations. There is a clear need for a more thoroughgoing reassessment of what motivates antiquities collectors, whether it is money, immortality, or self-esteem. But one thing seems clear: much antiquities collecting occurs for reasons that are personal or social and have little to do with the immanent qualities of the antiquities themselves. This emphasis on the social aspects of collecting suggests that many collectors might be persuaded to channel their passion for collecting into less destructive areas. Oscar White Muscarella of the Metropolitan, for example, notes that he has in the past been able to convince some people to stop collecting antiquities (Muscarella 2000: 27, n. 9) but that sometimes his museum colleagues have encouraged recidivism. Unfortunately, as long as academics and particularly the curatorial staff of large art museums continue in their acclamation of collectors and their admiration of the antiquities amassed, the practice of collecting will persist.

ANTIQUITIES AS ART

No matter what motivates the antiquities collector, the justification is always the same. The material object that is collected—the antiquity—is collected because it is an "art" object. But are all antiquities really art? This question is rooted in the Renaissance rediscovery of Greek and Roman sculpture and its subsequent impact upon the development of European visual art. Since that time, the world's antiquities have been transfigured by a creeping aestheticization, which has transformed what were once curios or objects of archaeological interest into individual works of art. After Classical sculpture, the accolade of "art" was awarded first to other Greek and Italian antiquities, particularly figure-painted pottery. But since the late nineteenth century artifacts from all areas of the world have come to be seen as significant artworks, or at least as possessing aesthetic qualities that appeal to the perceptions of Western taste, which has itself been characterized over the past 150 years by cumulative processes of protraction and diversification.

Pre-Columbian material has been known in Europe since the sixteenth century, but it was not until the mid-nineteenth century that it began to attract serious interest outside its countries of origin. This attraction was due largely to the explorations of various diplomats, illustrators, and early archaeologists, such as John Lloyd Stephens and Alfred Maudslay. The discoveries and revelations of their expeditions provided a "coming out" for Pre-Columbian material, which much nineteenth-century scholarship and museum exhibition in Europe and the United States defined as art. This attribution was based on its detailed and complex craftsmanship, which proponents argued was as impressive as anything found in the Old World. By the 1920s Pre-Columbian material had become a source of inspiration for European Cubist and Expressionist artists, who fostered an appreciation outside the circumscribed realm of specialists (Boone 1993: 331; Williams 1985). From this point forward the collecting of Pre-Columbian art matured, and in the United States large private collectors such as Alfred Stendahl and Robert Woods Bliss established themselves, first traveling to Paris to meet with fellow enthusiasts and later forming a cohesive network of Pre-Columbian scholars in the United States (Benson 1993: 18; Coe 1993: 275–81). By the 1950s Stendahl and Bliss dominated the field and sought advice from a host of archaeologists (Benson 1993: 21–25; Coe 1993: 275–81). Bliss and his wife eventually made a gift of their collection, together with their home and its grounds (Dumbarton Oaks), to Harvard University.

Similarly, it was not until the 1920s and 1930s that a viable commercial market for African artifacts became established, again due in part to the interest and promotion of European artists. At first, demand focused on wooden facemasks and ritual statuary, but as the supply of what Steiner calls those "classic genres" began to dry up in the 1950s, the trade expanded to include household or other utilitarian objects (Steiner 1994: 7). It also triggered a search for archaeological—in the sense of buried—objects, and since then there has been large-scale and illegal excavation of West African terra-cotta statuary, which was virtually unknown outside Africa before the 1960s (Brodie 2005).

The decorative art of China and Japan was highly esteemed in nineteenth-century Europe and North America and was in demand, but Asian figurative art was considered inferior to its European counterparts. The Hindu statuary of India was abhorred on account of its erotic and sometimes monstrous appearance, and Buddhist sculpture was considered lifeless (Mitter 1977). Both genres were rehabilitated in the early decades of the twentieth century, when it was argued that they were intended to represent spiritual rather than material realities, and by the 1950s South and Southeast Asian sculpture was flowing into U.S. art museums (Brodie and Doole 2004).

The aestheticization of much archaeological material has been due to the attention and opinions of artists who have seen in it a reflection of their own endeavors. But their reasoning is flawed, as can clearly be seen in the case of the German Expressionist *Der Blaue Reiter* almanac of 1912 (Lankheit 1974). *Der Blaue Reiter* presented a series of short texts written by artists interspersed with photographs of Modernist paintings and "primitive" works of art: medieval European art, drawings by children, ethnographic objects from various cultures around the world, and a couple of antiquities, one Pre-Columbian and the other Classical. The prime movers of this Expressionist manifesto, painters Franz Marc and Wassily Kandinsky, argued that the Renaissance project of mimetic realism had collapsed in the mid-nineteenth century and that the emerging goal of art was spiritual, to express a personal truth or idea—a goal they saw epitomized in the "pre-rational" work of "primitives." Following this early invocation in *Der Blaue Reiter*, by the 1920s Pre-Colombian, African, and Oceanic artifacts were increasingly being lumped together under the rubric of "primitive art."

Marc and Kandinsky understood, however, that the expression of an artist's creative urge was best communicated to viewers within a shared cultural environment, and ultimately this requirement for cultural community subverted the Expressionist creed. The artists themselves could only imagine the cultural worlds and artistic conventions within which their ethnographic and archaeological objects were produced, and therefore could not legitimately claim sympathy of purpose. They could no more grasp the intention of the objects' creators or the authenticity of original reception than their untutored contemporary public could engage with the visual emotion of their own paintings. For Gombrich, the Expressionists were guilty of "wrenching these works out of their cultural context in the interest of approximating them to the creations of twentieth-century art" (Gombrich 2002: 229), and it was an expropriation that highlights plainly the problems associated with the uncritical evaluation of antiquities as art—there is more to art than meets the eye.

Art turns out to be a concept that is difficult to define and resistant to critique. In the Western tradition, a work of art is meant to please or otherwise engage the senses, but it can also provide a window on the world of its making, or deliberately comment upon that world, or depict it from unusual perspectives. For the viewer, the appreciation of an art object is as much a cognitive as a sensory experience and is facilitated or improved by knowledge of the object's or its creator's biography, or of the techniques or circumstances of its production, or of its original purpose or function. In other words, the proper appreciation of an art object cannot proceed without knowledge of its historical context. Hence although a work of art embodies multiple purposes and insights, it can only be interpreted through the cultural lens of a more or less knowledgeable viewer.

On the surface, antiquities collectors ignore the importance of contextual knowledge and adhere to the belief that somehow an object can be appreciated as art outside the historical circumstances of its production and use. As noted by Tubb in chapter 16, George Ortiz has claimed a visceral connection to objects in his collection, declaring that certain objects "came to fascinate and move me, I let them speak to me, I let their content and spirit nourish me" (Ortiz 1996). There is no opportunity here for the viewer to bring anything to the encounter—the objects partake of a monologue. But Ortiz is quite clear elsewhere that his rationale for collecting is provided by the intellectual and political achievements of Classical Athens, which he sees reflected in Greek art of the period as an expression of the spirit of rational humanism. While Ortiz's equation of sociopolitical development and artist excellence can be criticized as harking back to nineteenth-century social evolutionism, it does provide a coherent structure for his collection, where pieces are judged according to their historical connection to Greece or their perceived spiritual (Greek) essence. *It also shows that his knowledge of the historical context of Greek art is an important part of his attraction.*

The importance of historical context is well understood by art historians. Art historical analysis is a powerful tool for the investigation of ancient cultures that have a strong aesthetic presence, but it incorporates other archaeological or textual sources and makes use of theoretical concepts derived from other disciplines. Art historical analyses of this sort are usually not possible for de-contextualized antiquities. The academic experts drafted in to write entries for catalogues of such material do their best to provide the outward trappings of scholarship, but their discussions are vitiated by lack of contextual information. Catalogue entries are rather formulaic: there is a description of the piece; then it is identified, if possible with reference to known comparanda in other collections and museums (preferably pieces from known contexts or controlled excavations); and finally, there is some speculation as to possible function or significance. Such catalogue entries merely describe pieces in light of what is already known and rarely add anything new to our understanding of the culture that produced them. These entries have the appearance but not, unfortunately, the substance of true scholarship. On the face of it, this lack of scholarship is not too much of a problem. Although the unscientific extraction of an antiquity from an archaeological site or monument is damaging, its subsequent reception into the corpus appears harmless. Nothing much new is learned, it is true, but the focus on description rather than detailed interpretation does avoid, to some extent, the production of false historical evidence. Unfortunately, this anodyne view of contemporary reception is increasingly being called into question, and it is becoming clear that such studies of decontextualized antiquities can in fact draw erroneous conclusions about their original purpose, function, symbolism, or significance or about the conditions of their production and consumption. Even for pieces belonging to traditions that are historically attested or well-known archaeologically, the danger of misinterpretation is ever present.

Nowhere has this been made clearer than for the example of sixth- and fifth-century B.C. Attic vases decorated with black and red figures. These pots, made in Classical Athens and exported to Etruria, have been dug out of Etruscan tombs—very few have been scientifically excavated—since at least the eighteenth century. They are sometimes marked with the name of the potter or painter, and their figured decoration draws upon a rich thematic repertoire to offer scenes from Greek mythology and legend. With so much intrinsic detail available for study, it is not surprising that they have been the object of more intense connoisseurship than any other class of antiquity, and the general consensus is that they were regarded in Greece and Etruria as works of art and that they would have been valuable or prestigious commodities. However, Vickers and Gill (1994) have argued that the scholarly celebration of their artistic quality and importance has endowed them today with a high market value, which has in turn created the illusion that they were similarly valuable in antiquity, when perhaps they were not. Instead, Vickers and Gill suggest that the pots, with their fine black glaze, were intended as cheap substitutes for silver vessels. Their argument is controversial, although in the absence of well-excavated assemblages it is difficult to refute or confirm, and it is perhaps ironic that information derived from depositional contexts—Etruscan tombs—has been used to develop a counter-argument (Spivey 1991).

It is disconcerting to find that our understanding of such a well-known corpus of antiquities as the Attic vases may be fundamentally flawed, but the argument of Vickers and Gill has a more general relevance. Any interpretation that locates ancient artifacts in modern regimes of aesthetic and monetary value necessarily situates them within the social and cultural structures that give those regimes meaning. But the dangers of misinterpretation and revaluation that face Attic vases are magnified many times over for material with less contextual control, and particularly for pieces that are likely to have been unusual in antiquity and that are not well represented in the archaeological record.

For example, in the collection of Shelby White and Leon Levy there is a painted ceramic jar in the style of pottery known from the sixth-millennium B.C. site of Hacilar, in western Turkey. The catalogue entry states that the piece is "among the earliest ceramics produced as fine art rather than as merely utilitarian objects" (Kawami 1990: 29). But painted pottery was not unusual at this time; in fact it is the most common type of artifact found on sites of sixth-millennium B.C. date throughout the Near East (Wengrow 2001: 171), and it was almost certainly produced in domestic contexts with a complex meld in mind of symbolic and functional purposes. The catalogue entry provides too much interpretation with not enough evidence and projects a twentieth-century viewpoint onto a culture almost entirely lost. George Ortiz, in his pursuit of the Greek spirit, likewise asks of a fifth-millennium B.C. terra-cotta figurine of a seated female from Thessaly, Greece: "Does this attest an artistic sensitivity beyond the context of its time, a fortuitous accident, or is this a premonition of Greek humanism that was to develop three and a half millennia later?" (Ortiz 1996: No. 44).

Identifications of fine art or of artistic sensitivity are invocations of what Alsop calls "art-as-an-end-in-itself," with all that this idea entails, as against his "art-for-use-plus-beauty," which would be more appropriate (Alsop 1982: 36). Imputations of art-as-an-end-in-itself in prehistoric contexts drive a wedge between "artistic" and "utilitarian" production, taking artistic expression out of the hands of ordinary people and placing it in the hands of individual creators. Quite transparently and inappropriately, this interprets past practice in terms of present socioeconomic structures.

The issues that attend the aestheticization of prehistoric objects are most acute and have been most successfully explored in the case of Cycladic figurines (Broodbank 1992, 2000: 58–65; Elia 1993; Gill and Chippindale 1993). Cycladic figurines are small, bleached-white marble figures varying in height from about 0.15 m to 1.5 m, with most falling in the lower end of the range, that were manufactured on some of the Greek Cycladic Islands during the third millennium B.C. When they first came to public attention in the nineteenth century they were considered ugly and barbaric, but by the middle years of the twentieth century they were viewed more positively thanks to the work of artists such as Brancusi, Modigliani, and Moore, who read into their purity of form and color an intimation of Modernist sculpture. Since the 1960s, this aesthetic revaluation has been associated with the widespread looting of cemeteries on the Cycladic Islands and the appearance of large numbers of figurines on the market and in museums and collections around the world. Acceptance of the figurines within the modern canon as art has brought all the trappings of connoisseurship, so that today, in trade and collecting circles at least, Cycladic figurines are classified as the work of "master carvers," which implies their production in a society with a socioeconomic system able to support full-time craft specialization (Chippindale and Gill 1995: 137).

A similar argument can be made for Classic period (A.D. 600–800) Maya polychrome pottery: ceramic vases and dishes with vibrant imagery illustrating life in ancient Mesoamerica. As discussed early in this chapter, private collecting and museum exhibition of Pre-Columbian material were well established by the 1950s, fostering an appreciation of non-Western aesthetics and pushing scholars to redefine what they meant by beauty and "art." Subsequent academic excavations, publications, and exhibitions have developed an idealized framework for interpreting much polychrome pottery as an elite ware, particularly pottery with "intricate scenes and hieroglyphic texts" (Reents-Budet 1994: 291), taken to be a hallmark of high status in the Maya world. Studies published during the 1970s, 1980s, and 1990s consistently argued that an elite-based artisan group produced such elaborate wares. The trade uses these publications, particularly those that appear as lavish, well-illustrated coffee table books (see Coe and Kerr 1997; Reents-Budet 1994; Schele and Miller 1986), to justify the increasing monetary value of polychromes, emphasizing the importance of a *Maya* link.

Yet looking closely at the archaeological data, one finds that much polychrome pottery from the Maya Lowlands is ubiquitous, found in large quantities in all contexts—from small hamlets to elite burials as well as residential garbage. Specific classes of polychrome pottery, particularly those with complex decipherable texts and intricate palace scenes, may be more restricted in their distribution but are still far from being a clear marker of elite production or consumption. The polychrome-is-elite hypothesis shares the same intellectual presuppositions as the argument for Cycladic master carvers. It has been taken as fact because of a Western aesthetic that validates specific non-Western traditions as "high art." The decipherment of Maya texts in the 1970s contributed further to the perception of these vases as elite wares, largely based on Western scholarship valuing hieroglyphic texts as representations of "a time-honored aesthetic tradition steeped in intellectual pursuits" (Reents-Budet 1994: 292). Artists of hieroglyphic texts have become "royal" scribes, even nobles, attached to high courts. It has been argued that "it was only the lowland Maya scribes of the Classic period who achieved a degree of elaboration, sophistication, and beauty in their writing that elevates it to the level of the great calligraphic traditions of the Old World" (Coe and Kerr 1997: 25; cf. Schele and Miller 1986: 14). Maya scholars further portray the intricate palace scenes and naturalistic representations of the body as great artistic achievements, particularly in comparison to what are described as the impersonal and abstract arts of the Maya "periphery." Study of these images "set the stage for the full recognition of Classic Maya polychrome pottery as a fine painting tradition to be studied in the same formal manner as European paintings on canvas" (Reents-Budet 1994: 292).

This emphasis on intellectualism and European canons of representation needs to proceed with caution. While we can legitimately ask what the possession and production of polychrome pottery meant in the Classic period in Mesoamerica, our investigation should proceed empirically with a view to testing hypotheses, rather than working from a preconceived idea of what constitutes high art. Much archaeological and art historical inquiry has turned away from a simple object-centered approach over the last two decades, but this new research has not been recognized by the trade, which appears to choose specific points from the scholarly literature that best reinforce to buyers the concept of high art. The problem is made worse by the fact that a good number of archaeologists and art historians have fostered the celebration of a "Maya heartland," and this framework has led to an academically constructed "core." It is no coincidence that it is these areas that are most targeted by plunder and that *Maya* is a term used by the trade to evoke high status in the past.

Thus for Cycladic figurines and Maya polychrome pottery there is an unwarranted equation between an aesthetically pleasing product and a creatively or socially circumscribed group of artisans (artists or craft specialists). This imputation of full-time specialist craft production implies a socioeconomic system with a marked and probably hierarchical division of labor and with relations of production and patronage similar to those that exist today. But the economic base of most prehistoric, usually pre-urban, societies was agrarian, with little capacity for surplus food production—at least not enough to support the work of *full-time* craftworkers or "artists" who were not engaged in subsistence-related activities. Even for more complex proto-urban or urban societies, the existence of full-time craft specialists or artists cannot simply be adduced from an apparently "artistic" product, the pleasing finish or developed iconography of which happens to appeal to the modern eye. Individual creativity in past societies may be open to empirical investigation if there is available for study a sufficiently large corpus of comparable objects with a complex style (Gill and Chippindale 1993: 638–40; Morris 1993); and the degree or nature of craft specialization can be assessed from the technology and standardization of production, the archaeological remains of workshops, and the nature of embedding socioeconomic structures (Costin 1991). But the mode of production remains something to be investigated, not assumed (Heilmeyer 2004).

Yet while it is possible to criticize interpretations of decontextualized antiquities for projecting modern, or at least recent Western, systems of production back onto ancient societies, evaluations of archaeological and ethnographic artifacts that are characterized as primitive art have been charged with the opposite solecism: without any contextual information to suggest otherwise, particularly about the identities of producers, it is easy to allege the communal authorship and spontaneous expression of these so-called primitive works and to contrast them with the individuality and reflection of Western equivalents (and sometimes imitations). But although primitive art is celebrated as more natural—or less cultured, which amounts to the same thing—this merely disguises racial stereotyping and other constructions of alterity (Hiller 1991: 2; Price 2001: 89).

Thus decontextualized artifacts are forcibly subject to bipolar conceptions of individual versus communal and rational versus irrational artistic production. This polarity is at the same time a product of, *and a reason for*, the Western separation of "civilized" from "uncivilized" societies. It is also essentialist. Cycladic carvers are individualized because they worked in an area that was to become known as Greece. This recursive relationship between conceptions of artistic production and schemes of historical and political categorization will persist until it is disrupted by the study of properly contextualized ethnographic and archaeological artifacts.

It cannot be assumed a priori that any well-made, aesthetically pleasing artifact is a deliberate work of art, in the sense of Alsop's art-as-an-end-in-itself. Although it is more than likely that some if not most antiquities were manufactured with a complex purpose in mind, including aesthetic expression, their reception today is problematic. Few antiquities are likely to elicit a response that is authentic for the time in which they were made. There can be no guarantee that the emotions inspired are those that were originally intended, and without evidence of context there is only a limited amount of external information that can be brought to bear. This conclusion removes the antiquities collectors' justification that anything they collect is art. Even when antiquities were produced as art, they cannot be appreciated as such on their own terms, and so they should not be collected as art. They can be admired because of qualities of style or form that they happen to share with modern art works; but without any demonstrable cultural or historical bridge, the resemblances can only be understood as fortuitous.

But although antiquities take meaning from modern conceptions of artistic production, they take meaning too from the commercial nexus of their trade and the destructive circumstances of their extraction. And today this plurality of meanings must be given our full attention. When antiquities are presented solely as art objects, a decision has been taken to suppress information about their recent history, and although this decision may be presented as an analytical one—a temporary but necessary bracketing intended to remove any distraction from an appreciation of appearance—it is in fact a political one. It hides the economic and cultural institutions that constitute the antiquity both as a commodity and as a work of art, and no mention is made of what Gill and Chippindale have called the "material and intellectual consequences of esteem" (Gill and Chippindale 1993). Nor is any criticism invited. But the reception of archaeological objects in modern society cannot proceed through an appreciation of appearance alone, which would be "a private activity with only slender public consequences" (Said 1993: 385). The unwelcome historical accretions of their immediate past cannot be ignored.

CONCLUSION

The antiquities trade is usually discussed or analyzed in terms of institutions or categories, as has been the case in this book. Thus the roles played by auction houses, collectors, and art museums are of intense interest. However, this abstract mode of analysis fails to grasp the fundamentally social nature of the trade. In reality, the antiquities trade is held together by people acting with a community of interest though driven by divergent personal agendas. The antiquities trade is a very human phenomenon and offers ample scope for the playing out of rivalries and conceits, for displays of power and largesse, for the pursuit and realization of overarching ambition, for broaching (or creating) social barriers, or simply for earning a living. These social interactions form the networks that constitute the trade, and they should be the object of future analysis.

The superficial reality of these trade networks is easily observed, and even participated in. Dealers, collectors, academics, museum curators, and museum trustees can come together at an auction or salesroom and interact, much as they would at a reception, a public lecture, or a gala opening. While the nature of their interaction may vary depending upon the setting—the commercial environment of the auction room, the hushed whispers of the lecture room, the convivial atmosphere of the gala dinner, or evening cocktails on the deck of a private Mediterranean cruise—the purpose remains the same: to promote antiquities as art, and to transact. Hoving's account of life as the director of New York's Metropolitan Museum of Art provides vignettes of such encounters (Hoving 1993). But it is the outcome of these interactions that is of interest: what exchanges of material, money, and expertise are agreed? Unless these simple questions are answered, a full understanding of the antiquities trade, and particularly of the secretive trade in unprovenanced antiquities, will remain elusive.

The presence of conventions and practices that protect the trade networks from too much unwelcome attention show that they also operate on a deeper and perhaps more sinister level. The anonymity that is a feature of auction sales provides one glaring example, and dealers too are unwilling to reveal details of their sources and customers, though perhaps understandably for commercial reasons. It is harder to understand why museums block access to information that pertains to the sources of their acquisitions and to their relationships with dealers, private collectors, and auction houses. Many collectors, who may also be museum trustees and company directors, are rich and powerful people, who can use their influence and political connections to obstruct inquiries and even close them down. For example, in 1991, the U.K. Foreign Office advised Scotland Yard in London that they should stop their inquiry into the origins of the so-called Sevso Treasure, a collection of fourteen pieces of Roman silver bought by the Marquess of Northampton during the 1980s (Renfrew 2000: 46–51). After his 1990s investigation into the involvement of some London Sotheby's staff in the illegal antiquities trade, Peter Watson was left wondering why no public prosecution had ensued (Watson 1997: 287). Until these closed networks of interaction that constitute the trade are rendered more transparent and amenable to investigation, the complex flows of money and material that they enable will remain hidden, and it will be difficult to design, evaluate, or enforce appropriate regulatory responses, whether they be voluntary or statutory. The trade in unprovenanced antiquities will continue unabated.

As discussed in the introductory chapter of this book, the commercial nexus of the art museums and of the antiquities those museums contain has become increasingly problematical over recent decades. It is incumbent upon art museums to adopt ethical acquisitions policies and to establish clear due diligence procedures that should be followed when checking the provenance of a potential accession. Museums should also carefully consider the impact that both exhibitions and any subsequent publications might make on the market, either directly, by acting as an unintentional and no doubt unwanted advertising campaign, but also indirectly, by reproducing the intellectual framework that values decontextualized objects.

Finally, as future research into the motivations and consequences of antiquities collecting beckons, research into the practice of archaeology and its relationship to the antiquities trade is necessary too. The archaeological methodology of excavation is, by its very nature, destructive; it provides a one-time opportunity to recover and properly document information. Such information is invaluable because it situates the excavated sites within a regional context, and thus archaeological features and objects are placed in specific relationships (e.g., burials, caches, houses, plazas, etc.). But although the information from known contexts is important, research focused on excavated finds is, *by default*, object-based. Hence collectors and archaeologists do agree on the importance of the *object* for understanding the past. What they disagree on is the importance of context. Archaeologists have made their position clear, supporting it with ample data: context is important, and looting destroys contexts. But collectors view context as secondary to objects, when they see it as relevant at all. They have not been persuaded by the value of scientific excavation and contextual analysis.

Many if not most archaeologists have chosen to separate themselves completely from the commercial world of collecting and dealing, and in consequence it is a world about which we know little. We do know that looting continues because we see it in the field. In fact, some new high-profile projects in Central America that have received press attention, academic recognition, and funding were initiated after looters had exposed impressive finds. But while archaeologists endeavor to preserve and understand these discoveries, and sometimes make commendable efforts to track down the looters, no one talks about tracking down the wealthy collectors—those responsible for creating demand—or about exposing the networks that constitute the trade. Perhaps we are frightened of losing research or excavation funding (much funding comes indirectly through private collectors); of damaging our museum and academic careers (similarly, many wealthy collectors are museum trustees or sponsor university departments); or of risking our ability to secure permits in foreign countries. Perhaps we are simply frightened of being involved in a police action or a court case. For whatever reason, most archaeologists are reluctant to explore or expose the antiquities trade.

Yet archaeologists must make more efforts to understand *why* people collect and *why* collectors are so little interested in context. Without monitoring or maintaining any relationship to the trade, archaeologists will not and cannot understand how our own research may be a contributing factor. Nor will we fully understand how field research influences the market for specific types of artifact, nor how theoretical concepts, such as the identification of individual artistic production, affect the monetary value of objects. From the work presented in this book it is clear that to some extent archaeological research does fuel the antiquities trade. To claim otherwise is naïve. It is also clear that collecting antiquities is a far more complex activity than previously suspected. Like doing archaeology, collecting involves a suite of social values, an established etiquette, and it is this ethos that we need to understand better.

BIBLIOGRAPHY

Alsop, Joseph. *The Rare Art Traditions*. London: Thames and Hudson, 1982.

Atwood, Roger. *Stealing History: Tomb Raiders, Smugglers, and the Looting of the Ancient World*. New York: St. Martin's Press, 2004.

Baekeland, Frederick. "Psychological Aspects of Art Collecting." In *Interpreting Objects and Collections*, ed. Susan M. Pearce, 205–219. London: Routledge, 1994.

Barnard, Charlotte. "Unlocking Asia Mysteries." *Art and Antiques*, February 2002, 48–51.

Belk, Russell W. *Collecting in a Consumer Society*. London: Routledge, 1995.

Benson, Elizabeth P. "The Robert Woods Bliss Collection of Pre-Columbian Art: A Memoir." In *Collecting the Pre-Columbian Past: A Symposium at Dumbarton Oaks, 6th and 7th October 1990*, ed. Elizabeth Hill Boone, 15–34. Washington, D.C.: Dumbarton Oaks Research Library and Collection, 1993.

Boone, Elizabeth Hill. "Collecting the Pre-Columbian Past: Historical Trends and the Process of Reception and Use." In *Collecting the Pre-Columbian Past: A Symposium at*

Dumbarton Oaks, 6th and 7th October 1990, ed. Elizabeth Hill Boone, 315–50. Washington, D.C.: Dumbarton Oaks Research Library and Collection, 1993.

Bourdieu, Pierre. *Distinction: A Social Critique of the Judgement of Taste*. London: Routledge, 1984.

Brodie, Neil J. "An Outsider Looking in: Observations on the African 'Art' Market." In *Safeguarding Africa's Past*, ed. Naill Finneran. British Archaeological Reports International Series. Oxford: Archaeopress, 2005.

Brodie, Neil J., and Jenny Doole. "The Asian Art Affair: US Art Museum Collections of Asian Art and Archaeology." In *Material Engagements: Studies in Honour of Colin Renfrew*, ed. Neil Brodie and Catherine Hills, 83–108. McDonald Institute Monograph. Cambridge, U.K.: McDonald Institute for Archaeological Research, 2004.

Broodbank, Cyprian. "The Spirit Is Willing." *Antiquity* 66 (1992): 542–46.

———. *An Island Archaeology of the Early Cyclades*. Cambridge, U.K.: Cambridge University Press, 2000.

Chippindale, Christopher, and David Gill. "Cycladic Figurines: Art versus Archaeology?" In *Antiquities Trade or Betrayed: Legal, Ethical and Conservation Issues*, ed. Kathryn W. Tubb, 131–42. London: Archetype, 1995.

Clifford, James. "Collecting Ourselves." In *Interpreting Objects and Collections*, ed. Susan M. Pearce, 258–68. London: Routledge, 1994.

Coe, Michael D. "From Huaquero to Connoisseur: The Early Market in Pre-Columbian Art." In *Collecting the Pre-Columbian Past: A Symposium at Dumbarton Oaks, 6th and 7th October 1990*, ed. Elizabeth Hill Boone, 271–90. Washington, D.C.: Dumbarton Oaks Research Library and Collection, 1993.

Coe, Michael D., and Justin Kerr. *The Art of the Maya Scribe*. London: Thames and Hudson, 1997.

Costin, Cathy. "Craft Specialization: Issues in Defining, Documenting, and Explaining the Organization of Production." *Archaeological Method and Theory* 3 (1991): 1–56.

Elia, Ricardo J. "A Seductive and Troubling Work." *Archaeology* 46 (January–February 1993): 64–69.

Fleischman, Barbara, and Lawrence Fleischman. "Preface." In *A Passion for Antiquities: Ancient Art from the Collection of Barbara and Lawrence Fleischman*, ed. Marion True and Kenneth Hamma, ix–x. Malibu, Calif.: J. Paul Getty Museum, 1994.

Gill, David W. J., and Christopher Chippindale. "Material and Intellectual Consequences of Esteem for Cycladic Figures." *American Journal of Archaeology* 97 (1993): 601–59.

Gombrich, Ernst. *The Preference for the Primitive*. London: Phaidon, 2002.

Graepler, Daniel. *Fundort: Unbekannt—Raubgrabungen Zerstören das Archäologische Erbe*. Munich: Walter Bierung, 1993.

Heilmeyer, Wolf-Dieter. "Ancient Workshops and Ancient 'Art.'" *Oxford Journal of Archaeology* 23 (2004): 403–15.

Helms, Mary W. *Craft and the Kingly Ideal: Art, Trade and Power*. Austin: University of Texas Press, 1993.

Hiller, Susan. "Editor's Foreword." In *The Myth of Primitivism*, ed. Susan Hiller, 1–4. London: Routledge, 1991.

Hoving, Thomas. *Making the Mummies Dance*. New York: Simon and Schuster, 1993.

———. *False Impressions*. London: Andre Deutsch, 1996.

Kawami, Trudy S. "No. 16, Ceramic Jar, Hacilar, South-Central Anatolia." In *Glories of the Past: Ancient Art from the Shelby White and Leon Levy Collection*, ed. Dietrich von Bothmer, 29. New York: Harry N. Abrams, 1990.

Kossak, Steve M. "Collector's Note." In *The Flame and the Lotus*, ed. Martin Lerner, 7. New York: Harry N. Abrams, 1984.

Lankheit, Klaus. *The Blaue Reiter Almanac*. London: Thames and Hudson, 1974.

Mauss, Marcel. *The Gift: Forms, Functions and Exchange in Archaic Societies*. Glencoe, Ill.: Free Press, 1954.

Mitter, Partha. *Much Maligned Monsters: History of European Reactions to Indian Art*. Oxford: Clarendon, 1977.

Morris, Christie E. "Hands Up for the Individual: The Role of Attribution Studies in Aegean Prehistory." *Cambridge Archaeological Journal* 3 (1993): 41–66.

Muscarella, Oscar W. *The Lie Became Great: The Forgery of Ancient Near Eastern Cultures*. Groningen, Netherlands: Styx, 2000.

Nørskov, Vinnie. *Greek Vases in New Contexts: The Collecting and Trading of Greek Vases— An Aspect of the Modern Reception of Antiquity*. Aarhus, Denmark: Aarhus University Press, 2002.

Ortiz, George. *In Pursuit of the Absolute: Art of the Ancient World*. Berne: Benteli, 1996.

Price, Sally. *Primitive Art in Civilised Places*. Chicago, Ill.: University of Chicago Press, 2001.

Reents-Budet, Doris. *Painting the Maya Universe: Royal Ceramics of the Classic Period*. Durham, N.C.: Duke University Press, 1994.

Renfrew, Colin. *Loot, Legitimacy and Ownership: The Ethical Crisis in Archaeology*. London: Duckworth, 2000.

Said, Edward W. *Culture and Imperialism*. London: Chatto and Windus, 1993.

Schele, Linda, and Ellen Miller. *Blood of Kings: Dynasty and Ritual in Maya Art*. New York: George Braziller and Kimbell Art Museum, 1986.

Spivey, Nigel. "Greek Vases in Etruria." In *Looking at Greek Vases*, ed. Tom Rasmussen and Nigel Spivey, 131–50. Cambridge, U.K.: Cambridge University Press, 1991.

Steiner, Christopher B. *African Art in Transit*. Cambridge, U.K.: Cambridge University Press, 1994.

Vickers, Michael, and David Gill. *Artful Crafts: Ancient Greek Silverware and Pottery*. Oxford: Clarendon Press, 1994.

Watson, Peter. *Sotheby's: The Inside Story*. London: Bloomsbury, 1997.

Wengrow, David. "The Evolution of Simplicity: Aesthetic Labour and Social Change in the Neolithic Near East." *World Archaeology* 33 (2001): 168–88.

White, Shelby. "A Collector's Odyssey." *International Journal of Cultural Property* 7 (1998): 170–76.

Williams, Elizabeth A. "Art and Artifact at the Trocadero." In *Objects and Others: Essays on Museums and Material Culture*, ed. George W. Stocking, 146–66. History of Anthropology, vol. 3. Madison: University of Wisconsin Press, 1985.

Appendix A. Law Enforcement Responsibilities Checklist

Investigative Protocol Involving Archaeological Resources

1. Has a crime been committed?
    1a. List and describe applicable laws
        1a1. Theft:
        1a2. Vandalism:
        1a3. Trafficking/illegal transportation:
        1a4. Trespassing:
        1a5. Illegal import/export:
        1a6. Human burial disturbance:
        1a7. Protected historic/heritage/sacred site:
        1a8. Violation of permit requirements:
        1a9. Poaching or violation of wildlife protection laws:
    1b. Did the crime/crimes involving archaeological resources concern other offenses against persons or property? If so, list:
    1c. Did the crime occur incident to military operations? *(If the crime occurred incident to military operations, consult the Rome Statute of the International Criminal Court document A/CONF.183/9 of July 17, 1998, amended and enacted July 1, 2002, for applicable laws pertaining to pillaging and destruction of cultural heritage property.)*
    1d. Sources of information that a crime has been committed
        1d1. Law enforcement patrol:
        1d2. Special investigative operations (task force, intelligence, or covert activity):
        1d3. Citizen informant(s):
        (In evaluating the credibility of informants, consider: possible relationship to the suspect; circumstances under which informant observed the crime [including distance from the action, lighting, and time of day]; motivation to cooperate with authorities.)
    1e. If the law violation was detected through surveillance, try to obtain photographs that show a suspect at the scene involved in illegal activity. *(If possible, videotape illegal activity during surveillance, and later videotape the crime scene and the in situ evidence.)*

1f. Make field notes to list specific observations of the suspect(s), to include:

1f1. Physical descriptions:

1f2. Actions or movements:

1f3. Handling of tools:

1f4. Attempts to disguise or camouflage activities or tools:

1f5. Any other actions that may help to show criminal intent:

2. Confronting the suspect

(Consider suspects as dangerous: they are escape risks and may be carrying weapons. Be aware that many crimes involving archaeological sites involve multiple suspects. A suspect at the crime scene may have an associate nearby.)

2a. When you confronted the suspect, note the following:

2a1. Was the suspect within the archaeological site or protected area?

2a2. Was the suspect in possession of tools, artifacts, and other physical evidence?

2a3. Did the suspect make any initial or spontaneous statements concerning intent, knowledge of the offense, or other damaging information?

2b. Observe, collect, and document any physical evidence associated with your suspect, to include:

2b1. Illegally removed artifacts:

2b2. Seizure of tools, materials, vehicles:

2c. Circumstances that might require delay in apprehending the suspect:

2c1. To develop additional suspicion or probable cause to arrest:

2c2. To determine if other suspects are involved:

2c3. To coordinate the investigation with cooperating agencies who may also have an active investigation pending that involves the suspect:

2c4. To await additional officers because of the remoteness of the area, numbers of suspects, observed weapons, or other safety considerations:

3. Processing the crime scene

(*Essential crime scene tools include bags, envelopes, or other receptacles for evidence; a camera and film; a tape measure; graph paper for a crime scene sketch; evidence tags; an evidence inventory form that documents the chain of custody.*)

3a. Determine the extent and nature of the crime scene and secure it from interference from *anyone* except the investigator or consulting archaeologist:

3b. Prepare crime scene file to contain

3b1. Complete field notes:

3b2. Photographs and photo log:

3b3. Evidence inventory form:

3c. Take evidentiary photographs

3c1. *Overall*—Entrance and exit points, including routes of travel, entrance and boundary signs, information signs:

3c2. *Intermediate*—Show relationship of evidence, features, and areas of damage:

3c3. *Close-up*—Each major item of evidence, such as vehicles, tire impressions, footprints, tool marks, and equipment:
(*If technically feasible, black and white film should be used to record footprints and tire markings, color film for court exhibits.*)

3d. Crime scene search and sketch

3d1. Use a thorough, systematic method to search for evidence:

3d2. Examine adjacent areas to locate a possible cache of tools, artifacts, or other damaged sites:

3d3. If possible, protect fragile evidence such as footprints, tire marks, fingerprints:

3d4. Enter the crime scene parallel to the suspect's footprints; note routes of travel, areas of activity (which may lead to adjacent sites, or caches, and may indicate a number of suspects):

3d5. *Before collecting any evidence*, it must be photographed, measured with respect to a datum, and located on the crime scene sketch:

3d6. Prepare a scale diagram or sketch of the scene:

3e. Evidence collection

(*Maintain fingerprint processing materials and a casting substance, if possible, along with a camera and film.*)

3e1. Photograph and sketch evidence before collection:

3e2. Collect fragile evidence first (footprints, tire marks):

3e3. If laboratory analysis of evidence is available, collect samples of soil, sand, or gravel at the crime scene, and of groundcover vegetation, and carefully package any tools of the crime for examination of soil or vegetal residue:

3e4. Collect control samples of soil and vegetation and note the control sample collection points on the crime scene sketch:

3e5. If possible, use gloves to handle archaeological evidence to avoid transferring prints and potentially destructive salts and oils onto the artifacts:

3e6. Mark each item of evidence for identification purposes; some fragile archaeological evidence should be marked on outside wrapper only. Consult with archaeologists for specific recommendations:

3e7. Maintain chain of custody on all evidence; be sure that the archaeologist understands the requirements for handling evidence:

4. Assessing site damage

(Refer to the checklist for archaeologists. Only a qualified archaeologist can compile an assessment of site damage. Further, suspects may have artifacts in their possession that may be forgeries or fakes. An expert's analysis may be required to ascertain a fake.)

> 4a. The archaeologist shall prepare a written narrative of his or her involvement in processing the crime scene, questioning suspects, or other matters:
>
> > 4a1. Include a brief statement of the archaeologist's training, experience, and qualifications:
> >
> > 4a2. Include a description of any evidence handled or examined by the archaeologist:
>
> 4b. The archaeologist shall collect and package all archaeological resources:
>
> 4c. The archaeologist shall perform any emergency restoration and repair of site damage *only* when authorized by the investigator:

5. Handling the suspect

(Applicable laws may require warrants obtained from a magistrate or other official to confiscate the suspect's property or to search for additional evidence.)

> 5a. Confiscate the suspect's shoes and clothing, taking care to preserve dirt, and if possible collect dirt from under fingernails:
>
> 5b. Confiscate all archaeological materials in suspect's possession:
>
> 5c. Confiscate all tools and equipment in suspect's possession, including
>
> > 5c1. Metal detectors:
> >
> > 5c2. Shovels, probes (flippers), trowels:
> >
> > 5c3. Screens:
> >
> > 5c4. Packaging gear (envelopes, bags):
> >
> > 5c5. Maps, brochures, books containing information on area archaeological resources:
>
> 5d. Suspect's vehicle
>
> > 5d1. Impound the vehicle and inventory contents:
> >
> > 5d2. Be sure to document and photograph the tire treads on all four tires:
> >
> > 5d3. If laboratory analysis is feasible, collect soil and vegetation evidence from trunk, floorboards, and undercarriage:
> >
> > 5d4. Confiscate as evidence any tools, equipment, or artifacts:
>
> 5e. Arrest or release of suspect
>
> > 5e1. Record suspect's statements, including admissions, alibi, excuses, inconsistencies:
> >
> > 5e2. If local laws require, release the suspect after complete identification and the seizure of evidence:

5e3. Consult with the prosecutor:

6. Preparing the reports

(If it is not in the report, then it does not exist!)

6a. Each member of the investigative team and the archaeologist shall prepare narrative reports:

6b. The investigator shall review each report for accuracy, completeness, conciseness, clarity, and fairness:

6c. Organize the report file logically to include:

6c1. An overview or synopsis:

6c2. Reports from all investigators and technicians:

6c3. Damage assessment report by the archaeologist:

6c4. Photographs and photo log (unless listed on the evidence inventory form):

6c5. Evidence inventory form:

6c6. Laboratory reports, if any:

6c7. Crime scene sketches, diagrams, maps:

6c8. Witness statements:

6c9. List of potential witnesses:

6c10. Documentation from the appropriate agency showing that the suspect neither applied for nor was issued a permit to excavate, survey, or otherwise disturb the site:

7. Site protection

7a. Confer with the archaeologist and appropriate local officials on the best way to stabilize and protect the archaeological resource:

7b. If appropriate and the technology is available, install remote sensors or arrange for periodic surveillance of the site:

7c. If feasible, meet with local residents with an interest in the resource, enlist them for occasional surveillance of the site, and instruct them on how to summon law enforcement:

7d. If human remains were disturbed, destroyed, or removed, or if the artifacts removed or recovered have known spiritual value, consult if appropriate with indigenous or tribal authorities about any rituals or practices that must be observed in handling and storing evidence, in recovering artifacts or human remains, or in presenting them in court.

7d1. Enlist a representative of the tribal or indigenous group as an *ex officio* advisor:

This checklist was adapted from course materials prepared by the Federal Law Enforcement Training Center, Glynco, Georgia.

Appendix B. Archaeologist's Responsibilities Checklist

Investigative Protocol Involving Archaeological Resources

Remember: The timeliness of your response is crucial. Law enforcement officers must protect the crime scene until your arrival. Be sure that you and the investigator understand one another's responsibilities. Your work contributes toward a successful prosecution. Your aim is to describe the vandalism to or theft of archaeological resources in a written report and place a monetary value on stolen artifacts or the cost of restoring or repairing the site. Help process the crime scene by diagramming and photographing it, carefully obtaining physical evidence, and labeling and packaging evidence or instruments of the crime.

1. If contacted by a law enforcement officer
   1a. Ascertain the facts (who, what, when, where):
   1b. Obtain a description of the crime scene *and* advise the investigator of the need to process it using archaeological techniques (and explain applicable techniques):
   1c. In consultation with the investigator, clarify the archaeological role:
2. Clarify applicable laws
   2a. Identify applicable state or national laws:
   2b. Ascertain if the suspect had appropriate permits:
3. At the crime scene
(Through discussion with the investigator, determine what you are allowed to do at the crime scene. Ascertain any hazards to performing the damage assessment. Help the investigator identify evidence.)
   3a. Bring the following, if available, *and ask whether officers can arrange to videotape the scene.*
   3a1. Camera:
   3a2. Trowel:
   3a3. Rigid trays of cardboard or plastic (if human remains):
   3a4. Twine:
   3a5. Tape measure:
   3a6. Folding measures:
   3a7. Photographic scale:
   3a8. Compass:
   3a9. Graph paper:
   3a10. Bags (both paper and plastic):

3a11. Gloves:

3a12. Shovel:

3b. Ask the investigator's instructions on labeling evidence:

3c. Ascertain where the evidence will be stored and in whose custody:

3d. *If* evidence is to be examined, stored, or otherwise retained by a museum or by you, obtain a clear list of guidelines pertaining to security of evidence and chain-of-custody controls *and* create a log showing entries *each time* the evidence is handled:

4. Post-incident analysis

4a. Identify and contact museum experts, as necessary, to evaluate artifacts:

4b. Ascertain the deadline for submitting your report:

4c. Maintain continual contact with the prosecutor to monitor developments and court dates:

4d. Verify existence and validity of permits:

4e. Write a narrative report including the following components:

4e1. Abstract or summary:

4e2. Chronological account of your involvement:

4e3. Drawings, photos, maps:

4e4. Significance/context of site:

4e5. Applicable archaeological principles and methods:

4e6. Description of damage to site:

4e7. Description and estimated cost of site restoration/repair:

4e8. Description and estimated commercial value of artifacts:

4e9. Description of any conversation with suspects:

4e10. Conclusion (what was learned):

(Remember that if you fail to include a fact in the report, then it does not exist.)

Appendix C. A Practical Exercise
in Criminal Investigation

PROJECT

Students will conduct a criminal investigation of a report of digging for artifacts on [*name of site*] property.

Goal

Students will portray a team of crime solvers, including police officers, crime scene technicians, photographers, and archaeologists. The team will respond to the complaint of witnesses who have seen someone digging up artifacts without permission. The student team will interview the witnesses, locate the looter, interview him or her, make an arrest if necessary, and process the crime scene. The mock crime serves as a focus for discussing how citizens and public officials should respond to thefts of and vandalism to our historic resources.

Objectives

1. Interpret the laws regarding historical resources and apply them to solving the case.
2. Explain the steps in conducting a criminal investigation of theft of or vandalism to historic resources.
3. Explain or define the following vocabulary:

trespass	historic resources	vandalism
theft	crime	probable cause/looting
instruments of the crime	artifact	crime
expert witness	archaeology	testify/testimony
defendant	relic	datum
suspect	charge	evidence
		fruits of the crime

Note: The term "historic" encompasses archaeological resources. "Historic" includes visible, above-ground monuments and structures.

Time Required

Two hours minimum

Skills

Making observations, inferences, decisions; analyzing and problem solving; working cooperatively with a group.

Materials and Requirements

At least eleven persons are required (one police officer, one police supervisor, one photographer, four crime scene technicians, one newspaper reporter, one witness, two members of the archaeological team). If the class is larger, appoint a maximum of two police officers, one police supervisor, two photographers, four crime scene technicians, two reporters, two witnesses, and three members of the archaeological team. If the class is very large, consider having two or more identical crime scenes. *Note that one suspect will be required: the suspect should not be known to the students.*

- Small notebooks and pencils for the police, news reporters, and the archaeological team.
- At least 15 evidence tags, two evidence/property forms, and two offense reports.
- Copies of relevant laws for the police officers.
- Minimum of one Polaroid camera with two ten-photograph packs.
- Casting powder and a water supply (preferred casting powder is that used by dentists; various brands available; powder requires a mix with water to the consistency of pancake batter; need sufficient powder for two casts).
- Plastic resealable bags (two sizes: sandwich size for artifacts or dirt samples; gallon size for mixing casting powder and water).
- Index cards (3 × 5 inches) for placing next to evidence or instruments of the crime found at the scene.
- Marking pens to mark index cards.
- Approximately 20 envelopes (9 × 12 inches) for evidence. Plastic bags can be used for evidence that is wet or messy.
- Crime scene technician tools: two tape measures, two rulers (for scale in photographs), graph paper for a crime scene diagram.
- Copy of a relic price guide.
- Sufficient role-play instructions for each function.
- Peel-off stickers to label the newspaper reporters, photographers, crime scene technicians, and witnesses. The police officers and their supervisor may wear badges, if available. It is helpful for the police officers to wear a tag that identifies them as such.
- Small artifacts appropriate to the site (e.g., coins, Civil War bullets, broken ceramics, pipe stems, and bottles).

- Looter debris: empty soda cans, empty cigarette packs.
- Optional: a "No relic hunting" sign to post in the vicinity.

EXERCISE

Arrange for the suspect to set up the illegal dig. Park the car nearby. The suspect should be unknown to students and should be kept out of view of students until the exercise begins. When caught, the suspect will not deny any digging for artifacts but will argue that he or she had permission to dig. The suspect will not be obstinate or uncooperative but will not volunteer any information.

The looter will be digging with a shovel, and by the time of his or her discovery by police, the looter should have dug a few small holes. The crime scene will be littered with some debris in the form of soda cans and cigarette butts. The looter will have retrieved some artifacts and placed them next to the holes or at some other nearby location.

The looter's car will be nearby, unlocked. A relic price guide will be on a seat, some soda cans on the floor (same brand as the soda cans at the site). The student/officers may or may not discover the car and recognize that it is part of the crime scene.

Police officers will watch the looter digging just long enough to establish that a crime is being committed.

On the assumption that this program is presented in conjunction with an archaeology lab exercise, course, or field study, without providing much in the way of background circumstances, inform students that a crime has been committed that involves artifacts.

State that the excavation site/historic property has received information that a looter is on the premises and is seeking artifacts. The looter has no permission to enter the property to obtain artifacts.

Briefly state that looting occurs on properties with historic resources and that it occurs for many reasons, including private consumption or commercial interest. Tell students that criminal acts have been committed when artifacts are removed from the historic property without permission.

Instruct students that their help is needed to investigate possible criminal acts. Explain that the matter will be investigated using the same techniques as in a real criminal investigation.

Ask for volunteers to assume the roles of police officers, a police supervisor, witnesses, photographers, crime scene technicians, an archaeological team, and news reporters. Once roles have been assigned, allow participants a few minutes to read them and ask questions.

After students have absorbed their roles, send the witnesses to a suitable vantage from which to observe the looting.

Assemble the police team (officers, supervisor, technicians, and photographer) and archaeological team and give them the equipment they will need to perform all tasks. Brief them that the police have received a call from the staff at the [historic property or archaeological site]. The staff members report that they have seen a person digging without permission on their property. The person may be digging up artifacts. The looting is in progress and staff members (witnesses) are observing the crime.

Students will gather their equipment and notebooks and walk out to meet the witnesses. The student police officers will interview the witnesses and take statements and proceed to the looting scene and observe at a distance. When appropriate, the officers will confront, interview, and possibly arrest the suspect. The rest of the team will process the crime scene. The crime scene technicians and photographers stand by until the police request them. Reporters may roam around at will to try to elicit information for their news story. The officers may learn that the reporters' movement may need to be restricted; the crime scene must be uncontaminated for processing.

The instructor must ensure that the police officers intervene as soon as possible to stop the digging. Even before the officers question the looter in detail, the crime scene technicians and photographer must be deployed to begin their work.

The crime scene technicians must begin processing the scene immediately. Many tasks must be performed: evidence and tools of the crime must be located and photographed; casts must be taken. If possible, take one cast of a footprint, another of a hole. The casts must be prepared and poured as soon as possible because they require about a half hour to harden.

The archaeological team must immediately collect information on the nature and history of the site. They may interview site staff members for relevant information. The instructor may notice the students becoming so preoccupied with their roles that they sometimes miss the larger picture: the looter may try to cover up holes once the police are at the scene, or the reporters or archaeological team may walk back and forth over the site before it has been processed. The crime scene technicians and the police may need reminding that the crime scene must be left intact until everything relevant has been identified, measured, and photographed. Only after these functions have been performed may the evidence be removed, tagged, and bagged.

The newspaper reporters may become a nuisance for the officers. Officers have a legal right to restrict the reporters' access to the crime scene while it is being processed.

The larger the group of students, the more likely that some will not apply themselves to the exercise or may not have enough to do. Students need to be meticulous with crime scene assignments; have them cross-check each other's work.

Following the field exercise, students will reconvene in the classroom and discuss the experience.

TOPICS FOR DISCUSSION

- Have each actor explain his or her role.
- Review the case: read aloud the offense report. Ask the class the purpose of a police investigation (answer: to support a prosecution). Review the laws: does the report show evidence of wrongdoing?
- Review the process: officers observe the offense, interview witnesses, and accost the suspect. The crime scene technicians and the photographer must document the crime scene and take evidence. Review the evidence for discussion by the class. Show the Polaroid photographs and the casts and evidence. Ask students why the processing had to be so meticulous (answer: to reconstruct the scene in court).

Thank all participants. Collect all equipment.

DISCUSSION QUESTIONS

1. Are the laws about looting and vandalism fair? Do they serve the purpose of helping to preserve the past? Is there a difference between local, state, and federal laws respecting archaeological resources?

2. What happens when a person is charged with breaking the laws regarding archaeological resources?

3. What did you learn in playing your role? Was it hard to perform?

4. How difficult were the laws to interpret?

5. How did you feel about this case? In your opinion, was it right to charge the suspect with a crime?

6. Compare what archaeologists do to tell the story of the past with what law enforcement officers do to tell the story of a crime scene. Differences and similarities?

7. Archaeologists use the terms "artifact" or "antiquity" when discussing the material evidence of the past. Collectors and looters use terms such as "relic." Do these terms reflect different assumptions and perspectives on the part of collectors, looters, archaeologists, and the criminal justice system?

8. In looting cases, archaeologists and law enforcement officers must focus on the monetary value of artifacts and on the cost to repair a damaged site. In archaeological excavations, however, monetary value is irrelevant: of concern is the information gleaned from the excavation. Discuss the implications of attaching monetary value to artifacts.

SOURCES

Course notes. Archaeological Resources Protection Act Training Program, Federal Law Enforcement Training Academy, Glynco, Georgia, n.d.
Model lessons from the journal *Archaeology and Public Education*, 1995–2005.
National Park Foundation. *Silent Witness: Protecting American Indian Archaeological Heritage* (learning guide). Washington, D.C., n.d.
Schermer, Shirley J. *Discovery Archaeology: An Activity Guide for Educators*. Special Publication, Office of the State Archaeologist. Iowa City: University of Iowa, 1992.

BACKGROUND SHEET: POLICE

Your job is to look into suspicious happenings and determine if a crime has been committed. As you look into this case, ask yourself: have any laws been violated? What are they?

Here is a checklist of what to do:

1. Find the witnesses or the people complaining. Find out what they saw or heard. Take notes.

2. Go to the scene of the possible crime and observe what is going on.

3. If you see a suspect, watch the person carefully, then go up to the suspect and ask questions.

4. Ask what the suspect is doing. Look around you very carefully: note what the suspect is wearing. Is a crime being committed? Does the suspect have permission to be there?

5. Walk up to the suspect. If you think the suspect might be dangerous, you can pat down the person's outer clothing for anything that feels as if it may be a weapon. You can remove the thing *only* if it may be a weapon. Here are some questions to ask:

Who are you?
Do you have any identification?
Why are you here?
Do you have permission to dig here?
Have you hunted relics here before?

6. If you think you have enough information to charge the suspect with a crime, read the person his or her rights before proceeding with questioning. Here are the rights:

You have the right to remain silent. Anything you say can be used against you in court. If you want a lawyer to help you before or during questioning, tell us now. Do you understand these rights? Now that you understand them, will you answer my questions?

7. If the suspect will not answer after you have read the rights, do not ask further questions. If the suspect does answer, continue questioning the person. The suspect can stop answering questions at any time.

8. If you need to make an arrest, tell the suspect that he or she is under arrest and say why. Then make sure that you take careful notes about everything that has happened, and make sure that your assistants collect evidence and map and photograph the crime scene.

BACKGROUND SHEET: POLICE SUPERVISOR

Your job as the police supervisor is to manage the entire investigation. You will put together the case file on this incident. Collect all evidence once the technicians have gathered it, and collect and assemble in a folder all of the reports. Make sure that the reports you receive are complete.

Instruct the police that they are to write an offense report, collect the evidence and evidence reports, and present them to you for review. Remember, any report must answer the questions: Who? What? When? Where? Why?

Check to see that every piece of evidence taken has been documented. Each piece of evidence should be labeled to show who found and packaged it and the date and time. Each piece of evidence should be marked on the crime scene map.

You should have:

- photos
- crime scene diagram
- police report
- archaeological damage assessment
- evidence

BACKGROUND SHEET: WITNESSES

You are the managers of the historic/archaeological site. One of your visitors told you of seeing someone digging holes on the property. The person appeared to be digging for relics. You go outside and observe the person digging several shallow holes and picking things out of them, but the activity is too far away for you to tell what kinds of things are being dug up. You call the police, and when the police team arrives, you show them where the suspect is. The suspect is still digging.

You are the experts on the historic/archaeological site. Be able to tell the police why the site is important and what is preserved there.

Background Sheet: Photographers

You are part of the police crime team that investigates looting cases. Your job is to take Polaroid photographs of the crime scene. Be sure to label each photograph you take with the date, the time you took the photograph, and your signature.

The officers will need the following photographs:

1. Show the suspect committing the crime, if possible.
2. A wide shot showing the entire crime scene.
3. Close-ups of the crime scene, including any evidence (artifacts; digging equipment or any other tools used to commit the crime; anything left behind by the suspect).

Background Sheet: Crime Scene Technicians

At least four crime scene technicians may be needed, divided into two teams. Do not move anything until it has been documented, measured, and photographed. (This is the universal rule of processing a crime scene). Carefully note any evidence at the crime scene. Evidence is *anything* that pertains to the crime.

First Team/First Technician

The first team will take plaster casts of shovel impressions in the dirt or footprints for later study in a laboratory. Take two casts, one of a footprint, the other of a shovel impression (a hole). Do not prepare too much casting material: put about two cups of powder in a plastic bag and slowly add water and knead the bag until you have pancake batter. This will do for a footprint. Mix a little more for the shovel impression. When the plaster begins to harden after you have poured it, scratch into it your initials and the date. Also take some dirt samples for lab analysis: if dirt is stuck to digging tools used by the suspect, cover them with plastic or paper so that the dirt can be removed in the lab. Take small samples of dirt from the crime scene, particularly from the holes dug, and put the dirt in baggies and label them.

Second Team/Second Technician

Your job is carefully marking and measuring every feature of the crime scene: the locations of any holes dug by the suspect, any evidence on the ground, and the relationship of the crime scene to a river, nearby road, building, or other fixture so that the judge and jury in court will know exactly what happened. Make a map of the crime scene and label on the map each hole, artifact, or anything else at the crime scene.

If one team finishes before the other, then help other crime scene technicians who are still working. Remember, each piece of evidence (artifact, dirt, tool used by the looter) must be bagged and tagged. Each tag must clearly show the name of the person who found and processed it.

Members of the archaeological team may assist in taking measurements only if necessary.

BACKGROUND SHEET: ARCHAEOLOGICAL TEAM

You are professional archaeologists who must write a damage assessment at the crime scene. Write a paragraph report on the site that has been looted or damaged. In your report:

1. Write down what you did in helping the police. Write down the date and time that you performed your work.

2. Describe the historic/archaeological site and why it is important. You may have to interview site staff to obtain this information.

3. Estimate how much it will cost to repair the site and put this information in your report.

4. Estimate the value in dollars of any artifacts taken or destroyed. If you can, estimate the cost of doing a professional archaeological excavation of the crime scene. Write down what information a professional excavation might produce.

BACKGROUND SHEET: NEWS MEDIA

Someone who listened to a police radio called to tell you about the possible looting at the archaeological/historic site. You work for the local newspaper as reporters. You go to the archaeological site and conduct interviews to write your story.

Your job is to get a story. The police, though, have a legal right to restrict some of your activities at the crime scene.

BACKGROUND SHEET: LOOTER

You are a machinist who has had a long-standing interest in relic collecting. You developed an interest in the Civil War some years ago and have broadened your knowledge by reading and visiting museums and relic shows. You have a metal detector and have visited some campsites to look for uniform paraphernalia or weapons. You have found some buttons, coins, and uniform badges. Your collecting interest has extended into other areas such as prehistoric Native American items. You have sometimes asked for permission to dig on private property, but not always. Today, you are digging for some relics on private, historic property where you have found a few items in recent years. You are in a remote area of the historic property, and you do not feel that you are disturbing anyone. You have dug a few holes and have found some objects, but you feel that you can take them because their commercial value is rather low. You believe that if you do not recover objects that you have learned to appreciate, then the objects will disappear and not be appreciated. Also, you intend to fill in the holes before you leave. You have not been stopped by law enforcement officers in the past for relic hunting. You are generally cooperative with law enforcement, but at the same time you do not wish to disclose all of your activities.

BACKGROUND SHEET: THE LAWS

Very short versions of the real laws are given to police team, archaeological team, and reporters. Here is a summary of state and federal laws about theft and vandalism.

Crimes under State Law

1. Entering private property without the permission of the property owner or remaining after the owner has told you to leave.

2. Damaging or destroying property belonging to another.

3. Taking property belonging to another without the owner's permission (theft).

4. Disturbing, destroying, or displacing any human burial or any human body part without permission of the state archaeologist. The burial can be on private or public property.

5. Disturbing, destroying, or defacing any monument or tombstone in a cemetery.

Crimes under Federal Law

1. Taking (or destroying), digging up, or defacing any artifact or feature on federally owned or controlled property without a permit. The artifact or feature must be at least one hundred years old and must have archaeological interest.

2. Selling, purchasing, or transporting for sale any Native American human remains or other artifacts, when you have no legal ownership or control over the remains or artifacts.

Offense Report

Case #: _____

Victim: _____

Phone number: _____

Address: _____

Location of incident: _____

Reported by: _____

Phone number: _____

Address: _____

Suspect Information

Name: _____

Address: _____

Race: _____

Sex: _____

Male _____ Female _____

Date of birth: _____

Offenses (list):

#1: _____

#2: _____

#3: _____

#4: _____

Suspect charged: yes _____ no _____

(If additional suspects, describe on reverse.)

Vehicle involved: Victim's _____ Suspect's _____

Description (year/make/model/color):

_____

If property/evidence was recovered, is an evidence recovery form attached?

_____

Narrative:

_____

_____

Officers reporting: _____

Date: _____

Supervisor: _____

Date: _____

Case #: Evidence Recovery Log

Date: _____

Time: _____

Offense(s): _____

Victim: _____

Evidence recovered by: _____

Supervisor: _____

Item	Description	Location Found	Container*
1			
2			
3			
4			
5			
6			
7			

* Enter E for envelope, P for plastic bag, and C for plaster cast.
Note: Label each bag or envelope with (1) case number, (2) item number, (3) description of item, (4) date/time found, and (5) officer's signature. For casts, as they dry, etch into each one (1) date, (2) time, (3) item number, and (4) officer's name.

Evidence Tags

Make as many copies as necessary.

Type of offense: _____

Item number: _____

Description of item: _____

Date/Time Found: _____

Where Found: _____

Officer/Technician: _____

Contributors

Neil Brodie is research director of the Illicit Antiquities Research Centre at the McDonald Institute for Archaeological Research, University of Cambridge. He is a co-editor of *Illicit Antiquities: The Theft of Culture and the Extinction of Archaeology*.

Patty Gerstenblith has been professor of law at DePaul University College of Law since 1984. She is the author of *Art, Cultural Heritage and the Law*, 2004.

John S. Henderson is professor of anthropology at Cornell University. He is the author of *World of the Ancient Maya*.

Robert D. Hicks recently retired from the Law Enforcement Services Unit of the Virginia Department of Criminal Justice Services, where he developed Virginia's Time Crime program on investigating crimes involving archaeological resources.

Julie Hollowell recently completed her Ph.D. at Indiana University. She is currently a Killam Fellow at the University of British Columbia.

Morag M. Kersel recently completed her Ph.D. in the archaeology department at the University of Cambridge. She is a co-editor of the Antiquities Market section of the *Journal of Field Archaeology*.

Juliette van Krieken-Pieters works with the Society for the Protection of Afghanistan's Cultural Heritage (SPACH), the Netherlands, and teaches at Webster University.

Paula Kay Lazrus is an assistant professor at St. John's University, New York. She has conducted field surveys in Italy, Israel, and New England.

Christina Luke teaches in the Department of Archaeology and the College of Arts and Sciences Writing Program at Boston University, and is a co-editor of the Antiquities Market section of the *Journal of Field Archaeology*. She conducts research in western Turkey, Central America, and Mesoamerica.

Lena Mortensen is the assistant director of the Center for Heritage Resource Studies, University of Maryland, College Park.

S. K. Pachauri is a member of the Indian Administrative Service. He is the former Commissioner of Archaeology in the state of Andhra Pradesh, India, and currently the secretary of the Ayodhya Inquiry commission.

Marina Papa Sokal is a research associate at the Accordia Research Institute, University of London, England. She has participated in fieldwork in both Italy and England.

Lyndel V. Prott was formerly the director of UNESCO's Division of Cultural Heritage. With her husband, P. J. O'Keefe, she is co-authoring the five-volume work *Law and the Cultural Heritage*.

Colin Renfrew is professor emeritus in the Department of Archaeology at the University of Cambridge. He is the author of *Loot, Legitimacy and Ownership: The Ethical Crisis in Archaeology*, 2000.

Christopher H. Roosevelt is an assistant professor of archaeology at Boston University and conducts field research in western Turkey.

Kathryn Walker Tubb is the coordinator of the M.A. program in Cultural Heritage Studies and a lecturer in the archaeology department at University College, London. She is the editor of *Trade or Betrayed: Legal Ethical and Conservation Issues*.

Peter Watson is a journalist and author and a research associate at the McDonald Institute for Archaeological Research. He is the author of *Sotheby's: The Inside Story*, an exposé of the auction house.

Index

CPSIA information can be obtained
at www.ICGtesting.com
Printed in the USA
BVHW071146120121
597455BV00002B/87